A Constant Search
for Wisdom

LIST OF PUBLISHED TITLES BY JOHN MATTHEWS

Arthur of Albion (Barefoot Books, 2008)
Arthur of Avalon (Calendar with pictures by Courtney Davis) Amber Lotus 2007
Arthurian Book of Days (with CM) (St Martins Press, 1998)
Arthurian Book of Days Diary & Address Book (with CM) (Eddison-Sadd, 1991)
An Arthurian Reader (Aquarian Press,1988)
The Arthurian Tarot: A Hallowquest (with CM) (Aquarian Press, 1990).
The Arthurian Tradition (illus.) (Element Books, 1994)
At the Table of the Grail (Ed) (Watkins Books, 2002)
Bardic Source Book (Cassell, 1998)
Barefoot Books of Knights (Barefoot, 2001)
Boadicea: Warrior Queen of the Celts (Firebird Books, 1988)
Book of Arthur (Chrysalis, 2002)
Celtic Warrior Chiefs (With R.J. Stewart) Brockhampton, 1998)
Celtic Battle Heroes (with Bob Stewart) Firebird Books, 1988,
Celtic Myths & Legends (with CM) Folio Society 2006
Celtic Seers Source-Book Cassell, 1999
A Celtic Reader Aquarian Press, 1991
The Celtic Shaman Rider 2000
The Celtic Shaman's Pack (Element, 1996)
Celtic Oracle (Barnes & Noble 2005)
Celtic Totem Animals (Red Wheel/Weiser, 2002)
Celtic Verse (Watkins, 2007)
Choirs of the God (Mandala, 1991)
Classic Celtic Faery Tales (Cassell, 1996)
Drinking From the Sacred Well (Harper San Francisco, 1999)
Druid Source Book (Cassell, 1996)
El Cid: Champion of Spain Firebird Books, 1988
Element Encyclopaedia of Magical Creatures (HarperCollins, 2005)
Elements of Arthurian Tradition Element Books, 1989
Elements of the Grail Tradition Element Books, 1990
The Encyclopaedia of Celtic Wisdom (with CM) (Rider 2000)
Encyclopaedia of Celtic Myth and Legend (with CM) (Rider, 2001)
Faces of Arthur (with CM) Folio Society, 2007
The Faery Tale Reader (with Caitlín Matthews) (Aquarian, 1993)
Fionn mac Cumhail: Champion of Ireland (Firebird Books, 1988)
From the Hollow Hills (Floris Books, 1994)
From the Isle of Dreams (Floris Books, 1993)
Gawain, Knight of the Goddess (Inner Traditions, 2003)
Giants Ghosts and Goblins (Barefoot Books, 1999)
Glastonbury Reader (Aquarian Press, 1991)
The Grail: Quest for the Eternal (Thames & Hudson, 1981)
The Grail Seeker's Companion (with Marian Green) (Thoth Books, 2004)
Grail: A Secret History (Godsfield Press/Barrons, 2005)
Grail Hunters (with CM) (Templar 2008)
Grail Tarot (Connections/ St Martins 2007)
Green Man: Spirit of Nature (Eddison Sadd, 2002)
Green Man Tree Oracle (Connections, 2003)

Hallowquest: Tarot Magic and the Arthurian Mysteries (with CM)(Aquarian 1989)
Healing the Wounded King (Element Books, 1997)
Household of the Grail (Aquarian Press, 1986)
King Arthur: From Dark Age Warrior to Mythic Hero (Cassell, 2004)
King Arthur: The Many Faces of a Hero (with CM) (Folio Society, 2007)
King Arthur's Britain: A Photographic Odyssey (Cassell, 1995)
Ladies of the Lake (with CM) (Aquarian Press, 1992)
Landscapes of Legend: A Journey Through the Land (Cassell, 1996)
Legendary Britain (with R. J. Stewart) (Cassell, 1989)
Legendary London (with Chesca Potter) (Aquarian Press, 1990)
The Little Book of Arthurian Wisdom (Element, 1994)
The Little Book of Celtic Wisdom (Element, 1993)
Malory's Morte D'Arthur (ED) (Orion, 2000)
Merlin in Calydon: Poems (Hunting Raven Press, 1981)
Merlin Through the Ages (with R.J. Stewart) Cassell, 1995
Merlin: Shaman, Prophet, Magician (Mitchell Beazley, 2004)
The Mystic Grail (Godsfield Press, 1997)
Paths to Peace (Century Hutchinson, 1992)
Pirates (Carlton/Harper Collins/Atheneum)
Pirates: Rogues Gallery/Most Wanted, Carlton/Atheneum 2007
Pitkin Guide to Merlin (with CM) (Pitkin, 2000)
Quest for the Green Man (Godsfield Press/Quest Books, 1999)
Richard Lionheart: The Crusader King (Firebird Books, 1988)
Robin Hood: Lord of the Greenwood (Gothic Image, 1993)
Secret Camelot (Cassell, 1996)
Secret Life of Elves and Faeries (Harper Collins 2005)
Secrets of the Druids (Black Dog Lebenthal, 2004)
Sidhe: Wisdom of the Celtic Otherworld (Lorian Press, 2004)
Song Of Arthur (Quest Books, 2001)
Song of Taliesin (Quest Books, 2000)
Sources of the Grail (Floris Books, 1996)
Story Box (with CM) (Templar Publishing, 2008)
Summer Solstice (Barefoot 2003)
Taliesin: the Last Celtic Shaman (Inner Traditions, 2002)
Trick of the Tale (With CM) Templar, 2007
The Unknown Arthur (Cassell, 1995)
Walkers Between Worlds (with CM) (Inner Traditions, 2003)
Warriors of Arthur (with Bob Stewart) (Blandford Press,1987)
The Winter Solstice (Godsfield Press, 1997)
The Wizard King & Other Enchanting Tales (Barefoot Books, 1997)
Wizards: From the Shaman to Harry Potter (Godsfield Press. 2004)
The World Atlas of Divination (Headline, 1992)

CD-ROM

Legends of Arthur (Castle Multimedia and Cromwell Interactive,1998)

DVD

King Arthur (Director's Cut). Background to the Movie

A Constant Search

for Wisdom

John Matthews

A Constant Search
for Wisdom

Edited by Jeremy Berg

Cover and Interior Art by Ann Amberg

Published by Lorian Press
2204 E. Grand Ave.
Everett, WA 98201

ISBN: 0-936878-19-3

Matthews, John
Constant Search for Wisdom / John Matthews

Library of Congress Control Number: 2007940682

First Edition: December 2007

Printed in the United States of America

0 9 8 7 6 5 4 3 2 1

Dedication

To all of those who bought my books and came to hear me speak – thank you for keeping me going for the last 30 years, and for all the good things you have said about my work.

Acknowledgements

First of all a special thanks to my good friend and spiritual brother David Spangler, for writing the foreword; to Jeremy Berg at Lorian for making this book possible; to Ann Amberg for the amazing cover art; to my wife Caitlin for permission to print the work to which she contributed – especially 'Graal: An Oratorio'.

Thanks to the estates of Michael Ayrton for permission to use the picture which appears on p 228 and David Jones for permission to quote from his writings in the essays entitled 'David Jones and the Arthurian Legend' and 'Sagging End and Chapter's Close'.

Every effort has been made to contact all copyright holders – where we have been unable to do so we invite them to get in touch and we will rectify any omissions in any future editions.

Finally to all the journals in which these writings first appeared – some are forgotten others now, but thanks to all the editors who asked for a contribution.

John Matthews - October 2007

Contents

FOREWORD

John Matthews is a Walker between Worlds. Ordinarily, this phrase designates someone who can travel between the physical and non-physical worlds, the worlds of spirit and of ordinary life. In his capacity as a practicing shaman, John certainly qualifies for this title. But as this book demonstrates, John's life and work give a wider definition than that. He is also a walker between worlds of history and imagination, art and myth, scholarship and magic, spirituality and ecology, folklore and everyday life.

Over the years I have been amazed not only by John's prolificacy as a writer—he can write at least five books in the time it takes me to write one—but by the scope of his knowledge and the depth of his scholarship. His topics range from the history of the Grail to the life and times of pirates in the Caribbean, from the deeds of King Arthur and his knights to the forests of Robin Hood and the Green Man. He has created numerous tarot decks (always of interest to me as someone who loves cards and games) written graphic novels, served as an historical advisor in films, and even written his own screenplays. He even inaugurated a whole genre of Celtic shamanism. What can this man not do?

I first encountered John through his books, in particular The Western Way, the brilliant history of Western esotericism which he and his wife Caitlin wrote. Then one day another friend of mine, William Bloom—an excellent writer himself and one of Britain's finest and most innovative spiritual teachers—came to visit while on a lecture tour of the United States. Coming into my office, he looked around at my collection of superhero and fantasy action figures, my Star Wars and Star Trek memorabilia, and a stack of board games and science fiction novels and said, "You don't happen to know John Matthews, do you?"

"No, only through his books. Why?"

"His office is exactly like this, even with the same toys. You two could be twins!"

It was at that point that I definitely needed to meet this man.

As it happened, I met his lovely wife, Caitlin, a prolific and brilliant writer in her own right, first. She and I were participants in a conference held in Britain near Sherwood Forest; at the time John was unable to attend. We had a train ride together back to London, and when we disembarked at the station, we had become good friends. And she also said, "You and John are so much alike, you could be brothers." This I took to be high praise indeed.

So I took it upon myself to organize a conference of my own at a retreat center near Seattle and invited John to come. Having now heard of me in encouraging ways from both his wife and William Bloom, he accepted. And thus it came about that John came to the Pacific Northwest of the United States for what became the first of many visits and the two of us were able to meet. And when he came into my office, he smiled with recognition that we were indeed two of a kind, collectors and fans of fantasy and science fiction in all its genres. And we discovered that though we were raised in different families in different parts of the world, we truly were—and are—brothers, sharing many common interests and ideas.

I mention this so I can for a moment bask in reflected glory. For aside from shared tastes in movies, comics, novels, and collectable action figures, John's work as scholar, teacher, and writer far exceeds my own. I step back in awe at all this man has accomplished in so many different fields. This is why it is such a pleasure to commend this book to you. It's a sampler of the richness of his thinking and writing. I have no doubt you will find much here to stimulate your thinking and to whet your appetite to explore his major books more fully.

What I most appreciate, besides the clarity and accessibility of his writing, is his caring. John loves knowledge, about that there's no doubt, and he's scrupulous in his scholarship. But what motivates him is caring. He cares for individuals and he cares for the fate of humanity. For all his accomplishments, he is exceedingly modest, for his intent—and this shines through everything he does—is not to forward himself or his own agenda but to provide tools and information that will enable others to find and foster the deepest Spirit within them. He is a true servant of the Grail, continually making his work a vessel from which others can drink from the wisdom of our own indwelling sacredness.

In our time when so much emphasis is on the quick and the facile, the glamorous and the trendy, John offers something deep and lasting. He bridges the ancient wisdoms of our past and the possibilities of our future. He calls himself a shaman, but I call him a sage. And as you read the treasures in this book, I believe you will as well.

David Spangler,
October, 2007

Section One:

ARTHURIANA

Chapter 1:

THE QUEST FOR WONDER
IN ARTHURIAN ROMANCE

This is one of several papers written for the Temenos Academy in London with which I have been involved since its foundation. It was read before an audience on October 24th 1994, which on this occasion included HRH Prince Charles. The theme of the search for wonder in everyday life has been an important one for me – hence the title of this collection - and it was inevitable, given my passion for all things Arthurian that I should write about its presence in the legends of Arthur and his knights. I would like to remember here the kindness and generosity of the late Kathleen Raine for many hours of discussion on this and other matters, for her always-generous support of my work, and for allowing me to be part of the vision of Temenos.

The sense of wonder can be invoked in us in a number of ways; through visiting a scene in nature, through viewing a great painting; through experiencing a major work of art, such as a play or a novel; or through coming in contact with a particular human being. It may also be brought about through the realisation that we are only a small part of a much greater whole. A wonder is also the thing seen, an object of desire if you will, a mighty and fruitful mystery such as the Holy Grail or an act of selfless love. It is both the object itself and the feeling it evokes.

This is what Marina Warner, in her anthology called *Wonder Tales* (Chatto, 1994) is referring to when she writes that:

> *'Wonder has no opposite; it springs up already doubled in itself, compounded of dread and desire at once, attraction and recoil, producing a thrill, the shudder and pleasure and of fear. It names the marvel, the prodigy, the surprise as well as the responses they excite, of fascination and enquiry; it conveys the active motion towards experience and the passive stance of enrapturement'* (p3)

From this we can see that the words wonder and marvel are virtually interchangeable, and I think that by looking at some of the instances of wonder and marvel which appear in the Arthurian tradition we shall see not only that this is indeed the case, but that most, if not all, the precepts mentioned above are also true.

However, first it is necessary to say something about the Arthurian tradition itself. It is not possible to state, with any final certainly, whether or not there ever lived a person called Arthur. If he did, he was most certainly not a king, did not wear shining armour, and in all probability was not accompanied by a band of noble knights who sat together at a round table.

The most likely truth is that Arthur was a 6th century war-lord, who helped bind together the factious Celtic tribespeople of Britain into a force strong enough to repulse the invasion of the Saxons, Angles and Jutes for a sufficient period for them to become settlers rather than invaders - and thus to found the beginnings of the English race.

Whatever the truth of the matter Arthur became a central figure in what we might call the mythological, or inner, history of this land. Earlier memories of a Celtic deity, Arth, of possibly several other heroes who bore this name, coalesced into the figure we know today. And, because most of the stories were written down in the Middle Ages, from the 11th century to the end of the 15th, the characters, dress, morals and motivation, are of that time.

This is why we have a medieval king with his medieval knights portrayed by everyone from Chretien de Troyes in the 11th century to Tennyson in the 19th, and in many of the poems, plays and fictions written in our own time. In each case it can be said - and so I would maintain - that Arthur and the adventures of the Knights of the Round Table are themselves a cipher of wonder, and that we would be just as correct in calling the stories which constellated around the figure of the king, 'wonder-tales' as the more commonly used term of 'romances'.

At the beginning of the great Middle-English poem *Sir Gawain and the Green Knight* we learn of King Arthur that

> *'He had sworn by his sovereignty he would start no meal*
> *On the festival so fair, before he was given*
> *Some strange tale about some most mysterious thing,*
> *Some mighty marvel that merited belief*
> *Of the Old Ones, or of Arms, or of other adventures... (GGK lls. 92-95)*

This is a theme taken up again and again in the Arthurian romances. In Malory's 'Book of Sir Gareth' he says:

> *'so ever the king had a custom that at the feast of Pentecost especially before other feasts in the year, he would not go that day to meat until that he had heard or seen some great marvel. And because of that custom all manner of strange adventures came before Arthur, at that feast before all other feasts.' (Works, p239).*

The fact that Pentecost is singled out as the most important feast where wonders should occur is clearly a reference back to the first Pentecost, where tongues of fire settled upon the heads of the Disciples of Christ, enabling them to speak in tongues. The importance of this 'wonder' in the Middle Ages was considerable, and is the chief reason for the repeated references to this festival in the Arthurian canon as a whole.

The earliest instance of Arthur's custom regarding wonder comes from the 13th century Old French *Vulgate Cycle*, a huge collection of stories collected and written down by Cistercian monks. Here it significantly occurs at the first gathering of the Round Table, which takes place after Arthur's marriage to Guinevere. Here the young king vows never to eat until he has seen a wonder.

In faery-tale, as opposed to medieval romance, wonder is most often encountered in the Otherworld. As Proinsias MacCana wrote in an article some years ago:

> *'The dimension of the supernatural, the otherworldly...is never absent from Irish narrative. Modern anthropologists*

3

have commented on the deep and continual concern in Irish rural communities of, say, thirty or forty years ago with the inter- relationships between the two worlds, and there can be no doubt that this is one of the underlying continuities from primitive to modern Irish society.' (Mythology in Irish Literature' p145. 1982)

Though MacCana was referring here specifically to Irish traditions, the same words apply just as well to what we might call the Arthurian world-view. The presence of the Otherworld is always at hand, and many of the marvellous events either take place within it, or else emerge from it, suggesting, as I shall hope to show later, a certain underlying tension between the two worlds which might almost be taken for a state of warfare.

But in the Arthurian Tradition wonder comes in many forms - beautiful, horrific, even tragic. We cannot, for example, help but feel wonder when we stand with Lancelot before the entrance to the Grail chapel and feel with him the desire to help and the experience of rejection that follows.

'So he came to the chamber door, and would have entered. And anon a voice said to him: Flee, Lancelot, and enter not, for thou oughtest not to do it; and if thou enter thou shalt for-think it...Then looked he up in the midst of the chamber, and saw a table of silver, and the Holy Vessel, covered with red samite, and many angels about it...And before the altar he saw a good man clothed as a priest. And it seemed he was at the sacring of the mass. And it seemed to Lancelot that above the priest's hands were three men, whereof the two put the youngest by likeness between the priest's hands; and so he lifted it up right high...And then Lancelot marvelled not a little, for him thought the priest was so greatly charged of the figure that him seemed he should fall to the earth. And when he saw none about him that would help him, then came he to the door a great pace, and said; 'Fair Father Jusu Christ, ne take it for no sin though I help the good man which hath great need of help.'
Right so entered he into the chamber, and came toward the table of silver; and when he came nigh he felt a breath, that him though it was intermeddled with fire...and therewith he fell to the earth, and had no power to rise...[and] lost the power of his body, and his hearing, and his seeing.' (Book XVII. Ch. xv)

But this is well into the story, and right from the start wonders accompany the birth and deeds of Arthur. His coming is itself a wonder, prophesied by Merlin in Geoffrey of Monmouth's book on the History of the Kings of Britain - the first romantic version of the stories as opposed to the earlier epic and folk-loric versions. Here, Merlin is brought before the usurper Vortigern and, though still a child reveals the wonder of the Red and White Dragons that fight eternally beneath the hill of Dinas Emrys in Wales. In the midst of a huge body of prophecy, Merlin declares:

'Woe unto the Red Dragon, for his extermination is nigh; and his caverns shall be occupied by the White Dragon that betokeneth the Saxons...But the Red betokeneth the race of Britain that shall be oppressed by the White. Therefore shall the mountains and the valleys thereof be made level plain and the streams of the valleys shall flow with blood. The rites of religion shall be done away and the ruin of the churches be made manifest. And at the last, she that is oppressed shall prevail and resist the cruelty of them that come from without. For the Boar of Cornwall [that is, Arthur] shall bring succour and shall trample their necks beneath his feet. The islands of the ocean shall be subdued unto his power, and the forests of Gaul shall he possess. the house of Romulus shall dread the fierceness of his prowess and doubtful shall be his end. Renowned shall he be in the mouth of the peoples, and his deeds shall be as meat unto them that tell thereof.' (Book VII ch.3)

Later on, a star is seen,

'of marvellous bigness and brightness, stretching forth one ray whereon was a ball of fire spreading forth in the likeness of a dragon, and from the mouth of the dragon issued forty two rays, whereof the one was of such length that it did seem to reach beyond the regions of Gaul, and the other, verging towards the Irish sea, did end in seven lesser rays.' (Book VIII. Ch 14.)

Called upon to interpret this sign, Merlin declares that the star itself betokens Uther Pendragon, Arthur's father. And he adds:

'the ray... that stretcheth forth toward the region of Gaul, doth portend that a son shall be born unto thee [Uther] that shall be of surpassing mighty dominion, whose power shall extend over all the realms that lie beneath the ray...' (Book VIII. Ch. 15).

This son is, of course Arthur, and the next wonder comes with his choosing as King of all Britain. Again, Merlin has a hand in this. You will, I am sure, be familiar with the story. Arthur is brought up in obscurity, ignorant of his own birth and destiny. These are shown forth through the wonder of the Sword in the Stone. Here is Malory's description of the event:

' So in the greatest church in London...all the estates were long or day in the church for to pray. And when matins and the first mass were done, there was seen in the Churchyard, against the high altar, a great stone four square, like unto a marble stone; and in the midst thereof was like an anvil of steel a foot on high, and therein stuck a fair sword naked by the point, and letters thus were written in gold about the sword that said thus: Whoso pulleth out this sword of this stone and anvil, is rightwise king born of all England.' (Book I. Ch.v)

Well of course it is Arthur who succeeds in pulling out the sword, where all others fail, doing so by accident as it seems, when his foster brother has need of a weapon. But Merlin reveals all and Arthur is proclaimed king and his true parentage revealed. It is the beginning of a reign of wonders.

Once crowned and established in his kingdom marvels continue to follow the young king. The magical sword that had proclaimed his heritage soon breaks and he must seek another. Merlin is on hand, as ever, to bring him to the place appointed where he will find what he seeks. Let Malory tell it again:

'Arthur said: I have no sword. No force, said Merlin, hereby is a sword that shall be yours, an I may. So they rode till they came to a lake, the which was a fair water and broad, and in the midst of the lake Arthur was ware of an arm clothed in white samite, that held a fair sword in that hand. Lo! said Merlin, yonder is that sword I spake of. With that they saw a damosel going upon the lake. What damosel is that? said Arthur. That is the Lady of the Lake, said Merlin; and within that lake is a rock, and therein is as fair a place as any on earth, and richly beseen; and this damosel will come to you anon, sand then speak ye fair to her that she will give you that sword.'

All falls out as Merlin foretold. The damosel, in answer to Arthur's request, replies: *'Sir Arthur, king, said the damosel, that sword is mine, and if ye will give me a gift when I ask it you, ye shall have it.'* (Book I ch. xxv).

So Arthur acquires the sword, which is the famed Excalibur. But the gift is not given without strings, as he will discover, later on, when the same Lady of the Lake, appears before him and demands

5

the head of one of his own knights, who had betrayed her. Such wonders are dangerous, as well as powerful.

Just before this there occurs another episode in which a remarkable creature, itself a living embodiment of wonder, is encountered by Arthur himself. The time is critical. The young king has not long been crowned and already the seeds of his eventual downfall have been sown. He has, though unknowingly, slept with his own half-sister, who has given birth to the son, Mordred, who will one day bring down his father.

The first intimation of this comes in a wonder-dream of the kind found throughout the literature of the day. In this dream Arthur sees many serpents and griffins come into his land, and though he fights, and at last defeats them, 'they did him passing great harm and wounded him full sore'. Waking, disturbed by his vision, Arthur chases a great hart until his horse falls dead beneath him, at which point he sits disconsolately beside a well. There he witnesses a wonder:

> 'And as he sat so, him thought he heard a noise of hounds, to the sum of thirty. And with that the king saw coming toward him the strangest beast that ever he saw or heard of...that had in shape a head like a serpent's head, and a body like a leopard, buttocks like a lion, and footed like an hart.... so the beast went to the well and drank and the noise was in the beast's belly like unto the questing of thirty couple of hounds; but all the while the beast drank there was no noise in the beast's belly: and therewith the beast departed with a great noise, whereof the king had great marvel.' (The Morte D'Arthur. Book I ch xix and Book IX ch. xii.)

This is Glatisant, the Questing Beast, which is destined to be followed, until death, by King Pellinore and later by Sir Palomides the Saracen. Malory gives no further explanation, and the Beast remains mysterious and enigmatic, like many of the wonders that appear in the Arthurian tradition. Elsewhere the story of the Beast - born to a woman who ordered her brother torn apart by dogs - gives more substance to the story, but the mystery, the wonder of the Beast which exists only to be quested after, remains a metaphor for the entire Arthurian tradition of errantry, in which the Round Table knights are ever riding forth in search of fresh adventure.

Not that they have to do so in any persistent way, since more often than not adventures come in search of them. If we move forward a little way we find Arthur, recently married and having sworn his all important oath not to eat until he has seen a wonder, presiding over the very first gathering of the Round Table Fellowship. And here a wonder indeed seeks them out. The scene is set for us, again in Malory's incomparable version, as follows:

> 'Then was the high feast made ready...and as every man was set after his degree, Merlin went to all the knights of the Round Table and bade them sit still, that none of them remove. For ye shall se a strange and marvellous adventure. Right so as they sat there came running in a white hart into the hall, and a white bratchet [that is, a small ladies' hunting dog] and thirty couple of black running hounds came after with a great cry, and the hart went about he Round Table as he went by other boards. The white bratchet bit him by the buttock and pulled out a piece, wherethrough the hart leapt a great leap and overthrow a knight that sat the board side; and therewith the knight arose and took up the bratchet, and so went forth out of the hall, and took his horse and rode his way with the bratchet.' (Book III. Ch v.)

These events are followed by the appearance, in rapid succession, of a lady on a white horse, who demands the bratchet; and a knight who rides in and carries off the lady! And as Malory laconically reports, 'When she was gone the king was glad, for she made such a noise...'

But Merlin reproves his master sternly. 'Ye may not leave these adventures so lightly; for these adventures must be brought again or else it will be disworship to you and to your feast.' Note the word 'must' - these adventures cannot be ignored; they are the trade of the Round Table, the wonders invited by the king himself. In this case three knights are dispatched: Sir Gawain to bring back the white hart; Sir Tor to bring back the bratchet; King Pellinore to seek out the lady and the knight who abducted her. It is a classic example of the quest formula: a task is set and the knight (or in this case knights) dispatched to undertake the solving of the wonder, rather like a riddle which must be answered before a magic door can open, or a spell be undone. These are wonders of a particular kind - they focus on what we might term adventures of the human spirit, which are here manifested in feats of physical courage, touched with a little of the unearthly. They often lead straight from the door of the king's castle into the forest, which is both a metaphor for the unknown and the unconscious, and also for the Otherworld, in which so many of these adventures take place.

A great deal of the Arthurian tradition consists of wonders of this kind - the scenario is repeated a hundredfold. A messenger or challenger appears at Arthur's court to ask for a boon, a gift or help in a task too great for they themselves to attempt. The definition is precise. It suggests that all of the stories that begin in this way are wonder-tales in their own right. And, though this is in part a literary convention, it has a venerable ancestry that goes back to the Celtic myths that underlie the Arthurian tradition at every level and every point.

Examples of this might include the medieval Welsh tale of Culhwch and Olwen or the 9th century poem, attributed to the great bard Taliesin, known as the *Preiddeu Annwn*, or 'Spoils of the Un-World'. Both these texts preserve a more primitive stratum of the Arthurian tradition, which, though nominally medieval, in fact contain material from a much earlier time. Here Arthur is already a king, with a mighty and magisterial court, but his followers are of another kind to the 'gentle, parfait knight' of Malory and elsewhere. In the story of Culhwch the hero is given the task of winning the hand of the daughter of the giant Yspaddaden Pencawr, a fearsome and at times bizarre character whose eyelids are so heavy that they require the services of two men to hold them up with huge forked twigs!

This intransigent father gives the would-be wooer a series of 39 seemingly impossible tasks which he must achieve before her can win the hand of the fair Olwen. In order to help him perform these tasks Culhwch approaches his uncle, King Arthur, and requests the services of certain of his heroic war-band. These characters - listed in the story to the tune of 150 names - are a far cry indeed from Lancelot and his kin. These are the heroes of Celtic wonder-tales, men like Sgilti Light-Foot who 'never took the road so long as he knew the way, but if there was a forest he travelled along the tree-tops, and if there was a mountain he travelled on the tips of the reeds, and never did a reed bend, much less break, so light of foot was he' (*Mabinogion*, trans J. Gantz p143), or Gwevyl son of Gwastad of whom it is said that then he was sad *'he would let one lip droop to his navel and raise the other until it was a hood over his head'. (Mab. pp145- 6).*

These are the people of the Otherworld - deriving, perhaps from real men with exaggerated features that became, in verbal hyperbole, cartoon-characters. They assemble to assist Culhwch find strange objects such as the comb and shears to be found behind the ears of the great boar Twrch Trwyth - the quest for which begins a great hunt across half of Wales, leaving a trail of destruction in its wake.

In the *Preiddeu Annwn* the poem concerns itself with a fantastic voyage to the Otherworld, lead by Arthur himself with three shiploads of warriors, in search of the Cauldron of Annwn, which will not provide food for cowards, but is otherwise inexhaustible. This is very possibly the earliest version of what was to become the quest for the Grail - and is every bit as wonderful. Here are two verses from the poem:

I am a pre-eminent praiser, my song echoed
In the four-tower caer, the Island of the Strong Door,
Where dark night is mixed with day,
And bright wine is set before the host.
Three shiploads of Prydwen we furrowed the flood -
Except seven, none returned from Caer Rigo
I merit better than the makers of clerkly books,
who have not seen Arthur's might beyond the Glass Caer,
Six thousand men stood high upon its walls -
It was hard to speak with its sentinel.
Three shiploads of Prydwen went with Arthur -
Except seven, none returned from the Caer Goludd.

In this text the clash is between heroes of the mortal world and guardians of the Otherworld. And it sometimes seems indeed, as if these beings were sending a stream of adversaries to test the Fellowship and its King.

Perhaps behind this lies another theme - that of Sovereignty. I do not wish to go into this at great length here - and I am sure that Dr Carey will have done so already in this series of lectures - but I will make a few brief points.

The idea of Sovereignty personified as a person - in particular as a woman - is especially strong in ancient Ireland. In several key texts of Irish myth - collected during the Middle Ages from earlier oral traditions, refer to the necessity of a newly elected king being required to marry or sometimes just sleep with, the Goddess of the Land, who gives him the gift of sovereignty. Essentially this results in a particular bond being formed between the King and the land over which he rules. Traces of this them are also to be found within the Arthurian tradition, and may well have resulted in the constant testing of Arthur and his knights which occurs throughout his reign. The theme of the Waste Land found in the mythos surrounding the Grail Quest, suggests that this is still an important theme. There, when the king is wounded the land withers - only when he is restored to health is the land likewise healed. If I am right in thinking that the king of this story was once Arthur himself, then the repeated pastern of test and trial becomes clearer.

Even the most innocent seeming adventures, which often begin with the 'damsel in distress' who appears at court and asks for a knight to help her or her mistress - even here the test is implicit, since the 'damsel' often turns out to be of otherworldly or faery origin. This has lead one commentator, the Breton scholar Jean Markale, to suggest that there is evidence of a war between the earthly realm of Arthur and the Otherworld - as represented by such figures as Morgan le Fay, Arthur's half- sister and his bitterest foe, and the various Ladies of the Lake, including Nimue who is ultimately responsible for shutting Merlin up in the earth so that he can no longer aid and assist Arthur. All of these women can be seen as not only Otherworldly, but as representing the Goddess of the Land, Sovereignty herself, to whom Arthur relates not always comfortably.

The greatest challenges seem to come from this direction. In the poem of *Gawain and the Green Knight*

8

with which we began, the Green Knight himself - a fearsome character with green skin and red eyes, offers to play a Christmas 'Game' with Sir Gawain, an exchange of blows with his huge axe. But whereas the Green Knight can pick up his severed head, Gawain cannot, and must undergo a series of fearsome tests of his honour before he faces the challenge and is spared. At the end it is revealed that the prime mover in all of this was none other than Morgane herself - here called 'Morgane the Goddess' in a fascinating hint at the regard in which she was once held.

Gawain, indeed, gets more than his fair share of such wonder- tests, as in the poem Gawain and Ragnall where after Arthur is confronted by the angry Gromer Somer Jour and given the task of finding what thing it is women most desire - a difficult quest then, as now - must wed the hideous Rangel in order to prove his loyalty to his king and the precepts of Chivalry. In the end of course all ends happily as Gawain's honesty and courtesy result in the averting of the spell that has made Ragnell ugly and restores her to her customary beauty. The answer to the question varies from version to version, but in a test one it is given as 'sovereignty' the right to be whom and what she will be - a theme which has taken on a powerful currency in our own time, but which once again refers back to the idea of the king's relationship with the land being personified by a woman.

These wonders are all of the type that I would call Otherworldly - they preserve a very ancient and frequently ritualistic heritage of human experience. Thus the challengers of Winter and Summer, the Green Knight and Gromer - whose name means Man of the Summer's Day - offer trials designed not only to test the human qualities of the king and his noticed, but also their atavistic spiritual selves - open doors into a past far more ancient that that of the Arthurian court.

But if the central experience of wonder in the Arthurian tradition comes from the individual adventures of the Round table knights, then by far the single most overwhelming instance of Wonder is in the Quest for the Grail. At every point in this story wonders abound. The first appearance of the Grail at Camelot sets the tone:

'And then the king and all the estates went home unto Camelot, and so went to evensong to the great Minster, and so after upon that to supper, and every knight sat in his own place as they were toforehand. Then anon they heard cracking and crying of thunder, that them thought the place should all to-drive. In the midst of this blast entered a sunbeam more clearer by seven times than ever they saw day, and all they were alighted of the grace of the Holy Ghost. Then began every knight to behold other, and either saw other, by their seeming, fairer than ever they saw afore. Not for then there was no knight might speak once word a great while, and so they looked every man on other as they had been dumb. Then there entered into the hall the Holy Grail covered with white samite, but there was none might see it, nor who bare it. And there was the hall filled with good odours, and every knight had such meets and drinks as he best loved in the world.' (Book XIII ch vii.)

This wonder is one that provides food of another kind - food of the spirit - and I believe this is an important aspect of wonder as it occurs and as it affects those who experience it.

But this is but the beginning of a marvelous parade of wonders. There is the coming of Galahad, the knight whose destiny it is to sit in the Siege Perilous - the one chair at the Round Table where only the best knight in the world may sit - and whose sole purpose for being on earth is to achieve the Grail. Wonders accompany him at every turn, until finally the greatest wonder is the achieving - a curiously muted climax coming on the heels of the excitement of the Quest.

The three successful quest knights: Galahad himself, Perceval and Bors, have taken the Grail to the mystical city of Sarras. There, Galahad is crowned king and the final events of the Quest are enacted.

Here is Malory again:

' Now at the year's end, and the self day after Galahad had worn the crown of gold, he rose up early and his fellows, and came to the palace, and saw to-fore them the Holy Vessel, and a man kneeling on his knees in likeness of a bishop, that had about him a great fellowship of angels, as it had been Jusu Christ himself; and then he arose and began a mass of Our Lady. And when he came to the sacrament of the mass, and had done, anon he called Galahad, and said to him: Come forth the servant of Jesu Christ, and thou shalt see that thou hast much desired to see. And then he began to tremble right hand when the deadly flesh began to behold the spiritual things. Then he held up his hands toward heaven and said: Lord, I thank thee, for now I see that that hath been my desire many a day....And when he had said these words Galahad went to Perceval and kissed him, and commended him to God, and said: Fair Lord, salute me to my lord Sir Lancelot, my father, and as soon as ye see him, bid him remember of this unstable world. And therewith he kneeled down to-fore the table and made his prayers, and then suddenly his soul departed to Jesu Christ, and a great multitude of angels bare his soul up to heaven, that the two fellows might well behold it. Also the two fellows saw coming from heaven an hand.... and ... it came right to the Vessel, and took it ... and so bare it up to heaven.' (Book XVII ch.xxii)

This belongs very clearly to the quest for Spiritual wonder - a growing closer to God that results in apotheosis, both of the body and the spirit. Nearly all of the vast and complex literature of the Grail falls into this category. For around every bend in the road lies another adventure, another wonder waiting to be experienced.

From this point on in the cycle of stories that make up the Arthurian tradition there is less wonder, as we would naturally define it. A grimmer note is sounded. The only wonder left to experience is the wonder of death - which in Arthur's case is itself wrapped in mystery.

It is also preceded by another wonder-dream, much like the one experienced by Arthur at the wellhead before he sees the Questing Beast. This time the vision is on Trinity Sunday at night just before the battle of Camlan, which will bring to an end the Fellowship of the Round Table and all that Arthur has striven for.

'King Arthur dreamed a wonderful dream, and that was this: that him seemed he sat upon a...chair, and the chair was fast to a wheel, and thereupon sat King Arthur in the richest cloth of gold that might be made; and the king thought there was under him, far from him, an hideous deep black water, and therein were all manner of serpents, and worms, and wild beasts, foul and horrible; and suddenly the king thought the wheel turned up-so-down, and he fell among the serpents, and every beast took him by a limb; and then the king cried out as he lay in his bed and slept: Help. And then knights, squires, and yeoman, awaked the king; and he was so amazed that he wist not where he was...' (Book XXI Ch.iii)

This is a straightforward image of the Wheel of Fortune, found throughout medieval literature in general and several times in Arthurian tradition. But here the dream is reminiscent of the earlier episode, down to the presence of serpents - though in this instance they attack the king's person rather than his lands. But the incident is generally an occasion for wonder - perhaps the cathartic kind that is intended to prepare Arthur for the coming battle in which he will receive a terrible wound and slay his own son.

The final wonder which attends him is in the manner of his departure - for this great hero cannot be allowed to die on the field of battle, he must remain asleep in the memory of the people, ready to

10

answer a future need. Though wounded, he is carried first to the side of the water, where his friend and companion Sir Bedivere restores Excalibur to the Lady of the Lake:

'he threw the sword as far into the water as he might; and there came an hand above the water and met it, and caught it, and shook it thrice and brandished, and then vanished away with the sword in the water' (Book XXI Ch v)

Then comes the departing of the king, a scene so famous that it hardly needs to be rehearsed - but I will read Malory's incomparable description anyway to round off this brief course through the life of the king:

'And where they were at the water side, even fast by the bank hoved a little barge with many fair ladies in it, and among them all was a queen, and all they had black hoods, and all they wept and shrieked when they saw King Arthur. Now put me into the barge said the king. And so he did softly; and there received him three queens with great mourning; and so they set them down, and in one of their laps King Arthur laid his head... And so they rowed from the land, and Sir Bedivere beheld all those ladies go from him. Then Sir Bedivere cried: Ah, my lord Arthur, what shall become of me, now ye go from me and leave me here among mine enemies? Comfort thyself, said the king, and do as well as thou mayest, for in me is no trust for to trust in; for I will to the vale of Avilion to heal me of my grievous wound...' (Book XXI ch v)

Even Arthur's passing is thus a wonder and a mystery. Malory himself is unable to tell us more, though he comments:

'Some men say in many parts of England that King Arthur is not dead, but had by the will of Our Lord Jesu into another place; and men say that he shall come again ... I will not say it shall be so, but rather I will say: here in this world he changed his life.' (Book XXI ch vii)

Another, earlier, text, known as the Didot Perceval after the discoverer of the Manuscript, suggests that with his passing into the realm of the Otherworld in this way, Arthur himself becomes available as a wonder.

'Then Arthur had himself borne to Avalon and he told his people that they should wait for him and he would return. And the Britons came back to Carduel and waited for him more than forty years before they would take a king, for they believed always that he would return. But this you may know in truth that some have since then seen him hunting in the forest, and they have heard his dogs with him; and some have hoped for a long time that he would return.' (Didot Perceval, Trans D. Skeels. p93)

That this idea became enshrined in the memory of the people is well attested by the number of local legends relating to Arthur's sleep beneath hills and in caves all across the land. This is indeed one of the central myths of Britain, referred to by Blake in the Prophetic Books as part of the inner life of the land that will one day wake, 'when Arthur shall awake from sleep, and resume dominion over earth and ocean' (*The Ancient Britons: Catalogue*. Keynes 577-8)

If we test our findings from these few brief glimpses into the extraordinary world of the Arthurian traditions against those definitions of wonder with which we began, I think we can say with a certain degree of certainty that the precepts are all of them met with. Wonders abound in Arthur's realm, evoking within the reader or listener the same response again and again. The sense of wonderful fear and surprised elation, the identification of the miraculous that is everywhere apparent though seldom recognised in our own time, is present within every level of the Arthurian world.

I am reminded also that the Latin word for mirror - speculum - also carries the meaning of wonder - questioning, speculating - suggesting that wonder itself offers a reflection of our human state - both our desire to perceive wonders and the degree of wonderment with which we face the world and our time within it.

And, since Wonder is a source of life-giving strength - of spiritual food like that given to the Round Table knights at the beginning of the Quest for the Grail - Arthur is right to refuse sustenance until he had received that food.

But the single most important factor that emerges from this examination of wonder in the Arthurian tradition is the sense of interaction that takes place between the wonder itself and those who perceive it. This is most often depicted in terms of a challenge. Thus the Green Knight, or Sir Gromer Somer Jour in the poem *Gawain and Ragnell*, the various coloured knights encountered by the hero in Malory's 'Tale of Sir Gareth', the Black Knights who invariably 'hove at the fiords' within the primal forest of Arthurian tradition - all, without exception, challenge the knights who encounter them, putting them to the most extreme tests of those universal precepts: courage, fortitude, and kindness... The quest for the Grail is not only a quest for wonder, it offers a challenge to all who seek it - a challenge of the spirit which requires that we enter into the mystery, the wonder, and help in the healing of the divide between nature and spirit characterised by the image of the Waste Land and the Wounded King.

In the Arthurian tradition wonders most often come about when the otherworldly reality impinges upon ordinary reality: they are symbolic messengers which speak of something which is not being addressed, of an injury or threat to sovereignty or to chivalry. The Arthurian wonder-tales serve the good order of the land.

The experience of wonder can and does change us. As the knights were affected by the appearance of the Grail, which caused them to see each other with new eyes, so does the experience of wonder change us, give us the ability to see with new eyes the world around us. This is something that, I would suggest, is desperately needed in our time, as we enter ever deeper into a new age of darkness. And it is fascinating that the Arthurian tradition itself came out of an earlier Dark Age period.

Wonder can only become more important to us as time passes, and it is heartening to see that in some places - and I would most certainly include the Temenos Academy among them - torches are being lit from the stuff of wonder, and are fuelled by wonder, so that the sense of it is not allowed to die - as so many would seem to want - but in fact is flourishing through the renewed interest in the ancient myths and stories - such as the Arthurian legends - not only here but in places all over the world. I would instance the growing renaissance in story telling, surely one of the central places to find wonder and to experience it. The sense of wonder recalls the treasures of the past in this way, evoking both childhood memories and the spark of past beliefs and traditions that might otherwise be lost. It can put us in touch with that child-like (but by no means childish) appreciation for the richness of life itself that is such an important aspect of the medieval traditions at which we have been looking.

In the compact of storytellers and listeners, we find wonder re- created afresh every day. But it takes our active participation at keep the spirit of wonder alive in the world. Yet if we all pledge our support to that endeavour, and trust that it will help turn back the tide of nihilistic pessimism that is everywhere present, we are actively involved in the creation of wonder.

As we began with Arthur waiting for a wonder to happen, it seems fitting to end with a wonder that sought out the Fellowship in a dramatic fashion. In the poem of Gawain and the Green Knight, with which we began, wonder comes in a fearsome but ultimately benign form. As the court prepares to sit down to their Christmas feast, the wonder desired by Arthur enters their midst.

> '...there passed through the portals a perilous horseman
> the mightiest on middle-earth in measure of height,
> from his gorge to his girdle so great and so square,
> and his loins and his limbs so strong and so huge,
> that half a troll upon earth I trow that he was,
> (J.R.R. Tolkien Sir Gawain, p28)

When asked what it is he wants, the Green knight answers *'nobbut a Christmas Game'* - though as we know, the game was neither simple nor innocent.

This is the challenge of wonder: to dare the Game even though it offers no assurances. It is the challenge we must all face if wonder is not to die out of the world forever.

Chapter 2:

CAMELOT AMONG THE STARS:
ARTHURIAN THEMES IN SCIENCE FICTION

This essay was commissioned in 1985 by my friend Peter Lamborne Wilson for the short-lived Journal Studies in Mystical Literature, published in Taiwan. It was an opportunity to bring together two themes that continue to fascinate me - Arthurian literature and Science Fiction. Inevitably it was made from a very personal selection of books and shows, and many more have appeared since (note the recent use of Arthurian themes in the TV space opera Stargate SGI). I had an opportunity to revisit this theme again in the book King Arthur: Faces of a Hero written with my wife and soon to be published by the Folio Society.

"This strangeness, this mystery, lies not simply in
common magical elements of folklore .... (but)
in the tantalizing suggestion ... that more is
meant than meets the ear."
R. S. Loomis: Celtic Myth and Arthurian Romance. (1)

It is less often the physical presences of Arthur and his Knights who inhabit the realms of Science Fiction than their ghosts. Such works as the *Dune* books of Frank Herbert *The Majpoor Chronicles* of Robert Silverberg, or the *Avalon* cycle of Roger Zelazny are noisy with their invisible presence. The concepts of Chivalry, the Eternal Quest, the endlessly varied themes of the Matter of Britain can be traced back, ultimately, to Malory, Chretien de Troyes, Wolfram von Eschenbach (2) and the rest, known and unknown, who first stirred the cauldron of story to produce the Arthurian mythos.

In the realm of Science Fiction, these themes have undergone their most radical reworking, but have emerged for the most part unscathed, though more often in strange garb. As Richard Monaco, responsible for some of the most enduring Arthurian fables of recent years, including 'Runes',' The Final Quest' and 'Grail Wars' has written

The strongest Arthurian tales are involved with literal and semi literal
history as much as with metaphor. They are anything but 'pure
adventure' stories. They are images of initiation; spiritual alchemy;
journeys into the secrets of the soul and the actual world." (2)

This seems to me the particular power of the best Science Fiction writing: the history of the future as it may or may not be; as some may wish and others fear it may be. The Arthurian mirror is held up to the nature of Futureworld again and again, giving us a foothold in its own reality, however strange.

Camelot, with all that the name can mean, shines amid the vast emptiness of space; her heroes and heroines transcending time and place to awaken in surprising disguises amid the clutter of robotics, ships, aliens and villains as strange as any encountered in ancient quests.

In the series of books by Arthur H. Landis, including 'Camelot in Orbit' and 'Magic of Camelot' set on a planet named Camelot, a complex system of chivalry, magic and superscience exists. The characters bear little resemblance to the Arthurian archetypes; but again and again they seem to embody the characteristic nature of the Arthurian world:

"In Galactic Foundation listings, Fregis was called Camelot;
the indisputable facts being that other than a classical medieval
culture and the like spells, enchantments, and dark wizardry,
as practiced by Fregis' sorcerers, really worked. Moreover
the planet was an occultists', alchemists', metaphysicians' paradise . (3)

This may seem more like the world of Sword and Sorcery than of Science Fiction proper, but here it is always the gimlet eye of science that observes, faintly surprised, the actions of older (not to say wiser) beings. In the fourth book of the series, *'Home To Avalon'*, actually a separate story expanded from the trilogy, the planet of that name has become the final goal for the doomed species of mankind. Only by releasing secrets hidden within a sleeping valley, frozen in time, can a disaster that has already overtaken Earth be averted. In other words, as we might guess from the name of another base on the planet Eden - this is the last flight of humanity to the realm of Paradise – a long promised home and perhaps ultimate goal of all quests. Like Arthur himself in search of healing, the last representatives of old Earth go questing - and if the 'island valley, deep bosomed, fair' of Avalon has the appearance of a time locked space capsule, we should not be surprised, for this is Future Avalon, where once before the quondam King found refuge with a triplicity of Queens.

This all serves to answer the question of what figures such as Arthur are doing in Science Fiction at all. After all, one might ask, is not the real stuff of Science Fiction mechanistic, futuristic, robotic? What have the heroes of myth and legend to do with the future? The answer comes in two ways. One can say, with Ursula Le Guin', that "Science Fiction is the mythology of today"(4), and go on to qualify the statement by declaring that only "submyths" such as Superman, Dr Strange and the multiform worlds of comic books are the real myths of the present. Or one can see it another way: that the mythos, heroes and quests of the ancient world are fuel for the mechanistic soap operas.

If there had never been myths of Titans like Prometheus, or heroes such as Herakles, would Superman have been the same? Would the galactic quests which feature so prominently in Science Fiction writing have had the same validity without, however distantly, knowledge of Odysseus' journey home or the Grail Quest of Arthur and his Knights? The idea of Chivalry alone has given rise to a whole ethos of modern heroes. Poul Anderson's Flandry, Robert Silverberg's Valentine, even Heinlein's muscle bound moralities would be unreal without the ghost of the Arthurian hero in the background.

As Le Guin points out in the essay already quoted, it is not that we can reduce the old gods to mere symbols of nature's elements but that those elements themselves are only aspects of the gods. We are talking about *transcendental* truths, and Science Fiction is where we are most likely to find them today. Where else might one find a story dealing with physical resurrection, the search for a lost soul, or the unmaking of creation? Yet they are all there, and more in the third *Star Trek* movie, "The Search For Spock (Paramount, 1984).

Indeed, anyone who watches the Classic TV series or the more recent 'Next Generation', with more than a casual eye cannot fail to recognize the archetypes. In the original series we have Captain James Tiberius Kirk, fearless but flawed commander; Mr Spock, shaman of otherworldliness; Leonard McCoy, honest and headstrong, the perfect foil to Spock's alien intelligence. These and others less immediately recognizable throng the decks of the USS Enterprise, comradely, adventurous soldiers of the future.

But what other archetypes can we see, standing in the shadows of Enterprise's circular bridge? Is there not something familiar about the Captain and his alien advisor? Call the one Arthur and the other Merlin and we already have the answer. Leading his band of brave adventurers, who 'boldly go where no man has gone before' from the centre of his starship, James T. Kirk is the leader of a new Round Table, with Spock his otherworldly guide; and in McCoy there is more than a shade of Gawain.

And in all the monsters, madmen and myths encountered during the 70 odd voyages of the Enterprise we have the futuristic journeys through 'lands adventurous' where Arthur and his knights went in search of adventure. In the *Next Generation* this continues of course – with Jean-Luc Picard as Arthur, assisted now by Data as his Merlin. Dr Crusher seems to me to share the qualities of Guinevere though never represented as a queen she plays the role of steady companion to Picard. Riker plays out the roles of Gawain here, while Guinan and Troy are otherworldly Ladies of the Lake, and Worf fulfils the place of the warrior cast from which arose the Fellowship of the Round Table.

Clearly we have in *Star Trek* a pattern of Arthurian themes, a Camelotamong--thestars whose mobile crew serve the same forces of goodness and justice as their mediaeval counterparts. Small wonder if the TV series and its movie spin-offs have found a place in the landscape of the human unconscious, as has George *Lucas' Star Wars* saga. Look at that unconsciousness and what do we see? A strange land inhabited by strange creatures, creations of our dreaming ('monsters from the id' as they become in that classic SF movie *Forbidden Planet)* – the real reason for most myth creation. Small wonder indeed if they keep on recurring, and if Science Fiction, which gives reign to almost everything, should play host to the latest cycles of rebirth which bring these archetypal heroes to the fore again.

II

Where do they come from, these shadowy heroes of the past, and what role do they play in the world of the future? The idea of the Eternal Champion seems to have been around for as long as myths have been formulated. The Nine Worthies, The Seven Sleepers, The King Under the Hill are ageold concepts, and all have been revived in recent years by Science Fiction writers. Indeed, Michael Moorcock, that doyen of the ultimate quest, has drawn much of his inspiration from the mythos of Arthureven though Camelot has not featured much in his pages in an obvious sense. Writing of his series of novels and stories relating to the albino champion Elric of Melnibone, Moorcock discusses the importance of the quest. When Elric's object of search, 'the Dead God's Book', supposed to contain all knowledge, finally crumbles to dust at his touch, Moorcock comments:

The Dead God's Book and the Golden Barge (from the book of the same name) are one and the same. They have no real existence save in the wishful imagination of mankind. There is, the story says, no Holy Grail which will transform a man overnight from bewildered ignorance to complete knowledge the answer clearly is within him, if he cares to train himself to find it. (6)

All this harmonizes with the idea of the Arthurian quest, and in his *WarHound and the World's Pain*, Moorcock takes this a step further. His hero, Graf Ulrich von Beck, is a brutal soldier of fortune hardly in the Arthurian mould, yet he is singled out by no less than Lucifer to go in quest of a cure for the world's pain which is, not surprisingly, the Grail. Lucifer's desire is to be reconciled with heaven, perhaps take up his former position there, but not all of Hell's denizens share this wish, and before Beck's quest is over he must face the legions of the damned. Beck does indeed find the Grail, and gives it to Lucifer, but it is insufficient to heal the breach between Heaven and Hell Lucifer is still not welcome in Heaven. Instead he is given the task of redeeming earth and of learning the true nature of the Grail. When both the Devil and mankind can do this, all shall be redeemed. But there is a warning. Lucifer declares:

"You are your own masters. Your lives are your own. Do you not
see that this means an end to the miraculous? You are at the
beginning of a new age for Man, an age of investigation and analysis."(7)

Where this "age of investigation and analysis" leads we well know; the hope is that a rediscovery of the miraculous will follow. If the trend in Science Fiction writing and current scientific thought is any indication, this may well be so; and Arthur is leading the attack.

The original Arthurian cycle ends in defeat and a strange victory. The Science Fiction treatment is a kind of resurrection a return of Arthur. In Martyn Skinner's neglected epic *The Return of Arthur*, the king does indeed return to set things right in a world of Satanic evil. Malice is reborn in the shape of Morgan la Fay. An ageold theme is the one which brings Arthur out of otherworldly retirement when the world needs him, and this is explored in several Science Fiction novels: *The Drawing of the Dark* by Tim Powers, *The Dragon Rises* by Adrienne Martine Barnes, and *A Midsummer Tempest* by Poul Anderson being three that are notable. AII are alike in attributing to Arthur the abilities and the desire to reaffirm what is threatened by destruction or undermined by evil.

In Tim Powers' book the Western world of the 17th century is threatened by the power of Sulieman's Turkish Empire it will fall unless the Fisher King, the Soul of the Land, is revived and brought to the field of battle. This can only be brought about by thwarting a plot to prevent the ancient monarch from drinking a special brew of beer, known as Hartzwesten Dark (a name not without significance). The only person who can save this from happening is Arthur, and he is long dead. But is he? In Powers' Science Fiction version of history Merlin, who is still active at this late time, discovers that Arthur's soul has been reborn in the body of an Irish mercenary soldier named Brian Duffy. With the help of Excalibur he succeeds in reawakening Arthur's memories in time to avert disaster the only problem being that when Arthur remembers *everything*, including his death at Camlann, he will once again withdraw.

In *The Dragon Rises*, it is the seven sleepers, of whom one is Arthur, who are revived. These are the heroes whose eternal task it is to guard the direction and fate of mankind. In this instance, the time is the far future and the players strangely named yet beneath the unfamiliar guises of Gilhame ur Fargon, Alvellaena and Pers Buschard lie the familiar figures of Arthur, Guinevere and Lancelot. Amid galactic adventure and universal mayhem these three play out the ageold pattern of love and friendship, lust and deceit. Yet this time there is a difference: always in the past the Dragon has returned to the

Glass Castle and the sleep of ages, awaiting his next call. This time he is able to transcend the eternal circle, move on to a new cycle of being; and Martine Barnes is the only writer who thus dares to break the mould of the original myth in giving her heroes a happy ending.

But then: what would it be like if . . . ? is a favourite device of most Science Fiction writers. In *A Midsummer Tempest*, the Arthurian theme is subliminal but none the less important. Here is envisaged a parallel time- line in which the Industrial Revolution has happened in the time of King Charles 1 and Cromwell, with the Royalist cavaliers standing against and the Roundheads for the progress of the mechanical over the natural. Prince Rupert of the Rhine, accompanied by faithful friends, invokes the aid of Oberon and Titania in a quest for the Staff and Book of Prospero. (In this world the works of William Shakespeare 'the Great Historian' are fact.) But when, after many adventures, the Staff and Book are found, the final confrontation takes place on Glastonbury Tor, home of Arthurian and Grail legends. Here Rupert invokes and succeeds in raising the Spirit of the Land, something older and more basic than the mere heroes of the past. Here also, Arthur and the knights of Avalon ride forth against the armies of Cromwell, the representatives of brick and mortar, wheels and cogs of mechanistic rule. Echoes here of Tolkien and the march of the Ents against Isengard, and here also Science Fiction seems to laugh at itself, taking the side of magic over science. The message is powerfully expressed:

"I am the land ... I have the right to raise the land I am.
In me alone the mightiness indwells, till I bestow it on my
messengers that they may bear my wrath across the world.
Mine is the outrage, mine was the love. Thou shalt not bind
me fast in brick and steel, nor make my people the idolaters
of little frantic leaders and their texts. If mystery and merriment
alike be human rights, I claim them for my folk."

Here is a timeless mystery that will not be shut out, which seemingly only certain contemporary writers are aware of, and some few poets. It is a mystery of time past and time future, of which Arthur and his knights, Avalon and above all the Grail are true symbols on which to draw.

III

Those works where the Grail appears produce a synthesis of the ageless myth represented by the Arthurian ethos, and what might legitimately be called the new mythology of Science Fiction. Sometimes, as in Roger Zelazny's *The Last Defender of Camelot*, the mystery will almost be explained awayonly to be replaced by another and greater one, which thank heaven – no one has yet succeeded in explaining. Or, as in work like Walter M. Miller's classic, *A Canticle for Lefflowitz*, or the more recent *Star- Spring* by David Bischoff, it looms central to the matter of the story.

In Miller's book, monks, hermits and pseudo-saints occupy a post holocaust wasteland where the Grail makes a fleeting but important appearance. Towards the end of the story, one of the characters, significantly called Mrs Grales, is making her confession to a latterday priest of this future earth. But Mrs Grales has two heads, one purely vestigial, a supernumerary growth that is dumb, lifeless, without expression. Whatever secret it may contain, cannot be conveyed by normal means. In the midst of her act of contrition, the church is struck by a missile, and the priest, Zerchi, pinned under debris. As he lies there, waiting to die, Mrs Grales reappears, unhurt but changed. Her vestigial head is now 'awake'

18

though still capable of repeating only whatever words are addressed to it. Zerchi notices also that the woman seems younger, and that her old 'Head' is gradually withering away. Something new has awakened in her. What happens next is extraordinary. Fearing that she may have suffered fatal exposure to radiation, Zerchi attempts to bless her. He is repulsed and suffers a temporary blackout from the pain of his wounds. When he awakens, he sees Mrs Grales kneeling before him:

> *Finally he could make out that she was holding the golden cup in her*
> *left hand and in her right, delicately between thumb and forefinger,*
> *a single Host. She was offering it to him . . .*
> *she made no conventional gestures, but the reverence with which she . . .*
> *handled it convinced him of one thing: she sensed the presence under the veil. (8)*

Thus, in the moment between death and life, with a new holocaust about to commence, a miracle occurs: the dead half of mankind awakens or is healed and dispenses a blessing upon the hurts of creation. The part that had been dead to the mysteries sees beyond the veils of matter into the heart of things. The symbolism of Eucharist and Grail is overt. Mrs Grales even has five wounds, one of which is described as caused by 'a spear of glass', like the wounds of Christ, and the Grail lance. With almost his last breath, the priest murmurs the words of the *Magnificat*, wanting

> *. . . to teach her the words as his last act, for he was certain that*
> *she shared something with the Maiden who first had spoken them ...*
> *he did not ask why God would choose to raise up a creature of primal*
> *innocence from the shoulder of Mrs Grales, or why God should give to*
> *it the preternatural gifts of Eden those gifts which mar had been trying*
> *to seize by brute force again from heaven since first he lost them ....*
> *(But) he had seen innocence in those eyes and a promise of resurrection. (9)*

It is precisely that 'promise of resurrection' which is inherent in all Grail stories; nor should it be necessary to wait for a distant future to discover it, The paradox may well be that in writing or reading of that future we somehow penetrate it, bringing back from the country *outside* time the knowledge we require.

Certainly, the knowledge is, as always, currently available, though it takes a certain ability to discover it, as is made clear in Bischoff's '*Star Spring*'. Described as a 'spaceopera' this odd book chronicles the struggle against the machinations of a two hundred year old millionaire named Edward Evers Hurt, whose determination to achieve physical immortality leads him to set up a scheme to gather all the finest artistic and scientific brains of the future age aboard a vast starship, and link them into a computercreated matrix which draws upon the imaginal quality of the human mind. With this Hurt intends to create an entry port into what Bischoff calls 'underspace,' a kind of super-collective unconscious which might more familiarly be called 'innerspace' in fact the dimension of spiritual reality. He thus attempts to 'storm heaven' or the reality of which heaven is but a vague shadow, and by this attempt aligns himself with another figure from the Arthurian corpus Klingsor, the evil magician who opposes the Grail knight in Wolfram von Eschenbach's Parzival, and who is best understood in Wagner's opera of the same name, or Richard Monaco's Grail Trilogy.

Into this ambitious and intriguing scenario Bischoff injects a somewhat bizarre Grail quest, where a symbolic Galahad, little more than a computer hologram with no sense of anything other than its own reality, is accompanied by the minds of two spaceborne secret agents transposed into the bodies of a lion and a donkey with a unicorn's horn. This unlikely trio travel across a twodimensional landscape invested with tactile reality by the computer matrix, in search of the Grail. The task is not self-chosen, but assigned to them, with maps provided. This seems curiously unlike the usual nature of the quest, but as one of the characters suggests the quest is:

> ...the process, I presume, that perhaps creates the votive
> qualities of the ... Grail." (10)

For Hurt, this is an active principle of the energy he desires to use to create a doorway into the infinite; the erstwhile Grail seekers see it as a possible way of hitting back if they can really discover the Grail they may be able to use it against him.

Soon after, they meet Merlin, and with his rather jaundiced help ('piss on this stupid Grail,' he remarks at one point) they penetrate deeper into the core of the living brain that the starship has virtually become. Finally, the seekers find themselves in 'The Fisher's Bar and Grail', where a strange version of the Grail Mass ensues and the 'realities' of the story are one by one shown to be masks. Nothing is what it seems, and even Hurt is only a dupe of a more sinister and alien evil. The end of the story is obscure but the Grail is central to the whole matter of the plot. A possible godfigure emerges as it were from the heart of the unconscious mind of humanity - not precisely to aid the seekers but in a mysterious way to watch over events. Herein lies an echo of the figure of Prester John, one of the titular guardians of the Grail, who seems to combine the images of Christ, Galahad and the Fisher Kings. But this is not taken up in the story.

Bischoff s book is a prime instance of the intricate mixture of technology and magic that lies at the heart of so much "Arthurian" Science Fiction. In Andre Norton's *Merlin's Mirror* the mixture is total. Here an alien installation, left on Earth centuries before, wakens to life and summons a ship sent forth from its own doomed planet with the accumulated wisdom of its makers lodged in its memory banks. This becomes the progenitor, by a species of artificial insemination, of Merlin, and thus of the whole Arthurian ethos. The story ends this time with a temporary defeat of technology by human emotion (Lancelot and Guinevere). Merlin retires to the depths of a mountain, where in cryogenic suspension, he begins an agelong dream until able to try again ...This theme is much used by Science Fiction writers who seek a paradigm of hope for the future out of the past and turn to the mythos of Arthur and the Golden Age of Knights and Ladies, magic and wonder, when the doors between the worlds were open without need of space flight and computer circuitry.

It reaches perhaps its purest form in the maxiseries comic *Camelot 3000*, where Arthur is revived from agelong sleep beneath Glastonbury Tor to help the earth against alien invaders. Merlin, Lancelot and Guinevere, Gawain and Tristan follow, appearing in reincarnation rather than revived form. But with the reawakening of Arthur other ancient powers stir again to combat him. Morgan la Fay, after unsuccessfully trying to combat the powers of Merlin, leaves Earth and drifts through astral realms across the galaxies until she discovers the home planet of the aliens and makes them into her new army with which to conquer Earth. Thus beneath the patina of Science Fiction an age old battle continues unabated. Even the evil president of Earth's security forces turns out to be a reincarnation of Mordred, who in a twist of the original story becomes the Grail thief and constructs out of it a suit of armour which makes him invincible.

Of course, good triumphs in the end, the aliens are routed and the old order, though broken, triumphs. Once again we see, in the Arthurian past, a world that can be transported into the present - though sometimes at great cost.

Roger Zelazny, in his brilliant short story *"The Last Defender of Camelot"*, makes the same point, but qualifies it interestingly. Here, it is Lancelot, preserved through time, who features as a representative of Cosmic Chivalry. Meeting Morgan la Fay in an Astrological Emporium he discovers that the reason for his preservation is the power of Merlin, whose last action before failing into enchanted sleep was to ensure that when he awoke, millennia later, the strongest knight in the world would be on hand to serve him. Morgan also implies that it could only mean the greatest harm for mankind if Merlin were once again at liberty to use his virtually unlimited power.

His desire to right wrongs would certainly upset the precarious balance of world power and bring about disaster. Merlin is mad anyway, she says, though Lancelot predictably finds this hard to believe. Indeed, it was Merlin who "arranged" the vision of the Grail to give fresh impetus to the failing energies of the Arthurian court. Lancelot, who believes that his preservation is a direct result of his ancient "sin" with Guinevere, is shaken by this; he believes he must still achieve the Grail before he can be redeemed. Nonetheless he sets out for England and arrives to find Merlin awake and the madness predicted by Morgan to be true. So it is Lancelot who becomes the "last defender", fighting a desperate battle against Merlin's magically operated 'Hollow Knight' (a kind of robot) amid a ghostly Stonehenge, half in and half out of the world. Watching Merlin and Morgan, locked in sorcerous combat, vanish forever between the worlds, and finally, wounded beyond healing. Beginning to age, he sees a vision of the Grail and follows it to his proper endthe end, Zelazny seems to imply, of the Arthurian quest for all time, and the death of Magic.

Except of course that there is no real end to the perpetual quest, at least not while a single blade of grass remains unredeemed, and Lucifer (vide Moorcock) fails to teach mankind the meaning of salvation.

Perhaps here we have the kernel of the use made by Science Fiction writers of the Arthurian corpus. It is possible to look back to the age of Arthur with fond nostalgia for what is gene, or to project it forward into the infinity of Futureworld as a pattern upon which to build a stable society or a workable world. We can further see in this the imperishability of myth, which continues to exert a potent spell upon all who have a hunger for it.

The Arthurian stories endure all that we do to them and our desire to inflict new forms upon them, but they lose none of their original power to move and inspire us. This, finally, is one of the best thingsScience Fiction hag to offer, this ability to make us better people than we were previouslywhatever one may mean by that. It is possibly the greatest gift of all great writing. The Arthurian theme is only one of many that can, and does, have this effect, if we let them, of course. As Zelazny says at the end of *The Last Defender of Camelot*:

QUO FAS ET GLORIA DUCUNT (11)

NOTES

1. R. S. Loomis, Celtic Myth and Arthurian Romance (NY, Columbia University Press, 1927).

2. Sir Thomas Malory, Le Morte d'Arthur Ed. John Matthews (London, Cassell, 2000); Chretien de Troyes, Perceval, The Story of the Grail (Totowa, NJ, Rowman & Littlefield, 1982); Wolfram von Eschenbach, Parsifal (Penguin, 1980).

3. Richard Monaco, Runes (NY, Ace, 1984).

4. Arthur Landis, Camelot In Orbit (NY, Daw, 1978), p. 7.

5. Ursula Le Guin, The Language of Night: Essays on SF (NY, Putnam. 1979); See especially "Myth and Archetype in Science Fiction".

6. Michael Moorcock, Elric At The End of Time (London, New English Library, 1984).

7. Michael Moorcock, The WarHound and the World's Pain (London, New English Library, 1982).

8. Walter Miller, A Canticle for Leibowitz (Philadelphia, Lippincott, 1960), pp. 275-.

9. Ibid., pp. 2767.

10. David Bischoff, Star Spring (NY, Berkley, 1982), p. 146.

11. Where duty and glory lead. Roger Zelazny "The Last Defender of Camelot" (I Books, 2002)

Chapter 3:

MERLIN'S ESPLUMOIRE

Towards the end of the 1990s R.J.Stewart and I put together a series of conferences exploring the figure of Merlin. We had some pretty high-powered guests for these – including the filmmaker John Boorman, the writer Peter Vansittart and the Merlin scholar Nickoli Tolstoy. Of course R.J. and I also contributed talks and out of this came two collections of essays about Merlin. Th one which follows here was originally published in a collection edited by R.J. Stewart called Merlin & Woman, (Blandford Press, 1988). Since then we have both published extensively on Merlin, with R.J. producing several books and The Merlin Tarot (1988) and myself the book Merlin: Shaman, Prophet, Magician (Mitchell Beazley, 2004). Here I wanted to show how there was a side to Merlin's character that remained little known – his relationship with women - which was far more complex than the better known stories of his fall to the wily Nimue.

It has become customary to view the end of Merlin's career in a certain light: as an ageing magician captivated by a young woman. In this scenario Merlin is beguiled into giving away his greatest secrets in return for sexual favours; once the temptress - whose name may be Nimue Niniane or Vivienne - has succeeded in extracting this knowledge she at once uses it to imprison her aged lover, sometimes under a great rock, sometimes within a hawthorn bush, sometimes in a glass tower. From here he is said to utter elusive prophecies or gnomic sayings, while in some versions the 'Perron de Merlin', Merlin's Stone, becomes a starting point for adventure, to which those in search of the strange or the mysterious resort, to await events or instruction.

Such is the story which Malory, for instance, gives us in the *Morte D'Arthur*, Book IV, Chap. i.

'Merlin fell in a dotage on the damosel that King Pellinore brought to court, and she was one of the damosels of the lake, called Nimue. But Merlin would let her have no rest, but always he would be with her. And ever she made Merlin good cheer till she learned of him all manner thing that she desired; and he was assotted on her, that he might not be from her ... And so, soon after, the lady and Merlin departed ... and always Merlin lay about the lady to have her maidenhead, and she was ever passing weary of him, for she was afeared of him because he was a devil's son, and she could not be rid of him by no means. And so on a time it happed that Merlin showed her in a rock whereat was a great wonder, and wrought by enchantment, that went under a great stone. So by her subtle working she made Merlin to go under that stone to let her wit of the marvels there; but she wrought so there for him that he came never out for all the craft he could do. And so she departed and left Merlin.'

Tennyson, four hundred years on, reinforced this in Victorian dress in his poem 'Merlin and Vivien' from *The Idylls of the King*; but there is another version. In this story, which we find in Geoffrey of Monmouth's *Vita Merlini*,' the *Didot Perceval* and various other texts, Merlin has reached a great age, or a particular stage of spiritual development, and decides to retire from the world of his own accord. He is, sometimes, still accompanied by a female companion, though, as in the Vita, it is more likely to be his sister than his lover, and the place of retirement may still be a tower, an island or a cave, but these are places of Merlin's own choosing or even construction.

The question is: which of these two versions is the right one, if indeed there is a right one; and which motivation - lust or continued growth should we believe? To answer this we have to ask another question: Why should Merlin withdraw from the world? I have already suggested one answer: that he sought further knowledge or the opportunity to grow. Fortunately there are several other figures, though from a different tradition, each of whom shares some of Merlin's attributes as prophet, mystic, and seer, and has a specific reason for withdrawing. Consideration of these figures may help to clarify matters.

The figures in question are generally known by the term 'hidden' or 'inner' kings, beings who have responsibility for a particular aspect of tradition or teaching and who continue to administer this even after they have withdrawn from active participation in the events of the world, although they are not actually dead. Among the most notable are Melchizadek, Enoch, Elijah and, I believe, Merlin himself.

Despite their many differences these figures share certain important aspects. They are all mysterious, shadowy beings, who appear at a time of crucial import, and who seem to have neither an orthodox beginning nor end to their lives. Finally, they each withdraw or disappear, leaving conflicting accounts of their actual existence, function or allegiance.

Melchizadek, was 'without beginning or end while Enoch 'walked with God and was not' but beyond this seems to have no point of origin. He is first mentioned, in Jewish traditional sources - significantly as we shall see - as living in a hidden place, from which he watches and records the deeds of mankind and holds occasional converse with God. Later he is represented as a king over men who ruled for more than two hundred years before being summoned by God to rule over the angelic hosts.

To this rather sparse account we can add, from various other sources, that Enoch visited heaven often while still in the flesh, and that he was instructed by the archangel Michael in all things, after which he wrote some 366 books, which may remind us of the 333 prophetic books of Merlin ...

When translated to heaven Enoch had bestowed upon him 'extraordinary wisdom, sagacity, judgement, knowledge, learning, compassion, love, kindness, grace, humility, strength, power, might, splendour, beauty, shapeliness and all other excellent qualities', and received besides 'many thousand blessings from God, and his height and breadth became equal to the height and breadth of the world, and thirty-six wings were attached to his body to the right and to the left, each as large as the world, and three hundred and sixty-five thousand eyes were bestowed upon him, each as brilliant as the sun ... " The description continues for several more paragraphs, outlining a truly cosmic figure. At the end it is revealed that Enoch - whose name, not surprisingly perhaps, means 'the enlightened one' received a new name. As the text puts it:

'A magnificent throne was erected for him beside the gates of the seventh celestial palace, and a herald proclaimed throughout heaven concerning him, who was henceforth to be called Metatron. God declares: —I have appointed my servant Metatron as prince and chief over all other princes in my realm ... whatever angel has a request to refer to me, shall appear before Metatron, and what he will command at my bidding, ye must observe and do, for the Prince of Wisdom and the Prince of Understanding are at his service, and they will reveal unto him the science of the celestials and the terrestrials, and knowledge of the present order of the world, and the knowledge of the future

order of the world. Furthermore have 1 made him guardian of the treasures of the palace of heaven, Arabot, and of the treasures of life that are in the highest heavens.'

Enoch has thus become a Lord of Hosts and a guardian of the Treasures of Life in heaven. More interestingly perhaps he is also said to have assumed the position left vacant by the fall of Lucifer. He is thus balancing out the uneven ranks of the angelic host, and perhaps it is not stretching the analogy too far to see here an echo of the place left empty at the Round Table, which will one day be filled by the destined champion of the Grail. 1 think also that in the description of the revelation of the sciences celestial and terrestrial, the knowledge of present and future, we have another analogy of the knowledge and wisdom of Merlin, derived from within his observatory with its 70 doors and windows.'

Many ages after the withdrawal of Enoch another figure appears to represent the mysterious hierarchy of the withdrawn kings. This is Elijah, who even in Biblical sources comes across as a rather cantankerous, argumentative character, not at all above telling God how things ought to be done. The story is told that when the time came for him to ascend to heaven, the Angel of Death was reluctant to admit him. Elijah argued so violently before the gates of heaven that God Himself was forced to intervene and gave permission for a wrestling match between Elijah and the Angel. Elijah was victorious and now sits with Enoch and Melchizadek, like them recording the deeds of mankind.' He is also seen as a psychopomp, detailed to stand at the crossroads of Paradise to guide the righteous dead to their appointed place. He is thus, like both Enoch and Merlin, a way shower, guiding travelers on an inner journey; and, like Enoch, he rules over a portion of Paradise.

Many stories are told of Elijah's travels through the world, and of his many disguises, through which he becomes something of a joker though always remaining a stern judge of human frailty.' Thus he is often to be found traveling the roads with some unsuspecting companion, behaving in an extraordinary manner or laughing unaccountably as one who knows the inner truth of the situation from an unknown source. In this he resembles Merlin closely, since there are several well-attested instances of 'Merlin's laughter', where he has perceived things unseen by others and finds the foolishness of men too funny to restrain his mirth."

Indeed there are so many similarities between Elijah and Merlin that it is very easy to pass from one to the other, especially if one considers one of the most significant accounts of Merlin's end. It is found in the medieval Grail Romance known as the Didot Perceval. Here Merlin declares that God *'did not wish him to show himself to people any longer, yet that he should not be able to die until the end of the world'*. To Perceval, he adds: *'1 wish to make a lodging outside your palace and dwell there, and 1 shall prophesy wherever our lord commands me. And all those who see my lodging will name it the Esplumoir [or Moulting Cage] of Merlin.'*

Now with this word Esplumoir we come to the heart of the mystery that connects Merlin to the Inner Kings and provides the reason for his withdrawal.

Much speculation has gone into the meaning of the word. What, after all, is this moulting cage? For a long while it was the term originated from a falcon's cage, and that because Merlin happened to share his name with an actual bird of prey, elaborate pun was intended. In one sense this was right, since birds moult in order to change, to grow fresh plumage, and Merlin himself, under another guise, is described as wearing a cloak of feathers and living like a bird in a tree.

However, the real meaning of Esplumoir is even more and takes us into some very strange areas. In Celtic tradition we find in episode from the Voyage of Maelduin' where the voyages arrive at an island where they see a huge bird renew itself in the waters of a lake. When one of the crew drinks this water he is said never again to be troubled with bad eyesight or toothache, so strong are the properties of the water. The same text adds a Biblical reference for the validity of this episode, from the psalm which says: 'You shall renew yourselves as eagles' and it is to a Biblical, or rather a Judaic, source that we must turn for a further definition of the Esplumoir.

In the Zohar,' one of the most important mystical texts from Judaism, we find a description of paradise which, both recalls the earlier passages dealing with Enoch and Elijah, and takes us a step further. In this passage we read of a part of heaven in which is 'a certain hidden place, which no eye has seen but those to whom God shows it, and which is called "the Bird's Nest" ... within this the Messiah [in Jewish tradition there are many Messiahs, so that Christ is not necessarily meant here] lies ailing in the fifth hall of Paradise, in the castle of Souls, the Bird's Nest, visited only by Elijah, who comforts him'."

This conjures up a scene that will be well known to students of the Grail. There, in many different texts, we find an old, ailing king, lying in the hall of the Grail castle (which could certainly be termed the Castle of the Soul) visited by Merlin. When we discover that, in a romance almost contemporary to the first known compilation of the texts which became the Zohar, this same king is called 'Messiahs' a word which could only have come from the Hebrew - the parallel is even greater."'

What, then, of the 'Birds Nest'? The text further describes it as a place of prophetic vision:

'The Messiah enters that abode, lifts up his eyes, and beholds the Fathers [Patriarchs~ visiting the ruins of God's sanctuary. He perceives mother Rachel with tears upon her face; the Holy One, blessed be He, tries to comfort her, but she refuses to be comforted. Then the Messiah lifts up his voice and weeps and the whole Garden of Eden quakes, and all the righteous saints who are there break out in crying and lamentation with him. When the crying and weeping resound for the second time, the whole firmament above the Garden begins to shake, and the cry echoes from five hundred myriads of supernal hosts, until it reaches the highest throne.'"

Merlin, also, when he enters his Esplumoir, is able to see things that others cannot: glimpses of British history just as the Messiah sees glimpses of Jewish history. There is, also, a marked similarity between the apocalyptic descriptions in the Zohar and the extraordinary visions of Merlin in both the Vita Merlini and the earlier Prophecies set out in Latin by Geoffrey of Monmouth, in the middle of the twelfth century.

Nor should we be surprised by these points of similarity between Christian and Judaic authorities; the barriers between the two cultures in the Middle Ages were far less severe than is often supposed. It is more than likely that any one of the widely read, much-travelled romance writers could have encountered the tradition embodied in the Zohar and elsewhere, and that it became a seed planted in the soil of their own vision.

In Celtic literature also, long recognised as a primary source for the Arthurian mythos, are descriptions of the Otherworld abode of the dead in which both Enoch and Elijah are described as living on a mysterious island until the Day of judgement; and in an early poem of the bard Taliesin," who also identified himself with Merlin, we find the line: 'I was instructor to Elijah and Enoch.'

Merlin likewise is said to retire to a glass house containing the Thirteen Treasures of Britain - including the Cauldron of Annwn, the Celtic Grail - and this also is on an island. (Indeed, an early nineteenth century scholar interpreted this in his own particular way, describing 'a museum of rarities in King Arthur's time ... which Myrddin ap Morfran, the Caledonian, upon the destruction of that place, carried with him to the house of glass in the isle of Enill or Bardsey ... This house of glass, it seems, was the museum where they kept their curiosities to be seen by everybody, but not handled; and it is probable that Myrddin ... was the keeper of their museum in that time ... !')"

Seriously, however, Merlin's Esplumoir is here both a treasure house and a place of prophecy, as is the Bird's Nest, and within it, like Enoch and Elijah, Merlin notes down the history of mankind to a clerk named Helyas, whose name is itself a corruption of Elijah, and who writes down all that Merlin recounts from inside his retreat.

Again, in the Vita Merlini, we have the description of Merlin's observatory, to which he withdraws with his sister Ganeida, to study the heavens and the mysteries of creation.' Here, the moulting cage is a place of study and learning, a place where, in the magical inner realm built by Merlin himself in another dimension, the prophet and wise man can put together the fragments of his knowledge to make a whole. This is Merlin as Phoenix, and we may remember that in the German *Parsifal* romance the Grail is described as a stone having the properties of renewal 'like that from which the phoenix renews itself when it is near to death, and from which it arises again restored'.

Before withdrawing, he was a king, but he rejects earthly sovereignty in order to discuss the meaning of meteorology or the purpose of the stars.

In the Jewish texts already quoted, we have seen that the Bird's Nest is a meeting place between the worlds; within the level of Paradise, or heaven, Enoch and Elijah enter the place where the Messiah sits, viewing the events of Creation. Is there anything within the stories of Merlin which further parallels this?

I believe there is. There are several references in Arthurian literature to an early name for Britain being Clas Merddin, Merlin's Enclosure, and it is said elsewhere that he built a wall of brass around this island to protect it from invasion or attack." Here, I think, we have the origin or seed-thought of the Esplumoir. Along with the references to Clas Merddin are many more which relate the island of Britain to the magical realm of Faery. In a text relating the adventures of Ogier le Dane, a hero once as famous as Arthur, we find him carried off to Avalon by Morgan le Fay, the great enchantress of the Arthurian legends. The description is interesting:

'The barge on which Ogier was, floated across the sea until it came near the Castle of Loadstone, which is called the Castle of Avalon, which is not far this side of the Terrestrial Paradise, whither were wrapt in a flame of fire Enoch and Elijah, and where was also Morgan le Fay...'?

This is very much the kind of description one gets when the Otherworld is being talked of, and here we also find not only Morgan le Fay but also both Enoch and Elijah. Again, in the *Vita Merlini*, we find a description of Britain that leaves us in no doubt that the tradition drawn upon here saw this island in a particular light. Britain is:

'foremost and best, producing in its fruitfulness every single thing. For it bears crops which throughout the year give the noble gifts of fragrance to man, and it has woods and glades with honey dripping in them, and lofty mountains and broad green fields, fountains and rivers, fishes and cattle and wild beasts, fruit trees, gems, precious metals, and whatever creative nature is in the habit of furnishing.`

This is Avalon as much as it is Britain; Merlin's isle, where adventure begins at the stone that bears his name, and where his voice may be heard upraised in prophetic utterance.

Together with Enoch, Elijah, Melchizadek and many more, Merlin has become a withdrawn or Inner King indeed, one who has chosen to enter an inner kingdom from which he will no longer play a direct role in the affairs of the world, electing instead to mediate events at a deeper level, where the barriers between humanity and the Otherworld are less defined.

This new house is the real Esplumoir, the moulting cage where we cut our ties with the world and move towards another state of being, guided by the withdrawn kings. There are parallels for this in many other areas of study, including Sufism or the Qabala. This shifting jigsaw of people and places happens outside time, where different names are given to the same people, manifesting in time and at each junction taking on a new aspect with an ongoing purpose. Thus a late medieval manuscript source wonders that so wise a man as Merlin could have allowed himself to be entrapped by a girl, and speculates as to the real nature of the story.

"For there are a variety of opinions and talk among the people, for some of them hold that that ... Merlin was a spirit in human form, who was in that shape from the time of Vortigern until the beginning of King Arthur when he disappeared ... After that, this spirit appeared again in the time of Maelgwn Gwynedd at which time he was called Taliesin, who is said to be alive yet in a place called Caer Sidia. Then, he appeared a third time in the days of Morfran Frych son of Esyllt whose son he was said to be, and in this period he was called Merlin the Mad. From that day to this, he is said to be resting in Caer Sidia, whence certain people believe firmly that he will rise up once again before Doomsday.'

Note that word 'before'. Merlin is evidently still seen as active from within the sphere of Caer Siddi, which is of course yet another name for the Celtic Otherworld, as well as a place where a famous prisoner, Gwair, or Guri, or Mabon, once resided.'

In the other, parallel version we have discussed, Enoch/Metatron begins as a replacement for Lucifer, righting the balance of power in heaven. He reappears as Melchizadek, initiating a line of priestly kings who lead to Christ, and beyond to the Grail itself. He reappears next as Enoch, who becomes Sandalphon, the way-shower, returns yet again as Merlin, who takes the Grail to the Nesting Place, the Bird's Nest, the Esplumoir, from where it passes to other hands.

This is all a far cry from the view of a lovesick old fool who allows himself to be tricked into an imprisonment from which he cannot escape. I hope I have shown that Merlin's withdrawal is a willing one, made from choice, to allow him the freedom of spirit necessary to enable him to grow and change. This can best be brought about within the chamber of the Grail, which is called by many different names, but had only one identity, like the withdrawn kings. They are the same, yet different, as is the Grail and all it stands for. Merlin is one of those figures who travel through the world for a while, only to withdraw again into the inner realm. This is how he was seen by the medieval writers who knew his story best; I believe it is how he should still be seen.

NOTES

1. *Vita Merlini*, Geoffrey of Monmouth, ed. and trans. J. J. Parry, University of Illinois Studies in Language and Literature, 1925. Edited with commentary. *Mystic Life of Merlin*, R. J. Stewart, Arkana, 1986.

2 *Didot Perceval*, trans. D. Skeels. University of Washington Press, 1961. 3 *Hebrews*, chap. 7, v. 3.

4 *Genesis*, chap. 5, v. 24.

5 *The Legends of the Jews*, A. Ginsberg, pp. 138-9.

6 *Ibid.* pp. 139-40.

7 *Ibid.* pp. 137-40.

8 *Vita Merlini op. cit..*

9 *Ginsberg op. cit.* pp. 137-40.

10 *Ibid.* p. 139.

11 *History of the Kings of Britain*, Geoffrey of Monmouth; Penguin, 1966. Cf. Gaster, M. *Legend of Merlin* (in) *Folk-Lore 11, P1). 407-26, Also *Mystic Life of Merlin*, R. J. Stewart, chap. 5, 1986.

12 *Didot Perceval*, p. 94.

13 *Ibid.*

14 Cf. Adolf, H. *The Esplumoir Merlin* (in) *Speculum*, 1946, XXI, pp. 173-93. Also, Neitz, W. A. *The Esplumoir Merlin* (in) *Speculum XVIII*, 1943, pp. 67-79.

15 *Voyage of Maelduin* (in) *The Voyages of the St Brendan the Navigator and Tales of the Irish Saints* trans. Lady Gregory, Colin Smythe, 1973.

16 *The Zohar*, trans. H. Sperting and M. Simon, V, pp. 281ff. and III, Pp. 21ff. 1931-34.

17 *Ibid.* III 22ff.

18 *The Vulgate Cycle of the Arthurian Romances*, ed. H. 0. Sommer, *The Carnegie Institution*, vols. 1 and 11, *L'Estoire del Saint Graal*, 1909-16. 19 *Zohar*, III, 22ff.

20 *Four Ancient Books of Wales*, ed. and trans. W. F. Skene, Edinburgh, 1868.

21 *Celtic Remains*, Silvan Evans, D. London, 1878.

22 *Prose Lancelot*, ed. and trans. L. A. Paton, George Routledge, 1929. 23 *Vita Merlini op. cit.*

24 *Parzival*, Wolfram von Eschenbach, trans. A. T. Hatto, Penguin, 1950. 25 *Le Roman d'Ogier le Danois*, fourteenth-century prose romance (unpublished).

26 *Vita Merlini op. cit.*

27 P. K. Ford, *The Death of Merlin in the Chronicle of Elis Gruffydd* (in) *Viator* no. 7, Pp 379-90, 1976.

28 *Mabon & the Mysteries of Britain* C. Matthews, Arkana, 1987

29 Matthews, J. "*Temples of the Grail*" (in) *At the Table of the Grail* Ed. J. Matthews Arkana, 1987. (reprinted on pp 00-00)

Chapter 4:

MERLIN IN MODERN FICTION

I wrote this essay in its original for an anthology called The Book of Merlin, Edited by R.J.Stewart (Blandford Press, 1987) This was one of two books that arose from the Merlin Conferences which Stewart and I organised in London from 1986 to 1988. Since then it has seen the light of day again in the more recent collection: Merlin Through the Ages, which we edited together (Blandford Press, 1995.) I took the opportunity then to update the text a little, and on this occasion I could not resist adding a reference to the memorable portrait of Merlin in the 2004 film King Arthur. New books about Merlin keep appearing, and undoubtedly always will. The ongoing series by Robert Holdstock, the first three of which have appeared recently under the title The Merlin Codex, are taking the character further then ever before.

"Because I am dark and always shall be,
let my book be dark and mysterious
in those places where I will not show myself".

This passage, from a medieval text about Merlin, makes a good point from which to begin this brief exploration, because it exactly describes what has happened. In no two versions is Merlin ever the same - even allowing for the idiosyncrasies of the various authors who have written about him, the divergence is so great that it would be difficult to imagine that it was the same character were it not for certain basic common factors which, ultimately, seem to reveal the figure at the heart of this constellation of disguises.

Merlin has remained 'dark and mysterious' despite everything. Yet somehow, none of those who have chosen to write about him have been able to resist asking the question: who - or what - is he? Their answers have been as diverse as they possibly could be, picturing Merlin as god or jester, as prophet, wiseman and sage; as an old lover caught in the silken wiles of his young pupil; as an alien being brought to earth on cosmic business; as a wondrous child or an Atlantean priest; as a servant of many gods or of one Goddess; as a charlatan and a liar and a madman. But always, between the disguises we glimpse another face, that of a grey-clad pilgrim and wanderer sent here long ago to guide and guard the destiny of kings and of men a majestic mage steering the barque of the island that has been named after him: *Clas Merdin* - Merlin's Enclosure, or, in Kipling's words:

Merlin's Isle of Gramarye
Where you and I will fare.

We perhaps know Merlin best in his most familiar guise - as the wise and foresighted wizard who stands behind Arthur in the early days of his reign and who acts as advisor and councillor to the young king until he himself is ensnared by a beautiful young woman who becomes his apprentice. Modern fictional versions of this basic tale do exist, but it is with some less familiar aspects that I wish to deal here, in the belief that an examination of the many facets of Merlin's character which they portray, will throw some light on the real Merlin, the enchanter in hiding.

Atlantean Origins

The span of his years is certainly immense; possibly, like the Biblical Melchizedek, 'without beginning or end.' Surprisingly, few writers in this or any age have looked for his beginnings. It is in the writings of the esotericist Dion Fortune (1890-1946) that we first find mention of Merlin as an Atlantean priest who fled from the destruction of the lost continent, bearing with him the princess Igraine, destined to become the mother of Arthur. Though Dion Fortune wrote no novel of Merlin himself, this idea has surfaced in two recent books of very different quality: *The Mists of Avalon (1982)* by Marion Zimmer Bradley, and *Merlin and the Dragons of Atlantis (1983)* by Rita and Tim Hildebrandt. In the latter, Merlin is a scientist from Lemuria, a land adjacent to Atlantis and far older. It has adopted more peaceful and mystical ways than those of its more powerful neighbours, who now seek to perfect a race of genetically engineered dragons to protect their vast cities and great domains. Merlin's thirst for knowledge brings him to join those working on the project, but when it is successful and the dragons are subsequently taken over by evil forces, he helps to destroy them, bringing about also the premature fall of Atlantis and the destruction of all that he loves. But Merlin himself does not die; he places himself in an induced state of hibernation from which he will wake to bring about the realization of a new dream, the creation of a new Atlantean state within the world of the Arthurian heroes. Then, we are told:

> *'he found his child and taught him well. The child grew with wisdom and knowledge into manhood. Thus for a brief second in history Merlin saw Arthur have his Camelot' (P.205)*

Dragons of Atlantis represents an effort to show Merlin as a tran-scendent figure, able to operate over vast distances of time, through the use of knowledge no longer current in our world. Atlantis is merely the latest image of the Otherworldly realm from which Merlin has always been recognised as coming, while the image of Merlin himself is much as we would expect him to be portrayed in our time: as a scientist rather than as a wizard or seer; as someone imbued with endless curiosity about the nature of creation and its foremost offspring: mankind.

Marion Bradley's book is both well written and imaginatively satisfying. However, for her, Merlin is a title borne by many rather than a name belonging to anyone figure. Here, as in numerous recent versions of the story, the setting is post-Roman Britain, in which Merlin acts as an agent of those who seek to unite the shattered country into an unshakable force under the banner of Arthur. But already, before that dream is even begun, a deeper split exists - a religious division between Christianity and those who follow the way of the Goddess of Earth. Bradley's interpretation seems to say more about the current spiritual divide between orthodox religion and eco-pagan groups than about any actual spiritual divisions existing in post-Roman culture. Nevertheless, her personal colouring of events gives the book it vigour and also allows her Merlin to voice a genuine observation:

'There are now two Britains ... their world under their One God and the Christ; and beside it and behind it, the world where the Great Mother still rules, the world where the Old People have chosen to live and worship.'(p15)

Igraine, soon to be the mother of the young king, remembers an earlier time, an earlier incarnation. In a waking vision, she stands on Salisbury Plain and watches the fiery sun rise over the great stone circle - and beyond,

'To the West, where stood the lost lands of Lyonesse and Ys and the great isle of Atlas-Alamesios, or Atlantis, the forgotten kingdom of the sea. There, indeed, had been the great fire, there the mountain had blown apart, and in a single night, a hundred thousand men and women and little children had perished ... "But the Priests knew" said a voice at her side. "For the past hundred years, they have been building their star temple here on the plains, so that they might not lose count of the tracking of the seasons ... These people here, they know nothing of such things, but they know we are wise, priests and priestesses from over the sea, and they will build for us, as they did before"...'(P. 63)

The speaker is Uther, who shares Igraine's reincarnational memories. From their love is soon to issue the young Arthur who with Merlin's aid will try to build a new and perfect expression of Human endeav-our. Here, we may see Merlin as representing the latest of a line of priests descended from the long-ago escapees of the doomed land, who have carried the seeded memories of the past within them until it can be brought once again into manifestation.

In a different way this is the aim of Merlin in Andre Norton's *Merlin's Mirror* (1975), where the image is a creation of a race of alien beings known as the Sky Lords, who in the infancy of the world leave behind them a hidden computer installation programmed to begin its work many thousands of years later, by the creation of heroes and leaders who will raise the race of men to their own height. There is an implication also that the Sky Lords will themselves have perished by this time, perhaps as a result of a long struggle with an opposing force called 'the Dark Ones'. These are not intrinsically evil, it seems, but are opposed to the actions of the Sky Lords and their aim to hasten the development of humanity.

In this science fiction version of the story, Merlin is created by means of the artificial insemination of a British woman who sees only a computer-generated image of a beautiful golden man - an ingenious twist to the story of Merlin's birth in Geoffrey of Mon-mouth's twelfth century *Historia Regum Britanniae*. But, just as Merlin represents the Sky Lords, so does Nimue represent the Dark Ones, and the ancient destiny of the King, his wizard, and the priestess who brings about their downfall, is here played out in images drawn from the cosmic world of the science fiction novel. In the end, Merlin, who has read all the future in his computer-operated 'mirror', sees that his dream of a united land under the figure of Arthur, is doomed to fail, and he retires, like the Merlin of the Hildebrand novel, into a self -induced sleep to await a more auspicious time when he may try again.

In Susan Cooper's *Dark is Rising* sequence (1965-1979) we are afforded a glimpse of Merlin once again in immortal guise, as a combatant against the powers of evil. To the world at large he is known as Dr Merriman Lyon, a professor of Arthurian studies and an archaeologist - two roles we may well imagine Merlin adopting in a twentieth-century setting. In reality, however, he is one of an immortal race known simply as 'the Old Ones', whose endless task it is to combat the ancient forces of the Dark. This is more openly dualistic than either Andre Norton or C. S. Lewis, but as in both of these writers, and in the work of the Hildebrandts there are echoes of Merlin's Atlantean origins. Once again his task is to guide the steps of human protagonists - here a group of children - rather than directly intervene in the age-old war of Light and Dark. As in his guidance of the young Arthur in the original romances, this role is one that requires him to adopt many faces and forms, becoming elusive and secret and unfathomable in order to perform his task.

Primary Task

We have seen already that Merlin is often shown to be a priest or councillor of kings, who comes from a far-off land where civilisation, or knowledge, may be more advanced than in the rest of the world. We can be sure as well that he is possessed of occult or prophetic knowledge, and we can extend our understanding of his role or function further by turning to another Merlin-type figure, who does not bear his name but who occupies a position in almost every way the same as that taken by Merlin. The relevant passage reads as follows:

> 'Warm and eager was his spirit ... opposing the fire that devours and wastes with the fire that kindles and succours in wan hope and distress; but his joy, and his swift wrath, were veiled in garments grey as ash, so that only those who knew him well glimpsed the flame that was within. Merry he could be and kindly to the young and simple, and yet quick at times to sharp speech and the rebuking of folly; but he was not proud, and sought neither power or praise, and thus far and wide he was beloved among all those that were not themselves proud. Mostly he journeyed unwearyingly on foot, leaning on a staff; and so he was called among men of the North Gandalf, the "Elf of the Wand".'
> J. R. R. Tolkien: Unfinished Tales pp. 390-1

Gandalf, of course, in Tolkien's mythology, is one of the Istari, emissaries of the Valar, great angelic forces who watch over the world and mediate between God and creation. This is completely in line with the primary task allotted to Merlin in the majority of the stories about him - to guide and shepherd the destinies of men. It is in this guise that we encounter him again and again, both in the medieval stories, and in the writings of modern authors - books as varied and far apart in scope as John Cowper Powys' Porius, (1951), Mary Stewart's Merlin trilogy (1970-1979), Peter Vansittart's Lan-celot (1978), and Linda Halderman's fantasy The Lastborn of Elvin-wood (1980).

The Merlin of Porius is half-man and half-god, a huge, slow earth-man, smelling of mould and green things. His work is devoted to the return upon earth of a new Golden Age, the age of Saturn/ Cronos, of which god he sees himself as a true avatar. Descriptions of him abound in Powys' extraordinary book. Here is just one:

> 'Myrddin Wyllt was dressed in his long black mantle; and at the place where his great beard reached the level of his navel, it was tied with the usual gold thread whose tassels hung down to his knees. His head was bare, and his long fingers at the end of his long arms were making slow majestic movements as if writing upon the interior darkness of the tent ... But it soon occurred to Porius that what the man was doing lent itself to another and quite different interpretation; namely, that instead of inscribing things on the air he was tracing out things that had already been written upon it!' (p405)

Powys' Myrddin Wyllt (or the Wild) is linked specifically with an ancient race of aboriginal giants, the very children of Cronos it seems, of whom the last remnant live out their days in the fastness of Welsh mountains. In Linda Halderman's book, Merlin is again associated with the destiny of a race of huge people - though here they have remained hidden, and have dwindled, becoming in time a smaller race, the denizens of Faery, who have no love for he whom they call 'the Old One', blaming his actions in a dim and distant time for their own present state. Their traditions tell how once their giant ancestors

> '... dwelt in the mountains to the north mostly, herding and farming and minding their own business. He, the Old One, lived alone in the south. What he is and where he came from, I cannot say. Perhaps your legend of him being the offspring of a demon has some truth in it. I don't pretend to know. We call ourselves the First Folk, because it is our belief that our gigantic ancestors were the first people to live on this island. Yet they called him the Old One [even then].' (P. 136)

The present day heroes, seeking to enlist his aid in the matter of two changelings, find the Old One living in semi-retirement in a cottage in the depths of the English countryside. On their way to visit him they discuss his history - the story of his being the son of the devil, and of his entrapment by Nimue:

> 'Ah yes, Nimue ... A naive ruse, but one that worked. It was the end of what he calls his political phase ... Arthur turned out to be a bitter disappointment, more interested in holding bloody tournaments than in planting gardens, [Mer-lin's great love] . . . and unnaturally preoccupied with his wife's activities ... Arthur is one of the main reasons he's down on the Celts ... he decided to retire. Arthur refused to let him go, so he paid Nimue to invent the cave story and slipped off to live in blissful solitude . . .' (P. 64)

Here we have a glimpse of a lighter side of Merlin's nature, yet he is still a difficult and even a dangerous character, who can be both chancy and unreliable in his dealings with humanity. Pete Vansittart, in his novel *Lancelot*, paints an even more oblique portrait. Here, Merlin is generally referred to as ' He' - a mark of respect and caution towards the Old One, whom one should never address by name unless invited to do so. 'He' seems, at first glance, an unprepossessing character:

> 'Despite the familiar dirt caking his ears, beard, bare feet, the sack like gown under gaudy robes, he repelled me less, his hierophantic mendacities more lively than the dismal hush that passed for entertainment with Artorius. Last year his hand motions had induced a snowfall when least required, his explanations being acceptable as minor poetry by anyone without scholarship or sensitivity. He had also acquired an adroit method of inclining his head so that a shadow of a bird or animal was reflected on the wall behind him.' (P. 144)

Merlin is brought back to life - literally since he is summoned from his grave by Ceneu, the current King of the Britons, to assist in the last desperate attempt to stem the tide of the invading Saxons - in Nikolai Tolstoy's *The Coming of the King: the First Book of Merlin.* (1988). This is the first in a projected trilogy, though a second volume is yet to appear at the time of writing - and follows on from Tolstoy's excellent study *The Quest for Merlin* which appeared in 1985.

The Coming of the King is an immensely long and discursive book, frequently interrupting the flow of the narrative for long digressions on matters of siege warfare or for huge set pieces such as the feast of Maelgwn Gwynedd, in which devils and daemons are conjured up to join in the baroque festivities. The setting of the book in Northern Britain two generations after the departing of Arthur, and consists in part of Myrddin's (Tolstoy opts for the more ancient figure and the traditional spelling) rambling memoirs, in which he recalls not only the time of Arthur but mythological time as well. He is conflated somewhat with the figure of Taliesin, which gives Tolstoy an excuse to re-tell the powerful myth of the shapeshifting bard, and to lead the way into the depths of Annwn itself. For this is not just a tale of historical characters and events - it is a vast spiritual tract, an allegory as dense allusive as Spenser or Bunyon

Tolstoy is primarily a historian and Celtecist, and the immense structure of his learning, which is intended to support the book only succeeds in hampering the story - almost drowning it in details which leave the reader alternatively gasping or reaching for a Welsh dictionary. The figure of Myrddin that emerges is, however, probably the closest anyone has got since Geoffrey of Monmouth to the real figure: immemorially ancient, powerful and merging almost with the land itself. In this Tolstoy is closest to J.C. Powys and C.S.Lewis in his delineation of the character of the old mage.

> 'It seemed to King Ceneu and his companions that there arose from the centre of the gorsedd a man greater far in stature than the men of their own time. His clothes were but the undressed skins of beasts, his hair thin and grey and flowing, and his aspect paler, emaciated, wild. He lacked his left eye, which was but a puckered, sightless socket. His gaze seemed to portend both pain and anger.... (p18)

This telling is bardic, drawing upon the Mabinogion and the old poems of Myrddin and Gwenddydd (see above, Part One) to fuel a powerful and extraordinary archetype.

Stephen Lawhead, in his trilogy *The Pendragon Cycle* (1988-89) again harks back to Atlantis and develops the theme farther than ever before, establishing an Atlantean community, ruled over by King Avallach and his son Prince Taliesin, within the land of Celtic Britain. The second volume of the trilogy *Merlin* (1988) concentrates on the figure of Merlin himself, Avallach's grandson and thus the inheritor of the Atlantean bloodline. He recalls listening to 'sad stories of Lost Atlantis' as he walks with Avallach 'The Fisher King' in the gardens of Ynys Wittrin (Glastonbury).

The book follows the outlines of the medieval *Vita Merlini* in its general shape and structure, though developing the character and story of Merlin far beyond the scope of the medieval tale. Here Merlin is both King of Dyfed and a reluctant seer, whose pain and passion in the wilderness is set forth in all its stark reality. The story is told in the first person, and at the very opening of the book Merlin recalls the various ways in which he has been recognised:

> 'Emrys is the name I have won among men and it is my own. Emrys, Immortal...Emrys, Divine...Emrys Wledig, king and prophet to his people. Ambrosius it is to the Latin speakers, and Embries to the people of Southern Britain and Lloegres.... But Myrddin Emrys am I to the Cymry of the hill-bound fastness of the west' (p15)

His long life, including years of wandering in the wilds of the hills are chronicled, as are his love for Ganeida, his association with Ambrosius, Uther and finally Arthur himself. Lawhead's long and intricately woven chronicle places Merlin squarely centre stage, and links him both to the dim and distant realm of Atlantis and to the founding of the great Arthurian kingdom that is so much his own work. Of all the recent portrayals of Merlin it is perhaps the best and certainly the most moving.

The Prophet

Merlin's prophetic gifts are so much a part of his character that they almost seem to pass unnoticed at times, though it is by this means that he is enabled, primarily, to bring about the shaping of the destiny of others. Mary Stewart, in her trilogy of books about Merlin *(The Crystal Cave, The Hollow Hills* and *The Last Enchantment)* makes these powers central.

In the first volume, Merlin discovers his ability to 'see' future events; but his visions are the product of fits brought on by staring into a pattern of crystals, rather than by inner or magical contact, and throughout the remainder of the book and those which follow it, ingenious solutions are found for many of the more mysterious aspects of Merlin's life. Thus we read nothing of his magic, only of his technical skills, which enable him to position the 'Hele Stone' of Stonehenge at its present site, rather than (as in the medieval stories) raising the whole monument or causing it to fly through the air or float across the Irish Sea.

This portrait of Merlin succeeds in flattening out the character in an effort to explain it - psychological motivation accounting for most of his life - though he remains a prime mover in the setting up of a stable kingdom under the enlightened rule of Arthur.

The third volume of the trilogy recounts the relationship with Nimue - almost the only attempt to tell this story fully since Tennyson debased it to Victorian drawing room melodrama in his *Merlin and Vivian* of 1890. In Mary Stewart's version, with Arthur estab-lished as king over all of Britain, Merlin retires to the wilderness. There, attacked by a subtle poison administered to him by Morgause, he is nursed back to health by a youth named Ninian, who of course turns out to be a girl, Niniane, or Nimue:

> *'The dim-seen figure in the mist, [seemed,] so like the lost boy, that I had greeted her and put the words 'boy' and 'Ninian' into her head before she could even speak. Told her I was Merlin: offered her the gift of my power and magic, gifts that another girl - the witch Morgause - had tried in vain to prise from me, but which I had hastened eagerly to lay at this stranger's feet.' (P. 365)*

The Lover

Thereafter, the story follows the more familiar track. Nimue becomes Merlin's pupil - until in the end, his powers begin to fade and she takes over the role of guardian of Arthur's realm. Finally, Merlin himself withdraws, promising to return. His end is left uncertain.

The only other significant treatment of Merlin as a lover is in a book by the American author, James Branch Cabell. Cabell is something of an oddity amongst those who have dealt with Arthurian themes in fiction in that he sets his book, *Something About Eve (1935)*, within the framework of a huge invented universe of chivalry and the erotic, spanning vast areas of time and space. In a chapter entitled 'The Chivalry of Merlin', the old wizard is summoned, along with King Solomon and Odysseus, to give an account of himself before he passes 'into the realms of Antan' (Cabell's name for the Otherworld), to discover the true meaning of his life:

> *'I was Merlin Ambrosius. The wisdom that I had was more than human ... but I served heaven with it ...' And then Merlin told about the child Nimue who was the daughter of the goddess Diana, and of how old, wearied, overlearned Merlin had come ... I to love her]. Then Merlin told to Nimue, because she pouted so adoringly, the*

36

secret of building a tower which is not made of stone, or timber, or iron, and is so strong that it may never be felled while this world endures. And Nimue, the moment he had fallen asleep with his head in her lap, spoke very softly the old rune . . .' (P. 190)

And Merlin confesses that he was happy for a long while in his tower, until he saw his 'toys', the men and women of the Arthurian age, begin to break each other and to become filled with hate and lust and barbarity. But even then he lingers on, happy with his child love and the peace of his tower - only now does he seek enlightenment in the Otherworld, where perhaps he may find reasons for the failure of his dream ... For, whatever Merlin's end, whatever his origins, he never ceases to be concerned with this world and the people who live in it. His function within what we may call the 'inner history' of Britain varies hardly at all from Geoffrey of Monmouth to Mary Stewart. As the prime mover in the setting up of Arthur's kingdom, and of the Round Table; and as prophet, guardian and sometime tutelary spirit of Britain, he remains true.

Thus, in Parke Godwin's *Firelord* (1980), when he assumes another guise, that of the Wonder-Child, it is to offer Arthur some cursory advice:

'The boy' was seated on a flat rock ... He looked maddeningly familiar with his shock of blond, curly hair and blue eyes glistening with secret excitement: things to do and tomorrows that couldn't be caught up fast enough. He shimmered all over, he made me tingle with the energy that came from him . . .'(PP- 5'6)

Here, Merlin is, in some sense, Arthur's own inner self, able to show him a vision of the future, of the great king and warrior whose presence draws the very utmost effort from the men who follow him - the man that Arthur is to become, driven by the Merlin within:

Deep in me, Artos stirs.
Stay away I tell him. Go back to sleep.
But Artos wakes ... opens his eyes inside me. 'It's time', he says.
Time for what?
'I know what Merlin wanted to teach me', whispers Artos in my soul.
'To be a king over men. To know what they are and the price of knowledge'. (p84)

The Teacher

Merlin's function is indeed often to teach -though he may choose to do so in some curious ways. In T. H. White's *The Sword in the Stone* he teaches by example, turning Arthur into animal, fish or bird. So that, from his encounter with a great pike that lives beneath the walls of his foster-father's castle, he learns that power for its own sake leads nowhere; while from a position high above the earth, Arthur as a bird discovers that boundaries are an illusion fought over without reason. And of course, all that he learns stands him in good stead when he comes to draw the famous sword from the stone - act that will make him King:

'All round the churchyard there were hundreds of old friends. They rose over the church wall all together, like Punch and Judy ghosts of remembered days, and there were otters and nightingales and vulgar crows and hares and serpents and falcons and fishes and goats and dogs and dainty unicorns and newts and solitary wasps and

goat-moth caterpillars and cockindrills and volcanoes and mighty trees and patient stones. They loomed round the church walls, the lovers and helpers of the Wart (Arthur) and they all spoke solemnly in turn . . .' (Pp279-80)

Nor is it surprising that Merlin should choose this method of teaching. His earliest incarnation was as the Wild Herdsman, the Lord of the Beasts, and even the trees and stones obey his call.

But it is as tutor and guide to the young king that we know him best, and as such he appears again and again in modern retellings. Catherine Christian in her excellent *The Sword and the Flame (1982)* has him arranging for Arthur to acquire his second, more famous sword, Excalibur. But in a variation from the more traditional episode, where he receives it from the Lady of the Lake, here Merlin assists in its forging by an ancient Smith God, from a lump of meteorite:

'It is now (says Merlin). Listen, Old One, the stream sings for it. The fire-spirits call for it. Fetch the King-sword here, to the anvil, and finish its forging, while the power of the Dragon and the power of the Merlin are together in this place to give you strength.' (p. 52)

That the shaping of King or sword may extend beyond a single lifetime is shown in those versions of the story where Merlin or Arthur come again, after a long sleep, in Avalon or the Hawthorn Tower, to continue the work left unfinished at the end of the Arthurian Age. In the final part of C.S Lewis' science fiction trilogy *(That Hideous Strength [1945])*, Merlin is awakened by the striving of the forces of good and evil - here represented by Ransom, Lewis' space voyager, and a totalitarian group seeking control over the earth. Here, somewhat as in Powys's version, Merlin is seen as almost a god - a force as old as time itself; a massive, primitive power virtually without limit. When he and Ransom first meet there follows a marvellous riddling exchange in which each tests the knowledge of the other. When Ransom has successfully answered a whole string of questions, Merlin asks another which he deems even harder: where is Arthur's Ring?

'The Ring of the King,' said Ransom, 'is on Arthur's finger where he sits in the House of Kings in the cup-shaped land of Abhalljin, beyond the seas of Lur in Peralandra. [Lewis' name for Venus.) For Arthur did not die; but Our Lord took him to be in the body until the end of time ... with Enoch and Elias and Moses and Melchisedec the King. Melchisedec is he in whose hall the steep-stoned ring sparkles on the finger of the Pendragon.' (p. 337)

Ransom is thereafter revealed as Arthur's successor, the new Pendragon, to whom Merlin once again pledges his service, and whom he aids in the final overthrow of the modern day forces of evil. References to Numinor (sic) and the 'Far West' in this book confirm the identification of Merlin with Gandalf in Tolkien's *Lord of the Rings*.

Reincarnation

The theme of the recurring acts of Merlin and Arthur is taken up again by the science fiction writer Tim Powers in *The Drawing of the Dark (1977)*. Here, Merlin is the guardian of the Wounded Grail King, who is kept alive, by a curious twist of the old story, not through the daily descent of a dove bearing a wafer in its beak, but by a yearly draught of a unique elixir - Hertzwestern Beer! Merlin, the owner of the inn where this mysterious drink is brewed, recalls the latest incarnation of Arthur in the shape of a seventeenth-century Irish mercenary named Brian Duffy, to help him protect the elixir against an ancient and implacable enemy. The substance of the book is concerned with Duffy's adventures and with his unwillingness to allow memories of himself as Arthur to come to the surface. But throughout the old story the figure of the old magus moves subtly. He is old, here, an undying figure who seems eternally destined to pit himself against the enemies of light.

In this guise also, he reappears in a children's book, *Merlin's Magic*, by Helen Clare (1953). Here Merlin calls upon figures as diverse as Walter Raleigh, Morgan-le-Fay, Francis Drake and the Greek god Mercury to aid him in frustrating an invasion of Robot-people who, because they lack the essential human function of the imagination, seek to steal it from mankind. Were they successful, Merlin implies, he himself, as well as Arthur and the other great figures, once mortal but now transformed into mythic archetypes, would all fade. The resulting loss to humanity would, of course, be almost without equal, and it is up to the great wizard to save the day again!

The Trickster

Despite Powys's version, which comes near to it, and perhaps also that of Tolstoy, we lack a truly shamanistic novel of Merlin. However, Merlin the trickster is not unrepresented. Apart from Linda Halderman's book there are two others: Robert Nye's *Merlin (1978)*, and to a lesser extent, Thomas Berger's *Arthur Rex (1979)*, which both deal with this strange, un-toward side of the magus' nature.

Berger is closest in many respects to Malory's version, though his book is a comic masterpiece shot through with gleams of the high fantasy of the original Arthuriad. In a scene near the beginning of the book, two knights seek out Merlin at an enchanted fountain in the forest:

'And both the knight and the horses, being sore thirsty, drank from the crystal water of the spring (into which one could see forever because there was no bottom) and by the time they had soaked their parched throats the men had been transformed into green frogs and the horses into spotted hounds. Now in despair and confusion the knights clambered with webbed feet from the steel armour which had fallen around them as they diminished in size, and the horses howled in dismay. 'None may drink of my water without my leave,' said a voice, and looking aloft the frogs saw it was the raven that spake. Then the glossy black bird flapped his wings twice and before their bulging eyes he was transformed into a man with a long white beard and wearing the raiment of a wizard, which is to say a long gown, a tall hat in the shape of a cone, both dark as the sky at midnight with here and there twinkling stars and a horned moon. And the next instant Merlin (for it was he) caused both knights and horses to return to their proper forms and only then did he laugh most merrily. *(P. 3)*

Robert Nye, on the other hand, aiming for a comedy of Eros, plumbs the depths of Merlin's character, as very few writers have managed to do. I make no secret of the fact that this is almost my favourite portrait of Merlin. It is funny, irreverent and profound, and underneath its scatological humour and endless word-play, there is a deeply researched picture which draws upon nearly all the many disguises of Merlin to reveal him, at last, as a strangely sorrowful creature, mourning for the even more sorrowful creatures over whom he has been given care.

From within the crystal cave of his retirement, Merlin views past, present and future with a jaundiced eye. He describes himself as:

'Merlin Ambrosius. Merlin Sylvester.
Merlin the magician. Merlin the witch.
The wisest man at the court of King Arthur,
and the greatest fool. Well, shall we say the only adult [...]

My mother was a virgin. My father was the devil'. (P. 3)

For Nye, this is the crux of the matter - Merlin partakes of *both* natures - human and non-human, good and evil, god and devil. Within him are the legions of hell and the armies of heaven. He is the battleground and the object of conquest and defense: ourselves - humanity. It is part of the subtle alchemy of Nye's book that he is able to show up the black side of human nature - as well as its silly side: all libido and bluster - and yet give a sense of the triumph of man over his own shortcomings. Merlin is the *deus ex machina* who stands ready to intervene, who laughs and plays the fool but who, underneath, *cares* for his children.

It is virtually impossible to get a proper feeling of Nye's book from a quotation - you have to read it all. Here are just two short extracts from the beginning and end of *Book 3:*

The boyhood of Arthur. The madness of Merlin.
Look.
A golden-haired boy running through a deep golden pool of sunlight falling into the trees in the deepest deep of the wild green wood.
Arthur running through the golden and the green.
His golden hair. His green tunic.
'Sometimes you seem mad, or a fool, or a boy like me.' [...]
I teach him. Merlin teaches Arthur. To KNOW
To DARE To WILL To KEEP SILENT.
Arthur is not a good pupil. . . (p. 150-2)

And at the end:

They bare away Arthur no man knows where.
(Unwise the thought: a grave for Arthur.)
The first queen has the face of the Virgin Vivien.
The second queen has the face of the Lady Igrayne.
The third queen has the face of the King's half-sister, Queen Morgan le Fay.
Now without a sail, without oars, the draped barge passed out from the shore. It is black upon the waters, and then gold.
Little pig, listen.
The wind in the reeds.
The laughter of Merlin! (P211)

There are echoes here of Malory, Geoffrey of Monmouth, old Welsh poetry, and even of Tennyson. Nye book is pure poetry and no other writer has so far delved as deeply into the very soul of the ancient magician.

Definitive Portraits

No one book has yet appeared which attempts to deal with all the aspects of Merlin's character, and perhaps there could be no such book. Robert Nye comes closest in my opinion, and there is the recent collection of stories by Jane Yolen, published under the title *Merlin's Booke (1986)*, which has great diversity, but lacks the coherence of a novel. Only one recent product of imaginative thinking seems to me to illustrate all the faces of Merlin, making it, for me, the definitive portrait to date.

I said imaginative portrait, because it is not a book. But I make no apology for including it here, because in every other way it fits the notion of a fictional retelling. I refer to the film *Excalibur (1983)*, directed and co-written by John Boorman and Rospo Pallenburg. At one time the intention was to call this film *Merlin* and it is the figure of the mage that dominates the action. Here we encounter him in each of his major aspects. As controller of destinies, he engineers the birth of Arthur, the giving of the magical sword, the shaping of the Round Table, and the quest for the Grail. But he is not of human blood and follows the old ways, which, as he tells his pupil Morgana, 'are numbered'; and, as he tells Arthur later, he is already fading: 'My time is almost over. The days of men are here to stay.' Like Gandalf, when his work is done, he must depart into the West to become 'a dream to some, a nightmare to others.'

Throughout the shifting patterns of the film, Merlin emerges, from Nicol Williamson's portrayal, as tetchy, loving, ingenious, amused, surprised. Possessed of god-like powers, vision and cunning, he is all of the Merlins in one. Finally, he is as baffling as ever, escaping before us like smoke, blown across the blood-soaked field of Camlan. Yet, it is in that dark ending that Merlin reveals himself most clearly. Let Parke Godwin's *Firelord* say it for me. In this scene Arthur is dying - or fading; however one wishes to see it. Merlin appears, as a boy again, juggling with brightly coloured balls:

> *The coloured balls soared higher, four of them now, five, six. The shimmering boy balanced and timed their flight so skilfully that they moved in a smooth circle like the sun. 'Don't they shine, Arthur? Shaped from the finest tomorrows. Not an easy job, you know. Another dreamer to be born in the same old place: where's he's needed'. He was my genius, this juggler, always the more impressive part of me. Or was I merely a facet of him, designed to lead and care for men? (p. 364)*

This is why Merlin will never be forgotten, why he keeps returning, under the guise of such diverse characters as Mr Spock in the television series *Star Trek*, or as Obi Wan Kenobi in the *Star Wars* saga. Even in novels like Lawrence Durrell's *The Revolt of Aphrodite (1974)* or Walker Percy's *Lancelot (1979)* we may detect the figure of the old mage, looming up against the backdrop of contemporary dreams or boardroom politics.

Nor can I pass on from the subject of Merlin in cinema without mentioning his most reincarnation there. This is in Jerry Bruckheimer's production of *King Arthur* (2004) in which Merlin, played by Stephen Dillane, is portrayed as freedom fighter, struggling to preserve his people (the Picts, who may be the oldest inhabitants of Britain) against both the Romans and Saxons. Script writer David Franzoni and director Antoine Fuqua chose to strip Merlin of most of his magic - though there are elements of the shaman still embedded in the character. Stephen Dillane's portrayal makes us aware of a raw power, scarcely held in check, which might at any moment break free. This promises to be one of the most interesting accounts of Merlin in recent years, and in its stark realism may come as close as possible to the human being behind the mage.

In Jane Yolen's collection of stories, *Merlin's Booke (1986)*, the story is brought up to date in a most intriguing way. The story is set in the near future, when a group of reporters have been summoned to a news conference at which it is revealed that Merlin's tomb has been discovered beneath Glastonbury Tor, and that along with the ancient wizard's mummified body is a strange box, which is to be opened by the Prince of Wales under the eyes of the world's press. Each of them sees something different, but one of Celtic origin, McNeil, sees more than any - though what, he dare not say:

'Could he tell them that at the moment the box had opened, the ceiling and walls of the meeting room had dropped away? That they were all suddenly standing within a circle of Corinthian pillars under a clear night sky. That as he watched, behind the pillars one by one the stars had begun to fall. Could he tell them? Or more to the point - would they believe? `Light,' he said. 'I saw light. And darkness coming on.' … Merlin had been known as a prophet, a soothsayer, equal to or better than Nostradamus. But the words of seers have always admitted to a certain ambiguity... `My darlings', he said, 'I have a sudden and overwhelming thirst. I want to make a toast to the earth under me and the sky above me. A toast to the arch-mage and what he has left us. A salute to Merlin: ave magister. Will you come?'

Among the new generation of writers who have added significantly to the Arthurian mythos is Charles de Lint, a Canadian whose perceptions of the darkly wooded world of the Celts runs as deep as any previous writer. In his novel *Moonheart* (1989) he introduced the figure of Taliesin into modern day Canada. In the sequel *Spiritwalk* (1992), a section appears called 'Merlin Dreams in the Mondream Wood'. This is almost a separate piece of writing from the rest, though it opens up themes that are further explored throughout the remainder of the book. In it one of the characters, Sara Kendell, comes to live in the Tamson House, a kind of gateway between the worlds where figures from the Otherworld enter and depart at will. Here, in the garden of the house, she encounters a mysterious being:

"In the heart of the garden stood a tree.
In the heart of the tree lived an old man who wore the shape of a red-haired boy with crackernut eyes that seemed as bright as salmon tails glinting up the water.
His was a riddling wisdom, older by far than the ancient oak that houses his body. The green sap was his blood and leaves grew in his hair. In the winter he slept. In the spring, the moon harped a windsong against his antler tines as the oak's boughs stretched its green buds to wake. In the summer, the air was thick with the droning of bees and the scent of wildflowers that grew in stormy profusion where the fat brown bole became root.
And in the autumn, when the tree loosed its bounty to the ground below, there were hazelnuts lying in among the acorns.
The secrets of a Green Man." (P. 6)

This Merlin is old, older perhaps than any of the others we have considered. He is both Arthur's Merlin and Geoffrey's Merlin and something else as well - the Old Earth Man, the Green One, the Walker in the Woods who had been on this earth for as long as the earth itself has been. De Lint's contribution, though slight in volume, is as significant of the way we regard Merlin as any other writer in this age or the past.

Thus we may see that as we get further from the time of Merlin, we seem to curve back upon our road to a time even earlier, when Merlin is almost a god, and when the elements which were to go into the creation of the character, were first stirring in the hearts and minds of the primal storytellers.

Merlin cannot fade. He is too much a part of us all, too deeply rooted in our hearts and minds and souls. He is as much the Spirit of Britain as Arthur, and it would be hard to imagine one without the other.

(1987-2007)

Chapter 5:

REAPPRAISING GAWAIN:
PAGAN CHAMPION OR CHRISTIAN KNIGHT

This is the text of a paper I gave at a conference in Oxford devoted to the work and life of Professor J.R.R.Tolkien in the late 1990s. I had by then written my book Gawain: Knight of the Goddess (1991, Reprinted by Inner Traditions, 2003) and knowing of Tolkien's famous edition of the English alliterative masterpiece Sir Gawain and the Green Knight – though this a good opportunity to follow up the connection with the figure of Arthur's greatest knight. Nearly 20 years later I was able to return to this theme in greater detail, (see Tolkien and the Green Man pp 188-197) exploring the presence of another character with whom Gawain was closely associated but on whom I could only touch in passing here.

I first discovered the work of J.R.R.Tolkien over thirty years ago. But it wasn't through the books for which he is justly famous, but through his scholarship that I first knew of him. I used his edition of the medieval poem *Sir Gawain and the Green Knight* done in collaboration with E.V.Gordon, long before I learned, from a friend, of 'a rather odd book' called *The Lord of the Rings*. Once I had my hands on that my life was never quite the same again, and though I very much regret that Tolkien never seemed to see as much value in the Arthurian traditions of this country as in the tales of the North, I have never forgotten that my interest in Gawain - the character whom I want to talk about today - was awoken by my reading of Professor Tolkien's work, and I like to think that he would have approved of the subject at least - if not of its conclusions!

It's my personal belief, incidentally, that the character of the Green Knight - in both his otherworldly guise and as his alter ego Sir Bercilak - of whom more in a moment - influenced Professor Tolkien in the creation of two characters in his own writings - those of Beorn in *The Hobbit* and Tom Bombadil in *The Lord of the Rings*. Though both these characters function very differently from the Green Knight, their power and larger-than-life characteristics seem to me to reflect those of their medieval counterparts very closely.

But now to Gawain - who is, in fact, probably the single most popular hero in the entire Arthurian cycle. He is the subject of some forty texts, in four languages, and plays a major role in 95% of the rest of those great tales. Yet, despite this popularity, a curious contradiction exists concerning the way in which he is portrayed. In the Celtic texts that record his earliest exploits, Gawain is a hero of tremendous stature and abilities. He "*never came home without the Quest he had gone to seek*" it says of him in the *Mabinogion* story of "Culhwch and Olwen". "*He was the best of walkers and the best of riders. He was Arthur's nephew, his sister's son, and the first among his companions.*" Elsewhere, in that marvellous collection of Celtic story-themes known as the *Triads of Britain*, we are told that Gawain is among the "*Three Fearless Men of the Island of Britain*", and that he was "*the most courteous to guests and strangers.*" In a later text, he very nearly becomes Emperor of Rome!

And yet, in the Middle Ages, from the 13th century onwards, and with few exceptions, a very different image is projected. Here, in texts like the *Prose Tristan* and the *Queste del Saint Graal*, Gawain is cowardly, discourteous, and something of a libertine. He is persistently criticised and unfavourably compared with other knights such as Lancelot and Perceval. Finally, in Malory's great book *Le Morte D'Arthur*, he is portrayed as a murderer, capable of fanatical hatred leading to a bloody vendetta.

How did this come about, and more importantly, why did it happen at all? Of what crime, or association, was Gawain guilty in the eyes of the medieval clerks and romancers, which called for this systematic blackening of his character?

The usual answer, from those who have noticed the phenomenon, is to say that other heroes displaced Gawain from his position of superiority - most notably Lancelot, who became the best of the Round Table Fellowship at the expense of earlier figures, such as Gawain. To a certain extent this is true, but I believe there is another reason, which I outlined in a book about Gawain in 1991.

Put simply, I believe that Gawain was a unique figure within the Arthurian tradition, who represented the last dying strains of an ancient theme - one which dated back to the very earliest days of Celtic story-telling, and which incorporated even earlier religious beliefs. Gawain, I believe, was the Champion of the Goddess.

It is difficult to say with any degree of certainty just what the Celts understood by the term Goddess, or what, for that matter, it meant to people in general during the Middle Ages. Celtic religious beliefs are still little understood, though we do know that they worshipped deities of wood and water, sky and sea - indeed that each of the elements was of prime importance to them. So that when they spoke of 'Goddesses' they were probably thinking of what we would call an abstract principle of nature, represented in the form of a woman.

The best example of this is the Goddess of Sovereignty, with whom Gawain, as we shall see, had a particular relationship. For the Celts, particularly the Irish, the concept of Sovereignty, as of Kingship, was of a unique kind of link with the earth itself. Thus the King was believed literally to mate with the Goddess of the Land - the otherworldly representative of the particular area over which he reigned. Without the sanction of Sovereignty thus gained he could not rule wisely or honestly, or ensure that the Kingdom remained strong and virile. This is all part and parcel of a much older idea concerning the sacredness of the land itself - which perhaps in some distant Foretime gave birth to the people who walked upon it - hence the concept of Mother Earth - or perhaps I should say, in this company - 'Mother Middle Earth'?

By the period of the Middle Ages much of this had been forgotten - or at least re-assimilated. The fact remains that it takes many hundreds of generations for a new set of religious beliefs to supersede an earlier strata, and that while the process is taking place a situation exists in which the shadowy forms of earlier traditions mingle with those of the new.

This is the situation that existed during most of the time the Gawain romances were being composed, in the period between the beginning of the 12th and the end of the 14th centuries - and reactions to it came in two distinct forms. There were those who took the stories that came to them, mostly from wandering singers and storytellers, and who simply turned them into Medieval romances by dressing them in the fashions of the time. And there were those who saw these same stories as an opportunity to put forward the tenets of Christianity in a unique form, and who recognised the "pagan" origins of much of what they saw. It is to these writers that we owe the degraded view of Gawain, who saw in him a Champion of the old ways and therefore sought to discredit him in the eyes of the world.

In considering this view we must not allow ourselves to forget that the subject of belief, of faith and theological teaching, was much more to the fore in educated society than it is today. Yet it was among the so-called "ordinary" people that the stories that went into the making of the Matter of Britain originated. In the process of becoming literary creations, they underwent a considerable degree of change and adaptation - to suit both the era and the audience.

Thus, since the majority of that audience was made up of knightly or noble classes, who loved to hear about chivalrous adventure above everything, so the epics of the Middle Ages concerned themselves with battles and tournaments and single combats. And when later on the concept of Courtly Love appeared on the scene, so that element too was tossed into the melting pot to add its flavour to an already heady brew.

The final element was the religious one - evidenced by the sudden outbreak of interest in the Grail story, which until the beginning of the 12th century had existed as part of an obscure collection of Celtic tales and Christian apocrypha, but which by the end of the 14th Century had become one of the most important, most widely written about themes of the time.

I have gone into all this in some detail - though it is still only a generalisation - in order to lay the ground for what I want to say about Gawain, because he seems to me to be a prime exemplar of the kind of thing I have been talking about. He began life as a simple Celtic hero, became one of the best-loved and most complex figures in the Arthurian cycle, and ended up as a dark and negative character a world away from his original origins. Even the authors who chose him for their hero - or who found him almost forced upon them - did not wholly understand him. Hence their often-ambiguous attitude to his character, which resulted in what becomes, at times, a misinterpretation of the facts.

Sometimes the treatment of Gawain is almost burlesque - as in the medieval story of *Merauguis de la Portlesgues*. Here, Gawain is discovered, having defeated an earlier incumbent, as Champion to the Lady of the Castle. Merauguis, had he succeeded in defeating Gawain, would presumably have taken on the same role - since we are told that whoever becomes the champion must remain there until a better man appears.

This is a very ancient theme indeed. You'll find it summarised conveniently in Sir James Fraser's *Golden Bough* under the heading "Rex Nemorensis" or King of the Wood. It dates back to a time before history when the idea of annual kingship was still practised. In this, the chosen candidate, having undergone various tests and trials - including his mating with the reigning Queen - became king for a year. At the end of that time he had to do battle with a new contender, a combat that he was not allowed to win. So a new King was appointed and the whole cycle began again.

Gradually, the period of rulership became extended. The Old King perhaps found substitutes who fought and died on his behalf. Only the Queen, the earthly representative of the Goddess, continued her uninterrupted reign, watching the cycle of Champions come and go. Eventually, the role of the champion likewise became subtly altered, merging with that of the King himself and extending beyond the boundary of a single year. It is this role that I believe Gawain inherited from the many nameless heroes who had gone before. It was to ensure his continuing fame, and at the same time cause him to be steadily degraded into the unsympathetic figure we find in Malory and elsewhere.

So much for the theory; what textual evidence can we find to support it? There is, in fact, a considerable amount, but before we look further at this we should pause for a moment to reflect on Gawain's origins.

I have stated already that the earliest references are in Celtic story and tradition. Here he is known as Gwalchmai, the Hawk of May, and earns a considerable reputation as a hero. However, it is his relationship to Arthur that is most often emphasised. He is generally described as being the son of Arthur's sister and King Lot of Orkney - the name of his mother being variously given as Anna, Gwyar, Morcades, and finally Morgause, which continues unchanged into the time of Malory.

Each of these ladies has an interesting history. Gwyar, whose name appears in several early texts, is believed to derive from an ancient Celtic word that has the meaning "to shed blood". The great Celtic scholar Sir John Rhys thought this probably meant that Gawain's mother had at one time been a Battle Goddess - and this is born out by the identification of Morcades/Morgause. Both derive, by a complex series of mythic relationships, from the figure of the Irish War- Goddess known as the Morrigan. She it was who became an implacable enemy of the hero Cuchulainn, eventually engineering his death where all others had failed. This in itself is significant because it can be proved that Gawain derives many of his heroic abilities from Cuchulainn, while the Morrigan also metamorphosed into an even more famous character from the Arthurian legends - Morgan le Fay. This, as we shall see, is also significant.

So, we have, at the beginning of the Middle Ages, a character whose adventures were still only circulating orally, but who was soon to become a great literary hero, who derives many of his abilities from even earlier heroes, and whose mother may well be a Goddess of War.

With these elements in mind it is not really surprising that the first major appearances of Gawain in Arthurian literature, show him as a brilliant soldier, and a valiant knight - for as such he is portrayed in several important Arthurian works, specifically Geoffrey of Monmouth's *Historia Regum Brittaniae*, the *Bruts* of Wace and Layamon, and the various anonymous Welsh chronicles which derive from them. The first signs we have of the direction which Gawain's career is about to take come in a much neglected Latin romance known as *De Ortu Waluuanii nepotis Arthurii* or The Rise of Gawain, Nephew of Arthur.

The title itself is important, because not only does it emphasise the importance now attached to the fact that Gawain is Arthur's nephew - rather than the son of Morgause, Morcades or Anna - thus indicating the failure of the later writer to recognise the importance of matrilineal descent - but because it is also prophetic of the literary rise of Gawain.

De Ortu Waluuanii tells a strange and extraordinary tale of Gawain's youthful exploits - how he was abandoned by his mother (here called Morcades) after she bore him illegitimately to Lot. Given into the care of some rich merchants, he is taken to Europe where a fisherman steals him again - along with considerable treasure - and brings him up as his own son. After a few years the fisherman travels to Rome and sets himself up as a wealthy nobleman. He soon comes to the attention of the Emperor and becomes his close confidant. His son (Gawain) is enrolled in the Emperor's personal guard and rises quickly through the ranks, astonishing everyone with his grace, courtliness and bravery. Finally, the fisherman turned courtier falls ill and, near to death confesses all, handing letters to the Emperor that prove that Gawain is the rightful nephew of King Arthur.

More adventures follow, as Gawain goes from strength to strength, being adopted by the Emperor, leading his armies against various enemies, defeating a pirate Queen, and finally, on the death of the Emperor, being offered the throne of the Empire. At this moment news comes from Britain of the Saxon invasion, and Gawain decides to lead a relief force to help Arthur. In Britain of course his real identity is revealed, and he decides to remain there, already beginning to prove himself a worthy knight.

This is an extraordinary story by any standard, and the brief summary given here scarcely does it justice. It shows to what extent writers at this point saw Gawain as an exemplary hero - and indeed there is a tradition that continues to see him in this light, despite an increasing number of texts that take a contrary view. It seems that the belief in Gawain as a representative of something important refused to die. In one version of the Prose Tristan - the most strongly anti-Gawain text of any - one reader or owner of the volume systematically crossed out the hero's name and substituted that of his less popular brother Gaheries - an early form of censorship!

Three texts which present Gawain in a wholly positive light - and which incidentally carry our argument to something like a triumphal conclusion, are the Middle-English *Sir Gawain and the Green Knight* - probably the most famous and well-known of his adventures - and of course edited by Professor Tolkien - the less well-known but no less remarkable poem *The Marriage of Sir Gawain and Dame Ragnall*, and a Middle High German poem by Heinrich von dem Tulin called *Diu Crone* , or The Crown.

The story of *Gawain and the Green Knight* is so familiar it scarcely needs summarising here. But just to recap briefly, you may remember that the Green Knight, a monstrous green skinned figure clad in green clothes and riding a green horse, rides into the hall at Camelot one Christmas and proposes a " game". He will submit to being struck a blow with his own huge axe on condition that he then be allowed to return the blow. At first no-one is prepared to take up the challenge, but when the Green Knight mocks the assembly and Arthur himself is preparing to go forward, Gawain requests that he be allowed to take the King's place. He strikes off the Green Knight's head, but sees him pick up the grisly object and hears him repeat his challenge - only that now it is to be postponed for a year. Gawain spends the time uneasily, then sets out, and after a long and arduous journey arrives at the castle of Sir Bercilak de Hautdesert, who makes him welcome and tells him that the Green Chapel, where his return meeting with the Green Knight is to take place, lies only a few miles distant.

For the three days that follow, the time leading up to the end of the old year, Gawain remains indoors, resting from his journey and reflecting on the coming encounter. He is entertained by Lady Bercilak, who while her husband goes every day to hunt game for the table, enters Gawain's bedroom and does her best to seduce him. Always in the most polite and courtly fashion Gawain refuses her - until on the last evening before he is due to leave he accepts a green baldric (or shash) that the Lady assures him will protect its wearer from any harm.

Next morning Gawain sets out for the Green Chapel and arrives to find the Green Knight whetting his axe. The "game" takes place, but after feinting twice the Green Knight only nicks Gawain's neck with his axe. He then reveals that he is in fact Sir Bercilak, who had been enchanted into his monstrous shape by "Morgue the Goddess", a hideously ugly hag whom Gawain had seen at the castle but failed to recognise as a danger. The two feints and the nicked neck are because Gawain accepted kisses from Lady Bercilak on two occasions and finally agreed to wear the green baldric. Returning to Camelot Gawain tells his story and the knights unanimously decide to wear green baldrics themselves in token of Gawain's courage.

Here, the Green Knight is clearly an otherworldly character, an elemental and magical being whose appearance at the Winter Festival marks him out as such - as do his colour and his ability to retrieve his head after Gawain's blow. This theme, the Beheading Game, has been traced without much question, to Irish mythology. The nature of the "Game" itself, which is clearly a partially confused memory of the old annual kingship, and the presence of Morgane the Goddess - or, as we know her better, Morgan le Fay, is also significant. That her real standing was recognised is made evident from this ascription, which is also repeated by Giraldus Cambrensis in his Speculum Ecclesiae. We have already seen that this same character, who is little more than a spiteful enchantress in most Arthurian literature, can be traced back to Morrigan the Battle Goddess. It is also more than likely that she was at one time Gawain's mother - which gives one pause for thought, since the lovely Lady Bercilak is clearly also an aspect of the hideous Morgane in the poem. But let us leave that for a moment until we have looked at another text, *The Marriage of Gawain and Dame Ragnall*.

This poem, which dates from the 14th century but is probably based on a much earlier text, tells a remarkable tale of love and enchantment, in which Gawain is tested to the utmost and comes through with flying colours, and in which he also establishes himself as the Champion of the Goddess.

There are two versions of the story, but the best known tells how, when Arthur was out hunting, he became separated from his companions in the magical woods around Tarn Wathelyn. There he encountered a powerful enchanter named Gromer Somer Jour, whose name is itself not without significance. Threatening to kill Arthur, Gromer gives him a chance to save his life by discovering the answer to a question: What is it that women most desire? He must return a year hence with the answer or face the consequences. Arthur returns to court and takes Gawain into his confidence. The two set out in search of answers, and in the year that follows collect sufficient to fill several books! Then, on his last journey before the year is up, Arthur encounters a monstrously ugly woman sitting by the roadside apparently waiting for him. She tells him that she knows the correct answer, but will only give it if Arthur promises to marry her to Gawain. Trusting in his nephew's honour Arthur agrees and returns to the court with the hag, who is called Ragnall. Though clearly taken aback Gawain agrees to fulfil the bargain, and preparations for the wedding are put in motion. (Guinevere tries to persuade Ragnall to have a quiet ceremony, but she insists on a full-scale celebration. The Court mourns Gawain as though he were about to go to his death, and Arthur sets off to keep his rendezvous with Gromer. There he gives the books of answers he and Gawain had collected but the enchanter throws them aside. Then Arthur gives Ragnall's answer and with a cry of rage Gromer admits it is correct - though he curses his "sister" who is the only one who could have told the King.

Back at the court the wedding of Gawain and Ragnall is celebrated and after a dinner in which Ragnall astounds everyone by her appalling table manners, the couple are escorted to the bridal chamber and left alone. Gawain can scarcely bear to look at his bride, but when she demands a kiss he courteously and gently obliges - to find that he now holds in his arms a beautiful woman! She explains that she was enchanted into this shape by - yes, you guessed it - Morgan le Fay, and that Gawain must now make a further decision - whether he will have her fair by night and foul by day, or vice versa. Struggling to envisage the outcome of either decision Gawain finally tells Ragnall that she must be the one to decide, since it affect her just as much as him. With a cry of joy Ragnall declares that the final part of the spell is now undone - for Gawain has, of course, given her the thing that women most want - sovereignty, which in this instance, as in Chaucer's *Wife of Bath's Tale*, which as you will have recognised tells much the same story - the sovereignty described is that of the woman over her husband (an important factor then as it maybe still is). The underlying meaning however, and of obvious importance to our theory, is the other sense of sovereignty, as something given by the Goddess of the land to her Kingly Champion.

Now in this story we have a similar situation to that which we found in *Gawain and the Green Knight*. There is the otherworldly challenger who must be met with again in a year. (And in the case of Gromer Somer Jour, whose name means Man of the Summer's Day, we are back in the ancient myths of Seasonal battles for the Maiden of Spring). Then there is the ugly old hag, who is under the enchantment of Morgan and the question of Gawain's fidelity, upon which the whole tale revolves. Also, I do not think we will be stretching matters too far if we see in the foul and fair aspects of Ragnall, the foul and fair aspects of Lady Bercilak, who is, of course, also Morgue the Goddess.

So you will see the point we have arrived at. Within the structure of these two poems, both of which originated in a part of the country - the West Midlands - rich in ancient culture and Goddess lore, in which Gawain is rigorously tested by the earthly representative of a Goddess. A test which involves the question of sovereignty in *Gawain and Ragnall*, and of the yearly test of the Beheading Game in *Gawain and the Green Knight*. The combination of these two gives us a scenario in which Gawain is tested by the Goddess, passes her trial, and receives as his reward her favours - marrying or mating with her just as the ancient Year Kings once did in order to win their tenure as her Champion.

By extension this leads to a further understanding - that Gawain, as Arthur's closest relative, his sister's son (long recognised among the Celts and elsewhere in the ancient world as a most potent relationship), is standing in for Arthur himself as Champion of Britain's sovereignty! So whether we see Gawain as Morgan's son, as her Champion, or her lover - in each of which roles we have seen him, and which reoccur in other texts not discussed - he is still fulfilling the same ancient archetypal role, as the Kingly Champion of the Land.

Just how clearly the medieval authors recognised these facts we cannot say with any degree of certainty. That they knew something of the truth is indicated by the manner of Gawain's gradual descent from hero to murderer and libertine. Yet even in the latter case, where he is constantly portrayed as light of love, as being unable to remain faithful to any one woman for more than a day - even here we can see a reflection of his original role. He who was the servant and Champion of the Goddess of course loved all women, but as her earthly representatives. To the medieval, and especially the Christian interpreters of the story this could only be seen in the way it was, by making Gawain an opportunist who played upon his fame and good looks to enable him to bed as many women as possible. Only in a few romances, such as those we have examined here today, did a distant echo of his original role remain, embedded in the marvellous adventures of the Round Table knights.

In short, the answer to the question posed in the title of this talk - is Gawain a Pagan Champion or a Christian Knight? - is that he is both, and that neither is mutually exclusive of the other since both roles are shown to overlap at almost every point.

One final thought. The greatest adventure open to the Round Table chivalry was the Quest for the Grail - itself a symbol which draws upon both Pagan and Christian imagery. In every single Arthurian text save one, where the details of this quest are related, Gawain is excluded from the final achievement, which is left to Perceval or Galahad. The one exception, the *Diu Crone* of Heinrich von dem Tulin, makes Gawain the unequivocally successful candidate. Nor should we be surprised to discover that this text, written in the 14th century, contains some of the most primitive Grail material. The suggestion being, as far as I am concerned, that at one time this adventure also had Gawain as its hero, and that the symbolism was once again correct - for the Grail, whatever else it may have become, began life in the Celtic traditions as a Cauldron of Rebirth and Inspiration belonging to the Goddess. Surely proof enough of Gawain's original role, if more is needed.

Chapter 6:

THE STORY NEVER ENDS
Arthurian Themes in Babylon 5

In 1998 the wonderful epic journey of Babylon 5 was first shown on TV. Over the next two years I, along, with thousands of others, thrilled to the adventures of the crew of the great space station at the edge of the universe, thronged with different species and fighting a war that seemed impossible against vastly superior odds. Within a few weeks of the show's beginning I realised that it was not only good – it was also Arthurian! After that I watched with extra interest and when in 1999 I was invited to give a talk at one of the first UK Babylon 5 Conventions, at which the show's creator J Michael Stazinsky himself was present, along with members of the cast. I decided to trace these themes in the (then still ongoing) series. When the show finally ended, it was followed by the equally exciting Crusade, in which further Arthurian elements appears as I had speculated in the talk that follows here. If you haven't seen Babylon 5 yet, I encourage you to seek it out on DVD. It remains one of the richest and most spiritually oriented shows ever seen on TV, and its ongoing story-arc can make you sit there spellbound for days.

"It was our last, best hope for peace."

Those who watched the unfolding of the extraordinary epic TV drama *Babylon 5*, created by Michael J. Stazinsky (1998 - 2000) will have heard this phrase again and again in connection with the Babylon 5 Station, but it could just as easily have been said about another place and another time - Camelot, the fabled city of King Arthur, in a time when it, too, was the 'last, best hope' for a group of beleaguered people surrounded by the dark.

Every work of the imagination has its influences, and only the author really knows what they are. That doesn't stop critics and commentators from playing guessing games with the authors - both living and dead, and it is therefore hardly surprising that a good deal of speculation has already gone into the possible sources of Babylon 5 (B5).

I've never been sure whether I agree with this process, which is a bit like scavenging in the brain of the author - but I can't help but be interested when a show of such richness and popularity as B5 includes references to the myths of Arthur and the Grail, which have been going strong now for around 1400 years and show no sign of losing their astonishing success rate. These stories turn up in so many different guises it's hardly surprising to find they have found a comfortable niche in Sci-Fi. As Emperor Londo Molari says towards the end of the episode titled 'In the Beginning' -"The Story never ends....', words that certainly apply to the Arthurian mythos as well as to any set of stories.

Parallels, then, exist, and I'm going to spend a little time looking at some of them. This is largely speculative of course, since we only have one of the authors present to agree or disagree. But we can be fairly certain of at least some of the details, especially as they appear in two episodes of the series - you know which ones they are - which are very clearly based on Arthurian sources. I could suggest a few other aspects that seem to me to have crept into other episodes - but after living with the Arthurian epic for 30 years I tend to see those everywhere. I might, for instance, suggest a number of Merlin like figures who appear through the first four seasons, or note that the *An la Shock* are more than a bit reminiscent of the Round Table Fellowship, and so on - Michael J. Stazinsky would be perfectly right in telling me that I was wrong - because only he knows the truth about this. And I might then respond that it was all unconscious, that he knows the stories and could have drawn on them without realising it. And so we might go on ... But at least with the two episodes we are on safe enough ground. So I'm going to look at them in some detail, but before that I want to say a bit about the Arthur stories themselves. This is for the benefit of those who don't know them well - if you already do I suggest you switch off for the next ten minutes or go and have a drink!

The Real Arthur

The truth is there are several 'Arthurs', not one. There's a very primitive, shadowy Bear god perhaps called 'Arth' or 'Artor' who may date back a thousand years before the time of the Celts, when the second Arthur figure, a real historical character, appears; and there's third Arthur, the mythical king of Arthurian legend, who we know best from movies like Excalibur or even Camelot, or the recent, disastrous First Knight. Each of these has contributed something to the ongoing legend, which has refused to die and keeps on coming back in places stranger than his occasional appearances on B5.

We really know nothing at all about the oldest figure, who is barely there at all except as a distant reflection in the Celtic tales from which the other Arthurs spring. The possibility is that there as an ancient bear deity who went into folk-memory and re-appeared when a hero came along who needed a name that would really resonate in the minds of the people. In fact it's possible that the 'real' Arthur took that name purposely to reinforce his position. But then we know very little about him either. The facts, meagre as they are, are as follows.

The Roman Legions had mostly left Britain by 385 and for the next two hundred years or so the Celtic tribes fought it out with each other in a struggle to find out who was top dog. At the same time the Saxons were raiding deeply into the country and establishing footholds everywhere. The British people would probably have been overrun by the beginning of the 6th century if someone hadn't come along who was able to bind those feuding tribes together into an army strong enough to overcome the invaders, and to keep them penned down around the southern and western coastlines for nearly forty years. That someone was Arthur. Whether or not he was really called that, or whether he took the name as a point of reference to an older time, or a previous hero, he did what no one else could do - and earned a place in the halls of fame for doing it. The sparse historical documents talk of twelve great battles, most of them fount in places we can no longer identify with any certainty, which ended at a pace called Badon Hill - possibly somewhere near Bath. This defeat was so sound that it kept the Saxons quiet for the next forty years - long enough for them to become settlers rather than invaders. At the end of that time Arthur died - or mysteriously vanished - around 537, and the stories began to spread and grow in the telling, until he was a full-blown legend.

By the Middle Ages, when the stories began to be written down, Arthur was a part of the folk-memory of Britain. Now, dressed in armour and with a court of medieval splendour, he and his knights became the single most popular subject for storytellers throughout Europe. Versions of the Arthur stories were told in Italy, Germany, France, Spain - even Russia - and everyone wanted to know more. Just as we hunger for more adventures of B5, so the medieval fans wanted more of Arthur and Guinevere, Lancelot and Galahad, Gareth and Gawain. The Round Table, a fellowship of knights devoted to defeating evil and defending all those in need of it, swelled their ranks with the likes of Owein, Bedivere, Perceval, Lamorak, - their names are legion.

Somewhere along the way, other stories, originally separate, became attached to the Arthur cycle as it now was. The tale of Merlin's capture and betrayal by Nimue - who was originally his sister - became part of the story. The Loves of Lancelot and Guinevere, Tristan and Iseult, Gawain and Ettare were added in; as was the tale of the fearsome Green Knight, who entered Camelot on Christmas Eve and offered to play the beheading game. The Lady of the Lake gave Arthur his second sword when the first one, the one pulled from the stone, broke in battle. Excalibur became one of the most famous swords in legend, making Arthur invincible in battle.

The story arc here, much as in B5, was long and extraordinarily flexible, allowing the insertion of countless new adventures and new heroes into the broad framework of the cycle. If you strip away much of this you are left with the tale of Arthur's rise to greatness, guided by Merlin, with the founding of the Round table and the many adventures of the knights in an enchanted land where anything was possible and where Goblins, giants, and even the occasional dragon filled the same place as Shadows, Centauri, and the other alien races of Babylon 5 - they kept the wheels of the story turning and added grist to the mill, opposition and aid in a complex pattern. In the end, the glory of Camelot is destroyed by human failure and lust. Arthur is seduced by his half sister Morgause and she bears him a son - Mordred, who is dedicated to destroying all that his father had built. By this time Merlin has withdrawn, or been spirited away by Nimue, so Arthur must fight on alone. The last blow is the betrayal of his friend Lancelot, who has loved Queen Guinevere for years and is finally caught in her chamber. Civil war follows, with both sides egged on by Mordred and finally, in a dreadful battle that takes place at Camlan - another site hard to identify - Arthur slays Mordred and receives a mortal wound. There then follows the famous scene in which Bedivere is told to throw the sword back into the lake and does so only at the third attempt, when an arm clad in white samite rises from the water and takes back the sword. We shall look at this again later when we comes to the episode 'A Late Delivery from Avalon.'

Now, as Arthur lies wounded unto death a ship carrying three queen, among them Arthur's other half sister Morgana or Morgain, who had hitherto been an opponent of all his work, arrives and they carry him off to the mysteries island of Avalon to be healed of his wounds and to await the time when he would be needed again. This is a crucial aspect of the story when it comes to looking at the Arthurian with B5, since it is Arthur's possible return that occupies the central part of the episode we'll be looking at shortly.

With this mysterious departure the way was left open for stories to be circulated that said Arthur was not dead but only in hiding. Some believed that he slept under various hills, awaiting the call to arms. Everyone wanted to hear about Arthur. There is a story that tells how a group of novice monks were listening to their master read from the scriptures. After a time it was hot and they started to nod off. The novice master stopped reading and said: 'I know a story about the great king Arthur' … immediately everyone was awake!

The Grail Quest

Another story that became attached to the Arthurian cycle was that of the quest for the Grail. Basically the story is about the search for an age-old relic that offers all kinds of rewards to the finder. This story goes back a long way, probably even earlier than Arthur. Celtic mythology is full of stories about quests for magic cauldrons, vessels that gave food, inspiration, and spiritual sustenance to those who sought them. One of the oldest surviving accounts of such an adventure, which includes Arthur, is a ninth century Welsh poem called

The Spoils of Annwn' - Annwn being one of the names for the Otherworld. It's an odd poem, attributed to the great bard Taliesin, who was possibly a contemporary of Arthur. But if you read between the lines you can get an idea of what it's about. Here's a verse to give you the feel of it:

'I am the pre-eminent praiser: my song sounded
In the four-towered caer, forever turning;
And of its Cauldron was my first song sung:
Nine maidens kindle the Cauldron by their breathing,
Of what nature is this vessel- the Lord of Annwn's Cauldron?
Enamelled iridescent colours at its rim,
It will not boil the food of a coward.
A flashing sword was thrust into it
And it was left in Lleminawg's hands.
Before the dark gates, light was lifted,
But when we went with Arthur - splendid labour -
Except seven, none returned from the Honeyed Caer.

From here there is big jump to medieval times, when the story of a quest for an ancient and sacred vessel becomes attached to the earliest Christian myths. The Grail, it is now said, is the cup used by Jesus to celebrate the Last Supper and which is afterwards used to catch some blood from his wounds. It thus becomes a twice hallowed object, and is put into the care of a particular family - that of Christ's uncle Joseph of Arimathea. Joseph sets out on a voyage from the Holy Lands and eventually arrives, with the Grail, in Britain, where he goes to Glastonbury, even then a place associated with ancient magic and wonder - and builds the first Christian church. Sometime after this the Grail mysteriously vanishes, and nothing more is heard about it until the days of Arthur, when it suddenly appears in the hall of Camelot floating on a beam of light. Everyone in the hall has a vision of sorts, and all the knights - remember we are in medieval times by now - vow to set out in search of the mysterious cup. So the great Quest begins. It will take countless years, and endless adventures before three of the knights will succeed in finding the Grail. Many will fail, some spectacularly, like Lancelot and Gawain. Others simply vanish without trace, lost somewhere on the roads leading between Camelot and the castle of the Grail. The three successful knights are Galahad, Lancelot's son, Perceval, a simple knight who stumbles through the quest in a dream; and Bors, the ordinary man who seems as though he along for the ride rather than the true objective of the quest. These three find their way to the country and finally the castle where the grail is kept and all undergo immerse visionary experiences, ending with the death of Galahad who has no other reason for living) and Perceval's election as the new guardian of the Grail. Only Bors returns to Camelot to tell what had happened.

Around this story is woven an immense network of tales relating to the various adventures of the knights. Gawain comes close to achieving the quest, but is too easily distracted by a pretty face to sustain the search; Lancelot, the greatest knight of Camelot, follows the quest with as much fervour as anyone, but is turned away because of his illicit love for Arthur's queen. In the end the Grail vanished again - though still in Perceval's care - to be sought for by subsequent generations. Which is where the story told in the episode called 'Grail', written by Christy Marx, comes in.

Apparently, the quest is still continuing in the 22nd century, as we learn when Aldous Gajic arrives on B5. He describes himself as belonging to an 'Order' though it is given no name, and he is in search of the Holy Grail, which he describes as 'a sacred vessel of regeneration', also known as 'The Cup of the Goddess' - actually a mistake as the Grail is not called this anywhere except perhaps in New Age writings.

The human reaction to Aldous' quest is somewhat negative: to them, the Grail is 'just a myth'. To the Minbari however, Aldous is an 'honoured seeker' who deserves proper acknowledgement. 'It doesn't matter that this Grail may or may not exist,' says Delenn, ' but that [Aldous] strives for the perfection of his soul.... and that he had never wavered or lost faith'. This is really a very good description of the purpose of the Grail Quest, which is not search for a lost treasure, but a journey in search of spiritual perfection. In the 13th century text, 'The Quest for the Holy Grail', the three Grail knights, Galahad, Perceval and Bors go aboard a mysterious ship, later identified as The Ship of Solomon. On it is written 'Beware he who steps upon me unless he has perfect faith'. Aldous, in stepping abroad B5, is also proving his 'perfect faith' that will be tested to the greatest extreme.

The first thing that happens to Aldous is his meeting with Jinxo, aka Thomas Jordan, a simple man who resembles Perceval more than anyone. In fact there are a number of interesting echoes in the relationship of the two men, which more than a bit resembles that of Galahad and Perceval. Like Aldous Galahad dies when he finally sees the Grail - though in his case it is as a result of seeing the sacred object rather than the reverse, where Aldous sees the Grail as he dies. But the passing of the mission to find the Grail from Galahad to Perceval is clearly echoed here when Aldous formally asks Sinclair to witness that Thomas is his heir.

The treatment of the Grail itself is interesting. It is regarded as a 'cult object' by the Centauri, and by Londo as a means to making money by researching the subject to see if there is any record of its being in their possession. Vir, who has already done the research, says it is not. Neither is it to be found among the Minbari - though significantly neither Delenn nor Londo deny knowledge of it. Unfortunately, the demands of the plot require that unfortunately we do not hear from either the Vorlons or the Narn, either of who might have had something to say about it.

The Grail itself is seen as something miraculous, something that has 'many names but one promise' and which offers healing. This again is very true to the original stories, which hold out the promise of healing to all who come into its presence. From the first the Grail is associated with the wounded king, its mysterious guardian, whose unhealing wound can only be cured by the achieving of the quest.

Aldous Gajec is every inch a Grail knight, even though he began as an accountant - not one of the most usual beginnings for a hero! It is only after the death of his family that he meets ' a man who was the last off his kind' who told Aldous that he was 'of infinite promise and goodness', a notion which he later ascribes to Thomas. After this 'the numbers begin to add up again - presumably a different set to the ones which had previously occupied him! The episode with the Na'ka'leen Feeder might have come out of any one of as number of Grail stories, where the seekers fate after cup must undergo encounters with monsters both inner and outer. The way that Aldous draws the creature out of the fake encounter-suit, with the words *'Nothing is in the dark. No fear. No pain. Only the light.'* show his true worth and purity. Even when he is wounded the Feeder seems to hesitate over him almost in a protective way, and is destroyed as a result. In some ways the Feeder is like one of the 'Enchantments of Britain', mentioned in several of the old texts. These enchantments take many forms, including the Waste Land, the dead area around the grail castle where nothing will grow, and which in B5 seems well represented by 'Downbelow'. The enchantments will only be lifted when the Grail is won; Aldous Gajic seems to echo the role of Galahad again here, since by his appearance on the ship he brings to an end the reign of terror perpetrated by the robber baron Deuce.

Interesting too is the character of Jinxo, which as I have said resembles the foolish Perceval. He sees himself as the cause of the Babylon curse, the failure of all four earlier stations. This echoes the fact that in nearly every Grail story Perceval is responsible for the continuing of the Waste Land when he fails to ask the all important question: 'Whom does the Grail serve?' This idea of service is central to the idea of the Grail. Only when we offer ourselves unreservedly, as do so many of the B5 crew, is the Wasteland healed and the Wounded King cured. There are echoes of this elsewhere, when Sinclair, questioned by the Emperor in the episode 'The Coming of Shadows' says that he wanted *'to serve something bigger than I was. Make a difference. Somewhere. Somehow.'* This is used as yet another opportunity for Delenn to hint at Sinclair's true nature when she responds to his doubts about Aldous' quest, and his own inability to pursue such a quest, with the words *'perhaps you don't know yourself as well as you think.'*

At the end of the episode Sinclair is still saying that it is hard 'to spend your life looking for something and never find it, in all probability referring to himself here. Delenn replies that everyone 'is looking for a reason...for everything.' She then gives Thomas a crystal that he must bury at Aldous' grave. It will continue to glow there for a hundred years. *'It is our way with all true seekers'* she adds, once again affirming her recognition of Aldous. At this point too 'Jinxo' formally acknowledges his real name, 'Thomas', just as Perceval, in the Grail story, only recognises his true identity when he is close to the Grail.

Aside from this I suppose the nearest thing we have to a B5 Grail is the mysterious Triluminary, which has the power to bring about change (Delenn in 'Chrysalis'), to read the souls of men (Sinclair in 'In The Beginning'), and to disable the guards of the dead Minbari leader Branmer (in 'Legacies'). It thus shares at least two, possibly three points with the Grail, which can and does transform those who go in search of it, indeed sees into the hearts and souls of those who seek it, and can bring about a static state as in the case of the Wounded King. There are, we are told, three Triluminaries in existence (the Minbari seem to share with the Celts a love for triplicities), but we know nothing more about them, or where they are kept beyond the one that (presumably) resides aboard the ship that carries the Grey Council. This idea, of a group of priests with a sacred relic in their possession, is of course very precisely the pattern of the Grail myth.

All in all, there are some very good parallels built into the Grail episode, which really marks the first direct outward show of Arthurian influences in season one. We had to wait until half way through season three before the next sampling of Arthurian lore appeared, in the shape of the episode called 'A Late Delivery from Avalon.'

Late Delivery From Avalon

This episode has had a hard time from critics and fans alike - but in fact it was one of the most popular among the general public - largely I think because of it's Arthurian connections - as well as the presence of Michael York in the role of the man who either is, or thinks he is, Arthur. Depending on your view, if you approach it from the Arthurian end, it's not at all a bad episode - and York's performance, if not outstanding, meets the necessary standard of 'Arthurness' - he's noble, brave and troubled all at the same time. Always on duty if you like. MJS had said of this episode that it was the heroic tradition he was interested in here, specifically *'the transition of someone who doesn't think he maybe worth of the crown being touched by destiny and then being propelled into a position where he has to achieve that destiny. Sometimes there's a price to pay, such as in the fall of Camelot'* (Killick: Point of No Return p119).

The price here seems to be the sanity of the Arthur figure who, according to Marcus (who seems to know a lot about the stories) needs to go full circle in order to be healed. This isn't quite the way it happens in the traditional ending of the Arthur story. There Arthur is given the sword Excalibur as a trust to defend the kingdom: when he's wounded by Mordred at the battle of Camlan that contract is considered to be at an end and so the sword goes back into the lake- thrown here by Bedivere rather than being handed back to the Lady herself by Arthur as happens in the episode.

The question of whether the man claiming to be Arthur is who he says he is, is kept open throughout the episode. Marcus is convinced from the start, when he welcomes Arthur by falling on one knee and says: 'Apologies my lord, we were not notified of your return.' He also states his belief that Arthur could have been taken out of time by the Vorlon and kept in suspended animation until he was needed, as in the promise at the end of the original Arthur stories. Franklin is opposed to this, and it is his research that identifies Arthur as David Macintyre, the gunnery officer on the ship which started the Earth-Minbari war. (and did you spot that moment in 'In the Beginning' where we fleetingly see Michael York's look of horror as he realises what he has done?).

The explanation for all this (or anyway the explanation as Franklin might see it) is that since Macintyre sees himself as the cause for the start of the Earth-Minbari war, and, in his Arthur-self, equates the accidental start of that war with the accidental start of the battle of Camlan, he must make reparation to Delenn, whom he sees as the representative of Sovereignty - the Lady of the Lake. This actually stands up quite well as a modern interpretation of the tale of the final days of Arthur's reign, and focuses on the often-ambiguous relationship of Arthur and the Lady.

Certainly Macintyre knows his Arthurian myth. He 'remembers' the events of his own final days, and of his passing into the care of the Nine Sisters (incidentally there is a mistake in the story where he says that the Nine Sisters and the Three Queens are in the boat which takes him to Avalon, in reality the Three are part of the Nine - which suddenly sounds like a Minbari saying when I think of it!). And he talks of the 'old wound' being re-opened. This sounds like a mixture of ideas, referencing the Wounded Grail King perhaps, or Arthur's role as the King of Britain in which he is himself wounded - by his failure to love Guinevere and his loss of the kingdom to his own son Mordred.

Anyway, the story keeps the possibility that Macintyre is Arthur going right to the end, where even after he is supposedly 'cured' of his 'delusion' by Franklin, he still talks like Arthur and is set to begin a new life organising resistance on Narn - a task surely well suited to an Arthurian hero who did exactly that in 6th century Britain. His words here, that he is healed, ' body and soul knitted together' seems to bear out this. G'Kar, appropriately enough, believes in Arthur as well - to him there are no historical or mythical overtones to latch onto: he simply sees the man for what he is, the stuff of which heroes are made. And of course G'Kar himself is a hero, who would have earned himself a place at the original Round Table just as he does at the new one on B5. Nor should be forget that he is knighted by Arthur as 'Sir G'Kar, the Red Knight'.

In the end I suppose it's down to the individual to decide what they believe. 'As Marcus says: 'Better the illusions that exalt us than any one truth.' Not surprisingly I have no difficulty in seeing Macintyre as Arthur, if not actually kidnapped by the Vorlon (which would, I guess, make one of them Morgana, since it is she who takes Arthur off to be healed and to await his needed return!) then perhaps reborn or called back from his sleep by humankind's struggle against the Shadows. Perhaps the Vorlons were themselves the Keepers of Avalon? They had preserved Jack the Ripper in an earlier episode, so why not Arthur also? As one of the characters says towards the end of the second part of 'War Without End': *The War is never completely won. There are always new battles to be fought against the dark'.* This is pure Arthur-speak: He is after all 'The Once and Future King, eternally ready to fight the soldiers of the dark.

In fact, there is another wonderful reference to this in 'War Without End part 1'. The triad of Sheridan, Sinclair and Delenn are described as being linked; Sinclair is the one who was, Delenn the one who is, Sheridan the one who will be. The exact words are: 'All is three as you are three, as you are one - as you are the one who will be, who was, and who is.' Of course the three in one idea comes right out of Christian mystical tradition, but it's also central to Celtic belief. Here it seems we are being given a pointer to another direction: that in some way these three people share one soul, or are linked through time by a bond that cannot be broken. There would be no difficulty in seeing Arthur in this way, as a great soul who was once and will be again, 'the king that was and the king that shall be' as it says on his tomb. Anyway, it's hard not to believe that MJS was thinking of this when he wrote that scene.

I suppose it's the scene at the end of 'A Late Delivery' that carries the clearest signposting for Arthurian speculation. The dialogue goes as follows:

"MARCUS (referring to Kosh) "Now, now, next thing you'll be saying is he's not Merlin. Merlin was a great teacher you know."
FRANKLIN: "I'm not hearing this."
MARCUS: '"They say he aged backwards. That was how he was able to foretell the future, by remembering it. Which means he came fro the future. Maybe he had Arthur form the Round Table by remembering us. We're forming one of our own after all. Which makes you Perceval. I'm Galahad, him being sinless and all. Sheridan is Arthur. Ivanova, perhaps Gawain. I think we both know who Mordred is. So the question is: Who is Morgan le Fay?"

There's certainly plenty to get to grips with here. It seems appropriate that it is Marcus, who is probably most like one of the Knights of the Round Table than anyone in the series, should say this, and who believes in the identity of the Arthur figure. Of course, he (or by his own admission, the author) is being somewhat tongue in cheek when he identifies himself with Galahad - though maybe not as much as one might think at first.

In fact we know that the author is himself being provocative here - he's gone on record as saying that he was 'having fun' with the fans in this scene. But the truth of the matter is that archetypes have a habit of biting back. Even if you take a set of people like Arthur and his knights, then upend them purely to send them up, things come across which very often even the writer didn't realise. So, let's take a look at these identifications in the face, forgetting that they were meant as a bit of private joke, and see how they stand up.

Kosh as Merlin

Well, this is at least a possibility. Merlin was, as you know, a powerful supernatural ally of Arthur, who operated from the background, and then withdrew when he felt he had got the ball rolling sufficiently for the King to go it alone. One thing that interests me here is the idea of Merlin living backwards. Now I've seen this ideas crop up a lot lately - not least in the recent TV movie *Merlin* with Sam Neil in the title role. But in fact this idea comes not from the old medieval stories, but from T.H. White's contemporary novel '*The Once & Future King*'. In Malory and elsewhere Merlin adopts the disguise of an old man because, as he says, 'People take more notice of you if you have a long white beard'!

But how does the identification of Kosh with Merlin hold up? I think quite well, for the reasons give above, and especially because he has the ability to appear in whatever form those who see him expect - another quality derived from Merlin. (Of course he also resembles Gandalf from The Lord of the Rings - but I refuse to go down that road!) But elsewhere he says that he is not interested in the affairs of other races.

In fact there are several Merlin like figures in B5 - Lorion for one - now there's a real Magus figure if ever there was one, and who departs as mysteriously as he arrived just as Merlin does. Or there's Zathras, who again seems to live backwards - as well as sideways through time. And I would suggest that there is more than a bit of a Minbari-Merlin in Draal - especially in the episode called 'Voices of Authority'. Then there is Dukhat, who is a Merlin-figure to Delenn and makes the first contact with the Vorlons.

The presence of so many 'Merlins' may mean no more than that any powerful, magical being who stands behind other characters and pulls their strings is a Merlin figure; but it can equally be said to demonstrate how deeply the wise old wizard character has taken root in our consciousness.

Franklin as Perceval

I'm not sure this one works - at least not for me. I can see that it might be arrived at by association. Perceval, who is the earliest of the Grail winners, is said to have healed the Wounded King, the Guardian of the Grail who has an unhealing wound - until, that is, Perceval asks a question - Whom does the Grail serve? - which brings healing to the king. In most of the stories which feature him Perceval is represented as naive to the point of foolishness - in fact one of his name is 'The Perfect Fool'. Now I don't now about you, but I really don't see Franklin in this way. He has a certain innocence, that's true, even a little naivety, but he is also full of wisdom, and I suppose the episode 'Walkabout' in which Franklin gone in search of his own soul, would make a fair parallel to the early quest of Perceval, in which he indeed wanders through a desolate land in search of the truth - about himself, about the strange wounded king, and about the Grail. So, while on the whole, I think we have to see that identification as something of a blind, there is enough of an Arthurian reference to hold up - at least to this informed gathering!

Sheridan as Arthur

This is a lot easier to go along with. Like Arthur, Sheridan becomes the focus for a group of freedom fighters that together defeat a much stronger opponent. The League of None-Aligned Worlds and later the Alliance, are clearly very like the group of tribes united by Arthur the Warlord into a fighting force which defeated the invading Saxons. On another level they are much like the Knights of the Round Table, who were also a mixed bag of heroes forged into a unit by the medieval King Arthur. So yes, on the hole, I think we can see Sheridan as Arthur working very well. Even to the way that he begins as an action figure and ends in the more passive role as President of the Alliance, just as Arthur retires to a more sedentary place as head of the Round Table and never seems to go on a quest again.

Sinclair as Arthur

While we're talking about Arthur figures, let's not forget Sinclair. Here we have, I think, an even better contender for the Arthurian crown. Not only is he the first commander of the B5 station, but he is also Valen ... Now we know less about Valen than we'd like, but one of the things we do know is that in the future he founded the An la Shok, and in the past he founded the Grey Council, both of which are not at all unlike the Fellowship of the Round Table. But, there's more to Jeffrey Sinclair than that. In esoteric terms he's what we would call a Withdrawn Master, a human beings who continues to influence events even though he is, to all intents and purposes, dead. Merlin is another such, and Arthur himself, you remember, retires to Avalon. So we might see Sinclair's withdrawal through time to Minbar as an echo of that. Nor should we forget that he was brought up and educated by the Jesuits, an august body of Catholic priests who have a lot in common with the Grey Council, and who acted as advisors behind the scenes for much of Catholic royalty during the Middle Ages. Another interesting point is the name. Sinclair. I've no idea how MJS chose that name, but it has a great deal of significance for those who are interested n the history of Arthur and the Grail.

There isn't time right now to go into the whole later history of the Grail, which I have been charting now for twenty years. But one factor comes up repeatedly. A single family has a very powerful link with the Grail, and that family is called ... Sinclair (sometimes spelled St Clair but always pronounced as Sinclair). There's a whole history of their connections with the Grail, including the fact that they were (or indeed still are) Templars. The Templars were a band of religious warriors who protected the Holy Land throughout the period of the Crusades. In this they were very exactly an 'army of light' of the kind founded by Jeffrey Sinclair. It's too soon yet to say exactly what path the new series 'Crusade' will take but we do have one quote from MJS that seems to suggest something interesting in this region:

> 'As the knights of the Round Table went forth to find the Grail, a cure for a troubled land, so too does Excalibur go out in search of the cure for a troubled world. As the first Excalibur brought hope and changed the world around it, so too will this Excalibur end up being a beacon of hope...'
> (Quoted in TV Zone No 106 Sept 1998)

This is, of course really exciting, and if I'm even a quarter right it might not be speculating too far to suggest that the crew of Excalibur (or should we say the wielders of Excalibur?) are going to look not unlike those warriors monks of the Middle ages ... who were guardian of the Grail... one of whose leaders was called Sinclair.... However you see this, let's not forget what is said of him in 'War Without End part I' - 'he is the closed circle, returning to the beginning' a phrase which can indeed be used of Arthur and which, by the way, was also said of the Arthur figure in 'A Late Delivery From Avalon.' It's also interesting to note that both Sheridan and Sinclair 'come again', as it were - Sinclair as Valen and Sheridan by returning from Z'ahadum.

Ivanova as Gawain

So, on to Ivanova as Gawain. Again I can't see this one very well. Gawain is Arthur's nephew and right hand man; he's hot headed and impulsive and a great ladies-man... Just how Ivanova fits this I'm not sure... If we turn it around then she would have to be Sheridan's right hand person, hot headed, impulsive and popular with the blokes.... Well, what do you think? For me, a far more worthy claimant for this identification is G'Kar. He is every bit as hot headed as Gawain (at times anyway) and his is knighted as 'The Red Knight' by Arthur. Gawain himself had red hair and was often portrayed as carrying a red shield.

Marcus as Galahad

As to Marcus as Galahad, I'm really not sure how to take this one. It's said very
much tongue in cheek by Marcus himself. But let's look for a moment at Galahad. He is, of course, best known in the quotation from Tennyson that says that 'his strength was as the strength of ten because his heart was pure'. Well, that's true of Marcus I think. Beyond this, if we look back at the medieval picture, Galahad is the son of Lancelot, so he comes with a heritage of strength and bravery. But, he is brought up by nuns in a convent and his sole aim and purpose is to find the Grail. Many have found him a priggish, rather insufferable character - so good that he will barely speak to his companions and always seems to be in a daze - talking to God. Not much resemblance to Marcus here - though I was struck by one detail when I reviewed the episode while writing this talk. Marcus is trained (as in 'brought up') by the Minbari, who teach him 'Direction, determination, patience and strength' in order for 'his actions to be pure.' This is a bit reminiscent of Tennyson I suppose. But, as I suggested earlier, I still think we have a closer approximation to Galahad in the character of Aldous Gajic. Perhaps it's best just to let this one lie and move on to firmer ground.

Mordred

Well we don't have to look far to see at least one candidate for this character, one who nearly shares his name: Mr Morden. Mordred is traditionally the bad apple in the Arthurian barrel. Arthur's son by his sister Morgause (not the same as Morgan le Fay by the way, as so often stated) his sole purpose is to destroy all his father has built, to bring down Camelot and the Round Table just as Mordern wants to bring down B5 and the rest of the Alliance. The only difference is that Mordred, as the sister's son, has a fair claim to being Arthur's legitimate successor - at least according to Celtic law - whereas Morden is a traitor to humankind. Here I think, beyond the broadest parallels, there is not much connection between the two. I would, however, suggest that we have another possible Mordred character in the person of Bester. There is - to me anyway - something very like Mordred about the cold, dark, tortured character of the PsyCop, but we have yet to see where the story will take him and whether he will change, rather as Londo did, from likeable to unlikable and back again.

Morgan le Fay

The suggestion has been made that the Morgan (or Morgana) figures is Anna Sheridan, who was amongst the crew of the ship Icarus, who were responsible for waking the Shadows. It is at this point that Morden becomes enslaved to them and becomes their human emissary. Anna returns in the episode 'Shadow Dancing' and tries to draw Sheridan away from the focus of the battle. This is a fairly Morgana-ish kind of thing to do, but I don't really feel the identification stands up. This is just an example of clutching at straws in order to bring in all the major characters of the Arthur story. Morgana is Arthur's half-sister, not his wife (assuming we accept Sheridan as Arthur) and she is also an otherworldly goddess figure, based on the Irish battle-goddess called the Morrigan. So, on the whole, I think we have to leave her out of the picture for the moment. What is interesting here is that there is a story in which Arthur has an encounter with a false Guinevere, who looks so much like the real one that he is persuaded to imprison his true wife and all is not revealed for ages. This adds even further to our Sheridan-as-Arthur argument.

Delenn as Lady of the Lake

Delenn as the Lady of the Lake is, of course, part of the plot line in 'Late Delivery from Avalon', which requires that she play the role to help Arthur/David finds his way back to sanity. But, one gets the impression that Delenn knows more about this character than she's letting on. It's not east to fill the shoes of an archetype unless you know something about it, and though we get no impression that Delenn bones-up on the role, she plays it with great aplomb - and well enough to convince Arthur/David. Maybe she was thinking of the Minbari saying: 'What is past is also sometimes future.'

Looking wider afield than this episode, there is no doubt that Delenn's role is not unlike that of both the Lady of the Lake (who is generally nameless except in one source where she is called Argante) and, to a certain extent, Morgana. Let me explain what I mean here. We are used to thinking of Morgana as the enemy, hence the way in which she is so quickly identified with the false Anna Sheridan; but in fact she wasn't always seen in this light. In the earliest Arthurian texts, she is regarded as almost a goddess, ruling over the mysterious island of Avalon with her nine sisters. Of course it's no more than coincidence that there are nine members of the Grey Council, but it's interesting none the less. Morgana's earliest role is as a helper, a behind the scenes character a bit like Merlin, who, in her Lady of the Lake aspect, provides Arthur with the sword Excalibur (and isn't it interesting that the ship in the 'Crusade ' series is named after the magical weapon?) In B5 it could be said that Delenn provides Sheridan with one of the most powerful weapons in the shape of the White Star squadrons - while her dawning love and the support she offers almost from the start make her his partner and therefore a kind of Guinevere figure as well.

Excalibur

Last, but by no means least, there is Excalibur the ship, constructed of combined Minbari, Vorlon and Human technology - and Excalibur the sword, forged by Wayland, Smith of the Gods according to one story, or by the Lady of the Lake herself in another. This was always the Sword of Power, so eloquently described in John Boorman's movie *Excalibur* as containing the strength of the Dragon, the unearthly power of the Otherworld that flows through the land and through its guardians, Merlin and Arthur. In the context of B5 we can see this as the unearthly power of the Vorlons and Minbari flowing through the half-mile long ship, empowering its crew in much the same way as Excalibur does for Arthur. And, in the episode we have just been looking at, it is significant that the discovery of Excalibur is what seems to trigger the 'Arthur memories' in Macintyre.

These are just some of the Arthurian themes I've located in *Babylon 5*. There are probably more that I've missed, and there may well be more to come. I personally think it is in these episodes and others like them where the themes are deeply connected to mythology, that the show excels. As Michael J. Straczynski himself says in the essay included in Andy Lane's *Babylon File*: 'it seems very clear that the element most emblematic of science fiction at its very best... is the sense of wonder.' I think it is in these kinds of episode that he comes closest to expressing that wonder for us all, and we should all be very grateful to him for doing so!

(1998)

Chapter 7:

AN ORKNEY CONNECTION

I have loved the Orkney Islands ever since I visited them over 30 years ago, so I was happy to be invited to lead a tour there in 1987. As part of this I gave the following lecture, exploring some of the less familiar aspects of the Arthurian legends and their connection with the Orkneys. It may still be useful – especially for those who confuse Morgane and Morgause or do not understand why Mordred behaved the way he did.

The Orkneys have always been considered somewhat strange and mysterious - especially by those who live in the South. In common with most of the more remote islands around the coastline of Britain, they were long held to be the abodes of the dead, borderlands between this world and the other. This stems in part from the fact that they were actual necropoli, burial grounds of the sacred dead. It's a well known fact amongst archaeologists that you can't walk more than a few hundred yards in any direction on the Orkneys without falling over a tomb or some tumuli, the final dwelling-place of some once famous chieftain or hero whose names are now long forgotten.

Fortunately however, some of the names associated with the Orkneys (or the Orcadies as they are sometimes called) are not forgotten - at least not to students of the Arthurian legends. Such famous knights of the Round Table as Gawain and Gareth are still remembered, and even their dark brother Mordred has not yet passed from the annals of the world. As for their mother - sometimes called Morgause sometimes Morgan le Fay - few would claim never to have heard of her.

The Orkney Clan, as T.H.White called them in his novel *The Once & Future King*, were a pretty explosive bunch. Lot, their father, was a piratical chieftain who was Arthur's bitterest opponent at the troubled beginning of his reign. Yet we find four of his sons: Gawain, Gaheris, Agravain and Gareth, among the first to sit at Arthur's Round Table in Camelot. Perhaps they were in reality political hostages to ensure there was no further rising amongst the Northern Tribes, but by the time we get to the great mediaeval romances of Arthur, other and subtler reasons lie behind the presence of Lot's sons. Not only was Camelot the greatest centre of learning and chivalry in those mythic times, but there was also a complex web of relationships between Arthur and his Northern knights.

You will probably remember how Arthur's father, Uther Pen-dragon, fell in love with Igraine, the wife of Gorlois of Cornwall, and how with Merlin's help, he was able to engender Arthur upon her, and with Gorlois soon dead able to make her his queen. Once this was done Uther lost no time in finding husbands for the daughters of his wife's earlier marriage. He sought them among the strong lords of the North and forged great alliances thereby.

The names and number of Gorlois' daughters vary according to which text you follow, but they are usually four: Morgain, Morgause, Anna and Elaine - the last-named quickly forgotten in the stories.

But Morgause is remembered for dark and terrible reasons and Morgain becomes famous as a sorceress. She was, according to Malory and others, put to school in a nunnery, where she learned a great deal of very unchristian knowledge. But this is merely a late interpretation by the mediaeval romancers for Morgain's joining a community of priestesses who served an older deity. Marion Zimmer Bradley has given us a very believable account of this in her novel *The Mists of Avalon*, and of the reasons for her deep and lasting hatred of her half-brother.

According to Geoffrey of Monmouth's 12th century book *Historia Regum Brittaniae*, as well as several other texts, Morgain is later married off to Uriens of Gore, another of the kings who fought against Arthur, but who became in time a firm alley and friend. Their son was Owein, of whom more later.

The second of the Cornwall sisters, Morgause, married King Lot of Lothian & the Orkneys, and gave him the four strong sons already referred to. After the wars in which Lot fell, his widow came to the court of the new king, bringing her young sons with her. And there, it was said, Arthur became enamoured of her, not knowing she was his half-sister, and so begot on her a child who was to be his nemesis - Mordred. This may have been Morgause' revenge for the death of her father at the hands of Arthur's father. Certainly, although she is not represented as such an implacable enemy as her sister Morgain, it seems likely that she knew of the forbidden consanguinity of her relation-ship with Arthur and deliberately seduced him. Incest was always a fearful thing, forbidden by the Church and abhorrent to God. The poet laureate John Masefield (1878-1967) gave this account of the events in his collection *Midsummer Night* (1928):

> *When berries were scarlet*
> *In the holly's dark green,*
> *To the court at Caerleon*
> *Came Morgause the Queen...*
>
> *Then she tempted Prince Arthur,*
> *The youth in command,*
> *Till she saw his eyes brighten*
> *At the touch of her hand...*
>
> *In her room hung with purple*
> *She baited her hooks*
> *With her sweet-smelling body,*
> *Sweet words and sweet looks.*
>
> *There she tempted Prince Arthur*
> *With beauty's delight,*
> *So that love was between them*
> *For one summer night...*
>
> *But in Orkney in winter,*
> *When waiting was done,*
> *She bare the boy Modred*
> *From the evil begun,*

And the father, the uncle,
Had a nephew for son.
(The Begetting of Modred)

Yet if we look at this story again, we will see that Mordred has a very real claim to the throne of Britain. He is both nephew and sister's son, which by the ancient laws of the land would have marked him out for particular favour in the eyes of the people. None of the texts name Mordred a hero, yet it is possible to see a context in which he might have found it easy to secure support for his claim.

Returning to Morgause, it has often been assumed by Arthurian scholars that Morgain and Morgause are in fact one and the same, a primal figure who has been - as were so many of the characters who make up the Arthurian world - split into two. If this is so, they may both have derived from the Celtic Battle Goddess known as the Morrigan. Certainly this ancient and fearsome deity shares a number of points in common with Morgain or Morgause. Each has the ability to change their shape, particularly into that of a crow; all are cruel and merciless; all are queens (Morrigan means literally 'Great Queen'), and all rule over the isles of the dead.

We may remember that at the end of the Arthur cycle, the King is put into a barge with three queens aboard, one of whom is Morgain, and taken to the island of Avalon to be healed of his wounds In another work by the 11th century author Geoffrey of Monmouth called the *Vita Merlini*, we find Morgain and her nine sisters ruling over an island to which, once again, Arthur is carried to be healed. Also of interest is the description, found in the story of Ogier le Dane, of the Castle of Loadstone, on an island ruled over by Morgan le Fay. Morgause was queen of the Orkneys after the death of Lot, and, as I said at the beginning, the islands were frequently identified as isles of the dead.

So we may, if we like, think of these islands as an outward symbol of the inner Avalon, the mysterious country of life and death, where the Goddess of the ever-living holds court over heroes and faery women.

But there is still one further possibility concerning these characters, which we might take a quick look at before we go on to talk about their children. Caitlín Matthews has dealt with this is some detail in her book *Mabon & the Mysteries of Britain,* so I will just summarise it here.

According to one of the ancient *Welsh Triads* (No 56 to be precise) Urien is married, not to Morgan but to Modron. Now this is the name of an early Celtic goddess (the name means simply 'mother') that appears in several Romano-British inscriptions along Hadrian's Wall and at Lydney in Gloucestershire. For Urien to have a goddess for his consort is not unusual in Arthurian romance - several of the knights keep such company. But the story of how this came about in Urien's case is interesting enough to warrant attention.

In a late 16th century MS the story appears in full - almost certainly recorded from a much earlier time. It tells of a place called the Ford of Barking, because all the dogs in the land come there to bark every full moon. No one else dares to go there because of its evil reputation. Urien decides to investigate and meets a woman washing clothes in the river. He lies with her and afterward she tells him that he has released her from having to remain at that spot until a Christian knight got her with child. She tells him to return at the year's end for his son. Nine months later she gives birth to twins, Owein and Morfedd.

Before Urien leaves she tells him she is the daughter of the King of Annwn, which is one of the Celtic names for the Otherworld and identifies her as Modron. Elsewhere Morgain is said to be the daughter of Avallach, again a name attributed to an otherworld king.

This seems to prove beyond a doubt that Morgain, or Morgause or Modron, whatever name we decide to use, is really a goddess ruling over an otherworld island not unlike the isles of Orkney. If we add that the Washer-at-the-Ford, in which guise Modron appears at the Ford of Barking, is a well-attested figure, sometimes identified with the Morrigan, who washes the shirts of those shortly to die in battle, I think this makes a satisfactory picture.

Small wonder then, if the sons of Morgause (who is also Morgain) live extraordinary lives. Gawain, the eldest and in some ways the most interesting, has a tradition stretching back into the mists long before he became attached to the great Northern family of later Arthurian romance. As *Gwalchmai*, the Hawk of May, he is to be found among Arthur's warriors in the earliest surviving texts: namely the *Triads of Britain* and the *Mabinogion*. There he has qualities attributed to him that are part of the heroic tradition. His strength waxes and wanes throughout the day in accordance with the passage of the sun across the heavens - thus clearly marking him out as a solar-hero. Later he is numbered amongst the greatest of the Round Table knights and the first to set forth on the Quest for the Grail. Later still, by one of those strange turns of fate which sometimes occur within mythological schemas, he is demoted from a prime example of chivalry and honour to a far less heroic figure - a womaniser who is not even above murder.

Why this was so I hope to show in a book I'm in the process of writing. It's called *Gawain: Knight of the Goddess* [published by Thorsons in 1990 and reprinted by Inner Traditions in 2002] In this I set out to show that Gawain's original allegiance was to the Goddess was well known, and that when later writers Christianised the stories they attempted first of all to make Gawain the Knight of the Virgin (this is why in *Gawain & the Green Knight* he carries a shield with a pentacle on it which is said there to be the symbol of Christ's mother but which is actually the five pointed star of the Goddess). Anyway, when this failed to work, Gawain's character was further blackened.

We can actually see this happening in one of the most famous stories about Gawain (who is, by the way, always referred to as 'of Orkney'). This story, *The Wedding of Sir Gawain & Dame Ragnell*, tells how when Arthur was out hunting he fell foul of an otherworldly knight named Gromer Somer Joure (the Knight of Midsummer). This powerful figure threatens to kill Arthur unless he can find the answer to a question: what is it women desire most? Well, this is pretty difficult question to answer at any time, but Arthur promises to try and returns to Camelot, sending all his knights out to find the answer. Of course, it is Gawain, the knight best loved by all women (don't believe every-thing you hear about Lancelot!) who discovers the answer. He gets it from a hideous woman he meets by the roadside who promises to help him on one condition - that Gawain should marry her: With wonderful courtesy he accepts her offer and returns with her to Camelot. One the year is up Gromer is confronted and the right answer given, and Gawain must now keep his promise. The wedding takes place, with much lamenting on the part of the ladies at the court, but that night Gawain makes an amazing discovery when he kisses Ragnell, the hideous lady - she at once becomes beautiful. But there is a catch (There often is in stories of this kind.) She can only be beautiful either by night or by day, not both, and Gawain must choose which it shall be. Without hesitating he refers the decision to her judgement and in so doing the spell is broken forever because the answer to the question of 'what every woman most desires' is 'freedom to chose', (Some have said 'her own way, but that's rather too sexist for me: The traditional answer 'to have sovereignty over men.' given in Gawain and Ragnell is of course derived from the ancient kingship testing of the candidate king by the Goddess of the Land. The one who successfully answers the question and embraces the hag finds a beautiful woman in his arms: she tells him she is the Sovereignty of the Land - kingly rule and the land personified.' This application of this to

Gawain is very interesting, showing how very important he was in the Matter of Britain.)

Ragnall belongs to a type of beautiful otherworldly women who appears at various times in the Arthurian stories; she is there to test the finest human qualities and in Gawain's case she finds him true to the test. She bears him one son and then, two years after, vanishes forever. Gawain could not be permitted to retain the favour of the Otherworld for longer, but we can see behind this another story, where the knight of the Goddess finds his true consort and is tested in her service.

There is more that could be said, but it will have to wait if we are ever to get around to the other Orkney brothers. Gaheris, the second eldest, is the most shadowy. There are few stories about him, though his name appears frequently in the lists of the knights of the Round Table. The one action for which he is best remembered is his worst and it concerns the end of Morgause. (In her separate character as sister to Morgan le Fay and wife of Lot).

Well past her middle years, she takes a young lover, Lamorak, one of the strongest of Arthur's knights. Gaheris, angered and incensed by this, surprises the two in bed and cuts off his mother's head. Everyone is horrified and sickened, but this was the middle ages and so he is forgiven, being merely exiled for a while until the scandal is forgotten. Later on however he and Gawain ambush Lamorak and murder him, an act that also goes unpunished and is part of the general downgrading of Gawain's character. Gaheris finally meets his end at the hands of Lancelot, killed in the melee when Guinevere is rescued from the stake after being condemned for adultery.

Agravain, the third brother, also shows up in a less than pleasant light. He is Mordred's chief supporter and is instrument-al in capturing Lancelot and Guinevere when they are together (innocently as it happens) in the Queen's bedroom. He pays for this with his life at the hands of Lancelot and no-one seriously mourns him.

The same cannot be said for the fourth Orkney brother and the best loved of all: Gareth, who was made a knight by Lancelot and always had a special affinity with him. He meets his death accidentally in the melee and Lancelot earns the undying hatred of Gawain. But that is at the end of the story. Gareth's first appearance at Camelot is as memorable as that of any of the great Round Table Knights. Here is Malory's description:

"Right so came into the hall two men well beseen and richly dressed, and upon their shoulders there leaned the goodliest young man and the fairest that ever they all saw and he was large and long, and broad in the shoulders, and well visaged, and the fairest and largest handed that ever man saw, but he fared as though he might not go nor bare himself but if he leaned upon their shoulders. Anon as Arthur saw him there was made peace and room, and right so they went with him unto the high dais, without saying any words.

Then this much young man pulled him aback, and easily stretched up straight, saying, 'King Arthur, God you bless and all your fair fellowship, and in especial the fellowship of the Table Round. And for this cause I am come hither, to pray you and require you to give me three gifts, and they shall not be unreasonably asked, but that ye may worshipfully and honourably grant them me, and to you no great hurt nor loss. And the first gift I will ask now, and the other two gifts I will ask this day twelvemonth, wheresomever ye hold your high feast'.

'Now ask', said Arthur, 'and ye shall have your asking.'

'Now, sir, this is my petition for this feast, that ye will give me meat and drink sufficiently for this twelvemonth, and at that day I will ask mine other two gifts.'

'My fair son', said Arthur,' ask better, I counsel thee, for this is but a simple asking; for my heart giveth me to thee greatly, that thou art come of men of worship, and greatly my conceit faileth me but thou shalt prove a man of right great worship.'

'Sir', he said, 'thereof be as it be may, I have asked that I will ask.'

'Well', said the king, 'ye shall have meat and drink enough; I never defended that none, neither my friend nor my foe. But what is thy name I would wit ?'

'I cannot tell you', said he.

'That is marvel', said the king, 'that thou knowest not thy name, and thou art the goodliest young man that ever I saw'.

Then the king betook him to Sir Kay the steward, and charged him that he should give him of all manner of meats and drinks of the best, and also that he had all manner of finding as though he were a lord's son."

(Morte D'Arthur, Book 7 Ch.1)

Malory may well have contributed more than a little of his own imagination to the story of Gareth; it is the only substantial part of the narrative of the *Morte d'Arthur* for which there is no exact source. There are several other versions - one of them concerning Gawain's son, which may have suggested to Malory the idea of using it for Gareth, but we cannot be sure. Some scholars maintain that Gareth and Gaheris were once one character, but there seems far too little similarity in what we know of them for this to be so. Gaheris, as we saw, is a violently jealous man; Gareth is gentle, kindly and suffers insults with great patience.

His first and greatest adventure happens soon after his curious arrival. He is still serving in the kitchens when a damsel appears to ask help for her mistress, held prisoner in her own castle by the terrible Red Knight of the Red Lands. Before anyone else can claim the adventure Gareth (who is still unrecognised as the son of Lot and brother of Gawain) demands the right to try it. He is secretly knighted by Lancelot, and sets forth with the Damsel, who is called Linnet, to help her mistress. But Linnet proves less than kindly disposed toward her champion, calling him ('kitchen knave' and 'Sir Greasy Hands.' and other such things, and gives him the rough edge of her very sharp tongue the whole of the way.

Gareth easily beats off larger and larger forces of robbers, and then defeats, one after the other, a whole series of knights, all brothers of the Red Knight of the Red Lands, each of whom wears armour of different colours. Despite all this, Linnet still refuses to acknowledge Gareth or his deeds; even when he finally defeats the Red Knight and rescues her mistress, she seems ill disposed towards him - though he has earned her respect if nothing more by then.

In the best of worlds, I suppose Gareth would have fallen for Linnet and she for him and all would have ended happily. Instead, more in keeping with reality, Gareth loves the lady, Lionors, whom he has rescued, and marries her instead. But they live happily thereafter and Gareth, until his untimely death, enjoys a brilliant career at Camelot.

We have now looked at all of the Orkney brothers save one - Mordred, the son of Arthur and Morgause. His name has become synonymous with evil in the Arthurian legends, although as I pointed out earlier, he had good reason for claiming crown and kingdom.

In her book *Arthur and the Sovereignty of Britain* (Arkana, 1990) Caitlín Matthews discussed Mordred's original role in some detail, so I won't repeat this here. Yet the evidence is there to suggest that he once had quite a different role to that of the later romances. He may, indeed, have been a legitimate child of Lot and Morgause (or lover), which would still have made him Arthur's nephew, with at least a vague claim to the succession. But it seems likely that he actually took a role similar if not identical to that of Lancelot - as the lover of Guinevere. Mordred may well have sought the sovereignty of Britain through marriage with his father's or uncle's wife, and to this end carried her off into a captivity from which

Arthur rather than Lancelot rescued her. This turns the story of the fall of Camelot very much upside down, but not without reason I believe.

Most of you know the end of the story. How Gawain drove Arthur to attack Lancelot and received his death wound at the hands of his old comrade. How Arthur returned to find Mordred usurping the throne and how they met and how Arthur slew his son at the last battle – which took place at Camlan, after which the King was borne away to Orkney out into the realms of the Otherworld by three queens: Morgain, Anna and Elaine perhaps, the three surviving daughters of Gorlois.

Thus Arthur entered the realms of the Otherworld and stepped outside time. It is interesting to note that Geoffrey of Monmouth, who mentions the Orkneys several times outside the context of Arthur's reign, names one of their kings as *Guanuasius rex Orcadum*, a name derived from the Welsh Gwyn ap Nudd, King of the Dead! Perhaps Geoffrey was aware of the reputation held by those islands whose name, Orcades, was derived from the Greek Orcus or death. Morgain too is known sometimes as Morcades, a clear enough indication of the way her role was understood in those times.

So it may be that we have, in some sense, entered the Otherworld here in Orcady, if not in actuality then at least in the sense that here the curtain between the worlds is very thin. Perhaps the words of Rudyard Kipling puts it best (and despite the fact that there are no legends of Merlin attached to Orkney, nevertheless Britain was known anciently as *Clas Merddin* or Merlin's Enclosure):

> *She is not any common earth,*
> *Water or wood or air,*
> *But Merlin's isle of Gramarye,*
> *Where you and I will fare.*

(1987)

Section Two:

The Holy Grail

Chapter 8:

THE GRAIL AND THE ROSE

In 1995 I was invited to speak at a remarkable conference exploring the mystical Brotherhood of the Rose Cross as it manifested throughout Europe in the 16th century. The setting for this conference was in the small town Cesky Krumlov, in the Czech Republic, where many of the original Rosicrucian brotherhood had met and worked. It was a magical place and I have the strongest memories of taking part in an event that had deep magical and mystical resonances for the World. It gave me the opportunity to explore a theme of the Grail history that has still seldom been written about. The text of this lecture was later printed in The Rosicrucian Enlightenment Revisited Ed. by Ralph White (Lindisfarne Books,1999) It is reprinted here with some slight revisions and corrections.

The Grail and the Rose: two streams of wisdom flowing side by side, sometimes entering the same channel and flowing together, sometimes separating again to lead into different enchanted byways of the soul. It seems particularly appropriate to be discussing these interrelated themes only a few miles from the Castle of Karlstein, which has associations with both subjects and in a sense conjoins them as I hope to do here.

To begin with the Grail. This is surely one of the supreme symbols of the Quest for absolutes - truth, wisdom, healing, and union with the Beyond - to come out of the Western Mystery Tradition. It begins obscurely, with the 12th century poem *Conte du Graal* by the French poet Chrétien de Troyes, but in the hundred years from approximately 1200 to 1300 it was the most popular strand of all that collection of wonder-myths known collectively as the Matter of Britain - the cycle of Tales and poems centring around the figure of the great medieval image of King Arthur. Before this the origins of the Grail recede into the mists of Celtic myth and hero-tale, and earlier still into the beginnings of human myth-making, with the image of the crater, the mixing bowl of the gods from which the very stuff of creation was poured forth. In this it prefigures its later incarnation in the *vas spirituale* the vessel in which the alchemists wrought their mysteries of the spirit.

But it is with the medieval, and specifically Christian incarnation of the Grail that we are concerned here - as the chalice in which some of the holy blood of Christ was caught, and which was used in the first great celebration of the Christian mysteries of the Eucharist. Here we already see aspects of the theme that will later find restatement in the mysteries of Alchemy and their subsequent importance to the Rosicrucian Enlightenment. From the beginning the Grail is a vessel that has contained some of the Divinity of God, the blood that is symbolised by the wine in Eucharistic symbolism. And it is the very embodiment of that transubstantiation in the mystery of the Eucharist. In the intensity of the Christian interpretation it is also the womb of Mary, in which the Divine seed is transmuted into the body of the infant Christ. Thus Mary herself, in the great medieval Litany of Loretto is praised as:

vas spirituale,
vas honorabile,
vas insigne devotionis..

spiritual vessel,
vessel of honour,
singular vessel of devotion...

In effect, Mary has become a living Grail, a vessel in which the blood and essence of Christ are both contained. The Litany makes this point even more powerfully when it calls the Virgin:

Cause of our joy
Ark of the Covenant
Tower of David
Tower of Ivory,
House of Gold,
Seat of Wisdom
Mirror of Justice,
Queen of Prophets,

Each of these epithets reflects an aspect of the Grail. It too was a vessel of the spirit and devotion, a cause of joy to those who came into its presence, an Ark of the New Covenant between God and Man. It is also associated with a house of Gold (the Temple of the Grail) with a Seat of Wisdom (the Siege Perilous in which only the one destined to achieve the mysteries of the Grail may sit) and with Prophecy, an aspect specifically attributed to it in the Medieval German poem of Parzival by Wolfram von Eschenbach.

In the full spectrum of medieval symbolism Mary is Queen of Heaven, as well as mirror, vessel, house of gold and star of the sea. Her supreme symbol is the Rose - Rose of the World, Rosa Alchemica, Queen of the Most Holy Rose Garden in which the Grail lies hidden - as Wolfram von Eschenbach puts it, the Grail is:

'The wondrous thing hidden in the flower-garden of the king where the elect of all nations are called.' (Parzival)

The mysteries of Mary, represented in Catholic tradition by the Rosary, are arranged in multiples of five: five decades (or tens) repeated three times, a total of fifteen decades. Five was thus the number of Marian devotion; the rose was always depicted in symbolic representation with five petals; Christ was wounded five times, in the hands and feet and side; the Grail underwent five changes....'the nature of which no one ought to speak ' according to the 13th century Grail-text known as the *Perlesvaus*. The last of these changes is into the form of a child - a restatement of the divinity held by the vessel of the spirit. Finally, in the elaborate and extraordinary symbolism of Courtly Love - that medieval dream which placed women on a pedestal while making her the subject of adulterous passion - the Rose Garden was the place where the Beloved awaits the coming of the Lover, who must pluck the Rose in order to achieve his desire.

All of this can be interpreted in both mystical and Alchemical fashion. According to Catholic doctrine Mary is the Vessel in which the Divine Child is brought to term. In Alchemical symbolism the vas mirabile is the vessel in which the Mercurious, the burning Child brought forth by the spiritual wedding of the elements, finds manifestation. The coming together of the Lover and the Beloved is the same allegory of Divine Love extolled by Dante, who fully understood the symbolism of the Rose. In the *Paradiso* he makes the rose the final symbol of revelation and union with the divine, granted to him at the behest of Bernard of Clairvaux, who prays for the intercession of the Virgin. The symbolism is interchangeable here; it works as well for profane (Courtly Love) sacred (the Marian impulse) and alchemical (the birth of the Wondrous Child).

Thus the infinite is born into the finite, Christ becomes man, the spiritual transformations of the Grail and the alembic are shown to be the same. As St Ephraim wrote in the 4th century, invoking Christ:

> *In the womb that bore you are Fire and Spirit,*
> *Fire and Spirit are in the river where you were baptised,*
> *Fire and Spirit are in our baptism too,*
> *And the Bread and Cup are Fire and Spirit.*

> *It is not surprising therefore if we find the Troubadours, who fuelled the Arthurian myths with their burning and joyful light, referring to Mary as 'the Grail of the World,' and applying the term with equal validity to the Lady of the Rose Garden - where 'The beloved one is the heart's Grail, her lover will not be alone, for she is to him the highest Grail, which protects from every woe.' (Fisher)*

Much of this symbolism is Catholic and founded on Catholic doctrine, though it also embodies a recognition of the importance of the Divine Feminine at a time when the established church was exoterically opposed to this. Devotion to Mary, while never criticised, was considered as secondary to devotion to Christ. The Grail stories, it seems, were giving voice to an undercurrent of belief that harked back to pre-Christian times when devotion to the feminine principle - the Great Goddess - was either as important or more important than that to the God. The Grail's own pagan heritage focuses this in a number of ways - by the implicit femininity of its form - the Cup or Vessel - and in the story of Dindrane, the only female Grail quester of which we have knowledge. Sister to Perceval, one of the three knights who achieved the mystery of the Grail, Dindrane not only foresees the coming of the sacred vessel in a vision, but actually sets forth in search of it. Her death is a parable of the feminine mystery - and of the Grail and the Rose.

Joining the three knights on their Quest, Dindrane gives up her life to save another, giving her life-blood to heal a woman suffering from leprosy. The blood that is taken is symbolic of the monthly blood loss of all women, of the blood in the Grail, and of death of the Rose. Charles Williams, a modern Grail poet puts it magnificently in the poem significantly entitled 'Taliesin in the Rose Garden'.

Taliesin is the magical poet of Celtic tradition, and in these lines he draws together a knot of symbolism - of the Grail itself, of the suffering of the Wounded King, the Guardian of the sacred chalice whose wounds continue to bled until he can find healing - something which can only be brought about by the successful accomplishment of the Grail quest itself.

Here is Williams:

'Woman's flesh lives the quest of the Grail
in the change from Camelot to Carbonek and from Carbonek to Sarras,
puberty to Carbonek, and the stanching, and Carbonek to death.
Blessed is she who gives herself to the journey.

The late Helen Luke, a brilliant Jungian analyst, says of these lines:

'Williams hints at the inner identity of the woman's menstrual blood, which tells her that she has not yet conceived, with the blood of the wounded Grail king, bleeding because he cannot bring to life the new consciousness of the Christ, the Self...Taliesin speaks of how woman may consciously give birth to the new keeper of the Grail, within herself, and so heal the wound in the psyche' (Luke p101)

Again the message is alchemical, and would, I believe, have found a receptive chord among those who gave voice to the Rosicrucian Enlightenment. They, who emerged from the new Protestant order, which rebelled against the strictures of Roman Catholicism, gave birth also to a new myth that, borrowing from the older story of the Grail, gave form to a new Quest - for the mystery of Christian Rosenkreutz and the Rosicrucian Vault.

At the end of the Arthurian era, in terms of literature and pursuit of the Quest, the Grail vanished for a time. As Adam MacLean rightly noted in his contribution to a collection of essays which I edited some years ago:

'The Grail mystery returned underground, wrapped itself again in its esotericism and waited for another time to unfold its inner revelation. Such a point was reached after the Reformation, when the inner Grail mystery...surfaced again in the Rosicrucian movement of the early seventeenth century. At this time...the Rosicrucians tried to incarnate an esoteric Christianity within the Protestant movement...in order to provide a much needed resolution of the polarities of Protestantism. Thus we should see the Rosicrucian movement as being inwardly related to the Grail mystery. The spiritual alchemy that was the esoteric foundation of Rosicrucianism can be seen as a development of the Grail impulse.' (MacLean 59)

This is indeed the case, and in the symbolism of the Rosicrucian Wedding we see an unfolding of the original Grail story in a new form. As so often in the past, and again in recent times, an esoteric core underpins an outwardly rigid spirituality. The Rosicrucian movement is just such an esoteric resonance, flowering within Protestantism just as the Grail myths flowered within the outwardly patriarchal form of Catholicism.

In the examination of the primary text of that movement, The Chymical Wedding, I follow a line of reasoning first set forth by my wife in her essay 'The Rosicrucian Vault as Sepulchre and Wedding Chamber' first published in 1985.

The Chymical Wedding is a rosary - a mystical sequence of, in this instance, seven beads - in which Christian Rosenkreutz gathers the roses of Lady Venus' wealth. Each day in a petal in the rose that surrounds him - the rose that is here called the Vault. At the centre of the rose is the hierogomy of Christian Rosenkreutz and the Lady Venus, for although the text is assumed to be about the symbolic marriage of the King and Queen, in fact the title is descriptive of the spiritual coming together of Christian Rosenkreutz and the Lady Venus.

If we turn the pages that lead up to Christian Rosencreutz's secret hierogomy, we glimpse the real Christian Rosenkreutz who, though his hair is grey and he accounts himself as no longer young, shares the same innocent earnestness as Perceval in the Grail myths at the outset of the Quest. Here is one who would sell all that he has for the possession of the pearl of wisdom, and who suffers the rigours of his initiation into wisdom with the greatest humility and determination. His approach is ideal for a candidate towards initiation, unaware that, although he has been invited to a royal wedding, he himself is the groom. In the same way, Perceval sets out to find the Grail and is at once the guest in the castle where it is hidden, though he does not know this, and sets out on a quest that will take him full circle, back to this point of beginning.

Christian Rosenkreutz and Perceval both suffer the lot of all men. They are thrust into incarnation, into the captivity of matter, where they are yoked to their fellows by the service they both offer to the Quest. We see this in the Chymical Wedding in Day One, where C.R. Dreams that he emerges from his dungeon with the help of 'an ancient matron'. He is wounded in such a manner that blood covers him from head to foot. He is released from the dungeon by the ancient matron and told that he should be proud of his wounds and 'keep them for my sake'. There are echoes here of the Christ-like Perceval and of the wounded Fisher King of the Grail.

C.R. arrays himself for the wedding with crossed red bands over his breast and four red roses in his hat. These roses proclaim his loyalty to the Goddess and show that for all its Protestant veneer, the Chymical Wedding is in fact an exposition of the mysteries of Venus, which can be traced back both to the practices of Pagan Europe and through the Grail myth itself in the parallels between the Venusburg of German folk-lore and the Holy Mountain (Muntsalvache) of Rosicrucian and Grail myths.

The roses themselves are a clear indication of the initiate's dedication to his task. As A. Bothwell Gosse says in his study of *The Rose Immortal*:

'The disciple, servant of the Rose and of the Cross, progressing along the narrow Path and passing through the narrow gateway of Initiation, keeps ever before his eyes the Goal, remote at first, but ever growing nearer. From the beginning he has been pledged to the finding of Unity, for Unity stands at the end of the Path.' (Gosse p43)

And that Path leads, inevitably, upwards, to the Mountain of Salvation, the place of Mystery, the site of the Grail Temple where the unutterable mysteries of unity with the Beloved are celebrated.

Suffering is a part of that path. Just as C.R. suffers in the Chymical Wedding so does Lancelot in the Grail Story. There, the great worldly knight comes to doorway to the Chapel of the Grail and looks within. There he sees:

'a table of silver, and the Holy Vessel, covered with red samite, and many angels about it...and before the Holy Vessel...a good man clothed like a priest. And it seemed he was at the sacring of the Mass...'(Malory Bk.17, ch.15)

Watching the events that unfold, Lancelot sees the celebrant holding aloft the image of a man, bleeding from hands and feet and side, as though he would make an offering at the altar. And, when it seems as though he would fall from the effort, Lancelot enters the chamber out of a simple desire to help. But he is struck down by a fiery breath, and blinded by the light that flows from the Grail. For Lancelot is a fallen man, and does not know his way into the presence of the Grail. C.R looking upon the form of Lady Venus is likewise blinded - by the Goddess's radiance.

Both of these events happen in a temple of the Mysteries, and it is in the account of two such temples – one devoted to the Grail and the other to the Rosicrucian Mysteries, that we find further analogies and links between the Grail and the Rose.

The earliest traditions relating to temple-building depict them as dwelling places of Deity, where the Creator, God or Goddess, invited to enter into his or her house, may choose to communicate with the created. The earth upon which the temple stands is thereby made holy - either through its being placed in that spot or by the hallowing which takes place through the touch of the divine, and which in a sense 'calls forth' the building as a marker for those in search of the sacred experience. It becomes, in effect, a temenos a place set apart, where an invisible line shows that here Divinity lives, and that to enter this space means to enter the sphere of the divine, the reflection of heaven on earth.

The imagery of the Grail Temple is consistent throughout the texts in which it appears. It is usually situated at the top of a mountain, which is in turn surrounded either by an impenetrable forest or deep water. Access, if any, is by way of a perilously narrow bridge. To make the entrance even harder, the whole temple, or the castle that contains it, may revolve rapidly, making it almost impossible to gain entry by normal means. Once within more perils awaited, and for those few who succeeded in reaching the centre, the heart of the Grail-Rose, the experience could, as in the case of Lancelot, be both parlous and chastening.

The most completely developed description of the medieval Grail Temple is to be found in the Middle High German poem *Der Jungere Titurel* (c1270) attributed to Albrecht von Scharfenburg. Here the lineage of the Grail knights is traced back to Solomon. According to Albrecht, Titurel, the grandfather of the famous Grail knight Perceval, was fifty when an angel appeared to him and announced that the rest of his life was to be dedicated to the service of the Grail. Accordingly he was lead to a wild forest from which sprang the Mountain of Salvation, where he found workers gathered from all over the world who were to help him build a castle and temple to house the sacred vessel.

So Titurel set to work and levelled the top of the mountain, which he found to be made of onyx. Soon after he found the ground plan of the temple mysteriously engraved on this fabulous surface. The completion of the temple took some thirty years, during which time the Grail provided not only the substance from which it was built, but also food to sustain the workmen. The Grail is thus seen to participate directly in the creation of its own temple, as perhaps the followers of CR did in the creation of the Vault. There, the uncorrupted body of CR lies in suspend animation, just as the body of the wounded Fisher King is preserved in the Grail Temple.

The allegory here is dense but perceivable. The image of the Temple as vessel, containing the holy matter of creation, relates to a fundamental aspect of both the Grail Temple and the Rosicrucian vault - the idea of the temple within, or, as we might say, the Grail as bodily vessel. This notion has been a common one since the earliest times. In the Chandogya Upanishad it is said that:

> In the centre of the Castle of Brahma, our own body, there is a small shrine, in the form of a lotus flower, and within can be found a small space. We should find who dwells there and want to know him...for the whole universe is in him and he dwells within our heart.'

Or, as one might say: in the centre of the Castle of the Grail, or the Vault of C.R., which is our own body, there is a shrine, and within it is the Rose, the symbol of the Grail of the Heart. We should indeed seek to know and understand that inhabitant of ourselves. It is the fragment of the divine contained within each one of us, the light that shines within everyone. The true quest of the Grail consists in bringing this rosy light to the surface, nourishing and feeding it until all can see its radiance.

But the way is hard, and the mountain steep, guarded by wild animals and powerful otherworldly opponents. In the Grail myths this takes the form of such challenging figures as The Black Maiden, sometimes called Kundry, who appears from time to time to urge the Grail knights on their way when they are beginning to fall by the wayside. However it is the mountain that remains the most fearsome and terrible trial.

In Rosicrucian terms we have the famous Rosicrucian allegory *The Holy Mountain*, which has been attributed to Thomas Vaughan. Here we find the following description:

'There is a mountain situated in the midst of the earth or centre of the world, which is both small and great. It is soft, yet also above measure hard and stony. It is far off and near at hand, but by the providence of God, invisible. In it are hidden the most ample treasures, which the world is not able to value. This mountain - by envy of the devil, who always opposes the glory of God and the happiness of man - is compassed about with very cruel beasts and ravening birds - which make the way thither both difficult and dangerous.' (Allan)

However, if you succeed in daring all these perils, in recognising that the mountain is not just a mountain and the treasure not just a treasure, you will find that:

'The most important thing [on the Mountain] and the most powerful, is a certain exalted Tincture, with which the world - if it served God and were worthy of such gifts - might be touched and turned into most pure gold.
This Tincture...will make you young when you are old, and you will perceive no disease in any part of your bodies. By means of this Tincture you will find pearls of an excellence which can not be imagined...' (Allan p395/6)

This is so like the function of the Grail it is hard not to believe that its author was directly influenced by the medieval texts - though it is more likely that both are an expression of a hunger for spiritual sustenance. However, if one turns to one of the most famous and esoterically based of the Grail texts - the Parzival of Wolfram von Eschenbach - we will see at once just how close the two streams are.

To begin with we find the following passage from Wolfram, which, when set along side the above extract from 'The Holy Mountain' seems to me to display remarkable similarities. The passage in question is where Wolfram describes the Grail and its effects:

'There never can be human so ill but that if he one day sees the stone [that is, the Grail] he cannot die within the week that follows...and though he should see the stone for two hundred years [his appearance] will never change, save that his hair might perhaps turn grey.' (Wolfram)

There is no time here to go into the mystery of the Grail as it is presented in this text in any detail. However it important to know that here the sacred object is, uniquely, described as 'a stone of the purest kind ... called lapsit exillis'. This phrase has been taken to be a reference to the lapis philosophorum, the Philosopher's Stone, the pursuit of which occupied the minds and energies of generations of medieval and Rosicrucian alchemists alike, and which symbolised the ultimate completion of the Great Work. If we consider alchemy here to mean a spiritual rather than chemical process we will see how apt the analogy is. The Grail transforms those who come into its presence. It preserves their bodies and extends their lives indefinitely. It feeds the hunger of the spirit that is present within every seeker. It is an alembic in which the transformation of base material into spiritual gold takes place - in other words it is an expression of the Great Work, of the resurrection, and of the flowering of the Rose and the Grail which takes place in both the medieval romances and the Rosicrucian allegories.

But there is yet another parallel between the story told by Wolfram and one of the most fundamental aspects of the Rosicrucian movement. In Parzival we read:

'As to those who are appointed to the Grail [that is, to be its guardians] hear how they are made known. Under the top edge of the Stone an inscription announces the name and lineage of the one summoned to make the glad journey.... Those who are now full-grown all came here as children. Happy the mother of any child destined to serve there! Rich and poor alike rejoice if a child of theirs is summoned and they are bidden to send it to that Company! Such children are fetched from many countries and forever are immune from the shame of sin and have a rich reward in Heaven.' (Book 9)

This, it seems to me, is so much in the spirit of that other great Rosicrucian document the Fama Fraternitatis, in which we learn of the existence of a brotherhood selected and called by God to bear witness to the great mystery of C.R., and whose task is to remain hidden until the time when the world is ready for their message. Robert Fludd, in his defence of the Rosicrucian Brotherhood, makes the connection even clearer when he says:

'Here then you have that House or Palace of Wisdom erected on the Mount of Reason. It remains however, to learn who are those...to whom this House is open. These most fortunate of men and their spiritual house are described by the Apostle in the following manner: 'To whom come, as unto a living stone...[the] chosen of God...[to whom] are built up a spiritual house, a holy priesthood, to offer up spiritual sacrifices, acceptable to God... A chosen generation, a royal priesthood, an holy community, a ransomed people, that you should practice the virtues of him who has called you out of darkness into his royal light. For previously you were not a people, but now you are the people of God.' *(Peter 2:4-5)*

This is certainly an echo of the 'Christian progeny bred to a pure life [who] have the duty of keeping [the Grail]' in Wolfram's poem. These are summoned to their task in the same way as the young knights in another Arthurian Grail text, the Perlesvaus who, long after the mysteries of the Grail are over in that age, hear rumours of the existence of the Castle of Wisdom and set forth in search of it:

'They were fair knights indeed, very young and high spirited and they swore they would go, and full of excitement they entered the castle. They stayed there a long while, and when they left they lived as hermits, wearing hair-shirts and wandering through the forests, eating only roots; it was a hard life, but it pleased them greatly, and when people asked them why they were living thus, they would only reply: "Go where we went, and you will know why". (Bryant)

This is the essential experience that those who seek the Grail have been undergoing ever since. It this which sends thousands to the little town of Glastonbury in Somerset every year, where the Grail was supposedly brought by Joseph of Arimathea - in search of the mystery which has reached out far beyond the simple story written down in the 12th century by Chretien de Troyes. It has in fact brought us together, in this castle, under the sign of the rose, just as those first disciples of Christian Rosenkreutz met together to discuss the mystery of their founder.

The alchemist Arnold of Vilanova said: 'Make a round circle and you have the Philosopher's Stone.' The Grail, whether as a stone, a cup, a container or that which his contained, remains at the centre of the circle, like the Rose at the centre of the Hortus Conclusus, the mysterious Rose Garden of the Beloved. But the centre is also the circumference, and all quests lead to this place of hallowing. The knights in their wanderings, like the disciples of CR, attain the goal that would have remained inaccessible had they gone purposely to the Grail castle by a direct route. In surrendering themselves to chance they are enabled to make the way ton the heart of the Mystery - where some at least recognise the truth, pluck the rose, or drink from the Cup of Truth.

I said at the beginning that it was especially appropriate to be discussing the Grail here in this place, not far from the castle of Karlstein, which is indeed only 12 miles from Prague, situated on a wooded hill near the river Beroun.

Karlstein was built between 1348 and 1365, soon after the first flowering of Grail literature, by the German King and Bohemian Emperor Charles IV, whose life and work prefigure that of the later monarchs of Bohemia who fostered the work of the Rosicrucian Enlightenment. Described by Rudolf Steiner as 'the last initiate on the throne of the Emperors', Charles understood the connection between the Rose and the Grail perhaps better than anyone before or since. Karlstein was consciously built to reflect this.

The following description shows just how deeply the two themes become one in this place.

'The adornment of the walls in the various chapels to be found in the castle, with their quantities of semi-precious stones and gold, the way in which the light is disused through these semi precious stones which - set in gilded lead - take the place of window glass, lead one to conclude that Charles IV knew about the [esoteric] powers of precious stones and gold. The small chapel of St Catherine, for example, is a veritable gem. The entire walls, up to the ceiling, are inlaid with semi-precious stones such as amethyst, jasper, cornelian and agate, while the cross vaulting above has a blue background, adorned with roses, according to the Rosicrucian motif. According to tradition it was here that Charles IV withdrew every year from Good Friday to Easter Sunday in order to meditate in undisturbed privacy....' (Allan p478)

This period is, of course, not only associated with the period of the Crucifixion and Resurrection of Christ, but also with the Grail mysteries that took place at the same time. This is reflected in the design of the Castle in a number of ways. Throughout the building are murals which reflect the shape of the Rosicrucian initiation - the releasing of the prisoner from his chains, the sowing of seed in darkness, its milling and baking - (all aspects of the alchemical process), the burial of the dead, the feast which reminds us of the Wedding Banquet in the Chymical Wedding - and finally, execution and dismemberment.

These images guide the seeker towards the great tower of the castle that is approached across a narrow bridge - the Sword Bridge of the Grail story. Within the tower is the Chapel of the Holy Cross, again decorated in semi-precious stones, beneath a roof representing the sun moon and stars, interspersed with the motif of roses. The windows are formed of pure topaz, amethyst and almandine, through which the light enters in bands of glorious colour. The symbolism is clear: the initiate makes his way through life, learning, forgetting, re-learning, following the path of spiritual alchemy, until he is able to cross the perilous bridge and enter the chamber of the Mysteries. The parallels need hardly be spelled out. This is the chapel of the Grail, where the Rose also blooms.

Rudolf Steiner understood this precisely when he said of Karlstein:

'I was recently in a castle in Middle Europe in which there is a chapel and where one can find, symbolised,

thoughts from the turning point of this new era. In the whole stairway are rather primitive paintings, but what can be found painted throughout this whole stairway - even if the paintings are primitive? - The Chymical Wedding of Christian Rosenkreutz! One walks through this Chymical Wedding, finally reaching the Chapel of the Grail.'
(Lecture on July 6th, 1918).

Here indeed, not too far from where we are now, the two themes with which we began, the Grail and the Rose, come together. To seek one is to seek the other. To follow one form of enlightenment is to find another. The Rose blossoms within and from the Grail - Rosicrucianism stems from the root of the Grail myths as a natural outgrowth of the spiritual search.

NOTES

1: Chrétien de Troyes Conte du Graal trans. N. Bryant, D.S. Brewer, 1982

2: Quoted in J. Matthews The Grail Thames & Hudson, 1981

3: ibid

4: Wolfram von Eschenbach Parzival trans. A T. Hatto, Penguin Books 1981

5: Perlesvaus N Bryant trans. D.S. Brewer, 1975

6: Matthews The Grail

7: Lizette A. Fisher The Mystic Vision of the Grail Legend and the Divine Comedy, AMS Press, 1966

8: Charles Williams, Arthurian Poems D.L. Dodds ed. Rochester, NY Boydell & Brewer, 1994

9: Helen Luke, "The Return of Dindrane," At the Table of the Grail ed. Matthews. London, RKP, 1982

10: Adam McLean "Alchemical Transmutation in History and Symbolism," At the Table of the Grail Ed. Matthews

11: C Matthews "The Rosicrucian Vault as Sepulchre and Wedding Chamber" The Underworld Initiation Ed. R.J. Stewart, Aquarian press, 1995

12: The Chemical Wedding E. Foxcroft, Trans. n.d.

13: A Bothwell Gosse, The Rose Immortal, J Watkins, 1958

14: Thomas Malory Le Morte D'Arthur ed J. Matthews Cassell, 2000. sacring is the consecration of bread and wine in the Eucharist

15: Albrecht von Scharfenburg Der Jungere Titurel W. Wolf Ed. Berlin, 1983

16: A Christian Rosenkreutz Anthology complied and edited by P.M. Allen Blauvelt, NY, Rudolf Steiner Publications, 1981

17: ibid

18: Parzival, Hatto trans

19: ibid

20 A Christian Rosenkreutz Anthology

21 Perlesvaus N Bryant trans.

22 see Carlo Pietzner's intro to A Christian Rosenkreutz Anthology

23 Ita Wegman "On Castle Karlstein and its Rosicrucian Connections" A Christian Rosenkreutz Anthology

24 A Christian Rosenkreutz Anthology p15.

(1995)

Chapter 9:

TEMPLES OF THE GRAIL

The way to the Grail lies within: this much is made clear by the nature of the Quest, in its imagery of the divine search for what is best in humanity. In this scenario the body, which has always been recognised mystically as an impediment to the realization of spiritual freedom, becomes a testing ground, where the good and bad aspects of the individual do battle, the one seeking to know God, the other running from Him. The Temple, of which the body is an image, performs a similar function, in the Grail story more especially so, where it reflects the duality at the heart of all matter, and the desire of humanity to conquer its divided self by stretching up to meet the descending love of creation. This essay was originally written for inclusion in a collection that I edited in 1988 under the title '*At the Table of the Grail*'.

I

When Sir Lancelot, in Thomas Malory's *Le Morte D'Arthur*, comes at last, after many adventures, to the Chapel of the Grail, an unearthly voice warns him not to enter. Hesitating outside the door, he non the less looks within, and sees:

> '*a table of silver, and the Holy Vessel, covered with red samite, and many angels about it ... and before the Holy Vessel ... a good man clothed as a priest. And it seemed he was at the sacring of the mass.(1)*

Watching the events that follow, Lancelot sees the celebrant holding aloft the image of a man, as though he would make an offering at the altar. And, when it seems as though he would fall from the effort, Lancelot enters the chamber out of a pure desire to help. But he is struck down by fiery breath, and blinded by the light that flows from the Grail. For Lancelot does not know the way into the presence of the Grail.

That way is a hard one, for it consists of entering the Temple of the Grail, which is so designed that it serves as an initiation test for all who wish to share in the mysteries. Lancelot's experience is echoed by many who set out unprepared, and who end by being blinded by what they cannot understand. Properly followed, however, the way towards the home of the Grail can offer a means of knowing, of understanding the light. Many temples have fallen in ruins, but it is said that the true Temple is never destroyed. We would do well to keep this in mind as we examine some of the images assumed by that imperishable temple throughout its long history, hoping that we may thus learn something of our own part in the continuing mysteries of the Grail.

The earliest traditions relating to temple-building depict them as liminal space, as dwelling places for God; where the Creator, invited to enter his house, may choose to communicate with his creation. The earth upon which the temple stands is thereby sacred earth either through its being placed at that spot, or by a hallowing touch of the divine that calls forth the building as a marker for those in search of the sacred experience. Thus it becomes a temenos, a place set apart, where an invisible border shows that here is sacred space, to enter which means to enter the sphere of the divine, the reflection of the heavenly on earth.

For this reason the forms most often incorporated into the design of the temple are those of the circle and the square, symbolic representations of heaven and earth, so that many consist of squared stones set up in circles (the Megalithic temples), or rectangular buildings supported by rounded pillars (Hellenic and Egyptian temples). These can also be seen as archetypal images of the masculine and feminine, so that the circle of the heavens and the square of earth unite in a single image.

This may be expressed graphically by a symbol known as the Vesica Pisces, two overlapping circles that illustrate the link between God and his creation that takes place in the temple, whether directly or through the agency of priests and seers. Plotinus understood this perfectly when he wrote (using a slightly different analogy), that the human is drawn to the divine 'like two concentric circles: they are only one when they coincide and only two when they are separated.' (2)

It is a state of spiritual separation that causes the failure of Lancelot and those like him, who seek the Grail for diverse reasons; and it is for this reason that the Grail temple exists, to show the way back to a state of unity with the divine impulse of creation.

It is for this reason also that we first read of the appearance of the Grail as an aftermath to the story of the Fall. It is said that the Grail was entrusted to Adam at the beginning of time, but that after the Fall it remained behind, since it was too holy an object to be taken into the world. But there is a tradition that says that Seth, a child of Adam and Eve whom the Gnostics revered as a hidden Master, made the journey back to the gate of Eden in search of the Sacred Vessel. There, he was permitted to enter, and remained for forty days, at the end of which the Grail was given into his keeping, to serve both as a reminder of what had been lost, and as a sign of hope and redemption to come - though this remained unrecognised until the time of Christ, when the symbol of the Grail as Chalice became established in Christian belief.

What is most especially important here, as the *Vulgate Grail Cycle* says, is that: 'those who possessed the Grail after [Seth] ... were by this very fact, able to establish a Spiritual centre destined to replace the lost Paradise, and to serve as an image of it.' (3) It is this image that is represented by the temple of the Grail, as a place where God and his creation can meet and converse as once they had in Paradise.

In this way the temple can be seen to represent a cosmic evolutionary diagram. It is as though the temple builders, by inviting God to descend into the temenos, were asking not only to be guided along the path towards the unity of perfection, but also anticipating that God would actually evolve through contact with them. For, God is spirit and humanity matter and the two cannot evolve separately - they are indeed linked like two interlocking circles, which are only complete when superimposed precisely one upon the other - at which they become one. Thus all temples and churches were intended as physical glyphs to be read by both mankind and their gods, as a mirror reflecting back images of the temporal and divine upon each other.

This imagery is continued in the iconography of the Virgin Mary, who becomes a human temple and a vessel for the divine, and whose reply to the Angel of the Annunciation in the painted imagery of the iconographers, is represented in reversed, mirror writing. This is done so that her words may be read by the angelic power above her, while Mary herself is sometimes referred to as 'a mirror of the greatness of God'.

Thus the earliest temples we know - the stones which gave Megalithic man his name - were erected in circles: set up on power points in the ground, so that they served as living extensions of the earth Herself - the Mother holding out her arms towards the Moon, the Sun and the Stars. These huge astrological observatories were built as much for the gods as for mankind - not just to honour them but to invite them to participate in the ritual living out of life in and around them. Or to quote Plotinus again:

> *those ancient sages who sought to secure the presence of*
> *divine beings by the erection of shrines ... showed insight*
> *into the nature of the All [perceiving that] though the Soul*
> *is everywhere its presence will be secured all the more readily*
> *when an appropriate receptacle is elaborated serving like a mirror to catch an image of it. (4)*

In its most complete and complex form, this cosmic mirror for the reflection of God becomes also an initiator into the divine mystery of creation, the most perfect object of the Quest. As such it may be expressed by the eternally fixed but changing pattern of the maze, and it is no accident that the architects of the Gothic cathedrals such as Chartres, in an endeavour to encode the mystery of the temple into the design of the great medieval churches of Europe, chose to include this form so often on both floors and walls. (5)

The temple of the Grail was a logical outcome of this, and it is not surprising to find how closely it conforms, throughout its many representations, to the traditional archetype.

III

The imagery of the Grail Temple is consistent. It is usually at the top of a mountain, which is in turn surrounded either by impenetrable forest or deep water. Access, if any, is by way of a perilously narrow, sharply edged bridge, which became known as the Sword Bridge. To make entrance even harder, the whole temple, or the castle that contained it, would often revolve rapidly, making it almost impossible to gain entry by normal means. Once within, more perils awaited, and for those few who succeeded in reaching the centre, where lay the Chapel of the Grail, the experience could, as in Lancelot's case, be both chastening and parlous. Nor was the castle without its human guardians; at an early stage in the mythos a family of Kings, supported by a specially chosen body of knights, appeared to serve and protect the sacred vessel.

The most completely developed description of the medieval Grail Temple is to be found in the Medieval German poem *Der Jungere Titurel* (c. 1270) attributed to Albrecht von Scharfenburg. Here the lineage of the Grail Kings is traced back to Solomon - a detail that, as we shall see, is of some importance - but the setting is firmly medieval in its details. According to Albrecht, Titurel, the grandfather of the famous Grail knight Parsifal, was fifty when an angel appeared to him and announced that the rest of his life was to be dedicated to the service of the sacred vessel. Accordingly he was lead into a wild forest from which arose the Mountain of Salvation, *Muntsalvache*, (6) where he found workers gathered from all over the world, who were to help him to build a castle and temple for the Grail - which at that time floated houseless in the air above the site, supported by heavenly hands.

So Titurel set to work and levelled the top of the mountain, which he found to be of onyx and which, when polished, 'shone like the moon'. Soon after he found the ground plan of the building mysteriously engraved on this fabulous surface.

The completion of the temple took some thirty years, during which time the Grail provided not only the substance from which it was built, but also food to sustain the workmen. Already the Grail is seen as a provider - a function that it continues to perform. But more rarely, and importantly for our argument, it is here seen as contributing directly in the construction of its own temple, making one a part of the other, the design non-human in origin, the execution attributed to the hands of man.

At this point in the poem Albrecht devotes one hundred and twelve lines to a description of the temple so specific in detail as to leave one in little doubt that he is describing a real building. (7)

The temple is high and circular, surmounted by a great cupola. Around this are twenty-two chapels arranged in the form of an octagon; and over every pair of these is an octagonal bell-tower surmounted by a cross of white crystal and an eagle of gold. These towers encircle the main dome, which is fashioned from red gold and enamelled in blue.

Three entrances lead inside: one in the North, one in the West, a third in the South from which flow three rivers (thus indicating a debt to the image of Paradise with its rivers and gates whereby they flow out). The interior is rich beyond compare, decorated with intricate carvings of trees and birds; while beneath a crystal floor swim artificial fish, propelled by hidden pipes of air fuelled by bellows and windmills. Within each of the chapels is a altar of sapphire, curtained with green samite, (8) and all the windows are of beryl and crystal, decorated with other precious stones.

In the Dome itself a clockwork sun and moon move across a blue enamelled sky in which stars are picked out in carbuncles. Beneath it, at the very centre of the temple, is a model of the whole structure in miniature, set with the rarest jewels, and within this is kept the Grail, itself a microcosmic image of the whole universe of creation.

It is clear that what is being described in Albrecht's poem is a type of Earthly Paradise. Details such as the three rivers, as well as the overall layout of the building, frozen and perfect in its jewelled splendour of artificial birds and fishes, all support this conclusion. The first home of the Grail is being rebuilt in medieval terms, but it remains a copy, a simulacrum of the true temple whose reality it merely mirrors.

But the image described in the poem is not limited either to mythical, or indeed literary, manifestation. It is possible to trace the origin of Albrecht's temple to an actual site, though this did not come to light until the 1930s, when the Orientalist Arthur Upham Pope lead an expedition to the site of the ancient Sassanian (Persian) temple known as the Takht-i-Taqdis, or Throne of Arches, in what is now Iran. Attention had already been drawn by earlier scholars (9) to the literary evidence suggesting a link between the semi-legendary Takht and the Grail Temple, but it was not until Pope published his findings that it became known that the reality of the Takht closely approximated the description of Albrecht's thirteenth-century poem.

The site contained evidence of a great central dome surrounded by twenty-two side chapels (or arches) as well as other architectural details similar to those described in the Jungere Titurel. Even Albrecht's mountain of onyx was accounted for by the presence of mineral deposits around the base of the site. These, when dried out by the sun, closely resembled the semi-precious stone.

Pope's excavations also confirmed that the Takht had once contained a complete observatory, with golden astronomical tables that could be changed with the seasons. A star map was contained within the great dome; and to facilitate matters even further the entire structure was set on rollers above a hidden pit, where horses worked day and night to turn it through the four quarters, so that at every season it would be in correct alignment with the heavens. Literary evidence from Persian writings such as the *Shah-Nama* further supported the details of the site, and made clear the nature of the rites that had been celebrated there. These were of a seasonal and vegetational kind, and, when performed by the priestly rulers of ancient Persia, ensured the fertility of the land and the very continuation of its people's life. Pope commented that the beauty and splendour of the Takht 'would focus, it was felt, the sympathetic attention and participation of the heavenly powers' (10) - so that once again we have an expression of the desire for the direct entrance of God into a man-made temple - a temple which furthermore revolved, as did both the Grail Temple and, according to some versions, the walls of the Earthly Paradise - without which it cannot be said to be complete.

IV

Many of the attributes discussed so far bring to mind an even more famous temple - that of Solomon in Jerusalem, the story of which is indissolubly linked with the history of the Knight's Templar and with the history of the Ark of the Covenant, which is itself an image that shares many of its attributes with the Grail. It is also the story of a chosen race and their communications with their God.

Built to house the Presence of God (the Shekinah) the Solomonic temple was the concretisation of an idea which began with the revelation of Moses, who created the first Tabernacle to contain the Ark and later extended it into the great image of the temple itself. From within this holy house God spoke 'from above the mercy seat, from between the two cherubim that are upon the Ark of the Covenant'. But the Tabernacle was never intended as a permanent home, and it wag left to Solomon to complete the fashioning of a final resting place for the Ark at Jerusalem.

Even this remained merely a pattern for the Heavenly Temple, the Throne of God, the Temple Not Built By Human Hands: it possessed also a secondary, spiritual life, made from stones crystallised from the river Jobel which flowed out of Eden. Here there is a sense of an image behind an image; while the link between the heavenly and earthly dimensions of the temple is part of the Edenic mystery, and therefore of the Grail - which in turn performs the same function as the Ark as a place for the meeting and mingling of God's essence with that of his Creation.

This can be taken a step further by reference to Jewish Qabalistic tradition, where the earthly temple is said to possess 'two overlapping aspects: one heavenly and one divine'. (12) Moses, who received the plan of the temple in much the same way as Titurel in Albrecht's poem, is enabled to witness the mystery performed in the divine dimension, where the high priest is the Archangel Michael. Beyond this is a still higher and more secret sanctuary, where the 'high priest' is 'divine light' itself. (13)

The mysteries of the Grail, which undergo a division into mind, heart, and spirit, echo the formation of the Solomonic sanctuary into the Temples of Earth and Heaven and the Temple of Light. In Jerusalem worshippers entering the outer court of the temple were said to have reached Eden; beyond this, in the Holy of Holies, the dwelling place of the Ark or the Chapel of the Grail, are the mysteries of the heavenly world, where the concerns of mind and body are left behind and those of the sanctified heart begin. Of those who went in search of the Grail, few except Galahad went beyond this point, and those who did were assumed into Heaven. It is as though, looking out of a window, the eye was lead beyond a glimpse of the immediate world, to gaze up into the heavens, and on looking there was suddenly able to see beyond, through all the dark gulfs of space to the Throne of God itself, there to be lost in light.

Lancelot was struck down and blinded by that light, for which he was unprepared. Only his son Galahad was allowed to look directly into the heart of the Grail, and then only at the direct invitation of God - an answer and a reversal of the continuing invitation of mankind to God to enter the temple built in his honour.

Of the several non-biblical accounts of the Solomonic temple which exist, that of the Islamic historian Ibn Khaldun is one of the most interesting, for in it he states that the vaults below the temple, which are still generally believed to have been the stables for Solomon's horses, were nothing of the kind; they were built to form a vacuum between the earth and the building itself, so that malign influences might not enter it from below. (14)

There is a suggestion of dualism in the opposing of the dark forces of the earth against those of the sky, and this is born out by what we know of the construction of Greek and Roman temples, where the adytum stretching below the earth was of equal or perhaps greater importance to the building above ground, and which served as a meeting place for the subterranean gods and their worshippers.

By medieval times, when the original site of the Solomonic temple had become a Muslim shrine, the chamber mentioned by Ibn Khaldun had become known as a place of entrance and exit for the spirits of the dead, while of the original structure nothing now remained above ground. The Crusaders however, continued to refer to it as the *Templum Dominum*, (Temple of God) and it became sacred to the three major religions of the time. For the Jews it was the site of Solomon's Altar of the Holocausts, while to the Muslims, as the place from which the Prophet had ascended to heaven, it came for a time to rival Makkah (Mecca), and was attributed with the property of 'hovering' above the earth. Thus the geographer Idrisi referred to it in 1154 as 'the stone which rose and fell' (lapis lapsus exilians), which interestingly recalls Wolfram von Eschenbach's description, in his 13th century poem Parzival, of the Grail itself as *lapis exilis*, (stone of heaven) sometimes interpreted as 'the stone which fell from heaven'.

It seems that here we have a paradigm for the whole history of the Grail and of the temple built to house it. The Grail, originating in Paradise, can also be said to have 'fallen' by being brought into this world by Seth. Through its use by Christ to perform the first Eucharist, it is hallowed, and the world, like the lost Eden, redeemed, so that it too 'rises'. Equally, the stones used in the building of the temple, and the design for its construction, as described by Albrecht, can be seen to have 'fallen from heaven'.

The Solomonic temple was to give rise to several imitations in the history of the Western world, one of which at least concerns us in our examination of the temple of the Grail. It became common practice among the Crusader knights to chip off fragments of the rock upon which the Temple had once stood. These they would take home as talismans of their visit to the Holy Land. One such man, a French knight named Arnoul the Elder, brought back one such piece to his home at Ardres in 1177, along with a fragment of the Spear of Antioch and some of the Manna of Heaven (though how he obtained the latter is not related). According to the Latin Chronicle of Lamber d'Ardres, Arnoul then proceeded to have built a castle to house these holy relics.

It was of curious design, containing rooms within rooms, winding staircases that lead nowhere, and 'loggias' or cloisters (a feature of Chrétien's Grail castle) and 'an oratory or chapel made like a Solomonic Temple'. (15) According to Lambert it was here that Arnoul laid to rest the objects he had brought with him, and it is interesting to note that these objects coincide precisely with the 'Hallows' of the Grail. The spear had long been identified with that which had pierced the side of Christ, and as such had become one of the features of the Grail temple. Manna, the Holy Food of Heaven, is the substance that the Grail provides, either physically or in spiritual form. The stone from Jerusalem was part of the 'stone which rose and fell' and thus recalled the Grail stone described by Wolfram von Eschenbach. So that we have, assembled in a temple or castle constructed to resemble the Solomonic temple, all the elements of the Grail Hallows originating from the Holy Land.

Nor do the links with Solomon and his Temple to the greater glory of God end here. Two important facts remain to be considered. The first concerns the Ark of the Covenant, which may be seen as the Grail of its age, and concerning which a well-founded tradition of the Ethiopian church maintains that it was removed from Jerusalem before the destruction of the Temple by Menelik, a child of Solomon and Sheba. It is still kept in the cathedral at Aksum in modern day Ethiopia, and has remained a central part of sacred practice within the Ethiopian Church. Known as the Tabot (from the Arabic *tabut 'al'ahdi*, Ark of the Covenant) it is carried in procession at the festival of Epiphany, to the accompaniment of singing, dancing and feasting, which recalls the time when 'David and all the house of Israel brought up the Ark of the Lord with shouting and with the sound of the trumpet. (16) Replicas of the Tabot are kept in every church in Ethiopia, and where these are large enough to possess a Holy of Holies, this representation of the Ark is kept within, as it was of old in the Temple of Solomon at Jerusalem.

Is it possible that we have here one of the contributing factors of the Grail story? It has been pointed out (17) that stories concerning a quest for a sacred object, undertaken by the fatherless son of a queen, may well have reached the West, where they became the basis for another story of a fatherless child (Parzival) who goes upon such a quest. Add to this the nature of the Ark itself, along with the fact that apart from the Kebra Nagast, in which this story is told in full, the only other known source is Arabic, suggests that the semi-mythical Flegitanis, to whom Wolfram attributes the ultimate source of his poem, and who was also of Arabic origin, may have been the disseminator of this narrative. Flegitanis/Wolfram speaks of the Grail as being brought to earth by a troop of angels where 'a Christian progeny bred to a pure life had the duty of keeping it',(18) Similarly, the Kebra Nagast tells how Menelik, the child of Solomon and Sheba, bringing the Ark out of Israel to reside in a specially protected temenos in Ethiopia.

Two further thoughts may be added. We have heard how Lancelot fared when he entered the chapel of the Grail to help the 'man dressed like a priest' who was serving at the Mass. Even though his intention is good, he is not permitted to touch or to look upon the mystery. So, too, in the story of the Ark's journey from Gebaa, described in the Biblical *Book of Kings*, when it had reached the threshing floor of Nachon, the oxen pulling the cart on which the Ark rode, began to kick and struggle and '*tilted the Ark to one side; whereupon Oza put out his hand and caught hold of it. Rash deed of his, that provoked the divine anger; the Lord smote him, and he died there beside the Ark.*'(19)

In a Medieval Grail poem attributed to Robert de Boron, we find the story of Sarracynte, wife of Evelake of Sarras, whose mother had for a time shared the guardianship of the Grail, in the shape of a host, and kept it in a box, which is specifically described as an ark. (20) She at least was allowed to touch it without harm, but such cases are rare in the mythos. Generally the mystery is too great to be looked upon or touched by one who is unprepared. A visit to the Temple of the Grail must come first, and its perils overcome, before the revelation of the mystery can take place.

V

We have already noted that one of the most frequently occurring forms in temple design is that of the circle and the square. These may be seen, in part at least, to reflect a polarisation of the masculine and feminine imagery that lies at the heart of the Grail myths. This mystery is born out by two seemingly unconnected things: a design incorporated into the great cities of Classical Rome, and an adventure of the knight Sir Gawain at the Grail Castle.

The plan upon which all Roman cities were based, like that of Titurel's Grail Temple, was supposed to have been divinely inspired, revealed to Romulus in a dream. It really consists of two separate designs, which together make up the total image of the city. These two designs incorporate the circle and the square; like the four square walls of the Earthly paradise, Rome is built on the principle of the rectangle.

The *urbs quadrata* is divided across and across by the cardo and the *decumanus*. The *cardo* corresponds to the axile tree of the universe, around which the heavens revolve, and is therefore a type of the same artificial, astrologically inspired plan as that of the Takht and the Grail Temple. The decumanus (from *decem*, 'ten') forms the shape of an equal armed cross when it intersects the cardo. Within this complex were situated the temples dedicated to the sky gods, the masculine pantheon inherited from the Greeks; while adjacent to the urbs or living quarters of the city, stood the citadel of the Palatine Hill, a circular form known as the mundus. This was the home of the dark gods of the underworld, and of the older worship of the Earth Mother, the Dark Goddess who held the secrets of birth and death in her hands. In token of this, the centre of the mundus contained a hole which went down into the earth, covered by a stone called the *lapis manalis*, which was only raised three times a year for the entrance and egress of dead souls, following the pattern established by the Greek temples and followed later by the Solomonic builders.

Here the hidden place at the centre is represented by the ancient Mother worship, existing within the place where male deities were honoured. The representation is reflected by the physical organisation of the city in the forms of circle and square.

In another dimension of the Grail Temple, known as the Castle of Wonders, we find another kind of adventure, that of Gawain and the magic chessboard. Gawain, the sun-hero whose strength grows greater towards midday and subsides towards evening, enters the feminine realm of the circular castle, where he finds a square chessboard set out with pieces that move of their own accord at the will of either opponent. Gawain proceeds to play a game against an unseen adversary - and loses. Angrily he tries to throw the board and the pieces out of the window of the castle into the moat, and it is at this moment that a woman rises from the water to prevent him. She is identified by her raiment, which is either red or black, spangled with stars, as an aspect of the Goddess, and after at first rebuking Gawain for his anger and thoughtlessness, she becomes his ally and tutor, reappearing later in a different guise as his guide on the Grail quest.

It does not take much stretching of the imagination to see that here we have a restatement of the masculine and feminine elements associated with the temple. Gawain enters a circular (feminine) temenos and finds within it a square (masculine) chessboard, which is none the less chequered in black and white, a reconciliation of the previously opposing figures. When he tries to dispense with the board, he is prevented from so doing by an agent of the Goddess who, in subsequently helping him, teaches the necessity of establishing a balance between the masculine and feminine sides of his nature.

This imagery is born out by a further story from the Grail mythos, which brings us back to the themes of both the Solomonic temple and the Ark of the Covenant.

In Malory and elsewhere there are numerous references to the Ship of Solomon, the mysterious vessel which carries the Questing knights or even the Grail itself, to and from the everyday world into the timeless, dimensionless place of the sacred. In fact, however, it does more than this, being in some ways not unlike a kind of mystical time machine, programmed to bear the message of the Grail through the ages, from the time of Solomon to the time of Arthur.

It was built, not by Solomon himself, but by his wife, who is called Sybyll in the medieval Golden Legend, and may be identified with Bilquis, the Queen of Sheba. She, according to another Grail tradition, gave a vessel of gold to Solomon as a wedding gift - a cup that later became enshrined in the cathedral of Valencia as a type of the Grail. (21)

According to the story related in the 13th century Queste del Saint Graal, certain objects were placed within the ship, which was then set adrift, unmanned, to sail through time as well as space to the era of the Grail quest. These objects were: Solomon's Crown, the Sword of King David, a great bed supposedly made from the Rood Tree, and three branches from the Edenic Tree of Knowledge, one of red, one of white, and one of green, which were arranged to form a triangle above the bed from which a canopy could be suspended.

We should not be surprised to find images of paradise contained in the Solomonic ship - for the vessel is clearly an image of the Temple, this time afloat on the sea of time, its destination the country of the Grail. But perhaps the most important detail is that it contains wood from the tree that supposedly grew from a branch taken out of Eden by Adam and Eve, and planted in the earth. From this tree, it was widely believed in the Middle Ages, the cross of the crucifixion was constructed, and part of it was used to make the Ark of the Covenant.

The presence of this wood within the floating temple of Solomon's ship makes for some fascinating speculation. The ship, as has been said, was built at the behest of Solomon's wife. It thus becomes doubly an expression of a feminine archetype, often regarded as a vessel, and sometimes shown ichnographically as an actual ship.(22) It becomes an emblematic prototype of all the traditional imagery of the human vessel, the womb of the earth and the womb of woman; Mary as the living Grail who carries the Light of the World within her, and the blood which will at length be spilled into the Cup which will in turn become the Grail. Within this female temple are placed the images of kingship: sword and crown; together with the three branches from the Tree of Knowledge, coloured in red, white and green, the colours of the alchemical process. Read in this way the myth becomes clear: it can be seen as an expression of the masculine contained within the feminine - of the square within the circle, images of the Grail Temple in all its aspects.

During the same account of the Quest, the Grail knights voyage together for a brief time in the mysterious vessel. When the healing of the Wounded King is achieved, the final act of Galahad and his companions is to carry the sacred vessel to Sarras, the Holy City that is itself an image of paradise on earth. They do so in the floating Temple of Solomon, and in token of his Christ-like role Galahad lies down on the great bed that had been made from the wood of the Cross. Symbolically, he is undergoing a species of crucifixion, and in doing so brings about the completion of the Grail work for that age.

After Galahad's death, however, we may believe that the ship returned to these shores, bearing the Grail hither again, to await the coming of the next Quester, and of the time when it would be redeemed again, and help thereby to redeem the time in which this far off event occurred - our own time perhaps.

But the image of the temple as vessel, and of the Grail as a human vessel, brings us to the most fundamental aspect of the Grail Temple - or indeed of the temple everywhere - the Temple in man. This notion has been a common one since earliest times. In the *Chandogya Upanishad* it is held that:

In the centre of the Castle of Brahma, our own body, there
is a small shrine, in the form of a lotus flower, and within

can be found a small space. We should find who dwells
there and want to know him ... for the whole universe is
in him and he dwells within our heart. (23)

Or, as one might say: In the centre of the Castle of the Grail, our own body, there is a shrine, and within it is to be found the Grail of the heart. We should indeed seek to know and understand that inhabitant. It is the fragment of the divine contained within each one of us - like the sparks of unfallen creation that the Gnostics saw entrapped within the flesh of the human envelope. This light shines within each one, and the true quest of the Grail consists in bringing that light to the surface, nourishing and feeding it until its radiance suffuses the world.

'Chaque homme porte a jamais l'age du son temple', 'each man is the same age as his own temple', wrote the traditionalist philosopher Henri Corbin, adding that the completion of the temple on Muntsalvache was a kind of second birth for Titurel who, after this, we next see four hundred years old but perfectly preserved. The Temple of the Grail is really a divine clearing house for the souls of those who go in search of it - a kind of adjunct to paradise, with glass walls that reflect the true nature of the seeker (like the floor of Solomon's Temple) and demand that he recognise himself.

The image of man is the image of the Temple, as writers as disparate as Corbin, Schwaller de Lubicz, Frederic Bligh Bond and Keith Crichlow have all noted. Man must make himself into a temple in order to be inhabited by God. This is the object of all the tests, the Sword Bridge and the turning door, the Perilous Bed and the blinding light of the Grail. The concept begins with the Egypt of the pharaohs, if not earlier, in the caves of mankind's first dwelling; and it continues through Platonic and Neoplatonic schools of thought. To them the temple was microcosmically an expression of the beauty and unity of creation, seen as a sphere. Expressed thus, it was reflected in the soul, and became indeed, 'a bridge for the remembrance or contemplation of the wholeness of creation' (24) words that could be as well applied to the Grail or the divine enclave of which it is a part.

This is the origin of the temple of light (the *haykat al-nur*), the macrocosmic temple which lies at the heart of Islamic mysticism, of which the Sufi mystic Ibn al-Arabi says: '0 ancient temple, there hath risen for you a light that gleams in our hearts,' (25) the commentary to which, states: 'the gnostic's heart, which contains the reality of the truth', is the temple.

Here we are back again in the world of the Solomonic Grail temple, the image of which, transformed and altered, together with that of the Earthly Paradise, were enclosed in the world of the Arthurian Grail mythos. And that world becomes transformed in turn, back into the Edenic world of primal innocence, the original home of the sacred vessel, possession of which 'represents the preservation of the primordial tradition in a particular, spiritual centre'. (26) The centre that is of the heart.

Ibn al-Arabi wrote (27) that the last true man would be born of the line of Seth. Do we not have in this statement a clue to the destiny of the Grail bearer who will come among us at the time of the next 'sacring' of the divine vessel? All the Grail knights were followers of Seth - who was the first to go in quest of it - and their adventures are transparent glyphs of the human endeavour to experience the divine. Most of us, if we found our way into the temple unprepared, would probably suffer the fate of Lancelot. But the Grail Temple exists to show us that the way is worth attempting, that the centre can be reached, if we are only attentive enough to the message it holds for us.

But what happens when we do finally reach the centre? If we look at what we have learned so far about the image of the temple on earth and in the heavens, we may begin to arrive at an answer.

All the temples are incomplete. They can only be made whole by the direct participation of God,

91

who must stretch down to meet and accept the rising prayers of his creation. So with the Grail, it too must be hallowed, made complete, as by the touch that makes blood of wine and flesh from bread. The Grail is made whole only when it is full, and it is not for nothing that the shape most often assumed by it is that of the chalice. If we see this as two triangles, one above the other, meeting at the apex point to form a nexus, we can see that it is an image of this divine meeting of upper and lower, temporal and divine. The same event occurs in the sanctuary of the temple, and is best expressed, as we saw earlier, by the figure of the Vesica Pisces, the two overlapping, interlocked circles which can represent God and mankind, and in the centre of which, outside time or space, the opposites are joined; the male and female, dark and light imagery we have been examining and which are represented, in the Grail story, by the Chessboard Castle.

We can see also that, in the human temple, this is expressed by the need of each individual to reach upwards and to be met halfway. We are all Grails to some degree, lesser or greater; but we are empty vessels until we offer ourselves to be filled by the light.

It is perhaps time that we looked finally at some of the imagery that has built up throughout this study. Indeed, there comes a point at which unsupported words can no longer make sense of the complex of ideas presented. In the simple image with which we began, that of the Vesica Pisces, we have most of the story. The centre of the design with the outer edges of the two circles taken away makes the shape of the Grail. Turned upon its side, it is still the same, except that now it represents the image of the Grail as Temple, the building above, the adytum below, or as they may be seen: the God / Goddess with, between them at the meeting point of time and place, the figure of mankind. And, in the temenos between, the reconciliation of opposites, the perfection of sacred space, sained by the touch of the divine which interpenetrates the temporal at the point of human experience. So that this experience can be shown as an exchange, to which we can contribute equally with God as was suggested earlier, the image of the temple is at once a glyph of creation and of the evolution of the gods.

The images of the ship and the chessboard castle, the urbs quadrata and mundus of the Roman world are also harmonised within this single point of interaction. The object of Gawain's visit to the Castle of the Grail was to be humbled and made to recognise the chequered pattern of all life, which is black and white, male and female in proportion. The importance of the containing vessel cannot be overemphasised. The lower part of the Grail is of this world, penetrating time and space at once, its upper part is already in the paradisal state of beyond time and beyond-space. At the centre is the Temple, the sacred space at the heart of the circle, lies the adytum that stretches below the earth but is open to the sky. Thus the ancient temples were the simplest and most direct means of contact with the divine, as today the most simple and direct method is the building and establishment of an inner temple, a temple of the heart.

Dealing with the response in mankind to the voice of God, the Word, the Gnostic Authoritative Teaching says: 'the senseless man hears the call, but he is ignorant of the place to which he has been called. And he did not ask ... where is the temple into which I should go and worship my hope....'(28). This could hardly be clearer. In the quest of the Grail, the failure to ask an important question is the cause of the failure of many knights who arrive at the castle. It is Lancelot's failure, and it is the failure of all who do not listen to the Voice of the Light.

Qabalistic teaching has it that 'the temple has been destroyed, but not the path of purification, illumination, and union that lay concealed in it'. (29) For when the perfected soul of mankind 'rises like incense from the golden altar of the heart and passes through the most inward curtains of his being to the holy of holies within' (30) then the two cherubim who stand guard over the Ark of the Covenant (of the heart) 'are united in the presence of the One in Whom the soul recognises its eternal life and its own union with Him. Henceforward the soul is called the eternally "living" [*hayah*], the "one and only" [*yehidah*]', (31) the perfect. The Light has come like veritable tongues of fire upon all who reach the centre of the temple and find there the seat of God in the heart of His Creation.

This was the aim of the Grail knights, of the Templiesen of Wolfram von Eschenbach, of the priest-kings who built the Takht-i-Taqdis or the Capitoline temples of Rome. Before them it was the desire of the people who erected their stone circles to echo the dance of the cosmos - waiting that moment when God would reach down and hallow their seeking with a touch. And so we wait now, who are modern Grail questers, for that touch that awakens the light within: as must all who seek to enter the Temple of the Mysteries.

Notes

1 Sir Thomas Malory, Le Morte D'Arthur, Ed. John Matthews (London, Cassell, 2000) Bk 17, ch. 15.

2 Plotinus, Enneads, quoted in K. Crichlow, Soul as Sphere and Androgine, Ipswich, Golgonooza Press, 1980, p. 23.

3 René Guenon, 'The Symbolism of the Graal', in Tomorrow, Winter 1965, vol. 13, no. 2.

4 Crichlow, op. cit., p. 23.

5 Louis Charpentier, The Mysteries of Chartres Cathedral, Research into Lost Knowledge Organization, London, R.I.L.K.O., 1972.

6 This later became confused with an actual site: Montségur, a stronghold of the Cathars in Southern France. From this grew a tradition that they were guardians of the Grail, a supposition that has yet to be firmly proved, though there is some evidence to support it. See John Matthews, The Grail: Quest for Eternal Life, London, Thames & Hudson, 1981.

7 Albrecht von Scharfenburg: Der Jungere Titurel, Augsburg, 1477

8 Green is a colour much associated with the Grail. In some versions the vessel originates as an emerald from the crown of Lucifer, the angel of fight, while in Islamic tradition, the Black Stone of the Ka'aba, recognizably an image of the Grail is carried on a cloth of green achmardi.

9 In particular Lars Ivar Ringbom, Graltemple und Paradies, Stockholm, 1951. For Pope's account, see 'Persia and the Holy Graal', The Literary Review (New Jersey), 1, 1957, pp. 51-71.

10 supra.

11 Exodus 25:22.

12 Zohar: Terumah 159a, quoted by Lee Schayer, 'The Meaning of the Temple', in Sword of Gnosis, New York, Penguin Books, 1974. supra, p. 363.

13 supra,

14 Ibn Khaldun, The Muqaddimah, London, Routledge & Kegan Paul, 1958.

15 see 'The Arthurian Tradition in Lambert D'Ardres', by Urban. T. Holmes in Speculum, XXV, 1965, pp. 100-2.

16 2 Samuel 6:15.

17 Helen Adolf, 'Oriental Sources for Grail Romances', Publications of the Modern Language Association, LXII, 1947, pp. 306-23.

18 Wolfram von Eschenbach, Parzival, trans A. T. Hatto, Harmondsworth, Penguin Books, 1980, p. 232.

19 2 Kings 6; 6-8.

20 Robert de Boron, Joseph D'Arimathea, trans. H. Lovelich, Early English Text Society, London, 1874.

21 Estha Quinn, 'The Quest of Seth, Solomon's Ship and the Grail', Traditio, XXI, 1965, pp. 185-222. I am indebted to this article, which contains a full treatment of the Ship of Solomon.

22 See the picture of the Virgin as Vessel in Matthews The Grail, op. cit., p. 86.

23 The Unpanishads, trans. Juan Mascaro, Harmondsworth, Penguin Books, 1965, 8A.

24 Crichlow, op. cit.

25 Ibn al-Arabi, The Tarjuman AI-Ashwaq, Acra, Theosophical Publishing House, 1978.

26 Guenon, op. cit.

27 Ibn al-Arabi, The Bezels of Wisdom, trans. R. W. J. Austin, London, SPCK, 1980.

28 The Nag Hammadi Library ed. and trans. James M. Robinson, Leiden, E. J. Brill, 1977, p. 282.

29 Quoted by Schayer, op. cit., pp. 364-5.

30 Ibid.

31 Ibid.

Chapter 10:

IN SEARCH OF HIDDEN WONDER

This is, in as much as any such thing is possible, my attempt to describe, very briefly, some of the most important things about the Grail, a subject on which I have written widely and have researched now for nearly thirty years. Despite this, I still feel that what I wrote here in 1994 is as near to the heart of the mystery as I personally can get, and contains some of my favourite quotations. The talk has been reprinted several times in different versions, but this was the first attempt and still in many ways, I think, the clearest.

The Grail is probably the most openly hidden secret in the whole of Western spiritual tradition. Though it has been often sought since the 12th century poet, Chrétien de Troyes, left his poem *The Story of the Grail* unfinished, it consistently resists being codified, identified, or pinned down to a specific space or time. Despite all the millions of words written every year about the Grail, it remains an object of mystery. It is hidden, a secret, as the medieval knight and poet Wolfram von Eschenbach wrote in his telling of the myth, the Grail is:

'The wondrous thing hidden in the flower-garden of the king
where the elect of all nations are called.' (Parzival)

The great mythographer Joseph Campbell has a passage in one of his books, which, though in fact referring to Biblical studies, sums up the attitude of many seekers for the Grail.

"It is" he says "one of the prime mistakes of many interpreters of mythological symbols to read them as references, not to mysteries of the human spirit, but as earthly or unearthly scenes, and to actual or imaginal historical events: the promised land as Canaan, for example: heaven as a quarter of the sky; the Israelites passage of the Red Sea as an event such as a newspaper reporter might have witnessed. Whereas it is one of the glories of the tradition that in its handling of religious themes, it retranslates them from the language of imagined facts into a mythological idiom; so that they may be experienced, not as time- conditioned, but as timeless; telling not of miracles long past, but of miracles potential within ourselves, here, now, and forever. (The Masks of God)

It is for this reason that the Grail is hidden - though the hiding is in plain sight. As Campbell said elsewhere, why should the medieval knights have needed to look for the Grail - which they saw as a chalice - when there was a chalice to be found on every alter in Christendom? In the same way, why do we still seek the Grail when it is in fact everywhere around us - and within us?

The Grail can be many things - it can be almost anything to anyone - or it may be something that has no form, or more than one form - it may not even exist at all in this dimension. The important thing is that it provides an object for personal search, for growth and human development. In fact, it is more often not the object those who seek it are concerned with - but the actions of the Grail - the way it causes changes to happen - in the heart, in the mind, in the soul.

In the traditions relating to Western teachings of alchemy, this is reflected in the mystery surrounding the transformational quality of the Great Work that lies at the centre of the alchemist's striving for earthly perfection. The transmutation of base metal into gold is a metaphor for the transformation of the human spirit - a transformation that takes place within the alembic of the Grail. Those who encounter the mystery are never the same again. They are caught up into an entirely new frame of existence, no longer bounded by time and space, they are transformed by what they encounter.

We are dealing here with high things, with a Mystery that is almost too much for us. But we can learn, and grow, from studying it, by sharing the adventure of the Quest with those far-off people of the Arthurian world - who in truth are not so far off at all. Whatever else it may be the Grail story is first and foremost pure myth. And like all myths it is filled with archetypes.

As we follows the Quest Knights through the forests adventurous of the Arthurian legends we see many turnings which lead to different places in the map of the soul's journey - nearly all of the characters are in some way archetypal - as are their adventures, their sufferings and their realisations. It would be wrong to regard the stories too literally of course - they are not and never were intended as parables - though it must be said, by way of balance, that the medieval writers were far more aware of what they were writing than they are sometimes given credit for. This is why we need to go back to the texts as often as possible - to their infinite variety, complexity and subtlety, where we may find ever-new meanings.

When, a few years ago, I edited a collection of essays by various hands, each of which sought to trace an aspect of the Grail in contemporary terms, I called this collection *At the Table of the Grail* because that is how I see all of those who go on the quest - as sitting down together at a great invisible table to share their realisations. In this book I quoted a passage from the 13th century romance of Perlesvaus, which seems to me to say a great deal about the reasons for the quest, now as much as then.

The scene is set not long after the Arthurian era. The Grail Castle, where so many strange and wondrous things have taken place, is describes as ruinous and empty, a place of ghosts with its once sacred and mysterious nature already beginning to be forgotten. To this place come two young knights in search of adventure, after the manner of the old heroes of the Table Round:

> *They were fair knights indeed, very young and high spirited and they swore they would go, and full of excitement they entered the castle. They stayed there a long while, and when they left they lived as hermits, wearing hairshirts and wandering through the forests, eating only roots; it was a hard life, but it pleased them greatly, and when people asked them why they were living thus, they would only reply: "Go where we went, and you will know why". (Translated by Michael Bryant)*

This is exactly the experience of the many people who have been "going there" ever since, seeking the mysterious object of which they have heard such marvellous report - more often than not failing, but sometimes discovering things about themselves and their own inner state. The Grail itself remains hidden, elusive, yet most have found that its "secret" is indissolubly linked with the idea of service.

And this brings us to the mysterious Grail 'Question', which though it is couched in several forms, is usually made out to be "Whom does the Grail serve?". Everyone who seeks the Grail has to ask

- and answer - this question sooner or later. It may seem an odd thing to ask when you have travelled however many hundreds of miles, undergone countless adventures and trials and arrived at last in the presence of the Wounded King and his entourage of Grail maidens and youths.

The Grail, you may remember, is born through the hall in procession with the spear that drips blood, a large shallow dish, and either a candelabra or a sword. The Wounded King is then fed with a wafer from the chalice. In some versions this is all, in others the entire company is fed with the food they most desire, which can be interpreted as actual or spiritual food. The point being that it is either the Grail King or the Company who are served, in the literal sense, by the Grail. Why then, the question?

In part, of course, it is a ritual question, requiring a ritual response which in turn triggers a sequence of events: the healing of King and Kingdom, the restoration of the Wasteland. In the texts, various answers are given: Whom does the Grail serve? Why, the Grail King, the Company of the Grail, all who seek it. It is this last answer that concerns us most.

The Grail is here shown to be a gateway, a nexus-point between two states of being - those that we may call, for convenience, the human and the divine, the worldly and the otherworldly. All who seek the Grail are in some senses seeking one of these alternative states. We can see this in the very shape most often assumed by the Grail, that of a Chalice. The upper portion is open to receive the down pouring of blessings of the spiritual realm; the lower half, stem and base, form an upward pointing triangle which represents our own aspirations. In the centre the two meet and are fused: the Grail operates its wonderful life giving properties - we are each served in the way that the Fisher King is served.

But this only happens in response to the need and urgency, the drive of the Quester. The answer is simple: the Grail serves us according to the way we serve it. Like the king who serves the land as the land serves him, we stand in similar relation to the Grail. Our service, our love or hope or desire is offered up, accepted and transformed into pure energy. And, if we have behaved in a right manner on our quest, we reap the rewards, the divine sustenance of the Grail. And, if we open this out still further, our service helps transform the land on which we live and walk and have our being. The Grail does not need to be in view - it is present all around us, in every act of service we do, whether it be, symbolically, for the king or the land.

While the king and the land are suffering the Grail cannot pass openly among us. It is as though a gap had opened between two worlds or states of being, leaving us shut out, lost in the twilight looking for the shining power of the Grail... or as some texts suggest, inhabiting a land where there are no chalices, no means of expressing our own love or hope for the world we inhabit.

A passage from a modern Grail story, War in Heaven by Charles Williams, sums it up. In this story, after many adventures, the moment has come when a celebration of the Eucharist is to be made, using the Grail itself as the chalice. Standing before it, one of the modern questers reflects on its long, strange history:

"Neither is this Thou" he breathed; and answered: "Yet this also is Thou." He considered, in this, chalices offered at every alter, and was aware again of a general movement of all things towards a narrow channel. Of all material things still discoverable in the world the Graal had been nearest the Divine and Universal Heart. Sky and sea and land were moving, not towards the vessel but to al it symbolised and had held...and through that gate...all creation moved.

Even here, where the Grail is still an object at the end of the search, it remains what it symbolises that is important, not the Grail itself - "through that gate all creation moved". The object is as mysterious, as 'hidden' as ever.

It seems that what we have to understand from all of this is that the Grail serves us in proportion to our service to the land and to the world about us. It is not some wonderworking artefact but an active principle touched off by the accumulated longing of mankind for what was once ours - for the perfect state of being which can still be ours. It is this that gives the aura of a lost golden age to Arthur's realm and acts.

The Grail is a symbol for now as much as for any time - a contemporary symbol of an utterly current aspiration. The King: call him Arthur or Christ or the World Soul, is wounded by as well as for us. His wounds impinge upon everyone, and when he is healed so shall we all be. It is the same story, an utterly simple one: the Grail serves us: we serve the Grail; it will heal us when we use it to heal the wounds of creation.

And, the wonderful thing is that each one of us is already engaged upon this quest. Each has a chance to redeem the time in which we live, to awaken the Sleeping King, to being the Wasteland back into flower. We are indeed all 'grails' to some degree, and the true object of the Quest lies in making ourselves vessels for the light that will bring about these things.

Only then can we ourselves be healed, the Fisher King within us regain his strength so that the land can flower. When that moment comes there will no longer be any need for a Grail, it will be everywhere about us no longer hidden but openly recognised - its presence felt in every particle of our being. As another contemporary writer, Vera Chapman, writes:

"Like a plant that dies down in winter, and guards its seeds to grow again, so you...must raise the lineage from which all Arthur's true followers are to grow - not by a royal dynasty, but by spreading unknown and unnoticed.... Names and titles will be lost, but the story and the spirit of Arthur [and the Grail] shall not be lost. For Arthur is a spirit and Arthur is the land of Britain. So shall Arthur conquer, not by war, nor by one kingship that soon passes away, but by the carriers of the spirit that does not die. " (The Three Damosels)

We are all carriers of that spirit, and by seeking the inner reality of the Grail behind the symbols and stories; we are taking part in an ongoing work without which all we hold most dear would long ago have perished. And if people look at us askance as we wander through the world with a strange look in our eyes, we have only to give the same answer of those knights who visited the ruined Grail Castle: "Go where we went, and you will know why."

SOURCES:

Bryant, M. (Trans.) The High Book of the Holy Grail (Perlesvaus)
    Rowman & Littlefield, 1978
Campbell, J. The Masks of God (Creative Mythology), Souvenir
Press, 1968.
Chapman, V. The Three Damosels, Methuen, 1978
Chrétien de Troyes, Perceval, or The Story of the Grail, D.S.
Brewer, 1982
Matthews, J. The Grail: Quest for Eternal Life, Thames &
Hudson,1981.
Matthews, J. Ed. At the Table of the Grail, reprinted by Watkins
Books, 2000
Williams, C. War in Heaven, Eerdmans,1988
Wolfram von Eschenbach, Parzival, Penguin, 1980

(1994)

Chapter 11:

GRAIL KINGS AND ANTI KINGS

This was a talk I gave sometime in the 80s in America - I can't remember where now – but in it I set out to say something about the darker side of the Grail quest – a theme seldom touched upon. Though this is perhaps not one of the best pieces of writing I have ever composed I think what it says makes it worth reprinting here.

All things have their opposites, and just as there is a Grail, and Grail Kings, and Grail Knights, so there is a black Grail, anti-Grail kings and evil knights who seek the ruin of the kingdom of the Grail.

These things are seldom spoken of, or written about, in out time, though the medieval writers knew of their importance. But they are a necessary part of the mystery - they provide a balance to pure goodness, just as pure goodness provides a balance to pure evil. At the nexus point, in the heart of the Grail, is a point of harmony, of resolution, of polarity, which is brought about through the interaction of the dark and light forces that surround the Grail.

To avoid this darker side of the Grail stories is to close our eyes to a very real problem. There is a great deal of casual-seeming cruelty in the Quest texts - the casual slaying by Gawain of pagans in a city which had become Christianised is one such example, though it would have seemed perfectly normal and proper to a medieval audience; or the episode where Bors is about to go to the rescue of a woman in distress when he sees his brother, Lionel, tied naked to a horse and beaten with a thorn twig by an evil knight who is carrying him into captivity. Bors has to make a choice between brotherly love and his knightly vows, and being the staunch Quester that he is he opts for the latter. But the woman he rescues is herself a demon in disguise, and although Lancelot rescues his brother, when Bors and Lionel next meet there is such anger on the part of Lionel that they almost kill each other.

This kind of situation is common throughout the Quest, and we are likely to encounter the same kind of thing on our own life journey - not literally the same of course, but no less difficult or painful because of that. What we must never expect is that the Quest will be easy, or that we will become miraculously sorted out people before we begin. Many, if not all the Grail mysteries are about self-discovery, hence the emphasised on questions. The Quest is a journey inward as well as through the lands of the Grail. For this reason it is useful to know about some of the adversaries the Quest knights encountered, so that we can recognise their like if, and when, they crop up.

Two themes that crop up continually in the texts that relate to the Grail are the Wounded King and the Waste Land. These are inextricably linked because the former is generally the cause of the latter. There are several stories that deal with this in detail, but let's look at just two of them for now. In Malory's *Morte D'Arthur* we find the following description of what is known as "The Dolorous Blow". It occurs when a knight named Balin kills an evil lord named Garlon, who attacks unsuspecting travellers whilst hidden by a cloak of invisibility. Balin catches up with Garlon in a castle and slays him. But the consequences are far more catastrophic than he could have supposed. The lord of the Castle, King Pellam, turns out to be the dead knight's brother and at once turns upon Balin:

"Anon all the knights arose from the table for to set on Balin, and King Pellam himself arose up fiercely, and said, 'Knight, hast thou slain my brother? Thou shalt die there-fore or thou depart'. 'Well', said Balin, 'do it yourself'. 'Yes', said King Pellam, 'there shall no man have ado with thee but myself, for the love of my brother.' Then King Pellam caught in his hand a grim weapon and smote eagerly at Balin; but Balin put the sword betwixt his head and the stroke, and therewith his sword burst in sunder. And when Balin was weaponless he ran into a chamber for to seek some weapon, and so from chamber to chamber, and no weapon he could find, and always King Pellam after him. And at the last he entered into a chamber that was marvellously well dight and richly, and a bed arrayed with cloth of gold, the richest that might be thought, and one lying therein, and thereby stood a table of clean gold with four pillars of silver that bare up the table, and upon the table stood a marvellous spear strangely wrought. And when Balin saw that spear, he gat it in his hand and turned him to King Pellam, and smote him passingly sore with that spear, that King Pellam fell down in a swoon, and therewith the castle roof and walls brake and fell to the earth, and Balin fell down so that he might not stir foot or hand. And so the most party of castle was dead, though that dolorous stroke. Right so lay King Pellam and Balin three days. (Book II, Ch xv)

Merlin comes to rescue Balin from the ruins but tells him that the spear he used to strike the blow was that which had been used to pierce the side of Christ and that its inappropriate use has brought a curse upon the lands around the castle.

Before we look at the second example, let's notice two things about this version. Firstly there is the way in which the blow comes to be struck - not just through Balin's impetuous actions, but also ultimately because of Garlon, the Invisible Knight. Secondly that the effect is local rather than general. It is the Fisher King's lands that are laid waste rather than the whole kingdom of Arthurian Britain.

The second text is called *The Elucidation*. It was intended as a kind of prelude and explanation to Chrétien de Troyes *Conte Del Graal* - although in fact it does very little to make things any clearer - not at first sight anyway. The beginning of the story goes like this:

"The kingdom turned to loss, the land was dead and desert in such wise as that it was scarce worth a couple of hazel-nuts. For they lost the voices of the wells and the damsels that were therein. For no less thing was the service they rendered than this, that scarce any wandered by the way, whether it were at eventide or morning, but that as for drink and victual he would go far out of his way to find one of the wells, and then nought could he ask for of fair victual such as pleased him but he should have it all, so long as he had asked in reason. For straightway, forth of the well issued a damsel - none fairer - bearing in her hand a cup of gold... Right fair welcome found he at the well... The damsels with one accord served fair and joyously all wayfarers by the roads that came to the wells for victual. King Amangons, that was evil and craven hearted, was the first to break the custom, for thereafter did many others the same according to the ensample they took of the King whose duty it was to protect the damsels and to maintain and guard them within his peace. One of the damsels did he enforce, and to her sore sorrow did away her maidenhead, and carried off from her the cup of gold that he took along with him, and afterward did make him every day be served thereof. Well deserved he to come to mishap thereby. For thenceforth never did the damsel serve any more nor issue forth of that well for no man that might come thither to ask for victual. And all the other damsels only served in such sort as that none should see them... In such sort was the kingdom laid waste that thenceforth was no tree leafy." (Trans Sebastian Evans)

Here we have a quite different version of the events that caused the Waste Land - the rape of the Maidens of the Wells and the stealing of their Golden Cups - but once again it is the actions of an anti-Grail character, Amangons, that is the direct cause.

Without getting too deeply into semantics, it is possible to show that the names Amangons and Garlon derive from a single etymological source, and that a third name, Klingsor, applied to the black magician in Wolfram von Eschenbach's Parzival, also derives from this same source. This suggests a kind of composite portrait of an Anti-Grail King, a dark aspect of the actual guardian. In the case of Garlon, he is actually described as Pelles' brother, and there is a suggestion that the same relationship once existed between Klingsor and Amfortas, the Grail King in Parzival. Amangons, though not related to Arthur by blood, functions as a kind of opposing force before the coming of Mordred later in the stories.

Each of these characters is then, in some sense responsible for the advent of the Waste Land, which, from a purely localised event, becomes more widespread and generally felt in the later Arthurian texts. So that by the time we get to the 13th century story of Perlesvaus, or The High History of the Holy Grail the failure at the heart of the Arthurian kingdom, which is illustrated by the Waste Land, has become more directly linked with the actions of Arthur himself, whose failure to take the initiative in the Quest - leaving it to his knights instead - is to be seen as a failure of will and the empowerment of his sovereignty.

In this sense the Waste Land has become indicative of a more general malaise - the heart of the Kingdom, its King, is ailing, and until both are healed, by the finding of the Grail, the sickness will not be cured.

In the same way, we have to cure our own inner ailments; our divided selves must be reunited just as, to speak for a moment in Gnostic terms, the innate goodness of the human soul desires to be reunited with its higher self - God. Not for nothing is Perceval referred to as "the Good Knight"- like the Gnostically inspired Cathars who called themselves parfaits, good men, and who carried their part of the Grail mystery into the heart of Medieval Europe, he is a distillation of the human condition. His tests and trials, his agonies, are ours, to a greater or lesser degree according to the depths of our involvement in the Quest.

Above all else the Grail Knights strive to reconcile the opposing forces that surround the object of their search. The Grail is a symbol of unity and reconciliation, and as such it requires that we lay to rest the ghosts of our own inner malaise. As one writer puts it:

"Imagine yourselves always in your spirit, as pure, deep, luminous vessels, open to the cosmos, standing on the earth but firmly closed against the outer world. The cosmic and divine streams flow into your cups and make the divine spark within them luminous and glowing. This luminosity then penetrates outside and streams as blessings upon all life. It is a wonderful ceaseless giving and taking, an eternal circulation which must never be disturbed by your own damaging thoughts, because only if your heart is pure all this can take place for the blessing of all life."
(Quoted by Anna Morduch: The Sovereign Adventure.)

If the Waste Land is to be healed and the Courts of Joy, which are its opposite and cure, are to be built we must each find a way to heal the wounds we ourselves bear. As the same writer just quoted puts it:

"Your thoughts and feelings, whether good or bad, the earth on which you live absorbs and digests. You provide her nourishment - if you love the earth and think kindly and divinely the earth is health and radiates. If you do not love her, and have dark and destructive thoughts, she becomes sick and dark, and one day her wounds break open." (ibid.)

Thus is the Wasteland caused by our neglect and our "dark and destructive thoughts", which are externalised in the form of characters like Amangons, Garlon and Klingsor. I have said that just as there was a Grail so there is a black Grail, and I had better qualify that. The Grail is the Grail is the Grail and can be nothing else but that - but there are always those who would misuse its power, which is neutral rather like the power of the neutral angels who, according to Wolfram von Eschenbach, first brought the Grail, described in *Parzival* as a jewel from the crown of Lucifer, to earth. And here again we see the paradox: the Angel of Light falls, is renamed Satan, the Devil; yet from his crown comes a fragment of the original, pure light he had once omitted. The Grail is as much within the keeping of the anti-kings as it is in that of the Grail-Family - Joseph of Arimathea and his kin. It is in our care also, and we must learn to use its power wisely.

All of which is just another way of saying what I'm sure most of you know already, that the Quest is unlikely to be easy and demands a level of service that is of the highest kind. But, once that initial commitment is made, once the first steps - however halting - are taken on the road through "the Grailless Lands", then already the rewards are prepared. It is up to us, finally, whether we overcome the negative aspects of the Quest within ourselves, the anti-Grail kings and their servants, and have in the end the satisfaction of seeing the duel aspects of the search united in one - the ultimate mystery of the Grail!

Chapter 12:

THE NINTH CENTURY AND THE HOLY GRAIL

The following introduction was written for the first English edition of a book that still deserves to be better known. The Ninth Century: World History in the Light of the Holy Grail (London, Temple Lodge Publishing, 1991) is the work of a great German scholar and anthropologist whose work laid down a strata of knowledge which later influenced the authors of The Holy Blood and the Holy Grail (1981) and more recently Dan Brown in his book The Da Vinci Code (2002). Yet, despite its depths and wisdom Walter Stein's work remains largely unknown outside Anthropological circles. It deserves to be better known and I hope that those who read this may be encouraged to seek it out for themselves.

The book that you hold in your hands has taken sixty years to reach print in English (although it was translated in the 1950s it remained in typescript in the Rudolf Steiner Library in London). Previously it has been known only through the writings of the late Trevor Ravenscroft, who met the author in 1945 and subsequently wrote about his work in two books, 'The Spear of Destiny' (Spearman, 1972) and 'The Cup of Destiny' (Rider, 1981). Both these books failed to give an accurate account of Walter Stein's work, and indeed misquoted it in several places. The theory of the Carolingian and Merovingian parallels with the Grail material, first advanced here by Stein, has been substantially extended in recent times by Richard Leigh, Michael Baigent and Henry Lincoln, in their best-selling book *The Holy Blood and the Holy Grail* (Cape, 1981) Yet though these theories have become increasingly well known, the present book and its author have remained in shadow, though there can be little doubt that *The Ninth Century: World History in the Light of the Holy Grail* constitutes one of the most valuable and original works on the Grail yet to appear in any language.

Walter Johannes Stein was born in Vienna on 6th February 1891. (1) He was educated at Schottengymnasium; a school run by Benedictine monks and at Vienna University, where he studied Mathematics, Physics, and the History of Philosophy and Psychology. He seemed set upon a career as a philosopher or a scientist; until one day he picked up a volume by Rudolf Steiner, the founder of Anthroposophy. It was *Occult Science: An Outline* (1909) and it changed Walter Stein's life forever.

For the next two months he read everything he could by Steiner - a not inconsiderable feat considering the latter's huge output. Then on the 19th January 1913, Stein attended a lecture in Vienna on "The Supersensible Worlds and the Nature of the Human Soul". During question time afterwards, his every thought seemed to be picked up and answered by Steiner, to whom he afterwards spoke, asking to become his pupil. Steiner told him to read Berkley and Locke and to write a thesis avoiding the mutually opposing directions of either. From this moment Walter Stein was Rudolf Steiner's pupil, and continued to support the work of Anthroposophy until his death.

The 1914-18 war followed, in which Stein served in an artillery unit. Under heavy bombardment, anticipating death at any moment he seemed to see Steiner, assuring him that his time had not yet come. He survived, completing his thesis in 1917 and receiving a doctorate from Vienna University.

After the war he joined the first Waldorf School, founded on Anthroposophical principles. Though his knowledge lay in the field of the sciences he was given responsibility for history and literature. Somehow Steiner had recognised that his pupil's real strength lay in this area, and he was to be proved correct when in 1928 Stein finally published the earliest version of his book on the Grail in 9th century history.

In 1924 Stein had the first of a series of profound religious visions, culminating in a recognition of his own past lives. Looking backwards at these lead him into the period of the 9th century and he began his long study of the period and its links with the mystical subject of the Grail.

Rudolf Steiner died in 1925, leaving others to continue his work. Walter Stein began lecturing to the Anthroposophical Summer School, delivering as many as 300 lectures a year. He became increasingly absorbed in matters of world economy. In 1924 he came to the attention of Daniel Nicol Dunlop, who was organising a "World Power Conference". Dunlop invited Stein to assist him in the work of preparing and publishing the conclusions of the conference, and having agreed to take up the post, Stein moved to England in 1933, where he was to remain almost permanently until his death in 1957.

It is clear that Stein saw the problems of economics as a type of Grail Question. Traditionally, that question is: Whom does the Grail serve? The answer, however phrased, is generally given as: Those who serve the Grail. To Stein the whole earth was a Grail and its resources were there for those who served it by their proper division throughout the world. Any possibility of such an event was crushed forever by the advent of the 2nd World War.

Stein's part in the great conflagration of 1939-45 has been much written about and considerably dramatised. It has been claimed that he met Adolf Hitler, in dramatic circumstances, in 1902. (2) Stein himself declared that he had first heard Hitler's distinctive voice at a meeting he attended in Berlin in 1932. There is no evidence at all that he ever spoke personally to the future *Furher*.

It has also been said that he was invited to England to advise Winston Churchill in the question of Hitler's occult practices. This is only partially true. We have seen that Stein actually came to Britain at the invitation of Daniel Dunlop. The truth of the matter seems to be that he was consulted as someone knowledgeable about the particular aspects of esotericism then rife within the Nazi party, particularly in the figures of Hitler himself (whom some have identified as a type of Klingsor) and Heinrich Himmler, the head of the SS. The latter was definitely interested in the Grail, sending a team under the command of the historian Otto Rahn to the ancient Cathar citadel at Montségur, where it was believed the actual vessel was hidden.

Stein's approach to the Grail was wholly different. For him it was not any physical vessel that made the subject unique, but the deeply spiritual reality that transcended all such objects. His book, the book you are about to read, took the form of a commentary on what many believe to be the most important of all the many versions of the Grail story - the *Parsifal* of Wolfram von Eschenbach, written sometime about 1220. (3) Within this work Stein found close correlatives to actual historic personages from the 9th century, and in particular from the Carolingian and Merovingian dynasties.

We are more used to hearing of the Grail as part of the traditions surrounding King Arthur. Stein saw in the deeds and accomplishments of Charlemagne a re-occurrence of the patterns found within the Arthurian myths, and was able to identify many of the characters in Wolfram's poem with figures from the Carolingian court. He read, in the account of the 12th century *Livre du St Graal* of the hermit who received the story of the vessel in AD 750; and in the account of the Holy Blood of Reichenau, learned how certain sacred relics, including an onyx cup containing the blood of Christ, were brought to the monastery of that name by its Abbot, Waldo. Delving deeper, he found Wolfram's description of the book from which he had taken his source for Parsifal, written by one Kyot of Provence from the teachings of the oriental Flegitanis, who wrote of the mysteries of the starry Grail. From these he began to perceive a new synthesis of material, drawn from Persian, Manichean, and other esoteric sources, which permeated the entire matter of the Grail. (4)

But Stein was not concerned only with sources. He states quite clearly the reasons for writing his book:

"The preoccupation of the Grail-Saga with the problems of Kyot, who interprets the starry-script and the signs of the times -now however for the nations - is literally a burning, present- day problem, What the present can gain by a spiritual interpretation of history, this is what we wish to show: for no other reason would we engage in research into the history of the Grail."

For Stein the starry book of Kyot-Flegitanis was a book of bloodlines, of a lineage descending from the ultimate foundation of creation - in fact, the Family of the Grail. Wolfram wrote of this at length, and of the way in which it was set in motion:

"Thus the Grail Its Maidens giveth,
in the day, and the sight of man,
But it sendeth its knights in the silence,
and their children It claims again,
To the host of the Grail are they counted,
Grail servants they all shall be."

Thus, whether hidden or revealed, the Family of the Grail enters the world and does the work of the vessel therein. This lineage has continued to percolate through history to the present time. Now it is made up of all the men and women who daily set out on their own search for the Grail, who have no need to explain themselves beyond the words of two medieval knights who visited the ruined castle of the Grail and when they returned, changed, could only say: "Go Where we went, and you will know why." (5)

Walter Stein had certainly journeyed to that castle many times, and always he returned with fresh insights and revelations into the great mystery. His book is not always easy reading - he makes demands upon his readership which 20th century education seldom meets - but the rewards for persevering are great; a fresh understanding of the relevance of the Grail to our own time, a teaching of the ways in which we may begin to heal the Wasteland of modern life. As Stein himself puts it:

"The Grail race has the mission of expanding to cosmopolitan proportions all that belongs to the narrow group, of enlarging separate interests to world interest. In our times this mission lies no longer within family group. How the present day faces this impulse will only become clear as through our consideration of the ensuing centuries, we step by step draw nearer to the problem."

Notes

1. I am indebted to Charles Lawrie and Bernard Nesfield-Cookson for all biographical information on Stein. See also my book: Household of the Grail (Aquarian Press, 1990), which contains a chapter about Stein: "Dr. Stone: Walter Stein & the Grail" by Charles Lawrie.

2: Ravenscroft, T The Spear of Destiny, Neville Spearman, 1972

3: A recent translation is by A.T. Hatto. Penguin Books, 1980

4: see my Elements of the Grail Tradition Element Books, 1990

5: cf. Perlesvaus Translated as The High Book of the Holy Grail by N. Bryant D.S. Brewer, 1978

Chapter 13:

THE MAGICAL CITY OF KITESCH

I first became aware of the book called Kitesch: the Russian Grail Legends by Munin Nederlander in 1988, when my friend Dolores Ashcroft Nowicki drew my attention to a large volume she had acquired while teaching in Holland. Knowing of my interest in the Grail and in Russian legends, she showed me the book, and together we decided to recommend its translation and publication in English by Aquarian Press. Happily, this was achieved and the book came out in 1990. I was asked to write a foreword to the volume and this is reprinted below. I still hope to find a publisher willing to publish a book further studying these fascinating parallels.

This book tells a strange and fascinating story, drawing some exciting parallels between the Russian legends of Prince Vladimir of Kiev and his Knights of the Golden Table and those of Arthur and the Round Table of Camelot. Although there are almost as many differences as there are similarities between the two cultures, the overlap between the two mythic cycles - between Camelot and Kiev - are indeed remarkable, and open up possibilities for deeper exploration still, which I myself hope to achieve during the next few years.

Of the great and mysterious city of Kitesch itself, little is known. It was supposedly founded in 1168 by Georgi (Juri) Vselodovich, a distant cousin of the same Vladimir around whom the cycle of tales referred to above first constellated in the Middle Ages. At some point, however, it vanished, rather like Arthur himself, and from that moment it became a place of legend, a withdrawn paradise to which only the elect could find their way.

This too is reminiscent of the Arthurian tales, in which the Knights of the Round Table go in search of the Grail, the final resting place of which is the holy city of Sarras, far to the East. In these Western-European Grail legends the Quest-Knights ride out in search of what they perceive as an object, which can heal the earth. In those of Eastern Europe the Grail is manifest as the earth itself, and the heroes of the Golden Table of King Vladimir experience its mystery in a symbolic relationship with their native earth through the presence of the invisible city of Kitesch. (This supplies the missing element of an actual Grail Quest in the Russian legends)

Munin Nederlander suggests that in a future time, mirrored by the past, all people will be able to enter the spiritual City irrespective of their nature. This belief lies at the centre of his book, which sets out to prove that the ancient mysteries of "Mother Russia", as embodied in the person of Vladimir and his Botaryi (Knights), reflects a future arc of history in which these symbolic stories will be re-enacted, but in a spiritual dimension.

This is all in keeping with Anthroposophical teaching, and "Munin Nederlander" (the name can be interpreted as meaning "Memory of the Underlands") is first and foremost a student of Rudolf

Steiner's intricate and fascinating vision. The book is written in a curious mixture of naivety and sophistication that characterises much Anthroposophical writing. The almost transparent mysticism is balanced by the precise and detailed commentary. The two interact to form a unity of surprising strength, and though the book is at times difficult to follow in terms of detail, it is very well worth the occasional effort for the gems of wisdom and insight this produces.

One of the most important aspects of the book are the translations (many for the first time in English) of the great cycles of heroic songs known as *Byliny*. These contain a fascinating account of a past heroic age, very little removed from that of the ancient west. Many parallels are evident, even at a superficial reading, and some are traced in the present book in extraordinary detail.

At a time when the Eastern and Western halves of the European continent are speaking to each other for the first time in many generations, this is indeed a timely and important book. It shows some of the ways this dialogue can be opened up to create a new spiritual unity between the USSR and the rest of the world. It is my personal hope that this is allowed to develop unchecked, and that further and deeper explorations of Slavic and Russian myth and spirituality are permitted to continue. The outcome can only be of the greatest value to both East and West.

(1990)

Chapter 14:

ARTHUR MACHEN
AND THE SECRET SCHOOL OF THE GRAIL

This was a talk given for the Arthur Machen Society in Wales around 1997. Machen has been a long time passion of mine and I wish more people knew about him. His writing has a particular quality, mixing the mystical and the adventurous in a bled that is unique to him. Many of his books are out of print, but you can still find them if you look around. Look out for his Horror stories – classics of the M.R. James school – and any of his magical writing about the Grail.

I seem to have been aware of Arthur Machen's work most of my life without ever having read very much of it. In fact, it is only recently that I have begun to read him in a more concerted way, and what I have found both excited and moved me. Through the courtesy of the Arthur Machen Society I was recently able to read, at long last, *The Secret Glory*, which had eluded me for nearly twenty years but about which I felt I already knew a good deal. Nor was I disappointed. It is in many ways a remarkable book, and it contains a number of fascinating references to the Grail - which, since that is my own personal way into Machen country, makes it a very good starting point for me here.

The longest and most interesting reference is in Chapter 2 of *The Secret Glory*, and I'd like to quote from it here. The young Ambrose Meyrick has gone with his father to visit old farmer Cradock, and on request an ancient aumbry is opened and an ancient cup taken out of it. The two men and the boy adore it or perhaps what it stands for:

"They knelt down, Cradock in the midst, before the cup, and Ambrose and his father on either hand. The holy vessel gleamed before the boy's yes, and he saw clearly its wonder and its beauty. All its surface was a marvel of the most delicate intertwining lines in gold and silver, in copper and in bronze, in all manner of metals and alloys; and these interlacing patterns in their brightness, in the strangeness of their imagery and ornament, seemed to enthral the eyes and capture them, as it were, in a maze of enchantment; and not only the eyes; for the very spirit was rapt and garnered into that far bright world whence the holy magic of the cup proceeded. Among the precious stones which were set into the wonder was a great crystal, shining with the pure light of the moon; about the rim of it there was the appearance of faint and feathery clouds, but in the centre it was a white splendour; and as Ambrose gazed he thought that from the heart of this jewel there streamed continually a shower of glittering stars, dazzling his eyes with their incessant motion and brightness. His body thrilled with a sudden in-effable rapture, his breath came and went in quick pantings; bliss possessed him utterly as the three crowned forms passed in their golden order. Then the interwoven sorcery of the vessel became a ringing wood of golden, and bronze, and silver trees; from every side resounded the clear summons of the holy bells and the exultant song of the faery birds; he no longer heard the low-chanting voices of Cradock and his father as they replied to one another in the forms of some

antique liturgy…" (The Secret Glory. New York, Alfred A Knopf, 1922)

This represents Machen's mature vision of the Grail. He had been fascinated by it as early as 1906, when he already saw it as representing a mystery that was at once hidden and open to all. In a letter to Sir Paul England of Feb 12,1906 he says:

"I have been amusing myself lately by going to the British Museum where I make researches into the origin of the Holy Grail Legend to gratify a curiosity excited by [A.E.] Waite's ingenious, but (I think) mistaken theory on the subject. He is inclined to believe the Legend the cryptic manifesto of the 'Interior Church'; he would love to connect it with Cabalism, the Templars, the Albigenses ... I am always telling him that nothing good ever comes out of heresy, but he won't believe me." (Selected Letters. Ed. Roger Dobson, Godfrey Brangham and R.A. Gilbert London, the Aquarian Press, 1988)

This was true. Machen wrote often and at length to his old friend A.E.Waite on the subject of the Grail, always trying to pull the latter away from the idea of the "Secret School" of Grail mysteries, which Machen saw as representing something else. In 1930 we see him maintaining:

"I have no belief in 'heretical sects' as a source of any Grail doctrine. Whatever the Grail may be, it is written in exaltation of the Sacrament at the Altar; and whatever heretical sect you choose, you will find, I believe, that its doctrine of the Sacrament is null, dull, and Protestant." (ibid)

I'm not sure how far I would go along with this. For me the Grail represents an idea that has been transmitted by various means from very early times to very recent times. The various methods by which it has made the transmission may well include such avenues as Templars, Albigensians, Bogomils, and many others - though this does still not, I believe, constitute a 'Secret School', heretical or not.

But Machen was seeking something deeper, more subtle and profound than this. Something Celtic indeed, and something which was an "open secret". In 1924 he wrote to Colin Summerfield of a miraculous book that tradition says belonged to St Columba. He notes particularly that the book was not meant to be opened, and goes on:

"This was important to me as illustrating one of the distinctions between the Roman and the Celtic Churches: the Romans exhibit their relics as much as possible to excite the devotion of the faithful: the Celts kept their relics in secrecy; it was dangerous for the unqualified to look upon them. You see how this bears on the Grail Legend; how it is one of the many small points which tend to establish the general, conclusion: the legend of the Grail is, in one of its aspects, the Legend of the Celtic Church." (ibid)

To Machen, the Grail mystery referred simply and directly to the destruction and loss of the old Celtic Church, which he saw as originating, with distinct differences to the Roman establishment, in the 5th century, and surviving as late as the 8th. After this, its systematic destruction by the now 'established' Church of Rome, brought such a sense of loss to the Celtic peoples that it gave rise to stories of forgotten relics, hidden in the hills of Wales, and of older doctrines, still continuing in shadowy form, among the valleys and groves of Machen's own mystic landscape.

Machen was able to see very clearly the vision he sought. In a brief sketch published in *Notes & Queries*, 1926, he returned to the theme in "The Mass of the Sangraal". The setting is the little - Methodist?

- Church of Llantrisant. Strange, unaccountable events have taken place, and wonders have been seen:

"There were a few who saw three come out of the door of the sanctuary, and stand for a moment on the pace before the door. These three were in dyed vesture, red as blood. One stood before two, looking to the west, and he rang the bell. And they say that all the birds of the wood, and all the waters of the sea, and all the leaves of the trees, and all the winds of the high rocks uttered their voices with the ringing of the bell. And the second and the third; they turned their faces one to another. The second held up the lost altar that they once called Sapphirus, which was like the changing of the sea and of the sky, and like the immixture of gold and silver. And the third heaved up high over the altar a cup that was red with burning and the blood of the offering."

Echoes of Sir Thomas Malory's *Morte D'Arthur*, and of the great Anglo-Norman Arthurian romances of the 12th to 15th centuries can be heard here. And of something older as well: an ancient Celtic primacy that gave rise to the legends, as we know them. It is these that intimately represent Machen's 'Secret School' - a far cry from Waite's elaborate and ingenious speculations in his book *The Hidden Church of the Holy Grail* (1909). For Machen it is no school at all, but a *"Secret Glory which is hidden from the Holy Angels"*, and which is certainly a description of the experience of the Grail and seems to be one held in common to mystics throughout time. It is an opening up to the true mystery at the heart of creation, a mystery which is present at all times and in all places openly - but which remains unseen and unrecognised by most people - partly because it is the most simple, beautiful, and innocent thing - and because there are no words to describe it. It may be no more than a feeling ... and yet how profound is a feeling ... can we truly describe any such thing? Most cannot. Those who do so are mystics, able to gather the bright and hidden mystery into net of words and relay their feelings of it to us. Machen tried to do so and, I believe, to some extent succeeded. Indeed, in the unpublished concluding chapters of *The Secret Glory*, there are passages that carry this thought to a triumphal conclusion, indicating that Ambrose Meyrick indeed found a way to the Glory even before his eventual "Red Martyrdom".

One may see it too in the words Machen wrote in *The Glorious Mystery* in 1924. There, he tells us what the Grail hero will find at the end of his quest:

"His are the delights which are almost unendurable, the wonders that are almost incredible - that are, indeed, quite incredible to the world; his the eternal joys that that the deadly flesh cannot comprehend; his the secret that renews the earth, restoring Paradise, rolling the heavy stone of the material universe from the grave whence he arises."

This, it seems to me, is as near as one can get to a mystical understanding of the Grail. It is also many other things to many other people; to Arthur Machen it was a wondrous object that transformed everything with which it came in touch.

(1997)

Section Three:

Celtic Mysteries

Chapter 14:

AUGURIES, DREAMS AND INCUBATORY SLEEP
AMONG THE CELTS OF BRITAIN & IRELAND

This essay was written for inclusion in another collection of papers from the Merlin Conferences, edited by R.J.Stewart: The Fourth Book of Merlin (Element Books, 1990), and I am still quite proud of it. It was an expansion of idea expressed in my book Taliesin: The Last Celtic Shaman (Inner Traditions, 20000) and presented materials which suggested that the Celts practiced incubatory sleep – or as we would think of it now - Dream Therapy. I feel there is still a great deal to be done with this method and hope to do more workshops on this one day.

"When the body is awake the soul is its
servant, and is never her own mistress...
But when the body is at rest, the soul,
being set in motion and awake...has
cognisance of all things - sees what is
visible, hears what is audible, walks,
touches feels pain, ponders."
Hippocrates: Dreams

Auguries

The search for omens and their meaningful interpretation is one that has long been recognised as a major concern of human beings. Ellen Ettlinger, in an article on the subject of "Omens and Celtic Warfare", sums this up precisely:

"The life of primitive man depended upon his unceasingly vigilant attitude towards the phenomena of nature. Among these were uncanny incidents, strange coincidences or vivid dream- impressions that took hold of his imagination. By pure intuition and without any analogy man interpreted a stirring natural happening as a warning of trouble ahead. Similar or recurrent experiences caused the attribution of...foreboding to a particular event. The newly won knowledge was passed on to the medicine man that handed the facts and the meaning of the "omen" down to his successor. As time went on the functions of the medicine-man gradually separated more and more from each other and developed along their own lines. Magicians, diviners, leeches, judges, and poets emerged and were initiated into the omen-language in order to satisfy the requirements of their respective activities." (1)

The first principle which of which we become aware when the subject of precognition among the

Celts is studied is the importance of dreams in which the subjects learn something of considerable import to their circumstances. A typical example of this is to be found in the Irish text of the First Battle of Moytura in which the arrival of the Tuatha de Danaan is perceived by King Eochaid in the following manner:

"I saw a great flock of black birds", said the king, "coming from the depths of Ocean. They settled over all of us, and fought with the people of Ireland. They brought confusion on us, and destroyed us." [And he said to his Druid, Cesard]: "Employ your skill and knowledge, and tell us the meaning of the vision". Cesard did so, and by means of ritual and the use of his science the meaning of the king's vision was revealed to him; and he said: "I have tidings for you: warriors are coming across the sea, a thousand heroes covering the ocean; speckled ships will press in upon us; all kinds of death they announce, a people skilled in every art, a magic spell; an evil spirit will come upon you, signs to lead you astray....they will be victorious in every stress." (2)

Two factors become immediately apparent from this: 1) that the king recognises his dream as important, implying that precognitive dreaming was a normal matter, and 2) that he required an interpreter for the meaning of the dream - in this case, the druid Cesard. A third factor, that the symbolism of the dream involved creatures (specifically birds), and water (the sea), will be seen to possess an importance of their own.

Prognostication from the actions of animals or birds is well attested in Celtic literature, and was a part of the substantial shamanic tradition once prevalent in Britain and Ireland (3). Two treatises preserved in a Middle Irish MS in the Library of Trinity College Dublin (codex H.3.17), refer specifically to the interpretation of the flight patterns and songs of the Raven and the Wren - birds long recognised as sacred in Celtic myth. Of the Raven, it is said that if it calls

"...from above an enclosed bed in the midst of the house, it is a distinguished grey-haired guest or clerics that are coming to see thee, but there is a difference between them: if it be a lay cleric (?) the raven says bacach; if it be a man in orders it calls gradh gradh, and twice in the day it calls. If it be warrior guests or satirists that are coming it is gracc gracc it calls, or grob grob, and it calls in the quarter behind thee, and it is thence that the guests are coming. If it calls gracc gracc the warriors are oppressed to whom it calls." (4)

Of the Wren we are told:

"If it be between thee and the sun, it is the slaying of a man that is dear to thee...If it be at thy left ear, union with a young man from afar, or sleeping with a young woman. If it call from behind thee, importuning of they wife by another man in despite of thee. If it be on the ground behind thee, thy wife will be taken from thee by force. If the wren call from the east, poets are coming towards thee, or tidings from them." (ibid)

The observations here are of a very general kind and are perhaps not to be taken too literally; however, they do indicate the divinatory importance of birds and suggest that at one time the practice was both more sophisticated and more precise.

Aside from this there were a number of specific kinds of omen that occurred frequently, notably before a battle: weapons that shrieked or cried aloud, the appearance of the Washer-at- the-Ford (see below), or the behaviour of animals - notably horses or dogs. Among the death omens that surrounded he last days of the great Irish hero Cuchulainn, is that in which he is offered a vat from which to drink before departing for battle. Hitherto this had always been a sign of certain victory for him, but on this occasion he finds the vat filled with blood.

Dreams

By far the most significant documentation of augury concerns precognitive dreams, not only of the kind discussed above, which are primarily spontaneous, but also self-induced visions, which may be brought on in a number of ways, including the position of the sleeper, bodily contact with other men or women, and with the skin of an animal on which the sleeper lay to have his or her dream. (5)

Several texts mention the positioning of the sleeper between two pillar-stones, as in the case of the Irish hero Cuchulainn, who could not sleep inside a house until a special bed was built for him at the behest of the king. First two tall stones were erected, then the bed was placed between them. Cuchulainn is then able to sleep - though when he hears "the groans of the Ulstermen", his comrades, in a battle, he stretches forth and breaks both the stones. Another text mentions Condla Coel Corrbacc resting on an island "leaning his head against a pillar- stone in the western part of the island and the feet against a pillar-stone in its eastern part" (6).

Neither character is described as having any vision or dream in this instance, but it seems likely that the depiction of this unusual method of sleeping with its orientation east/west, once held a greater significance as the position assumed by the seeker after dreams of predictive visions. Elsewhere we read that when the druids wished to make an important prognostication, and having tried all other methods available to them, made "round hurdles of rowan, and spread over them the hides of sacrificed bulls with the fleshly side uppermost..." (7) Whence it was said, remarks the historian Keating, that "anyone who had done his utmost to obtain information...that he had gone onto his hurdles of knowledge" (8)

The importance of sleeping on the skin of a particular beast is well attested throughout Celtic literature. The best-known example is in the story of 'The Dream of Rhonabwy' from the *Mabinogion*, in which the hero is in pursuit of an actual historical figure, known to have lived in the Middle Ages in Wales. Seeking shelter one night in the dank and evil smelling hut belonging to a hag, Rhonabwy sleeps on a yellow bull's hide and dreams a long and astonishingly complex dream of the hero Arthur and his men, who are all depicted as larger than life and much saddened by the fact that Wales has come to be occupied by such little men! (9)

Apart from the obvious shamanic nature of this idea, it is clearly a reminder of the *tarbh feis*, or "Bull-Sleep", practised by the Irish druids. In this, after having sacrificed a (usually white) bull and made a broth from its flesh, the druid wrapped himself in the freshly flayed skin and slept a profound sleep, in which he would dream the answer to a great question - usually the secession of a king or something of equal importance.

The eating of the sacrificed creature's flesh suggests a further connection with methods of prognostication described in Cormac's Glossary (10) a medieval compilation of lore that discusses such methods at length. Among the techniques mentioned is *Imbass Forosnai*, generally translated as "Knowledge that Enlightens". This was achieved by the subject chewing "a piece of (the) flesh of a red pig, or of a dog or cat", after which he "pronounces incantations on his two palms, and he lays his two palms on his two cheeks and (in this manner) falls asleep..." (ibid)

I have discussed the manner in which this relates to world- wide shamanic practice elsewhere

116

(11); but it is worth noticing that among the Okinawa, as among the Esquimaux, the Wintu and Shasta tribes of North America, and the African Zulus, shamans frequently receive their "call" in the form of dream or vision, and that often animals or bird are involved as in the examples of raven and wren lore quoted above. (12)

The practice of sleeping on a hide was attested as late as the 18th century, by Martin. Martin, in his Description of the Western Isles of Scotland of 1795, where he describes the rite known as *Taghairm* as follows:

> "*A party of men, who first retired to solitary places, remote from any house...singled out one of their number, and wrapp'd him in a big cow's hide, which they folded about him, his whole body was covered with it except his head, and so left in this posture all night until ...[he gave] the proper answer to the question in hand...*" (13)

This wrapping of the dreamer in a hide recalls the descriptions of patients at the Asklepion, who were wrapped in tight bandages, from which they were symbolically cut free after their incubatory period as a sign of their healed state. The objectives here are different, but the method of obtaining the vision once again curiously similar. We do not know whether this was practised as a mimesis of the swaddling clothes of small children, whose fontenelles would still be open to allow the ingress of spirits and visions, but this is a factor to be considered.

Finally, we must mention the idea of physical contact as a further means of enhancing the visionary state. We make not know if the priests of the Asklepion were present or watched over the patient during their incubatory sleep; it would seem, on the hole, unlikely. However, in most of the accounts from Celtic literature, the sleeper is described as being watched over by his friends, or by the druids who initiated his state of being. In some cases they are described as chanting "a spell of truth" over the sleeper (14), in others as being near at hand and shaking him awake after his period in a darkened room. Often there are four guardians mentioned, as in the description of the Bull-Feast mentioned above. Elsewhere, in the text known as *The Voyage of Bran* (15), one of the characters is described as ascending every day to the top of the royal rath with his three chief druids in order "to view all four points of the heavens that the *sid* [faery] men should not rest upon Ireland unperceived by him..." (16). We may guess from this that a watch was to be maintained at all times over the sleeper to ensure that his sleeping, or wandering spirit was not carried off into the Otherworld, as might happen all too easily at that time.

Whether or not the guardians were actually touching the sleeper is not stated, but in several other texts such a contact is specifically noted. In the *Mabinog of Math Son of Mathonwy* for instance we learn that Math spent most of his time with is feet in the lap of the royal foot-holder (17); while in a later story a child who is experiencing difficulty in remembering the Psalms has only to sleep with his head resting on the knees of the Irish Saint Aengus in order to awake with the entire canon of the scripture secure in his memory! (18)

This seems to point to the idea of the passing on of knowledge by direct contact with the master. It is no large step from here to the idea of knowledge gained from the dead, who were frequently consulted on matters of import, and whom could be contacted by either visiting their graves or summoning them in necromantic fashion. The Roman author Tertullian states (*De Anima*, 27) that the Celts were given to sleeping on the tombs of their ancestors in order to receive knowledge and inspiration; the same idea was current among the Norse: places where the dead rested being regarded as sanctuaries, and the act of sleeping upon them as likely to result in a revelatory experience. (19)

Incubation

The method of obtaining information from inner sources (primarily the Otherworld) most often attested to, not only among the Celts but also in a much wider sphere, is that of the incubatory sleep. This is especially true of ancient Greece, where the temples dedicated to Asklepios concerned themselves specifically with the healing of ailments through this method. Here the sufferer, after being suitably prepared, slept in a special cell in a part of the temple called an *abaton*, and there dreamed a dream in which he or she either received a visitation from the god himself, whose touch brought healing; or else was instructed in a method of self-cure - sometimes cryptically and in a form requiring interpretation; though this does not seem ever to have been done by the priests of the temple. (20)

To early man, who saw sickness as a reflection of spiritual health, if a person suffered from a physical ailment (excluding loss of limbs or wounds acquired in war) there must be something wrong with his soul. For this reason Asklepios, who became the god of physicians, was seen not only as a healer, but also as a "saviour" god, whose actions were intended to counteract those of other deities whom the patient might have offended, or whose observance he or she might in some way have neglected. Incubatory sleep was the god's principle method of working his cures - much as in modern psychoanalytical treatment, where the patient is encouraged to discover the disaffection in his or her soul through the study or interpretation of his dreams.

Unlike the modern practice however, the dreams were seen as specifically emanating from the god, and the whole process took place within a specific temenos, the sacred precinct of the god. (The word *incubare* is translated as "sleeping in the sanctuary"). The resultant dreams (and few seem not to have experienced something) either affected an immediate cure or gave a method by which this might be achieved.

Preparation for the ritual of dreaming was also carefully controlled. After undergoing rites of purification, involving a lustral bath and preliminary sacrifices (usually of a cockerel) to the god, the patient went to sleep in the place "not to be entered by the unbidden" (21). It appears that he or she underwent some period of waiting, until "called" by the priests, or even by the god himself, to enter the abaton. The importance of preparedness is stressed in every account of the Asklepiae; if the patients were not in a proper state of mind they were likely either not to experience a dream or to have one that was unsatisfactory. Those who did so were likely to be sent away, perhaps to try again later on, after a further period of preparation.

It is also clear that the period of incubatory sleep took place at night, an important point for our argument in the light of the stress laid upon absence of light on the part of the Celtic poets and prophets, who frequently gave forth their precognitive visions after being enclosed in a dark place, watched over by friends or priests, and afterwards brought forth into bright light. It is apparent that in the case of patients at the Asklepion who failed (perhaps from excitement or pain) to sleep at all, that they received some kind of direct vision of the god, in which they were instructed as to how they might achieve healing, in the same way as if they had experienced a dream.

Asklepios himself appears to have begun life as a mortal physician who, taught by the centaur Cherion, was struck down by Zeus after he had successfully raised the dead. A still earlier stratum suggests a more shamanic personality, in which his name is Aischabios and totemic animals - the dog and the snake - represent him. The latter continued to be Asklepios' theiromorphic form, so that whenever a new Asklepion was founded, one of the sacred snakes kept in the temple, was taken to be installed with due ceremony in the new one. (22)

The Asklepiae were generally founded near a grove of trees or a spring, indicating their connection with both the elements and the Underworld. As Dr. Chadwick has noted in her study of dreams in ancient Europe,

"The most striking features which these dreams share in common...are (1) that they generally relate to the underworld...and (2) that they are for the most part shared with the rest of the community." (23)

This in itself indicates the chthonic nature of the Asklepiae, and of the god himself, and it of course also recalls the accounts of sleeping on the graves of dead heroes or druids in order to obtain dreams in which their wisdom could be plumbed. That this was a very central aspect in the design of temple precincts where incubatory sleep took place is demonstrated by the account of the Greek historian and geographer Pausanius, who personally experienced initiation into the mysteries of Trophonios, an early Greek hero who became deified and took on many of the aspects of Asklepios. Initially he was shown to have lived in a cave at Lebadeia in Boetia, again an indication of chthonic aspects. Pausanius' account makes this even more apparent.

"When a man decides to go down to Trophonios, he first lives a certain number of days in a building which is consecrated to Good Fortune (Fortuna) and the Good Spirit (Agathadaimon). Living there he purifies himself and uses no hot water; his bath is the river Herkyna..." (24) The initiate is then bathed in the river Herkyna and anointed by pubescent boys, called the Hermai. *"From here he is taken by the priests, not straight to the oracle, but to the water-springs, which are very close together. Here he must drink the water of Forgetfulness, to forget everything in his mind until then, and then the water of Memory, by which he remembers the sights he sees in his descent...."*(ibid) After a period of worship here, he is taken to the mountainside above a sacred wood, which is surrounded by circular platform of white stone, about 5 feet high. On this are bronze posts that are linked by bronze chains. Passing through the doors down into a chasm, the initiate descends through the kiln-shaped orifice of the earth, descending twenty feet by means of a ladder. On floor level here is a small passage - one foot high and two feet wide to admit the initiate. *"The man going down lies on the ground with honey cakes in his hands and pushes his feet into the opening and then tries to get his knees in. The rest of his body immediately gets dragged after his knees, as if some extraordinary deep, fast river was catching a man in a current and sucking him down. From here on, inside the second place, people are not always taught the future in one and the same way: one man hears, another sees as well. Those who go down return feet first through the same mouth. "...When a man comes up from Trophonios the priests take him over again, and sit him on the throne of memory, which is not far from the holy place, to ask him what he saw and discovered.'*(ibid)

Pausanius' account says that only one person had ever been killed here. He himself had passed these dangers and wrote from personal experience. All who have consulted the oracle had to write down their story on a wooden tablet and dedicate it to the shrine. Such a collection of testimonies would be most interesting to read.

That mystery rites similar to these, and to those of Asklepios, were once current among the Celts, is evident from accounts in widely scattered sources. As these are pieced together we begin to see a pattern emerging.

Clearly water was seen as a conductor of healing or information from beneath the ground. Numerous instances could be quoted from Celtic literature in which omens or precognitive dreams are vouchsafed beside rivers or springs. In the poetry of the Welsh poet Taliesin (a probable contemporary of Merlin) there are more references to water than to any other element, and this can be seen to reflect the complex matter of visionary insight as it connects with both darkness and light, as in the story of Nechtan's Well, which those who looked into it unprepared were at once blinded by light from within, but whose waters also gave inspiration to those who had undergone the necessity preparation (as in the case of the visitors to the Asklepiae). (25)

Examples of omens received at or by rivers include the following from the story of "The Siege of Howth". (26) In this the king (Mes-Gegra) and his charioteer, have paused behind the main body of the army to rest awhile. The charioteer sleeps first and while he it watching Mes-Gegra sees a large not floating down river. Seizing it the king cuts it in half and eats the rest. As he looks he sees the charioteer "lifted up in his sleep from the ground" When the man wakes the king asks how he is: "I have seen an evil vision" replies the charioteer and asks about the nut. A quarrel then breaks out and the king is severely wounded and the charioteer killed. Though the connection between the dream and the nut is not made clear, we should remember that the nut is invariable connected with visionary insight, and of course once again we have the themes of precognition and water.

Badbh, the Irish War-Goddess, announced the approaching death of eminent heroes by taking the form of the Washer-at-the-Ford, who was to be seen washing out bloody clothes or blood- stained armour in the river near the site of a forthcoming battle - a possible memory of a time when priestesses, trained in the arts of prophecy, kept watch ar fords or springs, and were called upon to give prognostications before battle was joined.

There is no clear evidence for the existence of incubation temples of the kind discussed above in Britain or Ireland; however, one site has caused more than one commentator to suggest that it may have been put to just such a use - the inference being that if one such temple were operative in this country others may well have existed of which we have no current knowledge.

The site in question is at Lydney in Gloucestershire. It is of Romano-British provenance and was built between A.D. 364-367. It was excavated by Sir Mortimer Wheeler in the 1940s and found to possess a building consisting of several small cubicles. It was then noticed that the ground plan of the temple complex bore a marked resemblance to the layout of the Asklepion at Epidavros: including a bathhouse and dormitories. Casts representing a disfigured hand and a heavily pregnant woman were also discovered at the site, suggesting that these may have been representations of the ailments suffered by those who attended the temple. At Epidavros, similar effigies were found in profusion, having been hung up in the temple as thankful offerings by patients who had been cured.

All of this led Wheeler to suggest that

"Here, then, we seem to have a recurrent feature of some of the principle classical shrines of healing, and we may provisionally regard the Lydney building as a member of this series. On this line of thought it may be that the Long Building was indeed an 'abaton', used to supplement the 'chapels' in the temple itself for the purpose of that temple-sleep through which the healing-god and his priesthood were wont to work." (27)

If we accept this suggestion, the question arises as to whether the Lydney temple was the province of a native god, or was a copy of the classic foundations.

The dedication of Lydney was undoubtedly to the Celtic god Nodons, of whom little is, unfortunately, known. The presence of a priestly diadem at the site in Gloucestershire has lead some commentators to the belief that he was a solar deity, a belief substantiated by the great Celtecist Sir John Rhys (28), who also pointed out the probable links between Nodens, the Irish Nuada Argetlam

(Nuada of the Silver Hand) and the Welsh Llud Llaw Eraint (a title applied to Nodens in the hero list from "Culhwch and Olwen" in the Mabinogion) - both of whom derive from an earlier Brythonic version, Ludons Lamargentios. Nuada was, of course, the possessor of an artificial hand, made for him by the Smith god Creidne with the help of the leech-god Dian Cecht. Llud can be identified with Llyr Lledyeith (Half-Speech). These are interesting as they are both suffer from physical defects, and are connected with a god who may have been responsible for a healing temple....

However, the diadem mentioned above, which depicts the god in a chariot drawn by horses and surrounded by neriads and spirits of the winds, suggests not so much as solar deity, as a god of the sea. William Bathurst, who first drew attention to the Lydney site in 1831, translated the name Nodens as "God of the Abyss" or "of the Depths"(29), a suggestive appellation since it suggests connections both with the sea and with the chthonic depths of which, as we have seen, Asklepios was identified. Interestingly, like Asklepios, Nuada was eventually struck down at the battle of Mag Tureid by a bolt of lightning (30). Llyr was also connected with the sea, and together these watery references recall the provenance of so many Celtic dream visions beside streams or rivers - though this analogy should not be pressed too far.

It is possible, then, that we have in the figure of Nodens a native equivalent of Asklepios, and on the site at Lydney a British, Romano-Celtic temple where incubatory sleep was practised. We have seen from the evidenced presented above that the idea of sleep as a means of discovering information or precognitive vision was common among the Celts. That a tradition of shamanism was also current at least as late as the 6th century A.D. is also certain. The combination of these two strains of thinking and belief make it more than likely that the idea of incubatory sleep for healing purposes would have been readily acceptable; though whether it was imported from the Classical world or already existed in the native islands is less certain. However, one final piece of evidence does remain, which suggests that it may well have been current at least in Ireland.

We are used to hearing accounts of Sweat Lodges in the Americas, which are frequently associated with both healing and vision-seeking activities. What is not commonly known is that such practices were also current in ancient Ireland. "Sweating- Houses" (*Tigh 'n Alluis*) were known in the nineteenth century and seem to have been in use for much longer than that. A number of such houses have been discovered, notably on the island of Inishmurray. They are usually about seven feet long inside, and entered through a low, narrow door. A turf fire was usually kindled within and then the door closed up until the interior became like an inferno; then the ashes were swept out and those who wished went in and were enclosed until they were bathed profusely in sweat. (31)

The similarity between these structures and the ancient howes or burial chambers of Britain and Ireland is marked. Martin Brennan first drew attention to this in his book The Boyne Valley Vision, in which he noted that at sites such as New Grange, Knowth and Dowth, huge stone basins had been discovered in some of the side chambers. The use of these had passed unnoticed until Brennan realised that also present in the tombs were round stone balls that displayed signs of having been heated many times. He suggestion was that

"The enigma of these objects may easily be explained by filling the vessels and stone basins with water and be heating the stones and placing them in the basins. Water and heated stones produce steam and the chambers in the mounds contain steam, thus easily and efficiently creating a steam bath." (32)

Brennan goes on to note that this was an ancient and well-attested method of inducing an altered state among the shamans of many parts of the world. The combination of this idea with that of incubatory sleep and the Celtic love of augury, suggests a very strong argument in favour of these being such practices in these islands, perhaps from a very early date.

To end on a personal note. A few years ago, while suffering from a bout of 'flu, I received a visit in dream-state from an inner guide who communicated to me a specific method of helping myself to recover quickly. I had virtually forgotten about this until a few weeks ago, when I was again laid low with a virus. Lying in bed, suffering alternate bouts of hot and cold, I began to dream "lucidly". I recalled the previous instruction clearly: I must seek and find a pattern of negative promises: for example, I promise to feel very much more ill in a moment; I promise to bite my thumb very hard when I wake up. When I had successfully established this pattern I would awake refreshed. It proved extremely difficult to do. The tendency was to think: I will feel better when I awake; I will not bite my thumb hard on waking etc. I awoke feeling a great deal better and with an image in my heads of an ancient pillared portico seemingly hanging in pace.

Subsequent meditation on this has revealed more of the image: that of a temple portico, with seven pillars and a wide entrance standing open before me. It does not require too great a stretching of credulity to believe this is an image of the healing temple - whether the mother foundation of Asklepios or the native one at Lydney. Either way, it suggests to me very powerfully the continuing efficacy of incubatory sleep, as it was, I believe, once practised in these islands. (33)

To end I should like to append an "Incubatory Invocation", to be recited by the priest/priestess of the shrine over the sleeper. It was written by my wife after a discussion of the material presented above:

Learn to the gifted with the night,
With the words of wisdom;
From the depths of darkness' dazzling
The story will rise
As a circling snake.
May the sacred curve
Of Her arm enfold you!
May the stars of Her
Dark veil cover you!
May your sleep be founded
In the deep night of Her own lap!   *(© Caitlin Matthews)*

NOTES

1: Ettlinger, Ellen "Omens and Celtic Warfare" Man XLIII (1943) No 4. p 11-17. See pages 11-12.

2: Fraser, J. "The First Battle of Moytura" Eriu VIII (1915) pp1-63. See p.19.

3: Matthews, John. Taliesin: The Last Celtic Shaman (Inner Traditions, 2000)

4: Best, R.I. "Prognostications from the Raven and the Wren" Eriu VIII (1916) pp 120-126. See pp123-125.

5: Ettlinger, Ellen "Precognitive Dreams in Celtic Legend" Folk- Lore LIX (1948) pp97-117.

6: ibid.

7: Plummer, C. Vitae Sanctorum Hiberniae (Oxford, 1910.) vol I. p.cliv. n.5.

8: Keating, G. History of Ireland (London: Irish Text Society, 1908) vol. II pp348-50

9: Mabinogion Ed. & Trans. J. Gantz. (Harmondsworth: Penguin Books, 1965.)

10: Cormac's Glossary Ed & Trans J. O'Donovan. (Calcutta: Irish Archaeological & Celtic Society, 1868)

11: Matthews, J. Taliesin. See especially Chapter 7

12: Krippner, S. "Dreams and Shamanism" [in] Shamanism compiled by S. Nicholson. (London: The Theosophical Publishing House,1987.)

13: Martin, M. A Description of the Western Islands (London, 1703.)

14: Ettlinger, Ellen "Precognitive Dreams in Celtic Legend" p104.

15: Meyer, K., The Voyage of Bran (London, D. Nutt,1895)

16: Ettlinger: ibid. 17: Mabinogion

18: Ettlinger; ibid.

19: See especially The Underworld Initiation by R. J. Stewart (Aquarian Press, 1985) where this topic is dealt with in some detail.

20: Meier, C. A. "Ancient Incubation and Modern Psychotherapy" Betwixt & Between Ed. by L.C. Mahdi, S. Foster & M. Little. (Le Salle, Ill. Open Court,1987.)

21: ibid,

22: Kerenyi, C. Asklepios trans. R. Manheim. (New York: Pantheon Books, 1959)

23: Chadwick. N.K. "Dreams in Early European Literature" Celtic Studies. Ed. J. Carney & D. Greene. (London: Routledge and Kegan Paul,1968.) p38.

24: Pausanius. Guide to Greece vol I (Trans P. Levi) (Harmondsworth: Penguin Books, 1971.) pp393-395.

25: Ford, Patrick K. "The Well of Nechtan and 'La Gloire Luminesse' [in] Myth in Indo-European Antiquity Ed. G.J. Larson. (Berkley, University of California Press, 1974) pp67-74.
See also Matthews, J: Taliesin

26: Stokes, W. "The Siege of Howth" Revue Celtique VIII (1887) pp47-64.

27: Wheeler, R.E.M. Report on the Excavations of the Prehistoric, Roman and Post-Roman Site in Lydney Park, Gloucestershire (Oxford: Society of Antiquaries, 1932.) pp 51-52.

28: Rhys, John. Celtic Folk-Lore, Welsh & Manx (London: Wildwood House, 1980.)

29: Bathurst, W. Roman Antiquities at Lydney Park, Gloucestershire (London: Spottiswoode & Co, 1897)

30: Hersh, J. "Ancient Celtic Incubation" Sundance Community Dream Journal, III (Winter, 1979) pp81-90.

31: Joyce, P.W. A Social History of Ancient Ireland (vol I). (New York: Longmans Green & Co. 1903.) pp 626-7.

32: Brennan, M. The Boyne Valley Vision (Portlaois: The Dolmen Press, 1980.)

33: Several people are working with the idea of incubation at the present time. They include James Hersh of Salva Regina College, Newport RI; and Eugene Monick, who is a Jungian analyst practicing in New York City and Scranton, Pennsylvania. The Dragon Project Trust, under the guidance of Paul Deveraux, recently established a new program of experiments into incubatory sleep at ancient sites that have been found to possess unusual geophysical properties. (I am greatful to Paul Deveraux for putting me in touch with some of the material used in this essay, and for providing a copy of the artical by James Hersh.

(1990)

Chapter 15:

THE LANGUAGE OF TREES:
OGAM AND THE SACRED WOODS

This is a longer version of an article I wrote for the British magazine Prediction in 1997. I have explored the subject of sacred trees and especially the mysterious Ogham alphabet several times over the years – most notably in The Green Man Tree Oracle (Barnes and Noble, 2003) which I devised with the artist Wil Worthington and which brought together two of my favourite themes, the sacred trees and the Green Man. Here I was concerned to set out some of the fascinating lore of the Celtic world, drawing in part on what I had written about the subject in Taliesin: The Last Celtic Shaman (Inner Traditions, 2001

The Sacredness of Trees

Trees have always been considered sacred by most ancient cultures. The tradition of the sacred grove or *nemeton* was widespread throughout much of the western world. In central Asia Minor in about 280 BC the Gauls held a great council at a place called Drunemeton "the chief nemeton or sacred place", while later, in Caesar's time, the Druids were said to meet annually in the land of the Carnutes, believed to be the centre of Gaul. Nearly every tribe in the country seems to have possessed a nemeton or sacred meeting place, marked either by a tree or a stone pillar, and we may imagine that this was the same in Britain and Ireland, and that the local shaman held sway there at all times. Certainly, as the Roman military historian Tacitus says in the Germania:

'The grove is the centre of their whole religion. It is regarded as the cradle of the race and the dwelling-place of the supreme god to whom all things are subject and obedient'.

In Medieval Irish the word for "sacred grove" is translated as *fid-nemith* or *fid-neimid* that in turn derived from an older Celtic word *nemetos*, meaning simply "holy" or "sacred". This later became extended to mean a distinguished person or animal, or as a poet, a king, or a wise dignitary. In the *Irish Triads* it says:

"Three noble, scared things: groves or temples, filid or poets, rulers.
Three dead things that are paid for only with living things are an apple-tree, a hazel-bush, and a sacred grove."

This is reflected in the harsh laws laid down for the damage caused to certain trees in the Law Tracts. In *Senchas Mor*, at the end of the tract entitled 'Crith Gablach', it is stated that the fines for cutting certain trees are as follows: For the "Chieftain" trees: oak, hazel, holly, yew, ash, pine, and apple, the fine is a cow for cutting the trunks, a heifer for either limbs or branches. For the "Common" trees: alder, willow, hawthorn, mountain ash, birch, elm, and idha (possibly a species of pine), the fines are a cow for each whole tree and a heifer for the branches. For the "Shrub" trees: blackthorn, elder, spindle-tree, white hazel, aspen, arbutus, and test tree, the fine is a heifer for each tree. The "bramble Trees" are: fern, bog-myrtle, furze, briar, heath, ivy, broom, gooseberry. A sheep is the fine for each.

Each tree, like humankind, has its honour price or dire. Two poetic grades mentioned in *Sencus Mor* indicate the connection of poets with trees. The first of these is the "*cli*" poet,

> "*i.e. [he partakes of] the nature of the post (cleith)...[which is] strong and straight, and it elevates and is elevated, it protects and is protected; it is powerful from the ridge to the floor. It is the same with this grade in the poetic house, i.e. his art is powerful, and his judgement is straight in the circuit of his profession....*"

The second is the so called "*dos*" poet, so called,

> "*...from his similitude to a tree...i.e. it is through (dos, under) the name of a tree they learn their art...*"

The lore of trees itself was a significant part of the mysteries learned by all the bards and poets. It is illustrated, in a fragmentary way, by a whole body of widely separated texts.

The Lore of Trees

In Ireland there were five specifically named sacred trees: the Tree of Ross, the Tree of Mugna, the Tree of Dathi, the Tree of Usnach and the Tree of Tortu. They are listed in both The Calendar of Oengus and the Dinshencas, or Land Lore. The former says of them:

> "*Eo Mugna, great was the fair tree,*
> *high its top above the rest:*
> *thirty cubits - it was no trifle -*
> *that was the measure of its girth.*
>
> *Three hundred cubits was the height of the blameless tree,*
> *its shadow sheltered a thousand:*
> *in secrecy it remained in the north and east*
> *till the time of Conn of the Hundred Fights.*
>
> *A hundred score of warriors - no empty tale -*
> *along with ten hundred and forty*
> *would that tree shelter - it was a fierce struggle -*
> *till it was overthrown by the poets.*

*   *   *

How fell the bough of Dathi?
it spent the strength of many a gentle hireling:
an ash, the tree of the nimble hosts,
its top bore no lasting yield.

The Ash in Tortu - take count thereof!
the Ash of populous Usnach:
their boughs fell - it was not amiss -
in the time of the sons of Aed Slane.

The Oak of Mugna, it was a hallowed treasure;
nine hundred bushels was its bountiful yield:
it fell in Dairbre southward,
across Mag Ailbe of the cruel combats.

The Bole of Ross, a comely yew
with abundance of broad timber,
the tree without hollow or flaw,
the stately bole, how did it fall?"

The *Prose Dindshencas*, a remarkable collection of Irish traditional lore about the land, adds a few more details:

"Berries to the berries the Strong Upholder put upon his tree. [i.e. The Ash of Tortan]. Three fruits upon it, namely acorn, apple and nut, and when the first fruit fell another fruit used to grow. Now it was for a long while hidden until the birth of Conn of the Hundred Battles (when it was revealed). Ninine the Poet cast it down in time of Domnall son of Murchad King of Ireland (c 500 AD.), who had refused a demand of Ninine's. Equally broad were its top and the plain (in which it stood). Or it may have been that in the time of Aed Slane that this tree and the Bile Tortan fell together. Thirty cubits was its girth, and its height was three hundred cubits, and its leaves were on it always."

These are enigmatic references, clearly referring to cosmic world-trees of the kind worshipped among the Norse as scions of Yggdrasil, the World-Ash. (That three out of the five mentioned here are themselves ash cannot be without significance). The fact that the great Oak of Mugna is described as being "overthrown by the poets" is puzzling at first. That the poetic mysteries were intimately connected with tree-lore is beyond doubt; why, therefore, should the poets be described as destroying the sacred trees? For a possible answer we must turn to another text: The Settling of the Manor of Tara. Here we find the following account:

The Chieftains of Ireland having come together to discuss the seemingly over-large dimensions of the Manor of Tara compared to their own lands, desire to learn of the original reasons for the partitioning of the land. To this end they summon first of all two wise poets, who in turn summon five older and wiser than they - including Tuan mac Cairell, who underwent many changes of shape in order to present throughout much of the history of Ireland. However, none of these were able to answer, and all agreed to summon Fintan, who was agreed to be the wisest of them all. Fintan's discourse is long and rambling. Much in the manner of Taliesin he gives a poetic version of the history of Ireland, which he seems to be able to remember personally. Curiously, in the light of our present line of inquiry, he mentions another great tree:

"One day I passed through a wood in West Munster in the west. I took away with me a red yew berry and I planted it in the garden of my court, and it grew up there until it was as big as a man. Then I removed it from the garden and planted it on the lawn of my court even, and it grew up in the centre of that lawn so that I could fit with a hundred warriors under its foliage, and it protected me from wind and rain, and from cold and heat."

Fintan then goes on to tell the story of an assembly of all the Kings and lords of Ireland, together with all their principle story-tellers, brought together on the day of Christ's crucifixion by a wonderful being called Trefuilngid Tre-ochair, the Strong Upholder mentioned in the *Prose Dindshenca*. The text reads as follows:

"...We beheld a great hero, fair and mighty, approaching us from the west at sunset. We wondered greatly at the magnitude of his form. As high as a wood was the top of his shoulders, the sky and the sun visible between his legs, by reason of his size and his comeliness. A shining crystal veil about him like unto raiment of precious linen. Sandals upon his feet, and it is not known of what material they were. Golden yellow hair upon him falling in curls to the middle of his thighs. Stone tablets in his left hand, a branch with three fruits in his right hand, and these are the three fruits which were on it, nuts and apples and acorns in May-time: and unripe was each fruit.....”I have come indeed" he said, "from the setting of the sun, and I am going unto the rising, and my name is Trefuilngid Tre-ochair". "Why has that name been given to thee?" said they. "Easy to say" said he. "Because it is I who cause the rising of the sun and its setting." "And what has brought thee to the setting, if it is at the rising thou dost be?" Easy to say," said he. "A man who has been tortured - that is who has been crucified by the Jews today; for it [the sun] stepped past them [the Jews] after that deed, and has not shone upon them, and that is what has brought me to the setting to find out what ailed the sun; and then it was revealed to me, and when I knew the lands over which the sun set I came to Inis Gluairi off Irrus Domnann; and I found no land from that westwards, for that is the threshold over which the sun sets...."

Trefuilngid Tre-ochair then requests to know the history of the people of Ireland, and is given a much-abbreviated version due to the fact that there are apparently no lore-masters who know all the stories. Trefuilngid however, appears already to know more than they, calling himself "the truly learned witness who explains to all everything unknown". Indeed, he summons all the most learned men of the five provinces together and relates to them the entire history of the island. He then draws Fintan aside and tells him everything, since he is the oldest of all the wise, who has been alive since the coming of the first men. All this Fintan has remembered, and now relates it to the assembly at Tara, detailing the reasons for the partitions, what they are best known for, and an extraordinary catalogue of the people who originated all the greatest works and deeds in the land.

The text continues:

"So Trefuilngid Tre-ochair left that ordinance with the men of Ireland for ever, and he left with Fintan son of Bochra some of the berries from the branch which was in his hand, so that he planted them in whatever places he thought it likely they would grow in Ireland. And these are the trees which grew up from those berries: the Ancient

Tree of Tortu and the Tree of Ross, the Tree of Mugna and the Branching Tree of Dathee, and the Ancient Tree of Usnech...."

Thereafter the Kings of Ireland were accorded, and Fintan set up a great pillar on the hill of Usnech, in the centre of the land, marked with five ridges that showed the divisions of the Land.

This is an extraordinary text, so full of lore and wisdom relating both to the ancient traditions and to the cosmological legends of the Celts. Essentially, there are three ways in which we can regard what it tells us. On the one hand it is clearly a series of cosmological myths relating to the most distant past, when the world was created. On the other, we may choose to view the references to the trees as relating to the great lineages of Ireland, which were "cut down" or ended by time and circumstance conjoined. This is akin to the death of Tradition itself, the realm and responsibility of the shaman-poets and priests, and is suggested by the preponderance of names which translate as " Son of Oak" (Mac Dara), "Son of Rowan-Tree" (Mac Cairthin), Son of Yew (Mac Ibair) Son of Hazel (Mac Cuill) - indicating, incidentally, that some tribes had trees as their totems rather than animals. Certainly many settlements were built beside, or derived their names from, the sites of ancient groves. Fintan's reference to the tree which he transplanted from his garden to "the lawn of my court" reflects a reference to the nature of the ever-living tradition.

Thirdly, the idea of the cutting down of the ancient trees seems to have become synonymous with the spread of Christianity and the ending thereby of older ways. Perhaps the poets' deliberate cutting down of the trees of tradition can be seen in this light - as a desire to prevent their being felled by the axes of the monks! Certainly when we read in the *Calendar of Oengus* of "a certain great tree which was in the world in the east", and which was adored by the heathen until it was felled as a consequence of a Christian fast, we may feel this suggestion to be the case. Yet there is, to give the matter balance, a story of Columba that suggests that the sanctity of trees continued to be recognised.

When the Saint founded a church in Derry (which derives from *doire*, an oak wood) he burned the town and rath of the king in order to destroy utterly the works of men before re-consecrating the earth to God. "*So great was the fire and the blaze that it well-nigh burnt a grove of trees in that place.*" But Columba pronounced an invocation to protect the grove, and was so loath to fell so much as a single tree that he turned the oratory to face north and south instead of east and west. "*And he charged his successors to chop no tree that fell of itself or was blown down by the wind, till the end of nine days*", after which time it was to be distributed to the poor. He is later reported to have said that while he feared death, he feared much more the sound of an axe in the woods of Derry!

This great respect for the power and sanctity of the trees, especially when they were part of a grove, is reflected throughout Irish history and tradition. An equal importance was attached to language, and when these two major themes are brought together we find ourselves taken even more deeply into the heart of the Celtic tradition.

The Lost Language

The importance of language is emphasised again and again in Celtic tradition. Words themselves can be all powerful, as can song. One of the most important aspects of the bardic training was the learning of a secret language which could enable the initiated poets to converse with each other, if necessary in full view of a hall full of people, without anyone there being any the wiser.

This was done by means of Ogam, a linear alphabet found inscribed on stone or wood, apparently

129

devised by the ancient Celts. It has been called "the secret language of the poets" and in its long and complex history many theories have been advanced to explain its origin and purpose. Before looking in detail at some of these we should begin with what is known about Ogam from early texts.

"Early" here means medieval rather than ancient, but we do have an enduring testimony of another kind, in the shape of the many inscriptions in Ogam found carved on menhirs and standing stones throughout Britain, Scotland and Ireland. The purpose to which these were erected has long been debated. It is assumed, generally, that they were grave markers: "the stone of X", indicating where some great chieftain or hero was laid to rest. But there is at least one other possibility: that they were boundary markers, indicating the demarcation between one tribe's lands and another. This would explain the stones with more than one inscription, and is in line with the magical association of Ogam. A stone with the name of the tribe, its chieftain or clan mark would be as effective as a wire fence today - none would cross it without either permission or evil intent.

Many people have assumed that Ogham and Runic inscriptions must derive from each other, but this is not so. The former is a Celtic method, the latter a Scandinavian one. Both are concerned with arcane knowledge and under the patronage of gods of word- wisdom. Both Odin and Gwydion have reputations for weaving words and gaining wisdom.

The main source of written knowledge about Ogam comes from a 14th century Irish manuscript of *The Book Of Ballymot*. Contained in this are some eight pages, generally referred to as "The Ogham Tract". This has been edited by George Calder with extensive commentaries, and need not be reproduced here. However, certain salient points are worthy of note. The account begins, as one might expect, with the creation of Ogam:

"What are the place, time, person, and cause of the invention of Ogham? Not hard. Its place Hibernia insula quam nos Scoti habitamus. [in Hibernia where the Scoti dwell] In the time of Bres son of Elatha king of Ireland was it invented. Its person Ogma son of Elatha son of Delbaeth brother to Bres, for Bres, Ogma and Delbaeth are the three sons of Elatha son of Delbaeth there. Now Ogma, a man well skilled in speech and in poetry, invented the Ogham. The cause of its invention, as a proof of his ingenuity, and that his speech should belong to the learned apart, to the exclusion of rustics and herdsmen... The father of Ogham is Ogma, the mother of Ogham is the hand or knife of Ogma... This moreover is the first thing that was written by Ogham: i.e. (the birch) b was written, and to convey a warning to Lug son of Ethliu it was written respecting his wife lest she be carried away from him into faeryland, to wit, seven b's in one switch of birch: Thy wife will be seven times carried away from thee into faeryland or into another country, unless birch guard her. On that account, moreover, b, birch, takes precedence, for it is in birch that Ogham was first written."

This tells us several important things. Ogam was intended to be understood by the learned, noble class (i.e. the Druids) and not by the common people. Its first use seems to have been to inscribe a warning, and to have taken the form of a protective spell - if we are to understand the term "unless birch guard her" in this way. Also we are told that Ogma, whose rather complex pedigree is given, invented the alphabet. References to this same figure are found elsewhere, and it is clear from these that he was not a man at all (as in the "Ogham Tract") but a god - Ogma *Cermait* (Honey-Mouthed), *Grian-aineach*,(Sun-Faced), or *Trenfher* (Strong-man, Champion), a son of the great god Dagda. He is usually described as a god of literature and of eloquence, as his alternative epithets suggest. In Gaul he was called Ogmios and worshipped as a god of light and learning. The Classical author Lucian wrote that he was the Celtic Heracles, and gives a description of a painting which depicted an ancient figure drawing a group of men chained by their ears to his tongue. Puzzling over this Lucian found a native Celt at his side that was willing to elucidate:

"We Celts do not agree with you Greeks in thinking that Hermes is Eloquence: we identify Heracles with it, because he is far more powerful than Hermes. And don't be surprised that he is represented as an old man, for eloquence ...is wont to show its full vigour in old age.... This being so, if old Heracles here drags men after him who are tethered by the ears to his tongue, don't be surprised at that either: you know the kinship between ears and tongue."

Ogmios' title, *Trenfher*, suggests an actual identification with Hercules/Heracles, whilst his Hellenised name means "the Walker", and if we recall the original meaning of the word "pedant" is derived from scholar, or "one who walks up and down", we may see how this follows. Ogmios is clearly a god of Tradition, which binds men in chains of a kind, and which is shown to derive from the otherworldly realm of the gods. In an inscription found at Richborough Ogmios is depicted with rays of light coming from around his head and holding the whip of Sol Invictus (The Unconquered Sun.) He is thus in every way a suitable figure to be accredited with the invention of an alphabet which was to be associated with magical activities, with the transmission of secret knowledge, and with the writing of poetry.

The Ogam alphabet itself consists of various combinations of lines drawn across a vertical or horizontal stave. Each set of five letters has a name, as indicated, and the letters themselves have names, the most frequent being those of various trees. It is this association which has lead to Ogam being referred to as "the Tree Alphabet", or "Beithe, Luis, Nion" after the first three names of the sequence. (Which, occasionally varies from version to version) The complete list is as follows, adapted from several different texts.

Ogam Name	Letter	Tree
Beithe	b	birch
Luis	l	elm/rowan
Fearn	f	alder
Saile	s	willow
Nuin	n	ash
(h)Uathe	h	whitethorn/hawthorn
Duir	d	oak
Tinne	t	holly/elderberry
Coll	c	hazel
Quert	q	quicken /aspen/apple
Muinn	m	vine/mulberry
Gort	g	fir/ivy
(N)Getal	ng	broom /fern
Straif	str	willowbrake/blackthorn
Ruis	r	elder
Ailm	a	fir/pine
Ohn	o	furze/ash/gorse

Ur	u	thorn /heather
Edhadh	e	yew/aspen
Ido	i	service tree/yew
Ebadh	eba	elecampane/aspen
Oir	oi	spindle tree
Uilleand	ui	ivy/honeysuckle
Iphin	io	pine /goseberry
Emancoll/phagos	ae	witch hazel/beech

It will be seen from this that a number of variants exist as to the attribution of a particular tree or bush to a particular letter. Also the order has changed throughout its long period of development, so that we cannot always be sure of its original form. However, there are some interesting lists of 'glosses' attached to each of the letters that may contain more of their inner meaning. These lists imply a complex series of riddling references that must have been known to the poets, and could be applied to extend the meanings of the Ogam letters in such a way as to make them comprehensible only to those proficient in Ogam. Among them is the so-called tree-alphabet.

Doubt, first expressed by Charles Graves as long ago as 1847, and more recently explored by Howard Meroney as to the authenticity of the Ogham tree-alphabet, makes it clear that we must look again at the whole question of these identifications, which have been accepted quite literally by most commentators since the 1700s. The evidence points to them being copied and recopied until their original meanings became virtually lost, or so jumbled as to be virtually indecipherable. What appears to have happened is that the original glosses for the Ogham alphabet (still quite late as against the dating of the alphabet itself) were of a much more ordinary-seeming nature, and that these were changed, at some unspecified time (probably between the 7th to the 9th Centuries) to fit a purely arbitrary system of tree and plant names.

Lists of the various kinds of physically oriented Ogam (finger, nose, thigh foot etc.) also exist, and were used in a similar fashion - touching the part of the body in a certain way would indicate to those in the know a word or letter which could be interpreted in this fashion. Other kinds of Ogam listed in The Scholar's Primer include: Sow Ogham, River-Pool Ogham, Fortress Ogham, Bird Ogham, Colour Ogham, King Ogham, Water Ogham, Dog Ogham, Food Ogham.

The poet/druid/seer had thus to be familiar with a vast range of knowledge - not only of the general meaning of the Ogam character, but also to the many secret meanings which lay behind it. Thus the letter meant not only *ng*, but also all that *ng* stood for: tree, group of letters, phrase, part of the body and so on. The interpretation thus rested on a full spectrum of knowledge in which the relationship of the letter or letters to each other, to the remainder of the inscription, and to the context in which they were found - all had to be taken into account. Thus any one of the poetic epithets listed above could be interpreted differently according to their placement on the staves, and their relationship to each other.

R.A.S. Macalister notes that all of the Ogam signs could be easily made with the fingers - hence their grouping in fives - and that the five "extra" letters, which represent the vowel sounds and have often been suggested as late additions, are particularly appropriate for making with the fingers. From this he suggests that the earliest use of Ogham was as a sign language, and that only later was it adapted for use in the making of inscriptions. He also has some interesting perceptions on the possible origin of the alphabet, which he finds to be very nearly identical with a form of Greek known as the Formello-Cervetti alphabet. This was found inscribed on two vases dating from approximately 6th

Century BC. This, Calder believes, indicates they were borrowed by Gaulish Druids some time in the 5th Century and adapted to their own use.

Caesar remarks that the Druids used "Greek letters" to record their communications - though not their orally preserved religious teachings - which seems to bear out this idea. Certainly there was considerable interaction between the Celts and the Greeks for this curious borrowing to have come about. It establishes a date for Ogam of no earlier than 500 B.C. and lends weight to the belief that its original use was as a cryptographic system.

However, the story does not end here. An examination of the language of the Ogam inscriptions found in Ireland, Britain and Wales, shows that they contain archaisms that point to an extremely primitive language still being enshrined in stone long after it had ceased to be spoken. Macalister, who deals with his linguistic evidence at some length believes that it was Old Goidelic, the primitive language of the Celts, and from this infers that it continued to be spoken by the Druids, who taught it orally in their schools so that they were speaking a language no longer understood by their own people! References to "the dark speech" found in contemporary literature, suggest this may well have been the case, and add not only to the antiquity of Ogham, but also to the Druids themselves. All of this leads Dr Macalister to suggest that a reasonable translation of the word "Ogam" would be "the language", thus indicating its primary place in Celtic understanding.

There remains a good deal of disagreement over the order that the alphabet should follow, and over which tree or shrub belongs to which letter. The earliest lists we possess, and upon which the above examples are based, are those found in the Ogam Tract and the *Auraicept N-Eces* (The Scholar's Primer), which differ only slightly. R.A.S. Macalister, in his brilliant exposition of Ogam has given evidence to show that the order changed with phonetic requirements, so that the familiar Beith-Luis-Nion may well have been the earliest. After this there is a long gap in which various sources repeat the medieval lists more or less verbatim, until the 17th century version by Charles O'Connor, quoted by Edward Ledwich in his 18th century Antiquities of Ireland. This was defined again in Roderic O'Flaherty's *Ogygia* and later by the poet and mythographer Robert Graves. He included it in his "grammar of poetic myth" The White Goddess, in which he believed that it formed the basis for "a calendar of seasonal tree-magic". Unfortunately he made certain amendments to the original order of the trees, in an endeavour to bring the system into line with the overall picture of the Muse Goddess he wished to describe, and this may in part at least invalidate his theory.

The truth, or otherwise, of the existence of such an calendar must ultimately be for he individual to decide. The study of the materia however, leads to an increasing awareness of the importance of tree lore to the Celts, while the underlying magic of the Ogam letters cannot be denied.

(1997)

Chapter 16

TALIESIN:
BARDIC AND SHAMANIC TRADITIONS IN BRITAIN & IRELAND

I gave this talk in Boston in 1997, to a group of very enthusiastic students of Celtic history and Literature, some of whom disagreed very strongly with my findings while others applauded them! Much of what is here is reappeared in my book on Taliesin, but there are variations and some more up to the moment thoughts – hence its appearance here. For many years a being who names himself Taliesin has been something of an alter ego for me. His ever ready wisdom, a sharp; tongue and depths of knowledge always surprise me; and the warmth I feel both from and towards him is something I shall always be greatful to have known.

Much of what I am about to say is, academically at least, controversial, and I welcome any comments on the materials put forth here. But the story which underlies this account, and which can be read more fully in my book on the subject, is largely a personal one, undertaken in the conviction that a shamanistic tradition existed among the Celts from the earliest times until as later as the 6th century AD. This is a belief that few academics currently allow, perhaps because so much of the evidence is subjective. But that seems, to me at least, very appropriate, since the work of the shaman is very much an inner, individual experience which derives from a very deep level of human consciousness..

What I have set out to prove - for my own satisfaction as anything - is that not only did the Celts practice Shamanism, but that the literature, so much of it fragmentary, which has retained the essential elements of their beliefs and traditions, includes accounts of the shamanic experience. Thus when we read of Voyages to the Otherworld, undertaken by one or other of the great heroes of the Celts, it is possible to see, if we look at these accounts with Shamanic understanding, recollections of actual inner journeys, undertaken many hundreds of years ago and passed down, in the form of poem and song, generations after the people who experiences them were dust.

Ten years ago, when the writings of Carlos Castaneda were all the rage, I was frequently asked if there was any trace of Shamanism in Britain and Ireland, and at the time I replied with a qualified no. Then one day I happened to pick up a book of essays on worldwide shamanic traditions, and as I read I became increasingly aware that there was something familiar about the accounts of inner journeys accompanied by animal spirit-helpers, to realms that gave reality a subtle twist. These accounts gave such a unified view of an inner spiritual experience that people as far apart as Siberia and the Australian Continent seemed to be speaking a common language. Intrigued by what I had found, I set out to find similar materials within the literature and archaeology of the Celts.

I did not have to look far. I had been aware of the story of Taliesin for some time, as well as of the poems which had survived and which were attributed to this 6th century bard and seer. Until then I had tended to dismiss the poetry as largely nonsensical - indeed much of it is still considered to be so by the academic community. It existed, at this time, in 19th century translations that were considered - as indeed I found them to be - largely inaccurate.

Let me give you an example. The following is part of a much longer poem, called 'The Hostile Confederacy', translated by D.W.Nash in 1858.

A wonderful reciter,
A great singer of songs of praise,
Am I, Taliesin.
I compose songs in true measure,
Continuing to the end
To uphold Elphin.
Is there not a tribute
Of much gold to be paid?
When shall be hated and not loved,
Perjury and treachery?
I have no desire for benefits
By yielding imperfect praise
And salutations to the brotherhood.
Compared with me, no one knows anything.
I am learned in the principle sciences,
And the reasoning of astrologers
Concerning veins and solvents,
And the general nature of man.
I know the secret of composing songs of praise.
I have sung of the existence of God.
According to the saying of Talhaiarn,
For the gifted there shall be judgement,
And a judging of their qualities.
The poetic disposition
Is that which gives the secret virtue
Of a muse above mediocrity.
Seven score muses
There are in the inspiration of song;
Eight score in every score
In the great abyss of tranquillity,
In the great abyss of wrath,
In the depths below the earth,
In the air above the earth,
There is a recognition of it.
What sorrow there is,
That is better than joy.
I know the blessed gifts
Of the flowing muse;

To me it brings the rewards of skill,
To me happy days,
To me a peaceful life,
And a protection in age.
I am equal to kings, whatever their enjoyment,
I am equal with them through redemption.

And so on for another two hundred lines.

At first glance this may seem to have little meaning. But when I went back to the original Welsh, and with the help of my wife, who is an accomplished translator, began to work on a new version, I found a very different poem - or rather poems, because this is in fact a miscellany - hidden within. I also recognised that the problem with the earlier translations, was not so much that of faulty scholarship, but with a failure to recognise the real nature of the material and what the words themselves meant in the context of a larger whole.

To understand why this should be so we need to look for a moment at what is known of Taliesin himself and at the nature of the works that bear his name. Most of what we know about the great bard comes from two sources: a 16th century text called the *Hanes or* "Life" of Taliesin; and 70 poems contained in a 14th century volume known as *The Book of Taliesin* - one of the Four Ancient Books of Wales. Apart from these there are some references in the Mabinogion story of "Branwen Daughter of Llyr" and a list of famous living bards contained in the writings of the 6th century monk Nennius which includes Taliesin as among the best in the land.

It is this that helps us to date Taliesin to the 6th century - and this is supported by historical references in the poems themselves. However, although the mere fact of Taliesin's historical existence is fascinating and could lead us into some interesting areas - I want to concentrate of another Taliesin - a semi-mythical figure who is made up of a ragbag of references and memories to things that happened far earlier than the 6th century - things in fact that date back to the dim mists of antiquity, when the links between the earth and the people who lived upon it were more profound and real than at any time since. It's not a precise historical time zone, but more of a semi-mythical period when magic was taken as a matter of course and when almost anything could happen and probably did. Not that Taliesin lived in some kind of fantasy world. He was probably as real as you or I. The truth is that he, or rather his persona, became the inheritor of many of the beliefs of that time - a focus one might say for all the memories that were still locked in the subconscious minds of the people who lived in these lands both during the 6th century, and who were still half-conscious of a more primitive self as late as the 16th when the text known as Hanes Taliesin was written down.

Not that this is restricted to the Celtic world by any means - the foundations on which these stories, especially that of Taliesin rest, are built of both older and wider materials that any single culture. There are, I believe, enough references in the *Hanes Taliesin* and the poems to prove that he was the inheritor of a British shamanic tradition, and it is with the *Hanes* itself that we must begin.

In the time of Arthur there lived in the region of Llyn Tegid [Bala Lake in Wales] a nobleman named Tegid Foel [the Bald]. And he had a wife who was named Ceridwen, who was skilled in the magical arts. Tegid and Ceridwen had two children: one who was so ugly that they called him Morfran "Great Crow", but who came to be known as Afagddu "Utter Darkness", because of his extreme ugliness.

The Other child was a daughter, whose name was Creirwy, (Fair One) and she was as fair as Morfran was dark. Ceridwen thought that her son would never be accepted in the world because of his hideous looks, so she cast about for a way to empower him with wisdom, so that none would care about his appearance. And so she resolved to boil a Cauldron of Inspiration and Wisdom according to the Books of the Fferyllt, and the method of it was this: She must first gather certain herbs on certain days and hours, and put them in the Cauldron, which must then be kept boiling for a year and a day, until three drops of Inspiration were obtained. For the task of maintaining the fire beneath the Cauldron Ceridwen chose an old blind man named Morda, who was lead by a youth named Gwion Bach [Little], the son of Gwreang of Llanfair Caereinion in Powys.

At the end of the year Ceridwen stationed herself, with her son, close by the Cauldron, and there she fell asleep [alternately she is still out gathering more herbs and making incantations]. And while she slept [or was away] it happened that three drops flew out of the Cauldron and landed on the thumb of Gwion Bach, and so great was he pain therefrom that he put his thumb into his mouth and sucked it. And at once he knew all that there was to know, and foremost of that knowledge was that Ceridwen would destroy him as soon as she learned what had happened. And thus he fled. But the Cauldron gave a great cry, and cracked in two, and the waters flowed from it into a nearby stream and poisoned the horses of Gwyddno Garanhir. And Ceridwen awoke [returned] and when she saw what had occurred her anger knew no bounds. She struck the blind Morda so hard that one of his eyes fell out on his cheek, but he said that she had injured him wrongly.

Then Ceridwen knew all that had occurred and went in pursuit of Gwion, running. And he was aware of her and changed himself into the semblance of a hare; and she, perceiving that, turned herself into the semblance of a black greyhound. He ran to a rive and became a fish; and she pursued him as an otter-bitch, until he turned himself into a bird of the air and she into a hawk. Then, in fear for his life, he saw where a heap of winnowed wheat lay on the floor of a barn, and dropping amongst them, turned himself into one of the grains. Then Ceridwen turned herself into a black, red-crested hen and swallowed the grain of wheat, which went into her womb, so that she became quickened and bore Gwion in her womb for nine months. And when she gave birth to him he was so fair and beautiful that she could not bear to kill him, or to have another kill him for her, so she placed him in a leather bag [or in a bag within a coracle] and set him adrift on the sea [in a river or on a lake] on the 29th day of April [or on *Calen Gaef*, the 31st Oct].

Now there lived at that time, in the lordship of Maelgwn Gwynedd, a nobleman named Gwyddno Garanhir. He had a weir on the shore of the river Conwy [between Dyvi and Aberystwyth] close to the sea. And on every May Eve [All Hallows] he was accustomed to take from it salmon to the value of a hundred pounds. And Gwyddno had one son who was named Elffin, a hapless youth who had nothing but evil luck. Therefore his father told him that on this particular year he should have all that he could find in the weir. So Elffin went to the weir on May Eve and when he and his servants arrived they could see that there was not so much as a single salmon in the nets. Then Elffin began to lament, until one of the men with him pointed out where a leather bag hung upon a pole of the weir [or where a coracle lay in the arms of the weir]. Then Elffin took the bag from the water and cut a slit in it with his knife. And within he saw a bright forehead and cried aloud: "Behold, a radiant brow"(*tal-iesin*). And the child within the bag replied: "Tal-iesin it is!" [And it is said that he had been floating in the bag for nearly 40 years.] Thereupon Elffin took the child up and placed it before him on the crupper of his saddle and rode for home. And as he rode the child made a poem for him, which was the first poem that Taliesin made. And Elffin was filled with wonder, and asked the child how he came to compose poetry, and he so

137

young; and Taliesin replied with another poem, which was called The Life of Taliesin.

By the time he had sung it they were back at Gwyddno's court. Now when Gwyddno heard how Elffin had failed to find any salmon in the weir he bemoaned the ill luck of his son, but Elffin realised that he had from the weir something of far greater value. "And what is that?" demanded Gwyddno. "A bard" replied his son. And when Gwyddno asked how that would profit him, Taliesin himself replied: "He will get more profit from me than the weir ever gave to you." "Are you able to speak, and you so little?" demanded Gwyddno, and Taliesin replied: "I am better able to speak than you to question me." Whereupon Gwyddno asked him what more he had to say, and Taliesin replied with another song, which began: "Water possess the power to bless..."And so Elffin gave the child to his own wife to raise, which she did most lovingly. And from that day forth Elffin's luck turned, and he grew prosperous and was much favoured by his uncle Maelgwn Gwynedd.

There is more to the story, but it concerns us less here than the part I have told, which tells us a good deal about Taliesin. It says, quite clearly, that he was one of the Wondrous Children who appear regularly in Celtic myth, and who include Fionn MacCumail, Pwyll, Pryderi, Gwair, Goreu, and Mabon. Each of these was either born or obtained magical powers as children. Many, like Taliesin, were either assisted by animals or were transformed, at one time or another in animal shape - a very large pointer towards a shamanic underpinning. Later in the story Taliesin demonstrates not only his ability to perform magical acts, he also demonstrates his powers as a prophet and makes some extraordinary claims to have been in many places and times throughout history.

These boasts are echoed throughout the poetry, but we will be closer to the truth if we view these statements as elliptical references to a certain kind of inner knowledge, some which was, in fact, a product of Bardic/Shamanic initiation and training. It is this that is most clearly indicated by the *Hanes* account of Taliesin's re-birth. This whole episode is both a mishmash of stories from very ancient Celtic belief- systems, and a clear description of an initiation. There are references to this in more than one of the poems. In the Cad Goddeu or 'Battle of the Trees', for example, Taliesin says:

> *I have been in many shapes*
> *Before I assumed a consistent form.*
> *And in one of the many riddling songs he says:*
> *I am old, I am young, I am Gwion,*
> *I am universal...I am a bard.*

And in a memorable passage from the poem from which I have already quoted, 'The Hostile Confederacy', he relates:

> *A second time was I formed -*
> *I have been a blue salmon.*
> *I have been a dog;*
> *I have been a stag;*
> *I have been a roebuck on the mountain...*
> *I have been a grain discovered...*
> *A hen received me...*
> *I rested nine nights*

In her womb as a child....
I have been dead, I have been alive...
I am Taliesin.

It would be easy enough to read these as no more than mythological references, and so you may choose to do if you wish. But there is a coherence about the references that I find wholly convincing as accounts of another kind of experience - one that it is possible to see as shamanic.

It would be easy to fill the next hour or so with an account of Shamanism itself. But that is not my intention here. It must suffice to quote two writers on the subject who have contributed a great deal to our knowledge and understanding of the practice worldwide, and whose words evoke immediate parallels with the writings of the Celtic bards which we are examining here. The first is from *Dreamtime and Inner Space*, a remarkable book by Holger Kalweit, who though he is a trained anthropologist, keeps an open mind about the deeper aspects of the subject. Set alongside descriptions from Celtic records, we will at once see just how closely they resemble each other.

"The shaman is part of the age-old tradition of the Perennial Philosophy - the mystical teaching of unity of all things and all being. In the realm of magic everything is interrelated; nothing exists in isolation ... This level of consciousness, like a gigantic telephone exchange, affords access to all other realms of awareness. All mystical paths are agreed that such a way of experiencing requires a suspension of normal awareness and of rational thought by means of special techniques of mind training. An empty mind allows an alternative level of transpersonal experience."

This is the key to understanding the mysteries referred to again and again in the works attributed to Taliesin. They are by no means unique in the Celtic world, and an examination of the traditions of other figures like Taliesin would provoke a similar conclusion. However, this is to strengthen rather than weaken our case. The tradition, of which Taliesin is a prime representative, is at the heart of the Celtic world, and nowhere else is it so significantly representative of the shamanic tradition. To quote Kalweit again:

"Those that have returned from this world [the inner place of the Shaman] say that present, past, and future exist simultaneously, and that to enter this world is tantamount to enlightenment. Many people felt that in some inexplicable way they had gained total knowledge.... One person who returned said: 'It seemed that all of a sudden, all knowledge - of all that had started from the very beginning, that would go on without end - that for a second I knew all the secrets of the ages, all the meaning of the universe, the stars, the moon - of everything."

How better can we explain - if an explanation is required at all - Taliesin's extravagant claims: to have been present at the great events in the life of the cosmos, to know, literally, everything, to be familiar at once with the course of the heavens, the lives of stone and river and plant, to have penetrated so deeply into the essence of creation that he is able to state that he has been an endless number of things: a spade, a spear, a tree, a flower, a bird, a beast, a fish, a drop of water... the catalogue goes on virtually for ever.

And all of these things are part of the shaman's world. He, too, sees through everything, dies and is reborn, suffers the pangs of the world and sees into its darkest corners. As the Augustine monk Abraham of Santa Clara puts it: "Someone who dies before he dies does not die when he dies." The almost-death of initiation, the moment when Gwion becomes Taliesin, is the common experience of shamans the world over. Afterwards, they are never the same; everything has changed. They have known total knowledge and, to a degree according to their skills and strengths, have permanent access to it from that moment on. Some, like Fionn mac Cumhail, have to reactivate their wisdom through a ritual act - Fionn chews his thumb. Others, like Taliesin, seem able to command their store of knowledge at any time. It makes them unique, and it is not surprising that we find them awe inspiring today. They must have seemed so in their own time, when the understanding and appreciation of the inner realms was more generally recognised than it is now. But what is so astounding is that, in most cases, their words, where these have been recorded, still elicit a response from us today. We may not understand the poems of Taliesin at a first reading, but they speak to us at a level of which we are scarcely aware. We can still, if we wish, recover something of that original response, and of the miraculous knowledge that was part of the shamanic tradition. As we journey through the labyrinth of words which make up the Taliesin Tradition, we cannot help but be aware that we are walking in a world of crystalline wonder, a world where all things are possible and only the unexpected is to be expected.

Mircea Eliade, the greatest contemporary writer on the subject of shamanism, defines the shamanic experience as follows:

> '...in the strict sense, the mystical experience is expressed in a ....trance.....The shaman is pre-eminently an ecstatic. Now on the plane of primitive religions ecstasy signifies the soul's flight to heaven, or its wanderings about the earth, or, finally, its descent to the subterranean world...."

Shamanic abilities are generally brought on by personal crisis. However, where this was not naturally forthcoming, initiations designed to produce the effects of such a state were used to bring about this re-birth as a shaman. In the story of Taliesin, of course, this is clearly instanced by the episode of the Cauldron. Though elaborated into the form of a story, there can be little doubt that it hides a description of a shamanic initiation, in which the candidate was given a drink which caused him to undergo the kind of experience alluded to in the poems. The characteristic experience of the Shaman may be tabulated as follows:

1) He falls ill/ becomes unconscious/ecstatic
2) He encounters otherworld personages
3) He enters the otherworld itself
4) He journeys there for some time
5) He receives teachings
6) He faces dangers/ initiations
7) He returns "to life" at the moment he left

Each and every one of these points are encountered in the Taliesin tradition. In the form that they have come down to us the poems still record Taliesin's original experiences, overlaid by layers of complex manuscript transference. However, traces of their original shape and substance can still be observed when one looks at the poems line by line and verse by verse. If we take a brief sampling of quotations from various of the poems:

I have become a predicting Bard...
I have been with skilful men,

With Math and Govannon,
With Eunydd and Elestron...

I have been a sow, I have been a buck,
I have been a sage, I have been a snout,
I have been a horn, I have been a wild sow,
I have been a shout in battle...

I have been a cat with a speckled head on three trees
I have been a well-filled crane-bag, a sight to behold.
I am a harmonious one; I am a clear singer;
I am steel, I am a Druid.
I am an artificer, a scientist;
I am a serpent [of wisdom]; I am love...
I am the depository of song...

Three times I have been born, I know by meditation;
Anyone would be foolish not to come and obtain
All the sciences of the world from my breast.
For I know what has been, what in future will occur.
I know all the names of the stars from North to South;
I have been in the galaxy at the throne of the Distributor
I have been three periods in the Prison of Arianrhod..
I am a wonder whose origin is not known.
I have obtained the muse from the Cauldron of Ceridwen...

I have been an instructor to all intelligences,
I am able to instruct the whole universe.
I shall be until the day of doom on the face of the earth;
Nor is it known if my body is flesh or fish.
Firstly I was formed in the shape of a handsome man,
In the hall of Ceridwen where I was refined.
Though small and modest in my behaviour,
I became great in her lofty sanctuary.
While I was held prisoner, sweet inspiration educated me
And laws were imparted to me in speech without words;
But I had to flee from the angry, terrible hag
Whose outcry was terrifying.
Conspicuous when came from the cauldron
The three inspirations of Ceridwen...

And so on. All totally in line with the role of the shaman, who must know the heavens, the gods and the secrets of the elements, who must use all of his senses, including instinct and feeling, to act as a bridge between this world and the other. Three times, Taliesin tells us, he has been a prisoner in the court of Arianrhod, which is also the Northern Crown, the Corona Borealis - and now he is able to instruct all creatures, indeed the whole of the universe. He has learned the secrets of transformation, he has dwelled in the Court of Ceridwen and drunk from her Cauldron - in other words he has received initiation and is able to prophecy all the things that will be as well as knowing all the things that were.

The most important single aspect of Shamanism is at-one-ment with the Otherworld. All shamans are in touch with an inner self who is wiser, stronger, more balanced than they may appear in their normal selves. Trance states are used a great deal to keep in touch with the spirit world, including chant, drumming, and various hallucinatory substances. Drumming, the most commonly practised way of entering trance, does not seem to have been part of Celtic practice, despite the use of the bodhran by contemporary folk musicians, which seems to have no ancient tradition attached to it. Instead perhaps they relied upon a variety of methods that induced the trance state- including both a consciousness-altering drink and the use of darkness and light - what today we would terms sensory deprivation.

All shamans possess unique abilities to enter and leave the spirit world. Celtic literature abounds with descriptions of this place - descriptions that possess so many common elements that they could only derive from the very deepest levels of consciousness.

Amongst the various attributes of the shaman discussed by Eliade is the pole (originally from a tent) used by most Siberian shamans to represent the Centre of the Universe or the Cosmic Tree. Whilst climbing this the shaman would pause at various points to describe what he saw, each level representing a further stage in a voyage to an Otherworldly state of being. Similarly, the many stories of Immrama "voyages", from island to island across uncharted seas, represented a kind of map of the soul's voyage through life. In Ancient Egypt the same idea was current in the journey of the soul after death, in the Boat of Millions of Years.

The Celtic view of the otherworld is extraordinarily detailed. Perhaps in no other part of the world do so many full and varied descriptions exist that we can actually tabulate them and relate them to different states of being. David Spaan, in his study of the *Otherworld in Early Irish Literature* lists over a hundred different names for the Otherworld. The three central divisions were into the Otherworldly Paradise, which is usually situated on an island; the Land-Beneath-the-Sea, and the Underworld, which centred mainly on the lands beneath the various sidhe mounds. All three are at once very distinctive and yet so mutable in outline that they often overlap or blur into each other in a bewildering way.

The Underworld, pictured by Taliesin himself, seems a place where he felt utterly at home:

My chair is in Caer Siddi,
Where no one is afflicted with age or illness.
Manawyddan and Pryderi have known it well.
It is surrounded by three circles of fire.
To the borders of the city come the ocean's flood,
A fruitful fountain flows before it,
Whose liquor is sweeter than the finest wine."

In keeping with the poet's laconic style, he tells us of his own sojourn in the Otherworld, from where his poetic spirit (his Chair) comes. It is not difficult to imagine the shaman-poet conducting his listeners through the stages of the Otherworld in this way, climbing the world- tree, leaving them with

142

a series of magical images upon which to draw.

As already mentioned, another aspect of the world-wide shamanic tradition is the use of substances which cause the consciousness of the individual to loose its identity in a world of extraordinary inner vision. In the poem just quoted: "The Chair of Taliesin" the poet gives some {if not all} the ingredients of just such a sacred drink, which was imbibed by all who underwent the rigorous ceremonial which resulted in a series of visions. In Taliesin's case, this took the form of transformations into bird, beast and fish, just as we heard in the story of Gwion. Later, we may suppose, further self-induced trances gave him access to the pattern of history - hence his ability to be "present" at events which took place elsewhere in space and time, and which made him, effectively, into a seer and prophet.

This is all in line with my earlier statement - that the character of Taliesin became a repository for an age-old common tradition, shared in part by all initiates. We can learn more of his particular role from two sources: the Branwen story already mentioned and a poem contained in *The Book of Taliesin*, which has become perhaps his best known work. This is the *Preiddeu Annwn* or "Raid on Annwn", the Celtic Otherworld, lead by Arthur. In both texts the objective of the search is a cauldron with special properties that relate it to the Cauldron of Ceridwen from which Taliesin of course received his wisdom.

Preiddeu Annwn

In Caer Siddi Gwair's prison was readied,
As Pwyll and Pryderi foretold,
None before went there save he,
Where the heavy chains bound him.
Before the spoiling of Annwn he sang forever
This eternal invocation of poets:
Save only seven, none returned from Caer Siddi.

Since my song resounded in the turning Caer,
I am pre-eminent. My first song
Was of the Cauldron itself.
Nine maidens kindled it with their breath -
Of what nature was it?
Pearls were about its rim,
Nor would it boil a coward's portion.
Lleminawg thrust his flashing sword
Deep within it;
And before dark gates, a light was lifted.
When we went with Arthur - a mighty labour -
Save only seven, none returned from Caer Fedwydd.

I am pre-eminent
Since my song resounded
In the four-square city,
In the Island of the Strong Door.
The light was dim and mixed with darkness,

Though bright wine was set before us.
Three shiploads of Prydwen went with Arthur -
Save only seven, none returned from Caer Rigor.

Worth more am I than the clerks
Who have not seen Arthur's might
Beyond Caer Siddi.
Six thousand stood on its walls -
It was hard to speak with their leader.
Three shiploads of Prydwen went with Arthur -
Save seven only, none returned from Caer Goludd.

I merit more than empty bards
Who know not the day, the hour or the moment
When the chick was born;
Who have not journeyed
To the courts of heaven;
Who know nothing of the meaning
Of the starry-collared ox
With seven score links in his collar.
When we went with Arthur - that sorrowful journey -
Save seven only, none returned from Manawyddan's Caer.

I know more forever than the weak-willed clerks
Who know not the day of the king's birth,
Nor the nature of the beast they guard for him.
When we went with Arthur - lamentable day -
Save only seven, none returned from Caer Achren.

This is all most mysterious and repays more study than we have time for here. For the moment we should notice the references to the imprisoned youth, Gwair, the Cauldron warmed by the breath of 9 muses, the visits to the 7 mysterious Cares, and of course the fact that Taliesin is among the 7 who return "from Caer Siddi".

One possible explanation of this curious text may be found in the story of Branwen, which is also about a mysterious Cauldron. Bran, who is himself a god-figure, possesses a wondrous vessel that has the property of bringing the dead to life when they are placed within it - though they come forth dumb and unable to speak of what they have seen. When one of Bran's brothers, Evnissien, causes insult to the King of Ireland, Bran gives him, by way of recompense, this same cauldron, which had, in fact originally come from Ireland. The story of its discovery is especially interesting.

One day when Matholwch (the King of Ireland) was hunting near the Lake of the Cauldron, he saw a huge yellow- haired man coming from the Lake with a cauldron on his back. A woman followed him, who was also of great size. And because she was with child and the couple had nowhere to live, Matholwch invited them to return with him to his court. He soon regretted this, because the woman gave birth not to one child but to hundreds - one every month in fact, and every one a fully armed warrior. Needless to say this made them very unpopular, especially as their general behaviour was also terrible. Matholwch soon tried to get rid of them, having a specially built house prepared, made of iron, which was sealed as soon as the couple entered and its walls heated until they glowed white. But the terrible couple broke out and fled, taking the Cauldron with them. When they arrived in Britain, Bran received them using the woman's seemingly endless reproductive ability to garrison fortresses all over the land. Later on in the same story, when Bran and Matholwch are in conflict, the Irish use the Cauldron to restore their dead warriors, and it is only finally broken when Evnissien, who had caused all the trouble to begin with, crawls inside and stretches himself out, killing himself in the process. Of that fateful war only seven men escaped, including Taliesin.

Now if we look beneath the surface of this story it can be used to explain a number of things from both the Preiddeu Annwn and the Hanes Taliesin. Although the giant couple are called by other names in the Branwen text, they are clearly reflections of Tegid Voel and his wife Ceridwen. She herself was originally a goddess of gestation and birth, a Mountain Mother who in some stories is seen as letting fall from her skirt great stones that become mountains and hills.

The endless stream of warriors born by her confirm this identification, and it is perhaps possible to see the Cauldron itself as a symbolic womb - from which not only is life given, but also knowledge, wisdom, the awen or inspiration of the Poet. When the Cauldron is in the hands of other men, they are unable to create life, only restore those who were dead.

It is also clear that at some stage in the transmission of the various tales which went into the making of Branwen the original story concerned a voyage to capture the fabled cauldron of Rebirth and Inspiration, and that Taliesin, as an initiate of its secrets (they called themselves The Cauldron-Born) of course went along, and was, naturally enough, one of the seven - a mystic number - who returned from the Otherworld to tell the tale.

Taliesin is, then, someone who has access to the kind of knowledge which enables him to travel and return from the Otherworld. He experiences self-induced trances that give him insight into events both past and future. He is closely connected with a probable cult of initiates who traced their source of inspiration to the Goddess Ceridwen, who was the possessor of a cauldron from which Taliesin was said to have been reborn. He thus resembles in several points the shamans of other cultures, who also had the ability to visit the otherworld, who had visions of past and future, and who underwent various forms of initiation in which they were "re- born" with extended powers and deepened knowledge.

Taliesin, we remember, imbibes the wisdom of the Cauldron when he places his burned thumb into his mouth. This simple fact hides a maze of references to kinds of prophetic inspiration by the Celts and which are not limited to the story and writings of Taliesin. The principle character that shares this mode of magical transmission is the Irish hero Fionn mac Cumhail, who is sometimes called a poet, but who certainly possesses wisdom at least in some ways equal to that of Taliesin.

The story of Fionn's childhood, and his acquiring of wisdom is told in an Irish text The Boyhood Exploits of Fionn, which has been dated to the 10th century - though, as with the Taliesin material, the story it tells dates from a much earlier period.

At a certain juncture in his life Fionn went to learn poetry from Finneces (White Wisdom) who lived on the shores of the river Boyne, and who had been seeking for the Salmon of Wisdom that swam in Fec's Pool for seven years, since it had been prophesied that he would find it, eat it and know everything. However, when it was found, Finneces entrusted its cooking to Fionn who, though cautioned to eat nothing of the fish, nevertheless thrust his burnt thumb into his mouth when it was splashed by some of the liquor in which the salmon was cooked. So it was the boy, not Finneces, who received the wisdom of the salmon. The old poet immediately recognised the boy as Fionn, (The Fair One) naming him as the prophesied receiver of wisdom. In aftertimes, Fionn had only to put his thumb into his mouth to have prophetic knowledge.

At this point I would like to posit the existence of a figure that we shall call 'The Celtic Shaman'. We have already seen something of the evidence for his existence. What can we find in Celtic literature concerning his practice? If he is to conform to the nature of word-wide shamanism, he must be able to journey between the worlds, encounter and speak with spirits, and foretell the future.

In fact an image of the Celtic shaman stares back at us from one of the most familiar icons of the Celtic world - a relief from one of the inner panels of the Gundestrup Cauldron. It shows a man in a pose traditionally assumed by shamans the world over, cross-legged, upright, staring forth at a world only he can see. On his head are antlers, which may be seen either as a headdress, or as actually growing from his head. He is surrounded by beasts of all kinds, the spirit helpers which enable him to enter and travel unharmed through the realm of the Otherworld, and in his left hand he grasps the head of a serpent, a creature long associated with wisdom and magic. The name of this figure, long accepted by historians, archaeologists and mythographers alike, is "The Lord of the Beasts". He appears dramatically in several texts, nowhere perhaps as vividly as the following account from "The Lady of the Fountain", one of the stories contained in the medieval collection of Welsh myths and legends knows as The Mabinogion. In this the hero Cynon relates the story of his adventures, in which, having entered an obvious Otherworldly place and met with one of its denizens, he is instructed to go into a wood and there follow a path to a large sheltered glade with a mound in the centre.

"And thou wilt see a black man of great stature on top of the mound. He is not smaller in size than two men of this world. He has but one foot; and one eye in the middle of his forehead. And he has a club of iron, and it is certain that there are no two men in the world who would not find their burden in that club. And he is not a comely man, but on the contrary he is exceedingly ill favoured; and he is the woodward of that wood. And thou wilt see a thousand wild animals grazing around him...."

Cynon follows these instructions, and there, as foretold, encounters the strange figure of the woodward:

'Huge of stature as the man had told me that he was, I found him to exceed by far the description he had given me.... And he only spoke to me in answer to my questions. Then I asked him what power he held over those animals. "I will show thee, little man" said he. And he took his club in his hand and with it struck a stag a great blow so that it brayed vehemently, and at his braying the animals came together, as numerous as the stars in the sky, so that it was difficult for me to find room in the glade to stand among them. There were serpents, and dragons, and divers sorts of animals. And he looked at them, and bade them go and feed; and they bowed their heads and did him homage as vassals to their lord."

This whole passage is rife with shamanic overtones. It is clearly a very primitive story, despite the fact that it was not recorded until the Middle Ages. The depiction of the figure with one eye and one foot derives from a manner of casting a spell, in which the shaman or magician would stand upon one leg, with one hand behind his back and one eye tightly closed, before uttering his incantation. In Siberian tradition there are references to the birth of the shaman, where the Mother of Animals, who is responsible for all shaman, gives them, new-born - that is into their shamanic abilities - into the keeping of a spirit named *Burgestez-Udagan*, who has one eye, one hand and one leg. This clearly relates to an ancient idea of the shamanic initiator being hideous, just as Ceridwen is supposed to be. The fact that the figure is also black denotes his connection with the earth and with the underworld. Like all shamans he only answers when questioned directly. He is a master of beasts, including serpents and dragons - both of which are depicted on the Gundestrup Cauldron. His method of summoning the animals, by striking the stag so that it in turn calls the rest, seems to relate to an earlier scenario in which the shaman probably adopted the skin and antlers of the stag and summoned them by calling in the language of the beasts.

In a passage immediately following the one quoted above, the woodward instructs Cynon that if he would seek adventure he should go to a certain very tall tree in the midst of an open space "whose branches are greener than the greenest pine tree",

> *"Under this tree is a fountain, and by the side of the fountain is a marble slab, and on the marble slab a silver bowl, attached by a chain of silver, so that it may not be carried away. Take the bowl and throw a bowlful of water upon the slab, and thou wilt hear a mighty peal of thunder, so that thou wilt think that heaven and earth are trembling with its fury. With the thunder will come a shower so severe that it will be scarce possible for thee to endure it and live. And the shower will be of hailstones; and after the shower the weather will become fair, but every leaf that was on the tree will have been carried away by the shower. Then a flight of birds will come and alight upon the tree; and in thine own country thou didst never hear a strain so sweet as that which they will sing...."*

This whole passage reads like an account of a shamanic initiation. First Cynon must go to a great tree in the midst of a glade. This equates very closely to the idea of the World-Tree common to all shamanic beliefs. There he finds a silver vessel that may well have been a cauldron of the kind from which inspiration and knowledge were derived. Then he is instructed in the uses of weather magic that invokes a storm of hail so fierce that it will almost destroy him. Finally there is the wonderful image of the tree, stripped of its leaves, suddenly clothed again in the living bodies of birds, whose song is the sweetest he will ever have heard. Accounts of Shamanic visions abound with such descriptions, and the birds themselves are found throughout Celtic myth as the bringers of inspiration, or as conductors of the seeker into the Otherworld. Coming so close upon the description of the Lord of the Beasts, it can hardly be co-incidental, and we can only believe that we are reading a very ancient description, preserved in folk-memory, of real shamanic activity.

We can see from this that the references to what I have described as a 'shamanic' tradition are not limited to Taliesin alone - though even if this were the case it would remain a fascinating example of the preservation of a genuinely ancient tradition. Fortunately, there are a number of other examples that strengthen the case even further. Most are from the traditions that surround the origins and writings of the Celtic bards, and they lead me to believe that this body of people retained the last vestiges of a far more ancient tradition.

If we return to the poem by Taliesin with which we began we should have sufficient understanding of its shamanic content to understand it better. Editing out the other poems that had been mistakenly copied down as a single work, and interpreting the language in the light of the shamanic tradition, we are left with a work every bit as exciting and vital as any acknowledged great work of literature.

The Hostile Conspiracy

I am a wiseman of the primal knowledge,
I am an experienced astrologer,
I pronounce anger, I pronounce solutions...

I know the law
of fertile inspiration
when it is skilfully tuned to those happy days,
to a quiet life,
to the defence of the times,
to kings of whom long is the consolation
to the things which are on the face of the earth.

It is difficult to perform
such a task on a new instrument.
Why is the harp-string lamenting?
Why does the cuckoo lament? Why does it sing?
I know it as I know many pleasant things.
I know why Geraint and Arman
abandoned their camp, I know when the spark
of hardness works from the stones,
I know why the honeysuckle smells good,
why crows are the colour of silence.

I know the cup from which the wave has overflowed.
I know the end of the dawn.
I know who has preached
To Eli and Aneas.
I know the cuckoos of summer,
I know where they go in winter.
The inspiration that I sing
I have brought up from the depths.

Like a river it flows,
I know its length,
I know when it disappears,
I know when it refills,
I know when it overflows,
I know when it disappears,
I know which foundation
there is under the sea.
I know its measure,
I know everything that surrounds it.

I know how numerous are the hours of the day,
I know how numerous are the days in the year,
how numerous are the spears in battle,
how numerous are the drops of a shower
gently dispersing....
I know all the craft of Gwydion who made great mockery and nearly a disgrace.
I know who it is
who fills the river....
I know who averts
the present questions.
I know with what enduring patience
the sky was raised.
When the great knowledge of the stars is imparted
then will be understood every high thing.

I know when the spirit is working,
when the sea is pleasant,
when the race is valiant, when the most high is implored.
I know the extent over the earth
of the sun which shines upon us,
I know when the bird of anger goes to its rest -
the bird of anger goes to its nest
when the earth becomes green.

I know the number of the winds and streams,
I know the number of the streams and winds,
how many are its rivers.
I know size of the earth
and its thickness.
I know the sound of blades
reddened on all sides under the sun,
I know the Regulator
of the Heavens and of the Earth.

I know why a hill resounds,
I know why devastators win land,
I know why the vault of silver is restored,
why breath is black,
why it is better so,
why the valley is radiant.

I know why the cow is horned, why a wife is loving,
why milk is white,

why holly is green,
why the goat is bearded,
why the parsnip is crested,
why the wheel is round,
why the mallet is flat,
why the kid is speckled,
why salt is in brine,
why beer is a lively medium...

I know why the alder is purple coloured,
why the linnet is green,
why hips are red,
why a woman is never still,
why night comes,
I know the nature of the flood
but no-one knows why the interior of the sun is red.
I know who made the great pole
which connects earth and heaven,
I know the number of fingers in the cauldron.
I know what name of two words
will never be taken from the cauldron.

I know why the ocean rolls about us,
why fish are silent -
of sea food will their flesh be,
until the time when it will be transformed
when the fish will constrain the sea.
I know that the white swan's foot is black,
I know that the sharp spear is four-sided,
I know that the heavenly races are unfallen,
I know that there are four elements
(But I do not know their end).
I know the wanderings of the boar and the deer...

A second time was I created.
I have been a blue salmon,
I have been a dog, I have been a deer,
I have been a roebuck on the mountain,
I have been a trunk, I have been a beech,
I have been an axe in the hand,
I have been a pin in the tongs.

For a year and half,
I have been a white speckled cock,

among the hens of Dun Eiddyn.
I have been a stallion at stud,
I have been a battling bull,
I have been a yellow goat.
 Fecund and nourishing,
I have been a grain discovered
growing on a hill.
The Harvester took me
to free my essence
in a place full of smoke.

I have known great suffering;
a red hen took me,
she had red wings and a double comb;
I rested nine months
As a child in her belly.
 I have been matured,
I have been offered to a king,
I have been dead, I have been alive...

I am Taliesin
and I defend the true lineage
until the end of time
to the profit of Elffin.

This is a catalogue, not only of knowledge, but also of shamanic wisdom and understanding. Its author understood the rhythms of the seasons, the mystery of life itself, and had travelled deeply into the very fabric of creation. He is in absolute harmony with the natural world. This remarkable poem is filled with a sense of elemental power. Taliesin is master of the weather, of winds and waves; he has the strength of the bull, the keenness of sight that belongs to the hawk, the wisdom of the salmon, who has swum in the Pool of Knowledge; and he knows the way to and from the Places of Peace - that is the Faery Mounds - where he has learned to wield the fire of inspiration that burns in the head. He is wise also, in the lore of the heavens, knowing the ages of the moon, the rising and setting of the sun, and the dancing of the stars in the heavens. He wields air, water, fire and earth, and binds all to him through the elemental fire of his inspiration. All of these abilities are those of the worldwide shamanic traditions.

In my view, we can no longer ignore the evidence of these and other writings, which show the Celts as possessing a profoundly shamanic culture, and which we may still see, recorded in the writings that have survived.

(1997)

Chapter 17:

THE DANCING VISIONARY

Shamanism is the oldest spiritual discipline of which we have any knowledge and at one time it was practiced all over the world. Together with my wife Caitlin, I have done a great deal to establish the existence of a Shamanic tradition in Britain and throughout the Celtic world. I have now been teaching Shamanism for more than ten years and have seen hundreds of students though the first stages of a path that has the power to change their lives forever. I have watched them glow and learn and seen the light of joy dawn in their eyes as they discovered for themselves the wonder and wisdom to which they are granted access. The talk that follows was first given at the University of Seattle, where I was invited to speak to a class of psychology students in 1997. For more about the classes in Shamanic practice offered by us visit our website at Hallowquest.org.uk

Shamanism at the End of the 20th Century

The Way of the Shaman is just about as old as time itself. We have only to look at the ancient rock paintings, dating from the Palaeolithic era to see this. There we see the dancing, dreaming, journeying figures, who travel between the worlds and bring news of the subtle realms of soul and spirit; the wounded hero who tends to the spiritual needs of the tribe and watches over the physical, psychological and interior health of every individual. Later, in the writings of anthropologists who studied shamans still practising in tribal cultures at the dawn of the 19th century, we can read accounts of the astonishing abilities and visions of these people, showing that things had changed little over the millennia, and that their concerns were still with the soul's health and in establishing a balanced relationship with deity and with its expression in the living universe. In more recent times we have been privileged to read the words of various native practitioners who have offered first-hand accounts of their work. Finally, in the last few years, we have seen an extraordinary upsurge of interest in shamanism as everything from an emerging pattern of holistic living to a technique for healing many kinds of sickness.

Many varieties of shamanism have surfaced, and many claims have been made. You have probably read, or heard, a dozen different definitions, and as many refutations, of the word shaman, and what it means to 'be', a shaman. And the truth is, that probably most of those definitions - and the refutations - are right. Shamanism is, by its nature, difficult to define - though we can say a good deal about what the shaman is, and does. One thing in particular has remained constant through the ages - the work of the shaman takes place in the realm of the spirit, and the work which is done - healing work, divination, practical magic - concerns the health or otherwise of the soul and the links between the human soul and what we may term the soul of the planet - or the soul of the land if we want to bring it down to a more manageable size. It is also concerned with the balancing, the re-harmonising of the division between spirit and matter, between the inner and the outer, and between what we perceive as 'real' and 'not real'. The task of the shaman is one of healing, not merely the physical body but the soul, and to preserve the connection between the human psyche and the elemental word in which it found its home.

Many descriptions exist of what a shaman is and what he, or she, does (the word is non-general in its application). What to one person is shamanic, to another is not. The word ' shaman' happens currently to be a buzzword, and you'll find it on the covers and title pages of numerous books that have little or nothing to do with the subject. Even among serious practitioners it is often misapplied, and others take it to be no more than a nod in the direction of a current fashion. The word just happens to have been chosen from among a number of others by 19th century anthropologists, to describe a phenomenon of which they were becoming increasingly aware. Other, equally appropriate names could have been: *Babalawo* (Yoruba), *Angakok* (Esquimaux) *Kami* (Mongolian), *Sangoma* (Zulu), or *Bomoh* (Malay).

Indeed the use of the word is loaded down with a freight of received meanings that can often be misleading and are often applied with little or no genuine understanding of the concepts or practices involved.   To set the record straight - or at least straighter - let me say that the word 'shaman' comes from the dialect of the Tungusc peoples of North-Eastern Europe. The original sense of the word was probably 'to catch fire' or 'to burn with the fire of divine inspiration'. This perfectly describes the ecstatic nature of the shamanic experience, which literally burns through the ordinary view of existence and shows us a very different reality underneath.

When I began lecturing and teaching shamanic practices a few years ago, if I asked 'how many people here know how to journey?' maybe two or three would have raised their ands. Now, the majority seem to have experienced some form of shamanic journeying, whether learned from Indigenous tribal teachers or from what have been termed 'neo-shamans'. It is the reasons for this extraordinary upsurge of interest in the subject that concerns me here. I believe that Shamanism offers us one of the clearest and most effective ways of surviving not only the coming millennium but also the unknown reality of the 21st century, and that it is a - not always acknowledged - awareness of this which has brought about this current resurgence.

Shamanism is, by its nature, timeless. Most of what the shaman does takes place in the realm of the spirit, where there is no time. So that to say that the spirits are concerned for our well being in the 21st century is to some extent meaningless. However, what is very clear, both from my own personal experience and that of the hundreds of students with whom I have worked over the last few years- is that there are those in the spirit world who do care about us, and who recognise a lasting and powerful link between themselves and us.

This probably requires a certain degree of suspension of disbelief. We have not generally been taught to believe in disincarnate beings, and there is still a tendency to interiorise the experiences of journeywork and to ascribe it to the realm of the imagination. One of the most frequent reactions of the students I teach is to say, having completed a shamanic journey, is: 'That was a wonderful experience, but of course it's only my imagination.' Only my imagination - how sad those words always makes me feel. Because, the truth is hat the imagination is the most powerful magical tool we possess. It literal means 'to image forth', to give shape to the otherwise unknowable.

What happens when we journey is that we enter a different place - call it a parallel universe if you like - which is subject to its own laws and where the only thing you can expect is the unexpected. Our imaginations filter what we see, giving it a form that is acceptable to us. I can give you an example of

153

this from my own experience. For a number of years now I have had a relationship with an inner teacher whom I call Taliesin - he has a lot to do with how I came to be teaching Shamanism at all. I have a very clear sense of what he looks like, and a very aural impression of his voice. I had never thought to question this until David Spangler asked me if I had ever asked Taliesin what he really looked like. The next time I was in contact with him I asked this very question. In answer he simply 'peeled off' the outer body that I was used to seeing, revealing an amorphous shape of light. 'You see', he told me, "I take the form you usually perceive because you are comfortable with that. If I showed myself as simply light would you be as willing to listen to what I had to say?' I had to admit that I might not. The point being that, between my imaginative faculty and the design of my inner helper, an image had been generated which I could believe in. It was not something I had made up, invented, imagined in the way that we usually think if we use that word. Taliesin, then as now, is a very real being, utterly separate from me and expressing views that I would never hold. It was he who finally set my feet on the path to what I now teach - Celtic shamanism - though he himself has said (just to show you we don't always agree) that this is only another convenient tag with which to describe something that has been there from the beginning of time, and which will, in all probability, be there until the end of time.

So, what exactly does it mean to follow the way of the shaman? A recent writer on the subject summed it up very well as, 'An awakening to other orders of reality, the experience of ecstasy, and an opening up of visionary realms." (Halifax: Shaman)

This constitutes the primary functions of the shaman. I believe that each of these abilities is a necessary part of he human condition, and that each is needed if we are to continue beyond the millennium in any positive sense. In this instance shamanism can be seen as a science of survival, a way of making sense of the cosmos, and of bringing some kind of order into it. By this I don't mean that it restates the old idea that mankind has some kind of divine authority over the universe - far from it. What I do man here is that if we live in a chaotic way, at variance with the rest of creation, we can only end up suffering from an even greater sense of separation - a division between ourselves and the soul of the planet - and that shamanism offers us a way of restoring the ancient harmony of life, of making us once again part of the cosmos that gave us birth.

That there are many levels and degrees of shamanism is beyond question. Go to any of the major cultural areas of the world and you will find - just below the surface or hidden in plain sight - either a thriving shamanic community, or the remains of such a one. The commonality of experience within these various communities, suggesting a global network far more complex than the electronic networks that dominate so much of our lives, can be traced back to the primordial roots of our existence. The very simplicity, the directness of the experience from which shamanism grew, are what make it so vital. Shamans learned at the breast of the mother, from the dawn of creation, and from their own ancestors; they carry the encoded knowledge and wisdom of that primal time with them even today.

Shamans work equally in the realm of the spirit and in the outer world, and are able to dialogue with beings to whom the story of our existence seems as nothing, and who have perhaps already moved beyond the boundaries of time and space. From this perspective the idea of the millennium is as brief as the blink of an eye or a thought in the mind of God. By looking beyond the transitory moment in which we find ourselves, we enter a transcendental place from which we can perceive ourselves more clearly and with less of a sense of importance. We can - with a little prompting - see the division that has grown up between ourselves and the cosmos that brought us into being. And, we can even begin to see some ways in which to restore the primal sense of 'completeness' that began to dissolve from the moment we took our first shaky steps into 'history'.

And yet, this vast Shamanic overview is somehow made immensely personal. Though we may at times find ourselves carried to dizzy heights of realisation, or to the most profound of visionary states, yet we never loose touch with the simple fact of being human, of living on this blue-green ball of mud and rock and algae in an obscure corner of an obscure galaxy. There is no room for self-aggrandisement in shamanism. One simply acknowledges that there is work to do and, hopefully, gets on with it. If we do not, the spirits have their own ways of making life uncomfortable until we buckle down and get things done.

So, what is the purpose of all this? Why should these unearthly beings take the trouble to work with us anyway? As far as I can see - and I am by no means suggesting that I have the only answer to this question, simply that, based on my own experience, and on that of the many others with whom I have talked - the intention seems to be that we become re-aligned with the universe, that we find our way (to use an image which confronts us again and again in so many of the world's major religions) to Paradise. And, that when any one of us does so, not only does life becomes simpler and more comfortable for them, our helpers, but, by extension, for ourselves.

By Paradise I don't mean a kind of never-never land, a dream-place which has no links with the outer world in which we live out or lives, but a very real, very concrete place where we can find our roots and restore to ourselves the sense of direction and wholeness that is our rightful heritage. Joan Halifax, a writer who has explored the depths of shamanism both from a historical and a personal level, points out that many of the mythologies of the world speak of a time before time in which

'the cosmos had total access to itself. There was one language for all creatures and elements, and humankind shared that language. With the passage of time, the conditions of Paradise diminished … [But] Although the common language was lost, all phenomena in the cosmos are still interrelated, and the action of the human elements profoundly effect the state of nature and the spirit." (Shaman, p11)

One might say that the modern shaman's task is to re-learn that language of the cosmos, so that we can converse again with everything from a rock to a tiger, and learn what they have to tell us. If what we do as shamans is no more than this, we will have done something to insure that we survive the opening of the doors to the next millennium more or less in charge of our soul's journey, and that what we do with the wherever time is left to us - a moment in the life of the cosmos - is at least meaningful and at best magnificent.

Joan Halifax has also written powerfully on the importance of the Shaman's work in our time, and the effect it has on our joint consciousness:

"Even as the old gods are diminishing, the seers and prophets of the ancient times are yet alive; and for a brief period, a decade, perhaps two, we can embrace the entire sacred history of our planet before it dissolves in the powerful presence of the biochemical, trans-industrial age that is now upon us. Tens of thousands of years of history, yet alive, but predictably to die - and this century is the threshold of its passing. And so we turn our heads to regard our living heritage, perhaps for the last time, to explore the lifeways transmitted to us from the healer-priests of the Palaeolithic, to know their traditions, and to be introduced to the lineage of primordial visionaries that is perhaps coming to an end -or perhaps is to be renewed in a form not yet fully known." (Shaman)

Thomas Moore, in his wise book *Care of the Soul* expresses as similar idea in a telling phrase: 'we have replaced secret wisdom with information." At the present time we have access to more information that an any other period in history. By the pressing of a switch or the click of a computer mouse button, we can summon the collective knowledge of our race. But, do we gave access to wisdom? By putting everything in full view have we not lost great deal? Ultimately, I think, wisdom is a hidden thing - hidden because too great an access to knowledge freezes us. To put it another way, we need to be initiated, step-by-step, into the hidden mysteries of life. To be simply tossed all the information in one huge package is to be overwhelmed, paralysed. This is why we still need shamans, those who can enter into the realm of wisdom and knowledge and return with enough for our present needs, nurturing our souls as well as our intellects.

Our soul-life had been much neglected in recent times, and it is only in the last few years that we have begun to observe this fact and to attempt to do something about it. The current interest in Shamanism derives from the same need as that which has fuelled the current spate of books about the soul. Thomas Moore, Robert Sardello and others have spearheaded this, but like yet another current interest, in story, these all underlay a deeper, spiritual need -to be restored to wholeness, and to find a way back to the realm of the spirit, even to that paradisal state which, at the very root of our inner selves, we feel is rightfully ours.

The effects of this realisation is to fill us with a kind of rapture - a state of being that, as Mercia Eliade pints it in his seminal study of shamanism, is a common factor in all human experience. We have all been transported, at some time in our life, into a state of ecstasy - whether from the experience of love, or the effect of viewing a great work of art or listening to a great piece of music. Shamanism seeks to prolong that experience and to make it accessible at any time. The shaman enters into a state of ecstatic awareness, in which he senses are heightened, and in which he or she becomes one with everything. This enables her to travel a will into any part of creation, and to feel and experience with the sense of the rock, or the wave, or the beetle. It is this that enables the 6th century shaman-poet Taliesin to write:

I have been a blue salmon,
I have been a dog, I have been a deer.
I have been a goat on the mountain,
I have been the trunk of a beech tree,
I have been an axe in the hand,
I have been a pin in the tongs...

He is referring to the sense of identification with everything that occurs when the shaman makes a journey into the realm of subtle reality, where one literally 'becomes' everything and anything - tree, rock, cloud, deer, salmon, buffalo, gnat, mouse, spade, candle - whatever the experience that is required or sought.

And, most importantly, this is an experience that can be accessed without the use of mind-altering drugs (though these are still utilised by shamans in some cultures). We already possess the ability to reach the state of ecstasy that enables us to become part of the universal equation again - most of the time we live outside it, in self-imposed exile. The sense of coming home experienced when we return to this state is so powerful, and has been so widely reported, that to doubt its veracity is to doubt our own existence.

It is from this place - call it an inner sate or an actual concrete reality -that the shaman operates,

156

bringing healing, a re-awareness of the numinous and a sense of re-connection to the soul. It is from here that he or she undertakes the most profound elemental journeys, travelling up and down and around the world-tree of shamanic tradition, accompanied by spirits who take the form of human teachers, animal helpers, faery beings, otherworld gods and goddesses, heroes, heroines, cosmic travellers, and many more.

All of this strikes a deep and resonant cord at a fundamental level of human nature. We recognise these experiences, feel a growing sense of familiarity with the shape of the universe, and, slowly but surely, we begin to regain a sense of wholeness and balance which is instinctively recognisable as our rightful state of being.

In the spiritual reality from which the shaman works we find her at the Centre. It is from this vantage point, this deep awareness that everything flows - outward to the edge, inward again to the centre, in an endless tidal flow of imagery and sensual awareness. Every part of the shaman is engaged - every sense flows with energy, with power, and with a visionary acumen that we can seldom, if ever, attain in a state of 'ordinary' reality. Living at the centre enables the shaman to interact with what we might term the DNA of the cosmos - at a level that enables changes to occur at a sub-atomic level. The New Science, as it has been called, is in effect as old as time or older. The realisations, which are only now becoming part of our understanding of the universe, are no more than contemporary re-statements of truths which the first shamans experienced with the familiarity of old friends.

It is a truism to say that we all lived 'closer to the earth' in the past. But truism or not it is how things were. And it is just as true to say that we have come an immense distance from that time. Should we actively seek to return to that state of being and consciousness? The answer for me must be yes - not in an atavistic, backward-looking way, but by cutting ourselves loose from the parameters of time and space that hold us earth-bound and time-bound. A return to such a shamanistic view of creation will, if it comes about at all, emerge from a merging of past and future awareness, from a re-awakening of that part of ourselves which has merely been sleeping for the past few decades.

Much of the shaman's work involves transformation - of the self, of the soul, and of the intelligence. This can be terrifying and life changing if we are not prepared for it, and it requires a discipline that leaves most of us gasping. This is why so much of the imagery in which the shaman's experience is traditionally couched, takes the form of battles with demons, of titanic struggles against monsters, of dismemberment, death and re-birth. This is by way of telling us that the experience is often profoundly unsettling, that it can leave us feeling broken ands distraught. But this is not the whole story. If we persevere, if we continue in the face of opposition, both inner and outer, we can break through into a new sense of wholeness and visionary awareness. The following is a description of just such an experience by a Pomo shaman from North America. It could just as easily be from anywhere on earth, and it reflect a commonality of vision which is one of the strongest pieces of evidence for the truth an accuracy of the shamanic experience:

"Through rolling hills I walked. Mountains and valleys, and rolling hills, Ii walked and walked ... until I saw water, huge water - how to get through? I fear it's deep. Very blue water. But I have to go. Put out the first foot, then the next ... and I passed through. ... And I walked and walked and walked and walked. On the way you're going to suffer. And I came to a four-way road like a cross. Which is the right way? .... At this cross-road there was a place in the centre. North you could see beautiful things of the Earth, hills and fields and flowers and everything beautiful and I felt like grabbing it but I turned away. South was dark, but there were sounds, monsters and huge animals. And I turned away and Eastward I walked and walked and walked and there were flowers, on both sides

of road; flowers and flowers and flowers out of this world.

And there is white light at the centre, while you're walking. This is the complicated thing: my mind changes. We are the people of the Earth. We know sorrow and knowledge and faith and talent and everything. Now as I was walking there, some places I feel like talking and some places I feel like talking and some places I feel like dancing .... This is what I saw in my vision. I don't have to go nowhere to see. Visions are everywhere." (Alcheringo: Ethnopoetics, Vol 1. Boston, MA, 1975.)

One of the questions I am often asked by the students to whom I teach shamanism is, 'When do I have the right to call myself a shaman?' Now this touches upon the whole question of modern shamanic practice. There are those who would say that it is impossible for a twentieth century person, living unattached to a tribal community, to be a shaman - just as there are others who say, with some good reason, that only people brought up in a native tradition such as that which still flourishes in North America or Australia, can begin to understand what it is to be a shaman. These people may well be right, at least to a certain degree. The fist thing I tell my students is that I cannot make them shamans - only the spirits can do that, and only the spirits can decide when our apprenticeship is over. What I can do, and what in effect I do in my own practice, is to live shamanically - by which I mean in a close and personal relationship with the beings of the inner realms, and in a direct relationship with the cosmos. If doing this mans to be a shaman, then I suppose I am one, but I prefer the idea of being on a journey towards what is really more a state of mind than a role, rather than assuming that I have already reached it.

I can remember exactly the moment when I became aware that what I had been doing for years under another flag was in fact shamanism. I was on my way back from a workshop in Bath, where someone had asked, in effect, is here any such thing as a native shamanic tradition in Britain? My first answer was a qualified no - I knew there must have been shamans in this part of the world once, but I believed they had died out in the Stone Age. Then, sitting in the train, I opened a book I had bought in Bath - a collection of shamanic essays edited by Larry Dossy and, as I read, I experienced a waking vision in which it was born in upon me that there was indeed native shamanic tradition in Britain. It had been staring me in the face all along in the work I had been doing for more than twenty years on the Celtic traditions. From here onward I began to re-assess that work - and much that had seemed unclear at once fell into place. In the stories of Merlin and Taliesin, in fragmentary works attributed to them ,and in the vast archive of Irish traditions, I found accounts of a once active tradition - forgotten or hidden or given other names for hundreds of years. I remember hearing the voice of Taliesin - 'my' Taliesin that is - in my ear, saying words to the effect of: "At last! What took you so long!'

Since then I have taught many students to journey, to do shamanic healing and soul-work, and I have been continually astonished by the depths and power of the visions they bring back from the Otherworld. Just a few days ago I received a letter that included the following report. This student's guide is Merlin - or perhaps one should say an appearance of Merlin. He is a very strict mentor, and gives no peace until a task is accomplished. In this instance he urgently wanted some healing work done on 'Eyenhallow', the holy island of the Orkneys. What follows is a description of the journey that took place, not in the physical realm, but in the inner world - although as you will see the two at times overlap:

'As we flew off [on the back of my stag], I noticed that there was a kind of sticky red and dark brown aura over the land, interspersed with striations of a pure white light. Merlin said it was this light that we needed to brighten, and hat we were going to Eynehalow because it was placed over a very potent energy centre(Orkney legend has it that the island used to disappear), and that it was a gateway to many dimensions. He said that this centre had been growing dim, and that it was affecting the 'grid', and that it was worthwhile working here because the island is only visited once a year by tourists and has no electricity or phone lines to interfere with the energy...

We landed on Eynehalow and went straight to the old monastic ruins, which in the journey were actually whole and intact. We entered he church and went to the font that was dry. Merlin produced a large multi-faceted crystal from the depths of his cloak and placed it in the font. Hr said to hold our hands near to the crystal and to project as much love and light into [it] as possible.

This is where the journey [took] on [a] strange, trance-like quality.... As I projected love and energy into the crystal, this strange...breathing stated automatically, as though I was breathing something extremely fine and subtle from the air and blowing it out through my mouth over the crystal, and [then] my hands started to move in strange gestures... It was as though I was watching myself yet had no conscious control over my body, and as though I was existing on different levels at once. Whilst his was happening in the journey it was also happening to my physical body.

I also began to feel ecstatic, and my whole body was filled with a kind of bubbling feeling. I felt s though I was in deep peace and a part of everything ... in the cry of an eagle, the scales of the fish, the scent of the rose etc. Merlin seemed really pleased and after a while longer he said we should return....
As we journeyed back I looked down and saw that whereas the white light had been previously quite feeble, now seemed to pulse strongly and evenly...

On the journey back and even after ...I still felt full of peace and joy and again of being on several levels at once. I felt on another level that I had green skin, and shoots and branches growing out of my fingers, and on yet another level that I had just given birth to a golden child. The feeling of peace and serenity lasted about two hours after the journey, [and] the strange breathing carried on for about ten minutes after the journey actually ended."

You can see how, despite the contemporary language, the experience varies very little from place to place, culture to culture, time to time - and there are many more journey reports like this one. It is this which convinces me more than anything that there is a continuity within the practice of shamanism that links us just as assuredly with our ancestors as with the spirits (who are often one and the same), and that extraordinary things continue to happen, whenever we let go of ourselves and send our souls out on a journey into the infinite worlds.

Trends come and go. In a few years time another popular area of esoteric subject matter that will dominate the bookshelves. But Shamanism will have left its mark. There are already a number of very gifted people working in this field, and their contribution to the turning of the millennium is no small one. I remain convinced that the shaman's craft is one that offers us a unique perspective on the universe, and which offers a way to heal some of the many wounds that exist, both in ourselves and that creation of which we are a part.

'Visions are everywhere', said the Pomo shaman. If I had to sum up the shamanic experience in one sentence this would be it. And, it is out of these visions that a new sense of wholeness, of being in touch with the universe, comes. As long as we can journey to the otherworlds, talk with the spirits and learn the skills they have to teach, there will always be visions. And if we follow those we shall not go far wrong.

1997

Chapter 18:

There Were Giants in Those Times:
The Guardians of Albion

Among the more obscure aspects of British mythology, lore relating to giants has always fascinated me. There is something about the idea of these huge creatures stomping across the land, leaving signs we can still see, that is just too wonderful to ignore. I can't remember where or when I wrote this now; it must have been in the 1990s. I'm glad to include it here, next to the essay on New Troy, with which it shares a common place in the ancient history of Britain.

"There are giants in the sky . . ."
Steven Sondheim & James Lapine: Into the Woods

One of the earliest names for the island of Britain is derived from a giant, that same giant Albion written about by William Blake and earlier by that redoubtable historian of ancient Britain, Geoffrey of Monmouth. Once one starts looking at these (literally) huge figures, one begins to see deeper meanings to them. To our medieval ancestors, Giants were the residue of a primordial race believed to have first inhabited this island thousands of years ago. Similar stories have been told in most parts of the world at one time or another.

From this we might conclude that they are in fact a kind of ancestral memory of an ancient race of ordinary-sized people, who have grown larger with the passing of time; or maybe they are the distant memory of a pantheon of aboriginal gods, who may actually have been huge, or at least perceived as such by their worshippers.

We do tend to see the distant past through a distorting lens, making the older inhabitants of the land either bigger or smaller. The aboriginal inhabitants of Britain itself - we can call them the Picts, though there may have been others - having been forced to retreat into caves and holes in the distant North, became known as "the little dark people" and were quickly subsumed into the notion of the faery folk, who have also been seen as little, at least since the Middle Ages.

Where even more ancient races are concerned there may well be a tradition that made them gigantic. We may think here of the Welsh story of "Rhonawby's Dream," found among the great collection of myth lore known as the *Mabinogion*, in which the dreaming hero (who dates from c1300) encounters Arthur, who seems gigantic and comments on how the world is full of "little men" not like the great heroes of his time.

What we are actually looking at in the stories of these gigantic figures is almost certainly a series of foundation myths, stories linked with the primordial shaping of the land, with its first gods and its earliest heroes, and with a series of guardian figures who still remain.

161

So, with these thoughts in mind, let us briefly examine some of the traditions regarding giants in the ancient, myth-haunted land of Britain.

Geoffrey of Monmouth is as good a place to begin as any. His knowledge of ancient folkloric sources was considerable, and while his *History of the Kings of Britain* is unreliable as history, his eye for obscure detail is excellent. Here is what he has to say about the giants of Albion:

> *Naught gave him [Corineus] greater pleasure than to wrestle with the giants, of whom was greater plenty there [Cornwall] than in any of the provinces that had been shared amongst his comrades. Among others was a certain hateful one by name Goemagog, twelve cubits in height, who was of such lustihood that when he had once uprooted it, he would wield an oak tree as lightly as it were a wand of hazel. On a certain day when Brute was holding high festival to the gods in the port whereat he had first landed, this one, along with a score of other giants, fell upon him and did passing cruel slaughter on the British. Howbeit, at the last, the Britons collecting together from all quarters prevailed against them and slew them all, save Goemagog only. Him Brute had commanded to be kept alive, as he was minded to see a wrestling bout betwixt him and Corineus, who was beyond measure keen to match himself against such monsters. So Corineus, overjoyed at the prospect, girt himself for the encounter, and flinging away his arms, challenged him to a bout at wrestling. At the start, on the one side stands Corineus, on the other the giant, each hugging the other tight in the shackles of his arms, both making the very air quake with their breathless gasping. It was not long before Goemagog, grasping Corineus with all his force, brake him three of his ribs, two on the right side and one on the left. Roused thereby to fury, Corineus gathered up all his strength, heaved him up on his shoulders and ran with his burden as fast as he could for the weight to the seashore nighest at hand. Mounting up to the top of a high cliff, and disengaging himself, he hurled the deadly monster he had carried on his shoulder into the sea, where, falling on the sharp rocks, he was mangled all to pieces and dyed the waves with his blood, so that ever thereafter that place from the flinging down of the giant hath been known as "Goemagog's Leap," and is called by that name unto this present day.* (2)

This gives us the name and something of the history of Goemagog, to whom we shall return in a moment. For further information about Albion however we have to look to the romantic Elizabethan chronicler Raphael Holinshead, the source of so many of Shakespeare's plays, who gives us a more or less complete picture. According to Holinshead, the story of Albion takes us firmly into the realm of classical mythology, to the story of Hercules, in fact.

The Greek hero's tenth labor took him to Spain to recover a unique herd of cattle. On the way he passes through Gaul, where he and his companions are attacked by the Ligurians, who live near the mouth of the Rhône. The Ligurians are either giants themselves, or they are helped by giants, specifically, two sons of the god Poseidon. The same god, we learn, also sired Albion. Hearing word of this battle, Albion goes off to join his brothers.

Hercules is hard-pressed, and prays to his father Zeus for help. Zeus sends a shower of meteorites. The heroes use these as missiles and slay all the giants, including Albion. After this, the race of giants lives on for another 600 years in the island named after Albion (i.e., Britain) but in the end they dwindle until there are only a few left in outlying places such as Wales and Cornwall.

The great 16th century poet Edmund Spenser describes this vividly in his vast mythic poem, *The Faerie Queene*:

> *But far in land a savage nation dwelt;*
> *Of hideous giants, and half beastly men*

That never tasted grace, nor goodness felt

. . .

They held this land, and with their filthiness
Polluted this same gentle soil long time:

. . .

Until that Brutus anciently derived

. . .

Driven by fatal error, here arrived,
And them of their unjust possession deprived.

. . .

He fought great battles with his savage foe;
In which he them defeated evermore,
And many giants left on groaning floor
That well can witness yet unto this day
The western Hough besprinkled with the gore
Of mighty Goemagot, whom in stout fray
Corineus conquered, and cruelly did slay.
And eke that ample pit, yet far renowned,

. . .

[And] those three monstrous stones do most excel
Which that huge son of hideous Albion,
Whose father Hercules in France did quell,
Great Godmar threw, in fierce contention,
At bold Canutus . . . (3)

This story has several interesting aspects. First there is the connection with Hercules. Folklorists have long recognized that stories of the Greek hero were known in Britain and may have influenced our own native mythology.

There is a possibility that the giant chalk figure carved onto the hillside at Cerne Abbas in Dorset may represent Hercules - complete with club and lion skin (archaeologists found vestiges of a cloak once carried over one arm when the site was investigated a few years back). Some authorities have even pointed out that the Greek name *Ialebion* or *Alebion* might be the original of Albion, though this is not precisely provable. In the writings of the classical author Lucian there is also an interesting account that describes how the Celts saw Hercules as a god of wisdom, rather than as a hero:

We Celts do not agree with you Greeks in thinking that Hermes is Eloquence: we identify Heracles with it, because he is far more powerful than Hermes. And don't be surprised that he is represented as an old man, for eloquence . . . is wont to show its full vigor in old age . . . This being so, if old Heracles . . . drags   men after him who are tethered by the ears to his tongue, don't be surprised at that either: you know the kinship between ears and tongue.(4)

Two shadowy figures, or perhaps one, thread our history. In Geoffrey of Monmouth we heard about Corneas, the captain of Trojan Brutus' men, wrestling with the giant Goemagot. Long after this, two figures are said to have been carved out of the chalk on the cliffs above Plymouth. They are called

Gog and Magog, and were still to be seen as late as 1671, after which they vanished forever beneath the foundations of a new building. Gog and Magog are the names of the kings of the biblical land of Mesech, alluded to in *Chronicles* and *Ezekiel*. But how did their names get applied to the giants of Plymouth? The first editor of the Welsh version of Geoffrey of Monmouth's book, the *Brut Tysilio*, suggested that Gogmagog or Gomagot is a corruption of *Cawr-Madog* or "The Giant Madog," an ancient and now virtually forgotten Celtic hero. But there is another suggestion, which, if it is right, puts a whole different complexion on the matter of the giants.

This idea centers on the figure of Ogma, also called Ogmios in Gaul, where he was worshipped as a god of light and learning. It was this character whom Lucian identified with Hercules in the passage referred to above. So, if Ogma is to be identified with Hercules, and in Ireland the so-called "inventor" of the old secret alphabet called Ogham is also found in Gaul, we have at least two links between the giants of Albion and the classical giants - remember that we have Hercules fighting Albion and his brothers in Gaul, where Ogma is Ogmios, and that the Celts apparently saw Hercules as a god of wisdom, just as Ogmios was seen.

This is further born out by the land itself, in particular, the Gogmagog Hills in Cambridgeshire, where the archaeologist T. C. Lethbridge uncovered a somewhat controversial figure in the 1950s. This figure or figures seemed to show a primitive warrior in a chariot, carrying a club and with a cloak over his arm, another possible image of this merging of the hero Hercules with an older, Celtic figure, possibly Ogmios.

In London around 1522, two huge figures guarded the gate to the city. To some they were "Colebrand" and "Brandegore" (significant names, as we shall see), but they were popularly known as "Hercules" and "Sampson." These huge statues were paraded through the streets of the city on civic occasions, until they were destroyed in the Great Fire of London in 1622. After that two new statues, smaller than the originals, were lovingly carved out of wood and installed in the Guildhall. These were called "Gog" and "Magog," and survived until the blitz during World War II, when they were destroyed. The name changes cannot be without significance. My belief is that these two giant guardians were seen as British versions of Hercules and Sampson, even if no one really remembered why any longer, and that these ancient figures, once Cole and Bran, had become associated with the giants of Plymouth.

Later, when William Blake wrote his great series of prophetic poems, he made Albion in some sense represent an ideal version of humanity, the fall and salvation of Albion was also, symbolically, the fall and salvation of man. But Blake also wrote that "The giant Albion . . . is the Atlas of the Greeks; one of those . . . called Titans. The Acts of Arthur are the acts of Albion, applied to a Prince of the 5th century."(5) For Blake, Albion indeed represented a vast principle of human destiny, of whom Arthur was the merest offshoot, an earthly representative of the divine energy of God.

But what about those other names for the giants of London - Colebrand and Brandegore? Both these names have survived, in more ancient forms, as Cole (the same Old King Cole of nursery fame) and Bran, a very different figure, and one who is central to understanding the meaning of the giants in Albion.

Colebrand is almost certainly a distant memory of Coel Hen (the Old), a probable historic figure who predates Arthur and is described in several texts as a King of Britain. In one account he marries Helena (later Saint Helena) and their son is Constantine the Great, Emperor of Rome. Coel is also the supposed founder of Colchester<but none of this makes him a giant. Perhaps he was remembered as a great leader and warrior and, as we have seen happen so often in our own history, time makes him seem larger than life - literally larger!

But Bran is something else altogether. He is none less than the Celtic god *Bendigeid Vran* (Bran the Blessed), who is the prototype of the Wounded King of Arthurian Grail traditions. His story tells us a good deal.

Bran the Blessed is King of Britain and a giant. He arranges for his sister Branwen to marry Matholwch, the King of Ireland. At the wedding feast one of his brothers, Evnissien, takes slight at the Irish king and mutilates his horses. Strife seems immanent, but Bran offers Matholwch the Cauldron of Rebirth, into which dead warriors are placed and come forth alive again. Matholwch already knows of the Cauldron, which came originally from Ireland and was owned by a giant and his wife, Llassar Llaes Gyfnewid and Cymedei Cymeinfoll, who gives birth to a fully armed warrior every six weeks. They had been driven out of Ireland and had taken refuge with Bran. Branwen now went to Ireland, where she bore Matholwch a son, but was so unpopular with the people that she was forbidden his bed and put to work in the kitchens. There she trained a starling to carry a message to her brother, who, once he heard of her ill treatment, came with all his warriors across the sea. Matholwch retreats and sues for peace, which is granted on condition that he abdicates in favor of Gwern, his son by Branwen. At the feast that ensues, Evnissien again brings disaster by thrusting the child into the fire. Fighting breaks out and the Irish are winning because they put their fallen warriors into the Cauldron. Evnissien then crawls inside and, stretching out, breaks both the vessel and his own heart. Bran is wounded in the foot by a poisoned spear and instructs his surviving followers, who number only seven, to cut off his head and bear it with them. They journey to an island named Gwales, where they are entertained by the head of Bran and the singing of the Birds of Rhiannon for eighty-five years, during which time they know no fears or hardship and forget all that they have suffered. Then one of their number opens a forbidden door, and at once the enchantment ceases and they remember everything. Bran's head tells them to carry it to London and bury it beneath the White Mount with its face towards France, whence it guards the land of Britain from invasion until the time of Arthur, who orders it disinterred and reburied elsewhere.

The most important thing here is Bran's guardian aspect. He is not alone in this however. A number of such figures - the technical term for them is "paladians" - are recorded. For instance, Vortimer, the son of the fifth-century tyrant Vortigern, became such a well-loved hero that at his death he requested that he should be interred at the port where the Saxons normally landed, facing towards the enemy.

Another interesting point about the majority of the giants listed here is that they are nearly all associated with rivers, estuaries, or coastal areas. What if, like Bran, Vortimer, and his kind, these giants had originally been guardians of the coastline? The more I investigated the matter, the more certain I became. Let us look, for a moment, at one or two of these characters.

There is Treyryn, a Cornish giant<one of many such found in this area - who has a castle held up by a magical key. There is actually a rock, which may be seen to this day, called "The Giant's Lock." This rock has a hole in it with a round stone called "the key." It is said that if the stone is ever removed, the whole promontory will sink into the sea.

Then there are two giants at St Michael's Mount - Cormoran and his wife Cormelian. They are said to have raised the mount single-handedly and, it is also said, could demolish it just as easily!

Other guardian giants (in Cornwall alone) are:

Holiburn at Cairn Galva
Trebegan at Land's End

Bolster at St Agnes Beach
Bolster at Portreath
Ordulph at Tavistock (on the River Tavy)

Gog and Magog (or Cole and Bran), as we have seen, guarded London, on the river Thames. There is also Leon Gawr, who is said to have founded Chester (another river town) - he is almost certainly the same as Brandegore or Bran of Gower, mentioned in several Welsh annals, and who is probably not only the same figure as Bran the Blessed, but reappears throughout the Arthurian cycle under various guises as Brandelis, Brendegoris, Brangore, Strangore, and so on.

There are a number of references to giants in the Arthurian legends - and though this is not the place to discuss all of these, we must not fail to mention Ogryvan Gawr, who is said to be the father of Arthur's Queen Guinevere (he becomes Leodegran in the later stories). The interesting thing about this name is that the Welsh word *ogryvans* was applied to a bardic verse form which particularly applied to gnomic or wisdom poetry - suggesting that Ogryvan may well, like Bran, have been associated with the preservation of knowledge or ancestral memory.

This same idea is probably carried over into references to two other Welsh giants, Idris (or Arthur) who lived at the top of Cader Idris in Snowdonia, and Trichnug, from Plylummon. It is said that anyone who spends the night in Idris's chair - a natural rock outcrop, will waken in the morning either mad or a poet. Trichnug has both a chair and a bed. The chair has the same effect as Idris's, while the bed shapes itself to the height of anyone who lies on it.

In Wales we might glance, too, at a giant variously called Rion, Rhiance, Ritho, or Ron, who gives Arthur a lot of trouble at the beginning of his reign. He has a cloak trimmed with the beards of other kinglets he has defeated and killed. Accordingly he comes demanding Arthur's beard, and there is an inevitable battle, which of course Arthur wins. There is a variant to this story where Arthur goes to the help of Ogryvan (Leodegran) who is being attacked by Ritho - so here Arthur is helping one giant against another.

But by far the worst giant in Welsh tradition is Yspaddaden Pencawr, one of the chief giants of Albion according to the story of "Culhwch and Olwen" from the *Mabinogion*. The story is too long and rich to tell here, but briefly it concerns the quest of young Culhwch -Arthur's nephew - for Olwen, who is both the giant's normal-sized daughter, and a very clear memory of the goddess of spring. It is said of her that wherever she walks, she leaves a track of white flowers on the earth behind her<for which she is called Olwen White Track. The description of the first encounter with her father is so vivid that it is worth quoting here:

"The greeting of Heaven and of man be unto thee, Yspaddaden Penkawr," said [Arthur's men].
"And you, wherefore come you?"
"We come to ask thy daughter Olwen, for Kilhwch the son of Kilydd, the son of Prince Kelyddon."
"Where are my pages and my servants? Raise up the forks beneath my two eyebrows which have fallen over my eyes, that I may see the fashion of my son-in-law." And they did so.
"Come hither tomorrow, and you shall have an answer."
They rose to go forth, and Yspaddaden Penkawr seized one of the three poisoned darts that lay beside him, and threw it after them. And Bedwyr caught it, and flung it, and pierced Yspaddaden Penkawr grievously with it through the knee. Then he said, "A cursed ungentle son-in-law, truly. I shall ever walk the worse for his rudeness, and shall ever be without a cure. This poisoned iron pains me like the bite of a gadfly. Cursed be the smith who

166

forged it, and the anvil whereon it was wrought! So sharp is it!"(6)

There are several references in this story that suggest it was once part of a seasonal myth. Culhwch's mother is called Goleuddydd, which means "light of Day" and Culhwch himself is the youngest of twenty-four sons, a probable reference to the twenty-four hours in the day. One derivation of Yspaddaden's name is "Hawthorn," which prompted one commentator to suggest that he too was once a god associated with the springtime.

In fact there are enough references in these stories of the giants to suggest that they may be the memory of an almost forgotten pantheon of primal gods - a notion born out by such figures as the Scottish *Cailleach Bheur*, the Blue Hag, one of the few female giants of Albion. She really belongs to the "formative" type of giant - those who are involved in the "terraforming" of the land. As she walks she lets fall giant boulders from her apron and in Scotland she is known as "The Daughter of the Little Sun" - the sun of winter. She is in fact a kind of personification of winter -though she has other aspects as well, as a goddess of agriculture and deer - described as having a blue-black face, and hair like frosty twigs. As she walks across the wintry landscape, she is accompanied by deer, sheep, and wolves. Storm clouds are said to be "the Cailleach with her company of hags." When storms approach, local people still say "the Cailleach is going to trample the blankets tonight."

A whole myth has built up around the Cailleach. In her lair below Ben Nevis she holds the nymph of summer prisoner, imposing heavy tasks upon her. But one of the Cailleach's sons falls in love with the prisoner and they elope together in March/April. As they run off, the Cailleach sends wild weather to punish them, but her son responds by driving her ever deeper into the North, and when he finally overtakes her puts out her single eye. She is said to have two sons, one white with a single black spot on him, the other black with a single white spot - symbolizing the interaction and cyclicity of winter and summer.

There are a number of other giants who have only one eye - Balor, one of the major giants of Ireland, has an eye which (like Yspaddaden's) shoots out fire and is so toxic that it kills anyone who looks at it (the word "baleful" is said to derive from his name, and though that is etymologically inaccurate, it shows how he was seen.) The fact that the sun god Lugh eventually defeats Balor bears out his original status as a god of winter.

Interestingly, the giants of Scotland seem to be far more associated with foundation myths and the shaping of the land than those in Britain - perhaps simply because it is the gentle, more low-lying areas in the South that need guarding, while the highlands to the North were seen as a natural home of giant builders.

From all of this we can see that the Giants of Albion perform the role of guardians, wisdom-keepers, and foundation gods. They are also intimately connected to the landscape, which they helped to form. If we look at the sacred landscape of Britain and Ireland, what do we see? Stones. Stone circles. Megaliths. Standing stones. Henges. And what do these look like? Giants. In fact, there are literally dozens of stories that describe these ancient megalithic stones as giants, from Stonehenge, which is called "The Giant's Dance" to the Whispering Knights or the Rollright Stones in Oxfordshire - all of which are said to be giants frozen in stone. This suggests that it could well be memories of these ancient monoliths - themselves not infrequently set up as guardian stones, or as altars to ancient gods, as well as for tapping the energies of the earth -that gave rise to the stories of giants in the land. And I can't help thinking as well of something C. S. Lewis wrote in one of his letters to someone who asked about the giants in his Narnia books:

I have seen landscapes which, under a particular light, made me feel that at any moment a giant might raise its head over the next ridge. Nature has that in her which compels us to invent giants: and only giants will do. (7)

This makes more than perfect sense. Only giants will do. Only they are large enough to represent the huge forces of the earth involved in creation. They are literally emanations of the land; vast, semi-human forms that emerge from the earth and are its eternal guardians.

Notes:

1. Sondheim & Lapine Into the Woods. Simon & Schuster Inc, 2001.
2. Geoffrey of Monmouth. Historia Regum Britanniae, Book 1, ch. 16., trans. by Sebastian Evans, London, J.M. Dent, 1958
3. Edmund Spenser, The Faerie Queene, Book II, Canto X, vs. 7Þ_11. New York, Heritage Press, 1953.
4. Lucian, "Heracles," in Works, vol 1, trans. by A. Harmon. London & Harvard, Heinemann, 1913.
5. William Blake Poetry and Prose Ed G. Keynes. London, Nonsuch Library, 1975
6. The Mabinogion, trans. by Lady Charlotte Guest. London & Toronto, J.M. Dent, 1937
7. Letters of C.S. Lewis Ed by W.H. Lewis. London, Geoffrey Bles, 1967

Chapter 19:

NEW TROY: LONDON BEFORE HISTORY

I wrote this essay for a book called The Aquarian Guide to Legendary London (Aquarian Press, 1990), which I edited with the artist Chesca Potter. I lived in and around London for the first 30 years of my life and grew to love the secret heart of the city which today hides itself behind modern office buildings, but which then was a good deal more accessible to the solitary walker. This piece belongs along side the Giants essay, which also draws on the ancient and mysterious landscape of inner Britain.

The Trojan Kings

Until the end of the Elizabethan era it was still a commonly held belief that Britain had been colonised by Brute or Brutus the Trojan, a grandson of the famous hero Aneas. Even the sober, cautious John Milton, writing his *History of England* in 1670 reported that: *"Brutus in a chosen place builds Troia Nova, changed in time to Trinovantum, now London"*. (1)

To trace this extraordinary tradition back to its beginnings we have first to turn to the medieval writer Geoffrey of Monmouth, famed for what is perhaps the earliest novelization of the Arthurian legends in his History of the Kings of Britain, which begins, not with Arthur, but with Brute. The story he tells may be summarised as follows.

Aneas, fleeing from Troy, took ship for Italy with his son Ascanius. There he was honourably received by King Latinus whose daughter Lavinia he shortly married. Brutus was the grandson of Ascanius who, after he slew his father Sylvius accidentally in the hunting field, was exiled to Greece where he gathered about him the remnant of the Trojans who had escaped from the doomed city and who now flocked to him when they learned he was the grandson of the great Aneas.

With the help of the army he had thus raised Brutus defeated the Greek forces, and having taken their king prisoner demanded the hand of his daughter Ingoge in marriage and a fleet of well- equipped ships with which to seek a new homeland. Only two days out at sea they fleet sighted a deserted island called Leogicia, where stood a ruined city with a temple to Diana at its heart. Brutus made sacrifice there and that night dreamed of the Goddess, who told him to seek a land beyond Gaul in the country of the setting sun.

Voyaging on, the fleet sailed first to Africa, then on to Mauritania, through the Pillars of Hercules and into the Tyrrhene Sea, where they encountered a second Trojan colony ruled by Duke Corineus. Making common cause with them the Trojans passed onward to Aquitaine and the mouth of the Loire River, where they were attacked by the Gaulish people. Several mighty battles ensued in which the Trojans inflicted terrible losses on their enemy. But Brutus saw that he could not win in the end, and decided to follow the path of the sunset as the Goddess had advised. A fair drove the fleet ashore at a place called Totness on an island named Albion after its gigantic ruler.

Falling in love with the rich land Brutus and his followers establish a colony there and began to build a city. They were harried by the race of giants who dwelled in the island and fought and killed several of them. Finally they captured one, whose name was Goemagot, and the Trojan Duke Corineus, who was a famous wrestler, challenged him to a bout. The giant was a mighty fighter and broke five of Corineus' ribs before the latter, heaved him off the top of the cliffs into the sea, the place being thereafter known as Lamgoemagot or "Goemagot's Leap". After this the Trojans were left in peace and founded cities across the country. Brutus himself had three sons: Locrin, Albanacht and Camber, who became the governors of Cambria (Wales) Alban (Scotland) and Llogria (England) after the death of Brutus. (2)

Geoffrey goes on to extend the line of "Trojan" Kings into a complex dynastic chain extending to Arthur himself. The following genealogical tree, which first appeared in a more detailed form in Acton Griscom's edition of *The History of the Kings of Britain*, (3) gives some idea of the extent of Geoffrey's schema - which in fact far outreaches any simple "invention" such as his work has been consistently, until recent times, described. However much elaboration or decoration of his sources Geoffrey may be guilty of, he clearly had recourse to original material to produce a family of such magisterial proportions.

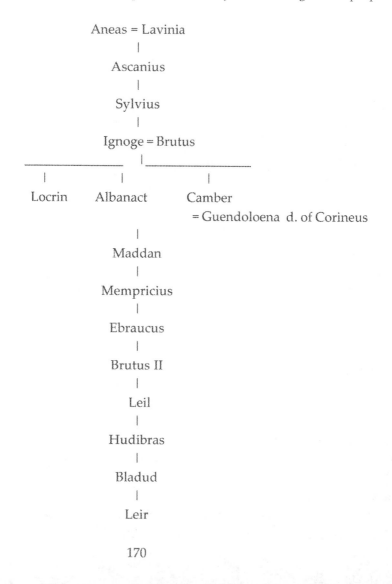

Aneas = Lavinia
|
Ascanius
|
Sylvius
|
Ignoge = Brutus
|
————————————————————————
| | |
Locrin   Albanact   Camber
= Guendoloena d. of Corineus
|
Maddan
|
Mempricius
|
Ebraucus
|
Brutus II
|
Leil
|
Hudibras
|
Bladud
|
Leir

From this, the character known to all from Shakespeare's play *King Lear*, the line extends down to Arthur, 90th in succession from Aneas of Troy. (An idea still being expressed in such great medieval Arthurian works as *Sir Gawain and the Green Knight*, (4) the opening of which describes Arthur's Trojan ancestry in detail).

When Caesar arrived in Britain he found a tribe called the Trinovantes living in the South of the country - were they the descendants of Brutus and his men? Or did the whole idea of the Trojan colonisation of the island spring from a medieval misunderstanding of the name Trinovante? It would seem, on the face of it, that we cannot know. Yet the tradition that Britain had been colonised by the Trojans is supported by a surprising detail. In Wales, as late as the 18th century, shepherd boys used to play a game called *Caer Droia* or "Troy Town", which consisted in laying out a maze-like pattern on the ground and holding contests to see who could reach the "City at the centre first. This indeed is a very ancient game indeed, possibly stretching back to Prehistoric times, when the maze or labyrinth was used for ritual purposes. Famous mazes in Crete and Egypt were described by classical writers, and were old even then. How there came to be such designs in Britain may be accounted for in a number of ways, including the assumption that a kind of universal religion was practices in the early world, or indeed that incoming conquerors (such as the so-called Trojans) brought the concept with them. (5)

The final word on the question of a possible Trojan settlement in Britain must await further investigation. We can however note that the idea of tracing one's descent to Troy was by no means unusual. The Roman poet Virgil himself did so, for his own people in *The Aeneid*, (6) and the Classical writer Ammenius Marcianus wrote of the Gaulish belief that they were of Trojan descent; while as late as 1514 an oration over the coffin of Anne of Brittany traced her lineage back to Brutus.

Certainly archaeological evidence suggests that trade routs between the Mediterranean world and Britain were established from a significantly early date. So that there seems no difficulty in believing that a group of people escaping from the fall of Troy (wherever and whenever we take that event to have occurred) might indeed have sailed to these shores and established a colony there. Whether Brutus really extended his sway over the entire country, so that it became known as Britain after him, is less likely to be true - though even here we may still be seeing a distant memory of an event that actually occurred.

Lud's Town

With the connection of London with Lud, Brutus's descendent, we enter the realms of both myth and religion. Geoffrey of Monmouth describes the foundation of Trinovantum in Book I. Chapter 17. The Welsh *Brut* offers its own idiosyncratic version, and is worth quoting in full from Lewis Spence's translation.

"And when he found a place lovely and fulfilling his desires, he built a city there [beside the Thames] and called it Troyaf newydd, and thus it was called for a long time; and then, by corruption of that name it was called Trynofant. afterwards it was possessed by Llydd, the son of Beli the Great, the brother of Casswallawn, the man who fought with Ilkassar [Caesar]. And when this Llydd got the kingship he strengthened the city with grants of lands and with walls of wondrous art and craftsmanship; and he ordered it to be called Caer-lydd, after his own name; and the Ssaissons [Saxons] called it Lwndwn....At this time Beli the Priest ruled in Judea and the ark of the covenant was in captivity to the Pilistewission [i.e. the Philistines]." (7)

The dating from the time when the Ark of the Covenant was in the possession of the Philistines is certainly startling - and just as certainly spurious - but it indicates the antiquity of the tradition, which was clearly seen as dating back to a very ancient past. Layamon, the Saxon poet who re-told Geoffrey's book in English, offers the king's name as Lud, the tower as Caerlud and adds:

"Afterwards came other dominion, and new customs, that men called it Lundin, over all this country. Subsequently came English men, and called it Lundene. Afterwards came the French, ...with their country-mannners, and Lundres it named. Thus has this burgh fared, since it first was reared." (Trans. Lewis Spence.) (8)

Once the city was founded Lud embarked on an intensive building plan, extending the existing town and instituting palaces and temples. Holinshed's Chronicle tells us more:

"[Lud] himself caused buildings to be made between London Stone and Ludgate, and builded for himself not far from the said gate a fair palace, which is the Bishop of London's palace beside [St.] Paul's at this day, as some think....He also builded a fairer temple near to his said palace, which temple (as some take it) was after turned into a church, and at this day called Paul's. " (9)

The mention of the London Stone is interesting, as it reinforces other claims that this ancient monument was erected by Brutus himself (For which reason it was also called Brutus' Stone in other texts). It was believed to have been erected on the site of a temple to Diana, whom Brutus worshipped after she prophesied that he should find his way to Britain. We should note here that a unique illustration in the 13th MSS of a work by Matthew Parris exists which shows Brutus sacrificing before the altar of a horned Goddess - indication of the validity still attached to the idea even as late as the Middle Ages.

Ludgate, also mentioned in the quotation from Holinshead, is the most tangible evidence we possess for the connection of London with the Trojan dynasty. Accounts exist of its restoration in 1215, at which time bricks from the houses of purged Jewish citizens were used to affect the repairs. These were discovered in 1586 when the gate was again pulled apart in order to rebuild it yet again.

In 1260 we hear of it being completely restored, with statues of Lud and other kings, though whether there were images present there before we are not told. Later, during the troubled reign of Edward VI, these statues had their heads knocked off, and were not repaired until Mary Tudor ascended the throne in 1553. Finally, in 1586, when the "Jewish" stones were recovered, the statues were again replaced with King Lud and others on the Eastern side of the gate and a new statue of Elizabeth I on the Western side. This cost the city the some of more than £1500, the equivalent of four times that amount in today's currency.

When the gates of the city were taken down in the 18th century the statues were bought by Sir Francis Gosling, who intended to install them in St. Dunstan's Church, Fleet Street. But it was found that they would not fit, and in the end only the statue of Queen Elizabeth was erected in its new home, while Lud and his sons languished "in the bone yard". What happened to them after that is unclear, and no one now seems certain of the precise origins of the statues which now stand in the porch of St. Dunstan's Church. They are much damaged and rather sad in aspect, though Lud himself still has a certain dignity, despite a chipped face and vestiges of paint that indicates that the images must once have been decked out in splendid colour.

As to Lud himself, there is every reason for believing that he may have been a god. The great Celtecist Sir John Rhys stared in his *Hibbert Lectures* (10) *"the association of Llud, or "King Lud", as he has come to be called in English, with London, is apparently founded on a certain amount of fact: one of the Welsh names for London is Caer Lud or Lud's Fort, and if this is open to suspicion as having been suggested first by Geoffrey, that can hardly be supposed possible in the case of the English name of Ludgate Hill. The probability is that as a temple on a hill near Severn associated him with that river in the west, so a still more ambitious temple on a hill connected him with the Thames in the east; and as an aggressive creed can hardly signalise its conquests more effectually than by appropriating the fanes of the retreating faith, no site could be guessed with more probability to have been sacred to the Celtic Zeus than the eminence from which the dome of St. Paul's now rears its magnificent form."*

Lud as a Celtic Zeus may cause a smile now, but there seems little doubt that Lud was indeed a god of some importance and power, and that his temple could well have been established in "Lud's Town, even at the present site of St. Paul's, which Holinshead thought to be the original site of Brutus temple to Diana, and where archaeologists did indeed discover traces of such a place after the last war. (11)

Perhaps, if there was a real "King Lud", descended from Trojan Brutus, he assumed something of the form and nature of an older god, much as the historical Arthur seems to have absorbed aspects of a primitive Bear God named Artos. Spence thinks he may have been a corruption of the Welsh Gwyn ap Nudd, the god of the Underworld, but this seems to be stretching a point, since the pronunciation of Nudd is "Nith" - although it must be allowed that the written form of the two names looks remarkably similar. However, there seems to be no precise overlay between the attributes of the Celtic god of the underworld and the guardian of Caer Lud, and in all probability we are looking at a figure of similar type to Gog and Magog, whose extraordinary history we must examine next.

Effigies of the Gods

One of the most intriguing references in Geoffrey's narrative, and one which touches most nearly on the legendary history of London, is the story of Corineus' battle with the giant Goemagog. The latter has an extraordinary and complex history, which is deeply connected with the mythic history of Britain, and with London in particular.

Although Geoffrey give the giant's name as "Goemagog", or even "Goemagot", other sources, in particular the Welsh *Brut Tysilio*, (12) which derives in part from the *History of the Kings of Britain* but which also contains independent material, gives the more familiar "Gogmagog", which the texts earliest editor, Peter Roberts, suggests was a corruption of Cawr-Madog - the Great Warrior of Madog. However, we may look further afield than this for the origins of the giant, digging back into the very foundation myths of this island.

Gogmagog (as we shall continue to call him) is the champion of the giant Albion, whose own legend stretches back to the mists of proto-history, where he is known as the son of Poseidon, the Greek God of the sea. Raphael Holinshead in his *Chronicles of England, Scotland, and Ireland* declared that after the Flood, Albion the Giant led a company of giants descended from a son of Noah's named either Ham or Shem to Britain - though it was not called that at the time - and how he overcame the original inhabitants through skill and cunning in warfare. After this the island was named Albion, a title which has remained embedded in the consciousness of its people to the extent that it can still be evoked today.13 The poet and prophet William Blake devised a whole mythology based on the Giant Albion, writing, in his Jerusalem (14)

"There is a Void outside of Existence, which if entered into
Englobes itself & becomes a womb; such was Albion's couch,
A pleasant Shadow and Repose call'd Albion's lovely Land.
His Sublime & Pathos become Two Rocks fix'd in the Earth;
His reason, his Spectrous Power, covers them above.
Jerusalem his Emanation is a Stone laying beneath.
O behold the Vision of Albion."

Elsewhere he wrote: "the stories of Arthur are the Acts of Albion applied to a Prince in the Fifth Century". (15)

Here Albion has become the tutelary spirit of Britain, an inner guardian not unlike the later Bran. Or indeed like another titanic figure also associated with Britain - the Greek God Cronos, father of Zeus, who is supposed to have been imprisoned in a cave beneath the island in an enchanted sleep until, like Arthur, he is recalled in some future time.

The myth of the sleeping titan seems inextricably linked with Britain. In c400 BC a Carthaginian explorer circumnavigated the island and included, in his subsequent report, in which its sophisticated populace refer to their homeland as the "island of Albiones". While later, the Greek Pythias recorded (c300 BC) a Western island known to be "the abode of Albion". Another Greek, Plutarch, described the sleep of Cronos, which had been "devised as a bondage for him, and round about him are many demigods as attendants and servants". (16) In the Mabinogion (17) the demi-God Bran commands that his head be cut off and buried beneath the White Mount in London, from which point it will guard the land. Arthur later has the head disinterred, so that he alone should be the guardian, and after his passing he is indeed believed to be sleeping beneath the hills of Britain, awaiting his country's call to arms. To this may be added the figure of the Celtic King Cadwallo who was embalmed and placed on the brazen statue of a horse above the Western gate into London - a position later to be assumed by Gogmagog - or rather, Gog and Magog after the giant became curiously divided into two characters, perhaps under the influence of Biblical traditions which referred to two giants by this name mentioned in Chronicles, Ezekiel and Revelations.

Descriptions of the 1554 pageant welcoming Philip of Spain to England for his impending marriage to Mary Tudor describe two effigies as being carried through the streets. Normally they resided in London's Guildhall. A reference in a work entitled the *Orthoepia Gallica of 1593* (18) seems to indicate that one of the two was of Corineus, Brutus' heroic captain, while the other was still of Gogmagog. While in Plymouth at this time and originating at least as early as 1494 there were two gigantic figures cut in the turf of the Hoe. Carew, writing in the Elizabethan era, describes them as

"the portraiture of two men with clubs in their hands cut in the turf, the one bigger the other lesser, whom they term Gogmagog and Corineus, intimating the wrestling to have been between these two champions and the steep rocky cliff affording aptitude for such a cast". (19)

Sir E.B. Taylor, in his book *Anthropology*, (1848) suggested that the idea of Gogmagog being thrown over the cliffs at Plymouth may have originated quite late on, as a result of fossilised dinosaur bones discovered there at various times. Lewis Spence, who has written most persuasively on the subject, quotes this information in his Legendary London, He also believes Corineus to have been an invention of Geoffrey of Monmouth, to form a link in the chain of semi-mythical Kings he represented as ruling Britain before Arthur.

Spence, in another book, *The Mysteries of Britain* (20) maintains the belief that Gog and Magog may have been the original (Celtic) deities connected with London, having their temples, or seats of power, on the twin hills either side of Walbrook. "They might actually have been those "Fierce ones" alluded to by Dr Henry Bradley in his derivation of the [old Celtic] name " Londinos", from which the spot took its name."

If this can be regarded as in any way true, we must immediately note that Magog may possibly be equated with "Mother Gog", an interesting speculation which supplies us with a much more likely male and female set of deities indigenous to the City.

During the Fire of London in 1666 the effigies at Guildhall seem to have been destroyed, and we hear in 1669 that the hall was to be restored and that "two new figures of gigantic magnitude will be as before" (Hatton: *New View of London, 1708*) The statues then erected were apparently carved by Captain Richard Saunders of King Street, Cheepside, sometime after this date. They are described in considerable detail by J.T. Scott in his *Ancient Topography of London* in 1815. (21)

The occasion was the restoration of the Guildhall, at which time one of the effigies - Gog - was taken down and stored in a specially constructed shed. Scott describes the statues as follows:

"I stood upright in the body of one of them. They are composed of pieces of Fir; and I am informed were the production of a ship-carver. It is also reported that they were presented to the City by the Stationers Company, which, if true, might have given rise to the [earlier] report of their being made of paper...[Gog]... measures fourteen feet, six inches in height, from the upper leaf of laurels to the lower point of the beard five feet, three inches, the nose is nine inches, the opening of th eyelids one inch and a half, across the shoulders about four feet, five inches and a half, from the wrist to the tip of the second finger, two feet, the feet are the length of the hands".

This truly monumental figure accords well with the later reconstructed figures which continued to stand in the Guildhall until WW2, when they were finally destroyed and not replaced.

What, then, are we to make of this strange mishmash of material? Who are, or were, Gog, Magog and Corineus? Are they totally inventions of Geoffrey of Monmouth's fertile imagination? Ultimately, we cannot be certain, but we can make some educated guesses.

The antiquarian Douce, again quoted by Spence, reports reading in *"A Very Modern Edition of the Celebrated Romance of the History and Destruction of Troy"* that after Brutus had captured Gog and Magog (here the brothers of the giant Albion) they were chained, as porters, to the gate of the palace built by Brutus on the present site of Guildhall. Spence adds that he has been unable to trace the reference, but traced or not, it has the ring of truth about it. If we are right in assuming that Geoffrey, as in so many other instances, was recording a genuinely ancient tradition, we should look for a possible source further back in time than the 12th century.

It may be that such a source does exist in the shape of the "Ancient Book in the British tongue" described by Geoffrey as his main source for the History of the Kings of Britain. Because no such text has ever been discovered it has generally been assumed to be a fabrication. However, it may well be that the book did exist, and that fragments of it may still be traced within the pages of Geoffrey's book, and elsewhere scattered throughout the various traditions relating to the early kings of Britain. The very nature of the early part of the *History*, and in particular the portion dealing with Brutus, may suggest the nature of this proposed text. Whatever, the true derivation of this story may be, it does, clearly, deal with a succession of incoming peoples, subjugating the native population and settling there permanently until they, in turn, are ousted. We may remember the references to Albion, of the same stock as Gogmagog, overcoming the indigenous races by his superior battle-tactics. Now again we find the Trojans overcoming the giants with a mixture of strength and cunning. Surely, what we are reading here is a kind of "Book of Invasions", similar in many ways to the famous Irish *Lebor Gabala Erin* dating from the 9th century but recording events of a far greater antiquity.

We can trace the names Gog and Magog or Goemagog, no further than Geoffrey, but if we look again at the evidence for the existence of the effigies at London Guildhall, we find that there were two such figures that predate the more familiar statues. These, according to an account of 1552, were called "Hercules" and "Sampson", an interesting detail in the light of numerous references to the former contained in the poetry of the 6th Century Bard Taliesin. Earlier still, they were known by names of even greater significance for the present argument: Colebrand and Brandamore, both of which contain references to important figures in Celtic tradition.

Both names contain the name Bran, a character whose life and deeds are well documented. He is also, it should not be forgotten, one of the giants who guard island from attack. The name Cole or Coel is also the name of an ancient British King (the "Old King Cole" of Nursery Rhyme fame), father of the famous Helen or Elen of the Roads (a semi mythical builder of pathways across Britain) and also mentioned briefly by Geoffrey of Monmouth.

What we seem to have, in this account of the battle between Brutus and Gogmagog is a distant, garbled memory of the overthrow of one set of people by another, and of their own subsequent enslavement at the hands of incomers from the fabled city of Troy. Perhaps also we may wish to consider the possibility that here we have a further reference to the mythic overlay of Julius Caesar's adventures in Britain, which in the hands of Geoffrey of Monmouth, taker on an epic quality of their own and contain references to an even older myth of the Goddess Fleur. Whether there is any historical foundation for any of this is doubtful, and the notion must remain purely speculative at this level. There is, however, a deeper stratum of belief, in the power of the hidden, inner guardians of the Land that accounts for the ability of these stories to move us still.

The myth of the dying god is universal, and needs no rehearsal here, beyond the statement that it entails the death, or sacrifice of the god for the sake of the people. Avatars as distant in time ands space as Arthur, Adonis, and Christ match this archetype. Bran, Gog and Magog, Cadwallo and Lud, each of whom has a strong connection with London, may themselves once have fulfilled the necessary role. Bran indeed, already does so, and it may well be that Gogmagog, meeting his death at the hands of Corineus, became a similar saviour figure to his defeated people.

Such interpretations require more space and time than the author has presently at his disposal. However, the fragmentary evidence for another London, before either history or archaeology establishes the physical city, is strong enough to recall Blake's line:

"O behold the Vision of Albion!"

NOTES

1: Quoted in Lewis Spence: Legendary London Robert Hale,1937, hereafter simply referred to as Spence

2: Geoffrey of Monmouth: History of the Kings of Britain, various editions including Lewis Thorpe, Penguin Books, 1976

3: Acton Griscom Ed. Historia Regum Britanniae, Longmans, 1929.

4: Sir Gawain & the Green Knight Edited by J.R.R. Tolkien and E.V.Gordon. Oxford: Clarendon Press, 1925

5: Rev. Peter Roberts. The Cambrian Popular Antiquities London, E. Williams, 1815

6: Virgil. The Aeneid, Translated by Robert Fitzgerald. London, Harvill Press,1984.

7: Spence.

8: ibid.

9: Ralph Holinshead: Chronicles of England Scotland and Ireland

10: Sir John Rhys: Celtic Heathendom London,1888.

11: Matthews and Potter: The Aquarian Guide to Legendary London

12: Brut Tysilio ed. Peter Roberts The Chronicle of the Kings of Britain, London, 1811.

13: Anthony Roberts. Sowers of Thunder, London, Rider & Co, 1978.

14: William Blake, Poetry & Prose Ed. by G. Keynes. London, The Nonsuch Library, 1975

15: ibid (see: A Descriptive Catalogue)

16: Plutarch. Moralia vol V. Trans by F.C. Babbitt. London: William Heinemann,1957.

17:The Mabinogion Trans G. Gantz Harmondsworth, Penguin Books, 1979

18: Spence.

19: ibid.

20: Lewis Spence: The Mysteries of Britain London: Aquarian Press,1970.

21: quoted by Spence.

Section Four:

The Green World

Chapter 20:

THE APPEARANCES & TESTS OF THE GREEN MAN

For more than 20 years my wife and I have run annual course just before Christmas at Hawkwood College in Stroud, Gloucestershire. This event has become somewhat legendary, with many participants returning year after year and forming an informal group known as 'The Company of Hawkwood'. We have had some great guest presenters, including Ari Berk, David Spangler, Brian and Wendy Froud and Robin Williamson. There have been many memorable times at these gatherings and we hope they will continue as long as we can give them and participants can come. The talk that follows was given as my own part of a course on the Green Man in 1990 and predates my later books on the subject. It was originally intended to include slides, so you will have to imagine you are seeing these magical images! It includes a brief mediation.

If you close your eyes for a moment you can imagine that a great green woodland has temporarily invaded this place. It surrounds us on every side, enclosing us in greenery and the sounds and scents of forest life. And, from between the leaves, from around the trunks of the trees, faces look out at us. Some are human and some are definitely not. Some are of the Faery race, some have pointed ears, some show mischievous expressions, some look serious and sad. One face in Particular catches our attention. It is a curious face, perhaps made up of leaves, perhaps looking out between the leaves. It is the face of the Lord or the Greenwood - the Green Man.

He has many forms and features besides this, and many names: he is Green Jack, John Barleycorn, the Green Knight, Robin Hood, Gromer Somer Jour, the Green Man of Knowledge, Robin Goodfellow, Puck, and many more. Despite their differences they all have one thing in common - they represent life in its most vital and verdant aspect -indeed they are life, personified, given a voice and a name, a character and story.

Let me invoke this figure in a magical poem by my friend Ari Berk

Anatomy

Wren left a polished stone within the oaken bower;
it was thus you came to know your bones.

Feathers were tied to blackthorn branches;
your coat was made from these.

Badger scribed solsticial sonnets on dark ash leaves;
on these your name was spelled.

A hedge witch boiled berries;
brought your blood up from the sod and soil.

Apples gave you flesh and scent
yet now they mould and rot and grow again

from hidden seeds;
thus your nature works its way.

There are mushrooms for a brain,
owl talons, vervain, mandrake,

and something else, unnamed,
that sets the shallow winter sap upon its face

and grants the Greenman motion
and binds him to the forest waste.

In the figures we shall be talking about, both the male and the female aspects of Nature come together, so that when we speak of the Green Man we are automatically speaking or the Green Woman as well. Both are so totally aligned with Nature that each contains the character of the other. In this way neither is dominant. Indeed one cannot exist without the other any more than human females or males can, ultimately, exist without each other. Without this polarity we would cease to exist - anyway in our present forms. The same can be said of nature, which has its own equilibrium and rhythm.

If we look at the origins of the Green Man as an image, we find them first in Classical Greece and Rome. Images of leaf-bearded Bacchus and ivy-crowned Dionysus, along with seaweed hung Okeanus are all seen as precursors of the European imagery. I personally believe that the image goes back much further, and may be recognised in the image of the horned man from the famous Gunderstrup Cauldron, who possess a leafy beard and hair.

All the Classical deities named above have one thing in common: they each have an association with the love of life and generation, the prime function or the Green Man as a representative of the generative power of nature. There is possibly no more powerful image or this than the great ithyphallic Cerne Abbas giant, carved into the chalk of a Dorset hillside perhaps 1500 years ago.

So strong is the belief in his virility that infertile women still go there to sleep on the hillside in the hope of bearing children.

But the Green Man is not merely a symbol of virility, or of the spirit of nature - but more of a direct manifestation of that nature. He is its guardian and champion also. And one of the most important aspects I want to consider here are the challenges and tests the Green Man offers to us - if we want them. From these we can learn much, not only about the natural world and its needs but also about ourselves.

Last year Caitlin and I took a group of people who were doing our Celtic Shamanism course to the great stone complex at Avebury in Wiltshire. Part of the work we asked them to do there was to find a stone to which they felt particularly drawn, to sit down with their back to the stone - or touching it in some way and when they had attuned themselves to its frequency, to ask if it had any instructions as to how they might work to heal the earth. Almost without exception they came back with the same answer - never mind about healing the earth, first you must heal yourselves.

The challenges the Green Man offers us are one way to heal ourselves and to reawaken ourselves to the power or Nature - both the Nature within us and the Nature of which we are a part. But this happens only if we want it to, only if we can overcome those negative aspects of ourselves which have separated us from Nature -greed, materialism, too great a dependence of Science, a belief that the earth is ours to take from whatever and whenever we wish.... It takes courage to face these things, and it needs more than a simple denial. It's no longer enough to say: I reject these things - we must go a stage further it we are to recover a real sense of the sacredness of the earth.

There's an old folk story that tells of the discovery of a Green Man in Britain during the Middle Ages. He was kept in a cage as a kind of freak and never once spoke until his death. It is this voicelessness that we are invited to reverse. The Green Man challenges us to help restore his voice, the voice of the green world and through that the voice of Nature and of the Earth. The rewards for this service are great, but so are the risks. It is no easy thing to accept the role of the Champion of the Sacred Land, and whether we live up to it or not is up to us. When we look into the eyes of the Green man we see a wildness and power that is an open challenge to us.

There are four aspects of the Green Man/Woman which express   this element of test and trial and I want to concentrate on these for the moment. Between them they form a seasonal and directional glyph which helps us orient ourselves towards them and all that they stand for and can teach us. Each one has its own consort, establishing the polarity of gender - each one issues a test or challenge of his or her own.

Each figure embodies an aspect of the Season and a Direction. Thus the Green Man of the North is a Winter King, who is embodied in the character of the GREEN KNIGHT whose role is that of a challenger. The story of his appearance at the Winter court of King Arthur is well known, but I'd like to read you the scene in a modern translation of the great medieval poem Sir Gawain and the Green Knight or, as he is sometimes called 'the Green Gome' a word which can also mean 'Goblin'. Here he is, entering before the astonished courtiers and their ladies.

From his neck to his loins so square set was he, and so long and
stalwart of limb, that I trow he was half a giant. And yet he was
a man, and the merriest that might ride. His body in back and
breast was strong, his belly and waist were very small, and all
his features full clean.
Great wonder of the knight
Folk had in hall, I ween,
Full fierce he was to sight,
And all over bright green." (trans W. Kirby)

This powerful and threatening figure offers to play "a Christmas game" in which he will exchange blows with any man there, on condition that whoever gives the blow will accept a blow in return. Gawain alone has the courage to face the giant, and with the Green Knight's own axe cuts off his head.

To the horror of all the company however, the monstrous visitor does not fall - instead he rises and taking up his head, holds it aloft. The lips move and the voice speaks, telling Gawain that he must journey to the Green Chapel one year hence to receive back the blow he has given. The Green Knight then mounts his horse and rides from the court, leaving everyone stunned and horrified and Gawain wondering what he has promised.

The second part of the poem tells of the turning of the seasons and of Gawain's approach to his terrible challenge. He sets out in search of the Green chapel and is at first unsuccessful until he arrives as the castle of Sir Bercilak, a fiercely hearty lord who tells Gawain that the place he is seeking lies close at hand and offers him hospitality and a guide when the day of the trial dawns.

Gawain willingly accepts the offer, and settles down to enjoy the elaborate hospitality of his host. Every day Bercilak rides forth to the hunt, returning with various beasts that he has captured and killed. Before leaving he proposes an exchange; since Gawain prefers to stay at home, he will give whatever he catches on the hunt in exchange for whatever prize Gawain wins at home.

Reluctantly Gawain agrees, expecting to win nothing. But his host's wife, the beautiful Lady Bercilak, intends otherwise. Every morning, as soon as her husband has departed, she enters Gawain's bedroom and offers herself to him. Gawain, whose reputation throughout Arthurian tradition is as a famous lover, but who is here described as the soul of chivalry and courtesy, refuses all but a chaste kiss, which he awards to the lord of the castle when he returns.

This curious exchange is repeated three times, and each time Gawain, fearing the inevitability of his death at the hands of the Green Knight, finds it harder to refuse the Lady. At last he is persuaded to accept a gift - a green baldric that she tells him will protect him from the death he fears. The day dawns when he must make his way to the Green Chapel. As promised Bercilak provides a guide and soon Gawain finds himself in a strange place. The poem describes it thus:

> *"At length a little way off he caught sight of a round hillock by the side of a brook.*
> *And there was a ford across the brook, and the water therein bubbled as though it had been boiling.*
> *The knight ... walked round about [the mound], debating within himself what place it might be.*
> *It had a hole at the end and on either side, and it was overgrown with tufts of grass*
> *and was all round and hollow within...." (ibid)*

The Green Knight now appears and Gawain kneels to receive the blow. Twice his adversary feints, then mocks Gawain's courage. Finally he nicks Gawain's neck and declares himself satisfied. To Gawain's astonishment and wonder he now reveals that he is really Sir Bercilak, and that he and his wife were placed under enchantment by 'the Goddess Morgane', whom Gawain had seen disguised as an ugly old woman in the castle. The whole business had been set up to test the courage of Arthur's court, and Gawain in particular. The only reason for the slight wound to Gawain's neck was because he had failed at the last and accepted the green baldric.

We can see at once what the challenge of the Green Knight is in this context. It is the challenge of death. Given that at one time the challenger probably really suffered decapitation this must always have been seen as a serious challenge. The loss of the head, especially among the Celts where this story originated, meant the loss of the soul as well, for they saw the head as a container of the soul and the strength of the warrior - which is why the Celts cut off their enemies heads in war and hung them from their chariots - and it is also why some Native American Tribes took the scalps of their enemies.

For us the challenge is different. We are asked to loose our lives in another sense - to give up our old lives and suffer a sometimes-painful awakening to the subtle energies of the greater world. To face the Challenge of the Green Knight means to loose our old life and rediscover a new way of being - one that entails re-establishing our connectedness with all of life - animal, human and vegetable. It is the first stage in giving back a voice to the Green Man.

Accompanying him we have LADY BERCILAK. She is a somewhat shadowy figure, yet few who have read the poem will forget her beauty and grace, as well as her bold sensuality. Her test is of the senses, and of honesty too, she forces us to come to terms with our approach to the physicality of life. Gawain deals well with her, despite his fearfulness over his upcoming trial, and wins her respect because of it.

The second aspect of the Green Man. who stands in the East and is the lord of springtime is ROBIN HOOD, perhaps the most familiar figure of the Greenwood. Robin's story is less clear than the Green Knight's and requires a summary constructed from a number of sources. On the one hand Robin is a medieval outlaw, hiding out in Sherwood Forest with his band of Merry Men, but on the other he is a far more ancient, ritual figure, 'The King of the Wood', whose role is to keep the groves of the Greenwood and to protect its denizens, both human and animal. He is thus also sometimes called 'The Lord of the Beasts' or 'Herne the Hunter'.

There is a clear cycle to Robin's life: he enters the Wood at springtime, where he is crowned King in the great medieval ceremony of the May Day Revels. As King of the May he rules for a year, accepting challenges from such powerful Otherworld figures as Little John. Friar Tuck and Will Scarlet, each of whom he defeats in combat and each of whom subsequently becomes part of his merry band. He also has to face the Champion of Winter, the Green knight himself, with whom he must battle to win the hand of the Spring Maiden,

Over the years the roles become blurred until Robin himself is seen as a kind of Green Gome, living deep in the Wildwood, and wearing a horned headdress, from which he becomes known as Robin-i-the-Hood, or Robin-o'-the-Wood, ritual titles dating back long before the middle ages. Ultimately he must die for the sake of the woodland, letting out his blood in a ceremony that is itself of great antiquity. The medieval ballad "The Death of Robin Hood", tells the end of the story.

Growing old and ill Robin decides to visit his 'kinswoman,' the Abbess of Kirklees Priory near Peterborough, who is a famed healer. Apparently sensing trouble, Little John tries to persuade his master to take fifty men with him, but Robin refuses and in the end is accompanied only by John.

On the way they encounter a strange old woman beside a stream, who appears to curse Robin. John is filled with foreboding but cannot persuade his master to turn back. At the Abbey John is locked out of the room where Robin is to be treated, and the Abbess begins to bleed her kinsman - a common enough treatment for most ailments in that time. However, as the ballad says:

And first it bled, the thick, thick blood,
And afterwards the thin,
And well then wits good Robin Hood
treason there was within....

With failing strength Robin blows his horn and Little John breaks in - too late to save his master, who has bled too much. As John begs to be allowed to burn Kirklees and all within it to the round, Robin rallies enough to say that he has never made war on women and will not begin now. He then begs to be helped to the window, and from there looses his last arrow, declaring that where it falls there should he be buried. John carries out this duty and erects a stone above the grave bearing only the words: Here lies bold Robin Hood.

In this story Robin meets his death by bleeding to death, a specifically ritual mode of dying. In the ballads the Prioress is represented as an evil woman in league with an old enemy of Robin's, but it is much more likely that she represents the memory of a priestess of much older times, whose task it was to let out the blood of the sacrificial King to give life the earth.

In this context, Robin is clearly a willing sacrifice - the King of the Wood who must die in order that the seasons may continue to turn. Once, as we have seen, this sacrifice was a central part of the annual celebration of the dying and rising king; by the time of Robin Hood the Outlaw, in the 13th or 14th centuries, such things were no more than a memory, all but forgotten save in certain neglected corners of the land such as Castleton and parts of Wales. But Robin Hood still reigned supreme, as had the Green Man through the ages, but in a new form. Ever renewing like the Greenwood he represented, he could not die, only change and take on a new disguise as 'the merry outlaw of Sherwood'.

The character of the Abbess, here seen as an evil enemy of Robin, must once have been a priestess whose role it was to let out the blood of the king in a ceremony intended to restore the potency of the earth. The fact that Robin meets an old woman 'banning' by a stream, equates well with this idea, since the Irish Bean-Sidhe or Washer-at-the-Ford is traditionally seen by those about fight in a battle, washing out their bloody clothing the night before they are to die.

The challenge of Robin is less obvious at first than that of the Green Knight. But if we consider the skill for which Robin is traditionally applauded we will see how it all fits together. Robin is, above all other men, skilled with the use of the longbow. He not only hits the centre of the target every time, he can even split his first arrow with a second - a rare feat indeed. In a little known ballad from the Robin Hood tradition, 'Young Gamelan', we find a description of an archer who can shoot between the cloth and the flesh of a man's leg, and in Celtic myth the wonder child Llew Llaw Gyffes performs a similar feat by shooting between the sinews of a bird's leg. Skills of this kind are mystical, and if any of you have ever shot with a longbow you will know that to pull the clothyard shaft back to the cheek and sight along it is a truly mystical experience.

At a deeper level it has to do with the concept of aiming the spirit with clear-sightedness and forethought. The skill of accuracy has more to it than simply being a good shot. So Robin's test is that of shooting skilfully, of learning to aim ones spiritual intent with clarity and insight. To face his challenge may mean wrestling or throwing a huge stone - all tests described in the ballad lore of the Greenwood. It may not seem as fearful or important as the Green knight's challenge, but it urges forward the Spring towards birth, and if you have felt the power of the dawning year between March and May you will know how powerful that can be. So with ourselves too we begin the return to our full heritage of strength and oneness with the earth at this time. It is the second stage of giving back a voice to the Green Man.

Robin Hood's partner is, of course MAID MARIAN, the May Queen, the consort of the King of the Wood. Her origins are shadowy and she only really emerges as a character quite late in the Robin Hood cycle, yet there is a unmistakable quality about her gentleness, gaiety, and sense of fun. She dances her way through life, and her test is the Test of True Love, of selflessness. She is best honoured in her Bower, woven of green branches and decorated with may blossom. As Queen of the May she brings a powerful feminine energy to match that of her Lord.

The third aspect of the Green Man is that of the Lord of Summer, and it is fitting that he should be represented by a figure who is in many ways the opposite of the Green Knight, and who is, incidentally, another challenger of Gawain. The figure I refer to is called GROMER SOMER JOUR which means 'Man of the Summer's Day, and he stands, appropriately enough, in the South, the season of Summer.

Gromer's partner is named Lady Ragnall. Given the appearance of a hideous woman by the Goddess Morgana she must seek a man willing to give her the freedom to choose her true appearance in order to break the spell. Only Gawain has the ability to do this. In the story she is represented as Gromer's sister though in an earlier version she would have been his consort. Her test is the test of Freewill. It is not until Gawain gives her the right to be herself that she is freed from the imprisoning spell. We might think of her as a representative of the Earth, which will only be set free when we give it the right to follow its own course rather than forcing it to follow our dictates.

Gromer is a representative of the Green Man of the Summer, a fiery lord whose testing of both Arthur and Gawain is every bit as extreme as the Green Knight's. It is a test of Truth, and it forms the third stage in giving back a voice to the Green Man.

The fourth and final aspect of this four-fold structure is the aspect of Fall and of the East. The figure that fits best here is known as GREEN JACK. In Europe and in England particularly Green Jack is as old as the hills. Stories are told of him all over the land, where he is also known as Jack-in-the-Green, the Berryman, John Barleycorn, and Robin Goodfellow. He is, primarily, a Trickster, though in our time he has more limited power. He plays merry pranks on the people, dances wildly in the streets, is 'cut down' and 'rises' again, and is sacrificed for the sake of the harvest. As such he stands polarised with Robin Hood in the West. They are in fact to a certain degree interchangeable ~ as are the Green Knight and Gromer. It would be just as easy to put Robin in the East and Jack in the West, but I have put them thus because there is a freshness and youthfulness about Robin, while Jack has a later-in-the-year feel to him which makes him more fit candidate for the golden days of the Fall.

There's an old traditional song about him that says it all.

John Barleycorn

There were three men came out of the West
Their fortunes for to try,
And these three men made a solemn vow,
John Barleycorn should die.

They ploughed him in the earth so deep,
With clods upon his head,
Then these three men they did conclude
John Barleycorn was dead.

There he lay sleeping in the ground
Till rain from the sky did fall,
Then Barleycorn sprang a green blade
And proved liars of them all.

There he remained till midsummer
And looked both pale and wan.
Then Barleycorn grew a long, long beard

185

Much like unto a man.

They hired men with scythes so sharp
To cut him off at the knee.
See how they served poor Barleycorn
They served him bitterly.

They hired men with forks and rakes
To pierce him to through the heart,
But the carter served him worse than that
For he bound him to a cart.

And then they brought him to a barn
A prisoner to endure,
And soon they fetched him out again
And laid him on the floor.

They hired men with crabtree sticks
To beat him flesh from bones,
But the miller served him worse than that
For he ground him 'tween two stones.

They flung him into a cistern deep
And drowned him in water clean,
But the brewer served him worse than that
For he brewed him into beer.

Oh Barleycorn is the very best grain
That ever was sown on land.
It will serve you more than any grain
From the turning of your hand.

Mysterious, and never represented as an image; cut down, threshed, flailed and beaten, ground between two stones and made into bread and ale, John Barleycorn is warmed by the rays of the sun and rises triumphant again as have all corn gods from the Nile Delta to the fields of England. In the eternal cycle of his life, death and resurrection is the mystery of all life.

The Jack's test is a simple one, and it is related to all the others. It is the test of Rebirth, and it involves dying in order to reawaken to a new life. It is not the same as the Green Knight's challenge however; to take upon the role of the Jack is to suffer death, to remain a while in the Underworld, and then to return, bringing knowledge and healing to the people and the land. It is about trust - about trusting that if you embrace this death you will return. So it is also the Test of Trust. It is the fourth and last stage in giving back a voice to the Green Man.

In Autumn, Green Jack's partner is the HARVEST QUEEN, who gathers the rich crop of berries and fruits in her cornucopia. In her we may discern the ancient Goddess of the Grain; but these days she is most often seen in the corn dollies that are braided from the last sheaf harvested from the fields and made into an   effigy of the Harvest Queen, trimmed with ribbons. Her test is the struggle for survival in the face of want. While Green Jack as John Barleycorn is cut down and made into beer and whiskey, the Harvest Queen is made into the bread that will feed us through the winter. Together, they bring the cycle back full circle to the North and give us a glyph of the Green Man's appearances and tests around the year.

Mediation

Now that we have now set up the four quarters with their resident powers and qualities, let us prepare to make a journey each of these directions in turn, there to communicate with one of these beings of whom we have heard. In each direction, take time to be with the beings that await you there. Each has something different to teach about healing yourself and healing the earth. Each one offers a test. You may, if you wish, commit yourself to undertaking that test or trial, at first in the subtle realm of your imagination, later in the world where you live and move and have your being. Or you may simply approach the figure and ask what they have to teach, how you can help to give back a voice to the Green Man.

Beginning in North I'd like you to stand and turn in that direction. Close your eyes and remember the images you saw for that quarter - the images of the Green Knight and Lady Bercilak. Imagine you are walking on the hills with the wind blowing in your face and that you meet with of them there. What will they have to say to you, what will you say to them?
Now turn to the East, and imagine you are walking in the forest. This time you will meet Robin Hood and Maid Marion. What will you have to say to each other?

Turning to the South imagine you are seated by a rushing river. Here are Gromer Somer Jour and the Lady Ragnall, waiting to talk with you. How will you address them and what will they say to you?

Finally, turn to the West and see yourself walking in a field of standing corn. Here are Green Jack and the Harvest Queen. What mysteries will you learn from them?

Last, turn back to the centre again, and still with eyes closed review all t you have learned in these few brief moments. Then slowly open your eyes and re-establish contact with the world around you. But do not forget, what the aspects of the Green Man and Green Lady told you - they may have far reaching effect on your life and the life of the world.

Chapter 21:

TOLKIEN & THE GREEN MAN

The Lord of the Rings has been a part of my life since I was about 12, when I first discovered *The Hobbit* and quickly graduated to the trilogy itself. It's hard to remember how powerful the effect of these books was on me. The vastness and beauty – as well as horror – of the world created by Professor Tolkien is something that has been discussed far too often to need repeating here. I enjoyed a very brief correspondence with the professor, who even sent me a poem, and the effect of the stories he told has remained with me ever since. I was delighted to be asked to read a paper at a 2006 conference in Oxford, where I live not far from the house where my great inspirer once lived. I chose a subject that is close to my heart – the Green Man – whose presence in Middle Earth is as powerful as it is in this world.

Like many others I first read '*The Lord of the Rings*' when I was in my teens. I also wrote a fan letter to Professor Tolkien, and in my 10-page missive mentioned the fact that I was writing a huge Arthurian novel - adding how much I admired the writings of his colleague Charles Williams. I don't think I expected a response, but I got one anyway, in which Tolkien expressed the fact that he was not a great lover of Arthurian romance and that he did not like what he called 'Charles Williams Arthurianisms'. Despite this he enclosed with his letter a poem called 'The Lay of Aotrou & Itroun' which makes reference to the great Arthurian forest of Broceliande, which just happens to be the title of my book!

Later on I heard about Tolkien's widely publicized statement that he had written the Lord of the Rings to provide a Mythology for England, and that he regarded the Arthurian legends as essentially French. By this time I'd spent years studying Arthurian literature and myth and I know that I reacted very strongly to this statement. I knew - as he must - and that the foundation for most of the Arthurian stories came not from French but from Celtic sources. And here perhaps lies the real problem Professor Tolkien had with Arthurian literature in general - that its roots were Celtic, while he loved all things Saxon. Given this, perhaps it would have been expecting too much for anyone to approve of a literature written those who had been one's enemies!

I think that every time I read the *Lord the Rings* after that - and again like most of you that's been quite a few times - I never stop looking for Arthurian parallels. I stand with another great British writer, who also lived close to Oxford - John Masefield - who wrote of the Arthurian legends, just before his death:

'Has not the time come for a re-making and re-issue of the epic [of Arthur] by a body of good scholars and writers? Is not the time ripe for an Authorized Version using old poems and fables little used by or unknown to Malory...? It is our English epic; we ought to make more use of it than we do.'

Tolkien did not, nor would he have wished to do any such thing – but he embedded so many Arthurian fragments in his books that he did go some way towards it. I could say a great deal about the Arthurian references in Tolkien, including the Merlin-like character of Gandalf, Aragorn as Arthur and so on – not to mention the very strong parallels between the character and situation of King Theoden and the Wounded King of the Grail romances. (Both are failing physically and as Kings and both have those who speak and act for them). I could also make out a reasonable case for a comparison between the One Ring and the Grail on Arthurian tradition. Instead of any of these matters I want to concentrate on a particular theme and on the characters that represents this in Tolkien's work. Specifically this has to do with his treatment of nature, which was clearly sacred to him in a very special way, not unlike the way it was understood by the pagans of the ancient world.

Despite Tolkien's dismissal (or should one say distrust?) of Arthurian literature, he had himself begin a long poem on 'The Fall of Arthur' (still, alas, unpublished!) and edited one of the most famous English Arthurian romances - an edition which is still widely used to this day. I refer of course to his edition, prepared with Professor Gordon, of the medieval poem known as 'Sir Gawain and the Green Knight'. We also have of course Tolkien's own translation of this, which was published posthumously. Though he refused to speak of them Tolkien acknowledged the presence of "ancient rituals... pagan divinities of the sun ... fertility ..." and of "the Dark and the Underworld, in the almost wholly lost antiquity of the North and of these Western Isles."(*Intro. to Gawain, Pearl & Orfeo* p17)

It struck me long since that there were some very interesting parallels between one of the characters in this poem and one of the leading characters in *The Lord of the Rings*. So, let we begin then with a brief summary of the poem for the benefit of those who are not familiar with it. 'Sir Gawain and the Green Knight' was written by an anonymous author living in the Midlands some around 1400. It tells the story of what happens one Christmas at Camelot when Arthur and the Knights of the Round Table are sitting down to supper. Just as they are about eat, thunder roles and lightning flashes - announces the appearance of a strange figure that enters the Great Hall of Camelot and confronts the king and his men, announcing that he is the Green Knight. He is indeed a most terrifying and unusual being. His skin and hair and his enormous bushy beard are green; as is his horse, his armour, and everything about him - except for his eyes, which are red. Over his shoulder he carries a huge axe, and in his other hand a club of holly. The Green Knight challenges Arthur and his men, addressing them in slighting tones, and suggesting they play a Christmas game with him - assuming that they have the courage to do so. The nature of this is that he will allow any man there to strike a blow with his own axe - on the understanding that he will then return the blow. Understandably perhaps Arthur hesitates before accepting this curious challenge - and in that moment his nephew, the great knight Sir Gawain, leaps up and offers to undertake the challenge on his behalf. The scene proceeds as follows: The Green Knight dismounts from his horse and hands the axe to Gawain, who raises it and strikes off the Green Knight's head. However instead of falling the body of the Green Knight marches across the hall, picks up the head and hold it aloft - at which point the lips move and the Green Knight announces that he will expect Sir Gawain in one year's time at 'the Green Chapel', where he will receive his return blow. The Green Knight then mounts his horse and, still carrying his grisly severed head, departs from the hall.

A year passes and Gawain sets out in search of the Green Chapel. Within a few days of the allotted time he arrives at a castle and is made welcome by its boisterous Lord Sir Bercilak and his beautiful lady. When he reveals that he is searching for the Green Chapel, Gawain is told that it lies close by and that Sir Bercilak will provide a guide to show him the way. Meanwhile, he insists that Gawain remain at the castle to rest and be entertained.

During the next three days we are treated to a detailed account of Gawain's stay at the castle. Each morning Sir Bercilak announces that he will go hunting, and offers to exchange any prize that he acquires with his guest. And each day, once the Lord has gone, Gawain is visited in his room Lady Bercilak, who attempts to seduce him. In each case Gawain is mindful of his knightly honour, and refuses her - accepting only a kiss. Each night Bercilak returns with the spoils of the hunt, and demands the exchange with Gawain, who is only able to offer up a chaste kiss on the cheek.

On her last visit, fearful for his life, Gawain accepts a talisman from her that will protect him from the Green Knight's axe. On the appointed day Bercilak provides the promised guide to the Green Chapel. The Green Knight appears and Gawain kneels to receive the blow. Twice his adversary feints, then mocks Gawain's courage. Finally he nicks Gawain's neck and declares himself satisfied. To Gawain's astonishment he now reveals that he is really Sir Bercilak, and that he and his wife were placed under enchantment by 'the Goddess Morgane', whom Gawain had seen disguised as an ugly old woman in the castle. The whole business had been set up to test the courage of Arthur's court, and Gawain in particular. The only reason for the slight wound to Gawain's neck was because he had failed at the last and accepted the protective talisman.

The Green Knight's game is an age-old one, well attested in mythologies around the world. The pattern is always the same: the God offers his life-blood for the sake of the people in return for their own courage and self-sacrifice. This exchange is at the heart of the Green Knight's story as it is at the heart of the Christian story. As the guardian of the natural world the Green Knight challenges people to acknowledge his yearly sacrifice by offering a willing service to all of creation. Gawain does not overcome the Green Knight but submits to a greener strength than his own.

So much for the story of this remarkable medieval poem, which seamlessly blends Christian and Pagan beliefs. I'd like to quote two passages from Professor Tolkien's own translation. The first is a description of the boisterous Sir Bercilak and the second describes the friendship and hospitality he offered to the knight.

> "Gawain gazed at the good man who had greeted him kindly,
> and he thought bold and big was the baron of the castle,
> very large and long, and his life at the prime:
> broad and bright was his beard, and all beaver-hued,
> stern, strong in his stance upon stalwart legs,
> his face fell as fire, and frank in his speech;
> and well it suited him, in sooth, as it seemed to the knight,
> a lordship to lead untroubled over lieges trusty.

Then:

> They took him between them, and talking they lead him
> to a fireside in a fair room, and first of all called
> for spices, which men sped without sparing to bring them,
> and ever wine therewith well to their liking.
> The lord for their delight leaped up full often,
> many times merry games being minded to make;
> his hood he doffed, and on high he hung it on a spear,

and offered it as an honour for any to win
who the most fun could devise at that Christmas feast-.
'And I shall try, by my troth, to contend with the best
ere I forfeit this hood, with the help of my friends!'
Thus with laughter and jollity the lord made his jests
To gladden Sir Gawain with games that night..."

Next to this I would like to place another quotation, this time from 'The Lord the Rings':

"There was another burst of song, and suddenly, hopping and dancing along the path, there appeared above the reeds an old battered hat with a tall crown and a long blue feather stuck in the band. With another hop and a bound there came into view a man, or so it seemed. At any rate he was too large and heavy for a hobbit, if not quite tall enough for one of the Big People, though he made noise enough for one, stumping along with great yellow boots on his thick legs, and charging grass and rushes like a cow going down to drink. He had a blue coat and a long brown beard; his eyes were blue and bright, and his face was red as a ripe apple, but creased into a hundred wrinkles of laughter. In his hands he carried on a large leaf as on a tray a small pile of white water-lilies". (p117 US Paper Edition)

This is, of course, a description of the redoubtable Tom Bombadil, one of Tolkien's most unforgettable characters. He is described as 'the eldest', 'the oldest of the old',
'The Master of Wood, water and hill', and is represented as a spirit so powerful so potent and so ancient, that not even the all-powerful Ring can affect him. His hospitality toward the Hobbits on their terrible journey reflects the hospitality of Bercilak to Gawain, also setting out on a life or death journey. Of course I am not saying that Tom Bombadil *is* The Green Knight, merely that the one may have influence the other. Tolkien himself, in various letters, admitted that he was reluctant to 'explain' Bombadil, and even professed not to fully understand him.

But there is more to it than this. Bombadil, along with the Ents, is very clearly a representation of the natural world, which Tolkien so often represented as being in a perilous state. In this alone he resembles the Green Knight, but the Green Knight, as perhaps is 'Old Tom', an aspect of one of the most ancient and potent symbols of the natural world that mankind has ever produced.

You can find this character represented in carved heads found in Middle-Eastern temples, in some of the most characteristic imagery of the classical world, and throughout the folklore traditions of Europe – and in the figure of the Green Knight. But by far the most significant appearance of this figure by far and in a series of extraordinary carvings found within the medieval cathedrals and churches of Europe. Known as foliate heads, these carvings represent humanoid faces that seem to be made from leaves, ought to be disgorging greenery that from now marls, eyes, nostrils, years. And they are found, generally speaking, hidden among the roof bosses them or on the highest areas on the outside of these buildings. It has been pointed out that few of these heads would have been visible to the congregation's worshipping below, and this has raised the question of why they were put there, and in addition who put them there, and what they represented.

You may not know it, but you have almost certainly seen more than one Green Man in your lifetime. If you have visited any of the magnificent gothic churches scattered over much of Europe, even as a curious tourist, you will have seen the foliate heads, faces which seem human but which when examined closely appear to be made of leaves. Indeed we have our fare share of them right here in

191

Oxford – some in the old Divinity School at the Bodlian Library, or all over the roof at Christ Church Alternately, you may have wandered into a museum and seen some of the fine medieval tapestries which depict scenes from the lives of some curious looking, leafy figures known as Wildmen. These too are green men - as is the figure of Robin Hood, the outlaw of Sherwood Forest, or the figure of Puck in Shakespeare's 'A Midsummer Night's Dream'. Here, as elsewhere, the Green Man lurks, almost in hiding, staring out from amid the trees of the forest of Arden or laughing down from the high transepts of Cathedral roofs.

But the story of the Green Man is made up of many strands, each of contributes to the whole. For some he is an ancient symbol of nature and fertility, which can be seen to represent mankind's connection with the earth. To others he is a symbol of wildness, of the untamed spirit that lives within us all and reflects the wildness at the heart of nature. In our own time the Green Man has become an unofficial icon for the environmental movement, pointing to the way in which we continue to interact with the world around us. He is also, I believe, very much present in Tolkien's great work

The idea of a 'Green' Man as a representative of the natural world probably dates back to the first agrarian peoples of the ancient world, who felt the power of nature and gave it a face and form. We have only to look at the way in which the green thrusts through, overcomes, glories in its strength to understand why a masculine image was chosen. Certainly among the tribal people who lived in the vast woodlands that once covered much of the European continent the Green Man ruled supreme as a spirit of these woods, a representation, in semi-human guise, of the abiding life force of the trees.

Both as an actual presence and as symbolic entities in their own right, the vast woodlands made a deep and lasting impression on the imagination of those who dwelt close to their shaded depths. Individual sacred trees featured in many cultures and often possessed the qualities of the deities to which they were dedicated. Though no truly ancient image of this kind has survived, we may imagine that certain trees could have been seen as representatives of the Green Man, and may well have been carved into his likeness. Even if this were not the case, the connection between trees and the sustaining of the world provided links with the energy of nature represented by the Green Man.

For the Norse people the entire world was founded on the roots and branches of the world tree Yggdrasil, while in ancient Ireland, the great yew, Eo Mugna, was considered a source of Druidic and territorial power. In the Mediterranean world the cult of the dying and rising god Attis, himself a type of Green Man, was represented by a pine tree, which was carried in procession during religious festivals.

In a severely deforested world, it is hard to imagine just how dense our woodlands once were. Forests were places of awe and mystery, into whose depths few would venture during the day, although the resources of the woodshore were useful to those who lived nearby. In North West Europe, these dense forests often contained groves of sacrifice or spiritual mystery. From trees in the groves dedicated to the Norse cult of Odin both human and animal offerings were hung, indicators of the powerful force of the ancient forest gods.

The oak groves of the Celtic world were the haunt of strange forest beings and awesome tree-spirits, their mysteries known only to the Druids, whose knowledge and understanding of the natural world was second to none.

All of this will, I am sure, be already recalling Tolkien's descriptions of Fangorn, and of its mysterious tree-herds, the Ents (a name found in Norse myths and was not coined by Tolkien). Let me quote you another passage:

"They found that they were looking at a most extraordinary face. It belonged to a large Man-like, almost Troll-like, figure, at least fourteen foot high, very sturdy, with a tall head, and hardly any neck. Whether it was clad in stuff like green and grey bark, or whether that was its hide, was difficult to say. At any rate the arms, at a short distance from the trunk, were not wrinkled, but covered with a brown smooth skin. The large feet had seven toes each. The lower part of the long face was covered with a sweeping grey beard, bushy, almost twiggy at the roots, thin and mossy at the ends. But at the moment the hobbits noted little but the eyes. These deep eyes were now surveying them, slow and solemn, but very penetrating. They were brown, shot with a green light. (pp452)

A better description of the Green Man you would, I think, be hard pressed to find!

There is a degree of wildness, a depth in Treebeard and the Ents, which can be released - as in the destruction of Isengard - and this too is present in the many forms of the Green Man. You can see it in the leaf mask carvings discovered in the Middle Eastern cradle of civilization lead us to the Sumerian epic of Gilgamesh (c 700 BC) where we encounter a figure who represents just such a power: Enkidu, a wild and primitive being whose great strength and passionate soul embodies the energy of Nature itself. Jealous of his power, the gods condemn Enkidu to die, prompting his friend, the hero Gilgamesh, to undertake a journey to the otherworld in search of a cure for death itself - a plant called 'The Old Man has Become a Young Man Again'. Although Gilgamesh finds the plant, he loses it again to a serpent, which at once sloughs its skin in a symbolic image of rebirth.

In the poems that make up the Gilgamesh epic Enkidu represents an overflowing life force, wild and untamed. He stands out as one of the oldest representations of the potent energy of the Green Man that was to reappear later, during the Middle Ages, in the figure of the Wildman, who represented a return to the idea of living closer to the natural world. Though considered barely human, the Wildmen (and Women) represented a return to nature long before Rousseau proposed it.

Elsewhere, in ancient Egypt, where water was scarce and the annual rising of the Nile waters was essential to all life, green gods and goddesses played an important part in the spirituality of the two lands. The colour green was honoured above all, and to 'do green things' came to mean doing good; while ' to do red things' meant to do evil. Osiris, perhaps the most important deity in Egyptian life, was both a god of vegetation and resurrection. In the Pyramid Texts, he is known as 'the Great Green' and is depicted as green skinned in acknowledgement of his life-giving energy.

The story of Osiris tells of his murder and dismemberment at the hands of the jealous god Set. Afterwards his wife Isis recovered the scattered parts of his body and restored him to life. Thereafter this cycle of dismemberment, death and resurrection was honoured as a symbolic reference to the flooding of the Nile delta, by which the fields were greened with new growth when the waters rose. In token of this, miniature mummy cases representing Osiris were sown with grain and left out in the rain until they sprouted - an emblematic statement of life rising from death and a perfect expression of the energy that flowed in the veins of the Green Man.

In the Classical world also we find references to older, wilder forces than the orderly deities of Mount Olympus. Just as among the Celtic peoples every tree, stream, hill and grove had its own dryad, nymph and tutelary spirit.

The god Pan, whose name means 'universal,' was a major deity of nature. As the protector of the wild, he could appear anywhere in the natural world. Those who came across him at lonely, unfrequented places were said to be consumed with panic at the sight of him. This experience of solitude, of a numinous sense of wild, god-filled nature is one seldom experienced in a world that has tamed so much of the earth. But Pan could not be tamed or controlled, any more than Dionysus (or his

Roman equivalent, Bacchus), could be made to obey the desires of his followers. The wild green power of Dionysus, like that of Pan, overcomes the ordered world of humanity in much the same way that plants penetrate concrete. His growths overwhelm man-made structures, and his ferment enters into the human body so that we can experience for ourselves the ecstatic life of plants. Both gods represent an energy that is an essential aspect of the Green Man.

I asked a question earlier: Why are Green Men found almost hidden among the roof bosses and far up on the outer walks of the churches and cathedrals of Europe? During the Middle Ages, woodlands were managed and coppiced to provide cover for deer and sport for the nobility. Forests were administered by royally appointed foresters and Woodwards and became forbidden to ordinary people. But the loss of the forests and the building of the great cathedrals coincide.

The early Church Fathers, perhaps with reason, was suspicious of the woods and what went on there – as well as what inhabited them; despite the fact that it was partly in acknowledgement of the importance of the ancient treescapes that so much of the architecture of medieval churches was designed to make them look like stone forests. It is not really so surprising to find the Green Man there; his presence was too deeply embedded in the consciousness of the ordinary people to be forgotten.

But other factors underlie these carvings. The dependency upon the harvest had not yet been replaced by modern methods of preservation and freezing. If the harvest failed, so did life - no one was exempt. The great cathedrals entailed the cutting down of prime trees to provide scaffolding for the huge stones to be raised. This enormous undertaking required its own harvest of men, skilled craftsmen who learned their trade through respect of their materials - stone, iron and wood. It was they who carved the foliate heads and placed them high above the heads of the worshippers. And, like all men engaged in dangerous work, they needed their talismans, carving their protectors in places of honour in acknowledgement of their powers. For the first time men had climbed higher than ever before. Were they aware of the hubris of climbing higher than the tallest trees, even in the service of God's glory? Lest the woodland spirits be offended, their green images were set higher than the holy images upon the altar.

Ideas and realisations of this kind passed into the folk-life and customs of ordinary people, along with the distant memories of devotion to the power of nature. Scraps of lore and imagery became embodied in dance, story, song and legend, underpinning the traditions of a world that still acknowledged the presence of the Green Man despite an increasing sense of separation from nature.

The story does not end here however. The Green Man has continued to reappear throughout the ages, reflecting, in the way he is represented, in the forms he takes, the changing relationship of humanity with nature. Often, and not at all surprisingly considering our constant attempts to subdue the earth to our needs, he comes as a challenger, seeming at times more than a little threatening. Yet beneath this fearsome aspect lies an unquenchable fountain of delight, which finds outlet in many ways - notably the exuberant festivals of Mayday and Midsummer, which continue to be celebrated in our own time and which become at times an all-out honouring of the Green Man in his many forms.

Like many of the gods of the ancient world, the Green Man is ever-present in the cycle of the growing year. He makes his youthful appearance amid the first green unfurling of spring, growing sturdily into the full panoply of summer manhood before beginning his descent into the rich reds and browning tints of his autumn age. As the bare, withered branches of winter reveal the skeletal woods, he is still present in the evergreens of the forest. The Green Man is a constant companion throughout the year and his presence is acknowledged at the many festivals that celebrate the turning of the seasons.

As the emerging green of early spring covers winter's bareness, it is time to herald the beginning of summer with festivals celebrating the Maytime. The Green Man appears as the King of the May, whose consort is chosen from the fairest maidens of the village. At this time the Green Man is young, desirous, the bringer of fertility and ecstatic celebration. When summer's basket is full, he reappears as the mature Harvest King, his beard full-grown, echoing the full ears of standing grain in every field. Then he is cut down with ritual solemnity, his sacrifice becoming the stored bounty of barns, the flour to make bread, the grain to ferment beer and distil spirits. When the cold blasts of winter blow the last leaves from the trees, his spirit returns as the King of the Winter Woods. His celebrations are fearsome games and contests, full of riddles, wrestling and combat. At the hub of the winter-locked wheel of the year, his games give the vigour to spin the wheel of life once more, to begin the cycle of green growth without which we could not live. His pastimes, feasts and contests literally pass the dead time of midwinter, making us grateful for his gifts that keep us alive when all else is dead.

From earliest times the ancient pattern of planting, growth and harvest was supported by rituals designed to ensure that the yearly cycle continued. At one time sacrificial offerings - some human - were made to appease the gods of the natural world and ensure the health and fertility of the earth. In many parts of the world, especially throughout the Mediterranean, vegetation and harvest cults sprang up with their attendant mysteries of the dying and rising god. One of the most widespread stories focused on the sacrificed god-king, sometimes called 'The King of the Wood.' or 'Rex Nemorensis', a man chosen to reign for a year, then killed, his slayer taking over his role for a further twelve months.

A figure that unites the characteristics of the sacrificial Year King with the spirit of the forest and woodland is Robin Hood. Most familiar as the leader of a band of 12th century outlaws in Sherwood Forest, he is in fact a far more complex, myth-based character, whose historical existence is at best doubtful, but whose life, as told in medieval ballads, follows a universal pattern.

Of unknown or doubtful parentage, Robin appears fully-fledged, living in the greenwood with his outlaw band, the Merry Men. Their trickster-like adventures, which conceal a darker historical truth in which Norman overlords ruthlessly oppressed their Saxon serfs, marked them out as semi-divine beings hiding behind the appearance of medieval freedom fighters.

The eventual death of Robin Hood, betrayed and bled almost to death by a priestess-like figure, show him to be a type of Rex Nemorensis, while Marion, Robin's greenwood sweetheart, represents the Queen of the May, a figure as old as the Green Man himself, decked out in flowers and garbed in white. Together these two ancient beings ruled over the riotous Mayday Games - often referred to as Robin Hood's Games - which celebrated the arrival of Spring with a wildness and abandon that is very much an embodiment of the Green Man.

The appearance, from the height of the Middle Ages, of Robin, Marion, and the Merry Men in the folk-plays of Britain make it clear that their true nature was recognised by the ordinary people, who continued to celebrate the mysteries of the green year in this way under the suspicious eyes of the Church.

Underlying both the Robin Hood myth and the story of the Green Knight is a far older myth - that of the battle between the Kings of Summer and Winter for possession of the Spring Maiden. This theme goes right back to the rituals of the Year Kings and the Rex Nemorensis, and underpins a vast cycle of myth and legend from many different cultures. The two combatants, or their champions, fight annually for the hand of the Maiden, and also for rule over the opposing halves of the year. Since the pattern of the seasons always follows the same path, there can only ever be one outcome - the King of Summer must defeat the King of Winter and win the heart of the Maiden of Spring. But since the natural progression of the seasons was not always perceived as inevitable, the ritual enactment of the struggle of one against the other was regarded as a serious event, and this is reflected in the myths that describe it.

Thus in the cycle of Robin Hood myths, the battle is replayed in Robin's continuing struggle with his arch enemy, the Sheriff of Nottingham; while in Gawain and the Green Knight (just in case you thought I had strayed too far from the subject!) the hero's contest with the Green Knight harks back to the older battle with, in this instance, Lady Bercilak carrying the role of the Spring Maiden, Gawain acting as the champion of the Summer King (Arthur) against Bercilak as the Winter King.

In our own time, the Green Man has returned though a resurgence of interest in 'green' living, and increasing concerns for the survival of our natural habitat. Even the works of contemporary fantasists, such as the immensely popular 'Mythago Wood' novels of Robert Holdstock, or the urban fantasies of Canadian writer Charles de Lint, reflect a growing interest in the story of the Green Man. And here of course we return to the works of Professor Tolkien. There is, for me anyway, no doubt at all that Treebeard, and perhaps to a lesser degree Tom Bombadil, have brought the presence of the Green Man into the lives of countless readers, while comic-book heroes such as 'Green Lantern', 'Green Arrow' and 'Slaine', and the popular TV series 'Robin of Sherwood', have helped keep us aware of the character and purpose of the Green Man in some of his many guises.

The struggles and challenges offered by the Green Man draw us back to a realisation of our own perilously eroded relationship with the environment, which Tolkien recognised long before it was fashionable to do so. A desire to conquer the natural world, to rob it of its resources, to decimate its productivity in the name of progress and financial gain, has caused us to come perilously close to the destruction of the natural world foreshadowed by the machine-like intent of Saruman. The return of the Green Man in our time as an unacknowledged icon of the ecological movement can be seen as only the latest chapter in an age-old story that begins in the shadowy forest world of early man and continues to this day in the ongoing struggle to save the green world from eventual extinction.

In a time when the world's tree cover is being steadily eroded, the ancient respect for the green is being recovered, not only as a spiritual, but also as a practical necessity. Trees stabilise the atmosphere, exuding the oxygen that earth's living beings need to exist. Our symbiotic partnership with the green world is in the air we breathe, as the trees process the carbon dioxide that we exhale. The Green Man's domain is also ours. Mythic and historic knowledge need the balance of ecological awareness - a living acknowledgement that, without the green world, we would not be here.

Nature's wisdom is an oral tradition that we can all experience. It is to the greenwood that we look to provide the paper on which to record our own store of wisdom in book form. We still need the nurture of the green, through the grains, nuts and fruits that it provides. We cover our bodies with clothes derived from the wood pulp and fibres of the green world, coloured by vegetable dyes. The power of herbs, plants and trees restores us to health when we are sick. Truly, there is no end to our symbiotic connection with the green.

Professor Tolkien would, I am sure, have endorsed this, and were he still living might have been an active voice in the cause of the green movement. For me this is made clear by every line in the Lord of the Rings that describes the natural world. Tolkien is among the foremost writers of our time when it comes to describing the landscapes through which his heroes and heroines walk. Let me leave you with just one example, which is as full of the unseen (but not, I think, unacknowledged) presence of the Green Man as the medieval poem Tolkien loved so much:

Day was opening in the sky, and they saw that the mountains were now much further off, receding eastward in a long curve that was lost in the distance. Before them, as they turned west, gentle slopes ran down into dim hazes far below. All about them were small woods of resinous trees, fir and cedar and cypress, and other kinds unknown in the Shire, with wide glades among them; and everywhere there was a wealth of sweet- smelling herbs and shrubs ... Here Spring was already busy about them: fronds pierced moss and mould, larches were green-fingered, small flowers were opening in the turf, birds were singing ... South and west ... looked towards the warm lower vales of Anduin, shielded from the east by the Ephel Uuath and yet not under the mountain -shadow, protected from the north by the Emyn Muil, open to the southern airs and the moist winds from the Sea far away. (P636 US Paper Ed.)

(2006)

Chapter 22:

ROBIN HOOD AND THE GREEN MAN

I grew up watching the old BBC series Robin Hood, staring Richard Green. Every week I would sit myself down in front of the TV and listen to the theme song:

Robin Hood, Robin Hood,
Riding through the glen,
Robin Hood, Robin Hood
With his band of men…

I think there as no child in the whole of Britain in the 50s who did not know this and go about singing it while re-enacting the adventures of Robin. Later, in the 80s, came the wonderful series Robin of Sherwood devised and written by Richard (Kip) Carpenter, with whom I became friends. Mark Ryan, who played the enigmatic Saracen Nazir in this series, is also a great friend, and in 2003 we worked together on the movie King Arthur, with Mark as sword master and myself as historical advisor. Meantime, there was Robin and Marion with Sean Connery as the ageing outlaw; Robin Hood Prince of Thieves, with Kevin Costner – a far better film than many give it credit for; and Robin Hood with Patrick Bergin. As I write I hear of a new adventure, Nottingham, with Russel Crowe as the Sheriff, which will appear in 2009. All of this has kept Robin Hood in our minds and hearts. But there is more to him than just a glamorous screen outlaw. In 1993 I wrote a book called Robin Hood: Green Lord of the Wildwood (Gothic Image) and soon after gave the first of two talks (both included here) at a Robin of Sherwood convention in London.

When it comes to it Robin Hood is as elusive today as he appears to have been in the Middle Ages. The reasons of course are different. In those days Robin was hiding from the law - in the shape of the Sheriff of Nottingham and his men; today he hides from us in a number of deferent ways - mostly through the wide diversity of images his name conjures up. Are we to see him as a Bold Outlaw, as a Green Man figure, as a Native British Trickster, or as a mixture of all of these and perhaps of something more as well?

In fact, despite the large amount of literature written about Robin, there is really very little hard information in any of it. Aside from a few scattered references in medieval chronicles the main sources for the legends are a handful of popular ballads - some twenty judged to be genuine products of the Middle Ages - and a few more which date from the 16th and 17th centuries and later. Even here, as in the character of Robin himself, there is disagreement as to which of the ballads is the oldest - and how old that is - which are genuine and which pastiche, and which contain clues to the possible historical characters that can be 'identified' with Robin Hood.

The best of the ballads is " The Little Gest of Robin Hood" printed in 1508 but maybe written earlier - 'Gest ' means life but it is really more of a mini-epic running to 456 stanzas, and combining the best of the stories. It tells the most familiar story of Robin, with all the usual characters, and some of the best known adventures - the meeting with Little John and Friar Tuck, the battles with the Sheriff, the meeting of Robin with the King of England - not Richard Lionheart but Edward I. There is no Maid Marion however and a good deal of the text is very bloody and savage - as in the episode when Robin, having finally killed the Sheriff, cuts of his head and mutilates it savagely before displaying it on the end of his bow - a far cry from the more usual image of Robin as a 'merry' character - though less far from some of the older associations we shall look at in a moment.

At the end the *Gest* peters out with a brief reference to Robin's death at the hands of the Abbess of Kirklees. We have to turn to one of the several versions of another ballad "the Death of Robin Hood" for the end of the story. Even here the versions we have are curiously conflicting and fragmentary and there has been much debate as to their real meaning. However, it is possible, with only a little effort, to understand what is being said.

Growing old and ill Robin decides to visit his 'kinswoman,' who is Abbess of Kirklees Priory near Peterborough, and a famed healer. Apparently knowing that she was also the mistress of Roger of Doncaster, an enemy of Robin's, and sensing trouble, Little John tries to persuade his master to take fifty men with him, but Robin refuses and in the end is accompanied only by John.

On the way they encounter a strange old woman beside a stream, who appears to curse Robin. John is filled with foreboding but cannot persuade his master to turn back. At the Abbey John is locked out of the room where Robin is to be treated, and the Abbess begins to bleed her kinsman - a common enough treatment for most ailments in that time. However, as the ballad says:

And first it bled, the thick, thick blood,
And afterwards the thin,
And well then wits good Robin Hood
treason there was within....

With failing strength he blows his horn and Little John breaks in - too late to save his master. As John rages and begs to be allows to burn Kirklees and all within it to the ground, Robin rallies enough to say that he had never made war on women and will not begin now. He then begs to be helped to the window, and from there looses his last arrow, declaring that where it falls there should he be buried. John carries out this duty and erects a stone above the grave bearing only the words (in this version) HERE LIES BOLD ROBIN HOOD.

It's not hard to see in this a version of the death of a Divine King, his end foretold by an old woman who seems very like the Celtic *'bean sidhe'*, or Washer-at-the-Ford, who traditionally appears to heroes about to die in battle. But we need to go further yet and deeper to find the real Robin Hood.

Lewis Spence, one of the most outright champions of a mythological identity for Robin, gives some pretty heavy clues in an article written in the 1930s. Robin was, he says, no lesser person than,

' the King of the May, and his Maid Marian the May Queen....His May Day ceremonies seem to have given rise to tales capable of arrangement into three classes: stories of single combat, stories of feats with a bow, and tricky stories... These are all suggestive of a system by which the king reigned from one May Day to the next, when he

had to fight for his title, if not for his life, and possibly also for the possession of his consort. Here, then, we are...face with the ...theory of the king whose waning vigour made it necessary to remove him or put him to death and replace him by another. The second class of story is due to the popularity of the long-bow in England in the fifteenth century...Lastly, the tricky stories may be due to a confusion between Robin Hood and Robin Goodfellow, the familiar fairy.' (Hibbert Journal)

This last point gives us another strand in the mystery of Robin's identity - his connection with the people of Faery. It may well be a truism that the Faeries dressed in green and wore hoods, and that Robin and his men did likewise - but it is from this point that we begin to see a connection between Robin and the Faery Race.

No one knows the origins of the Fairies. Perhaps they were the first people in this land, the Little Dark People, or the Picts, the Old Ones. Perhaps they were gods once; perhaps we only dream them - but no two people can ever agree as to their   appearance. Some say they are small, others of normal human size, while still others see them as tall and stately; and though it is generally accepted that it was the Victorians who opted for small and cute, and who added the tinsel wings still associated in many people's minds with the idea of fairies, there seems little reason to doubt that just as they were sometimes perceived as tall, beautiful and powerful, they were equally often seen as small in statue.

One of the few things that most accounts agree upon is that the favourite colour of the faery folk was green. It is for this reason that some people still think of green as unlucky, since it could only be worn by the people of faery and to copy them was to court their anger.

The tradition that Robin and the Merry Men wore 'Lincoln' green is probably a late one, though if we are right in supposing that Robin is a relative of the Green Man, then it would be natural enough for him to wear this colour.

But what about Robin Goodfellow? Almost everything we know about this character comes from a curious 17th century pamphlet which rejoices in the title Robin Goodfellow, alias Puck, alias Hob: his mad pranks, and merry jests, full of honest mirth, and is a fit medicine for melancholy. It was printed in 1628 but almost certainly drew on a whole range of earlier faery lore as well as lore concerning Robin Hood and the Green Man. The story contained in the pamphlet may be summarised as follows:

This Robin's nascence is described in a manner very reminiscent of the birth of Merlin. Oberon, the Faery King, visits a maiden at night, but in the day vanishes 'wither she knew not, he went so suddenly.' As with Merlin's mother, the outcome of these nightly visits is a child, who shows no unusual traits until, aged six, he began to be so troublesome and to play such knavish tricks upon the neighbours that his mother was in despair. Finally she promised him a whipping, and since this did not please him he ran away. A day from his home he settled to sleep in a field, and there dreamed of bright-eyed folk who danced around him all night to music he deemed as fair as Orpheus might have made. In the morning he woke to find a scroll beside him on which was written, in words of gold:

"Robin, my only son and heir,
How to live take thou no care:
By nature thou hast cunning shifts,
Which I'll increase with other gifts.
Wish what thou wilt, thou shall it have;
And for to fetch both fool and knave,
Thou hast the power to change thy shape,

To horse, to hog, to dog, to ape.
Transformed thus, by any means,
See none thou harm'st but knaves and queans:
But love thou those that honest be,
And help them in necessity.
Do thus and all the world shall know
The pranks of Robin Goodfellow,
For by that name thou called shall be
To age's last posterity;
And if thou keep my just command,
One day thou shall see Fairy Land."

Robin at once tested the promise of wish granting by asking for food; a dish of fine veal was set before him. He wished for plum pudding: it appeared. Then, being weary, he wished himself to be a horse. At once he became a fine spirited beast, and thereafter changed himself into a black dog, a green tree and so one, until he was sure he could change himself into anything he wished. Then he wished to try out his newfound skills by playing more of the tricks for which he had been recently chastised, and forthwith he set forth into the world, where he began to play so many merry jests that soon his name was known throughout the land. He played tricks on clowns, on burgurs, on old and young; he turned himself into a chimney sweep (for which reason he was a patron of sweeps until the Victorian era and appeared in procession with them in the May Day Games). Finally, so many were the complaints of Robin Goodfellow's trickery, that his father Oberon summoned him to Faery.

Robin rose from his bed at once and went where he was called. Here he met with Oberon and many other fairies, all clad in green. Throughout the night they danced to faery music, and after this Robin is said to have remained in Fairyland for *'many a long year'*.

Thus ends the curious little story, which on the face of it bears little resemblance to anything to do with Robin beyond the name of its hero. However, as we dig a little deeper unto the origin of the work we begin to glimpse some common points, which suggest its origin in a more distant past.

Kathleen Briggs, the great modern writer on Faery lore, catalogues this Robin, together with Puck, as a type of Brownie, a hobgoblin or sprite whose characteristics were chiefly to cause trouble for mortals and to clean up houses where they were made welcome. This is generally in line with the instructions Robin Goodfellow is given in Oberon's scroll: that he harms none who do not deserve it. Generally, the victims of his pranks are indeed unworthy people, and despite the anger he causes by his at times outrageous deeds, there is little or no real spite or cruelty in them. Indeed, like Robin Hood he more often helps the poor at the expense of the rich.

Like other heroes of myth, such as Taliesin, he is able to change shape at will - not only into animal, bird and fish, but also into such things as trees, bushes, rocks and clouds. In this, and by the nature of his birth, he proclaims himself more than a simple fairy. Like Robin he is a hero of the common people, with powers far greater than his pranks would suggest. Indeed, it seems that he really never grows up, but remain forever the little six-year old boy, even after he has attained his rightful place beside his father in Faery. Like the young Merlin and the youthful Taliesin he loves playing tricks that more often resolve mysteries or which display his abilities to make things happen. His characteristic 'ho,ho,ho' is reminiscent of Merlin's laughter, while his shape-shifting abilities are like those of the famous Welsh bard.

This leads me to think that we could see Robin Goodfellow (and therefore Robin Hood) as a native British trickster. The other leading contender for this title is the Puck, who is most familiar to us from his appearance in Shakespeare's *A Midsummer Night's Dream*.

Puck is nearly always seen as virtually interchangeable with Robin Goodfellow, as the title of the old pamphlet discussed above also makes clear. Yet he does have an existence of his own, and is still remembered all over Britain in place names like Pickwell, Pickhill, Pickmere, Peckham, Puckholm etc. His name, in fact, is probably derived from the Middle English 'pook', or 'pouke', which today gives us 'spook' but which originally meant an elf or sprite.

But there is more to Robin than these tricky folk. In 1936 Sir James Fraser, who is generally seen as one of the founding fathers of modern anthropology, published the thirteenth and final volume of his book *The Golden Bough*. The central theme of this monumental work is the worldwide myth of the sacrificed god-king whom Fraser called 'The King of the Wood. This king, who could be regarded either as a god or a priest, was usually selected to reign for a year, at the end of which time he was killed and his slayer took over his role for a further year. In this way the eternal round of the seasons are preserved, without hindrance, and the human and animal realms remained in balance and harmony with the rest of Creation.

Such was the essence of Fraser's theory, which he elaborated over many hundreds of pages, drawing on traditions from all over the world. Among the Celtic people of Britain, Ireland and Gaul in particular Fraser draws our attention to a large number of celebrations centring on two periods of the year: Spring and Autumn. These two gateways are seen as key turning points in the progression of the seasons, and it is during this time that the most significant examples of sacrificial acts are to be observed. He also noticed that one such set of beliefs, native primarily to Britain, concerned a figure known as the Green Man.

Now it's a well-known fact that many Medieval Christian churches in Britain contain a significant number of carvings representing this figure. These generally take the form of foliate heads, faces from the eyes and lips and ears of which sprout leaves, so that the faces sometimes seems to be peering from amid the leafage, and at others to be actually made of leaves.

The historian of religion, E.O. James, calls Robin Hood *'a further development...[in]...themes associated with the Green Man, or Jack-in-the-Green, as the annual victim in the vegetation drama, the prototype of the Fool garlanded in greenery.'* James adds that until the 14th century Robin was almost certainly the product of the ballad maker's muse, but that *'his equation with the Green Man and the May Day revels and Maid Marian brought him into the fertility drama and its seasonal death and resurrection ritual. As its central figure he had to die by the chance flight of an arrow and like Adonis bleed to death, and then be restored to life, while Maid Marian assumed the role of the Man-Woman. In the capacity of Robin-of-the-Wood, he was essentially a vegetation sacral hero rather than the leader of a robber band in the forest, of the highly skilled archer of the ballad and romance..."*

For Medieval churchmen, the symbolism was something other. In the man-made forests of the gothic cathedrals the Green man is pent, the old pagan wildness tamed in frozen stone. It must have been a cause of supreme satisfaction to the church Fathers to see the image they regarded as 'devilish' caught and pinned on the roof-bosses of their own stone forests. That the masons and worshippers perhaps had the last laugh is a matter of conjecture - certainly the protruding tongues and grimacing faces of the foliate heads may be interpreted in more ways than one - as strangled or beheaded gods on the one hand, or as grinning, nose-thumbing caricatures on the other.

The question is how do these figures relate to Robin Hood? The answer is complex and leads us back to a basic premise: that all the aspects of the Green Man/Woman derive from a central theme - that of the vegetation myth already described. This is denied by many modern folklorists precisely on account of the wide variety of evidence and the disparate nature of such figures as the Green Jack, the Wild Man, the Green Knight and Robin himself. However, what we have to look at is the underlying pattern of meaning that is bodied forth by all of these figures. All represent, in some way, fertility and the greenness of growth and of life itself. Essentially Robin Hood is one of the great fertility and vegetation figures of this land. As the Wild Man he is a representative of the old shamanic traditions of this country, dating from the most distant times and refocused by the Celts and the Saxons.

Such figures as Suibney Gelt in Ireland, Lailoken in Scotland, Merlin in Britain and Taliesin in Wales, all in their own way represent the vital, life-giving greenness. Whether as Green Jack, May King of Summer Lord, Robin-o-the-Wood or Maid Marian, they are all expressive of the power of greenness, of growing things, of ripening corn. The symbolic death and resurrection of these figures, from the Green Knight to Robin himself, is part of a vast ongoing cycle that will continue until the end of time (or until we become so mechanised that we forget our origins entirely). All these Green and wonderful figures exist to remind us that we are a part of the natural world, and that we are still able to celebrate the ancient holy traditions of the earth and the greenwood.

All of this leads towards the central point I want to make - that the way to understand Robin, Marian and the Merry Men is to see them as central to the ancient fertility games celebrated around the time of May Day. These revels celebrated the death of winter and the arrival of spring, and took place all over England in the Middle Ages.

Then, once the may-blossom flowered, a kind of divine madness took possession of the people. Everyone, from Kings to commoners, took part in a variety of celebrations of the dawning spring, when the shackles of winter were thrown off, and a new light was everywhere apparent. The May Day Games, or 'Revels' in fact took place at almost any time throughout the Summer, as well as on May 1st and, from at least the 1500s, until the end of the 17th century, were almost continually ruled over by Robin Hood, to the extent that the celebrations became known as 'Robin Hood's Games'. Maid Marian was present as well - though not specifically named until later - taking upon her the role of the May Queen just as Robin assumed the guise of the May King - thus bringing back to his role characteristics which had originally belonged to him but which had been absent for generations.

An anonymous 17th century pamphlet expresses this clearly.

May *"was considered the boundary day that divided the confines of winter and summer, allusively to which there was instituted a sportful war between two parties; the one in defence of the continuance of winter, the other for bringing in the summer...The mock battle was always fought for booty; the sprig was sure to obtain the victory, which they celebrated by carrying triumphantly green branches with May flowers, proclaiming and singing the song of joy..."* (Brand)

Other sources elaborate upon this, indicating that the battle was fought for the possession of the Spring Maiden, who is elsewhere called the May Queen, or Maid Marian. Robin, alias the King of Summer, alias the King of the Wood, fights the King of Winter, alias the Green Man, for the hand of the Queen of the May, alias Maid Marian. Gradually, as time passed, these roles became blurred; Robin became a permanent resident of the Greenwood, a full time Champion of the Goddess of Spring, at the same time absorbing many of the attributes of the Green Man. In time, Robin becomes the Green Man, and rules over the time between summer and winter, the time of the May Day revels. Later still he becomes the outlaw of Sherwood.

There is an abundance of evidence of this kind, descriptions of games and sports, fairs and races, held between May day and Midsummer, which make it clear that annual fairs, in all probability connected with solsticial worship, were firmly established as early as the 13th century (the time in which the Robin Hood ballads were circulating widely). That they were, even then regarded as dangerous and of pagan origin is made clear by the number of attacks mounted upon them by the Church.

Thus Bishop Latimer, in a sermon delivered before King Edward IV in 1549, relates how he came to a place on his way back to London where he had given prior warning that he intended to preach there in the morning

'Because it was a holy day, and me thought it was an holy day's work; the church stood in my way; and I took my horse and my company and went thither; I thought I should have found a great company in the church, and when I came there the church door was fast locked. I tarried there half an hour and more, and at last the key was found; and one of the parish comes to me, and says: Sir, this is a busy day with us, we cannot hear you; it is Robin Hood's Day....'

He continues, perhaps not unreasonably, on a pained note:

'It is no laughing matter, my friends, it is a weeping matter, a heavy matter, under the pretence of gathering for Robin Hood, a traitor and a thief, to put out a preacher, to have his office less esteemed, to prefer Robin Hood before the ministrations of God's word...This realm hath been ill provided, for that it hath had such corrupt judgements in it, to prefer Robin Hood to God's word.' (Quoted in Ritson)

We may be tempted to smile at this picture of the outraged bishop, languishing outside a locked church while his parishioners were off gathering for Robin Hood, this offers a clear enough indication of just how important the May Games, as ruled over by Robin Hood, were to the people of Medieval England.

Just as the introduction of the Green Man into the Gothic cathedrals of the Middle Ages represents the entrance - by the back door, - of the old pagan force of nature into the Christian architraves, so the May Games of Robin Hood represented the entrance of a forest law into the realm of the city and the everyday. Wildness, of a kind deplored by so many puritan writers that it must have had a strong hold, broke out everywhere once the May Pole had been erected. These poles, most often of oak, elm or birch, were brought from the forest and erected in town and village alike, where they became the focus of joyful and uninhibited games, feasting and general merriment.

'There can be no doubt' asserted Lord Raglan in his book *The Hero*, that

...[May Day] was of pagan origin - that it was, in fact, the spring festival which was theoretically superseded by the Christian Easter. We should expect a pagan festival to be associated with a pagan deity, and we should not be disappointed. We have in Robin Hood a deity particularly associated with spring and vegetation. He was the King of May, and Maid Marian was the Queen of May.'

The insistence of certain scholars that Robin Hood was only associated with the May Day celebrations at a late (i.e. Elizabethan) period, fails to take in the whole of the picture. If we are correct in our supposition that Robin was but the latest aspect of the age old figure of the Green Man, then what is far more likely is that the wheel of tradition came full circle, returning Robin to his rightful place in the celebrations after a time of absence from them. This much is evident when we consider the ritual aspects underlying the May Day celebrations, each of which, in one way or another, suggests the half-glimpsed presence of Marian and Robin as Green Lady and Green Lord.

There is little doubt that the May Day sports were once the decoration around a far more serious 'game', in which the chosen champion of summer or winter was beheaded. That a form of this theme continued into the 19th century, is demonstrated in the journal *Folk-Lore* for 1901, where S. D. Addy collected descriptions of May day ceremonies in the isolated village of Castleton in Derbyshire. His description, somewhat paraphrased, reads like this:

'It appears that on the 20th or 29th of May the church bell rings at 2 o'clock to call all the ringers together to make a garland of May flowers, which have been gathered by the villagers in the morning. This so-called garland is rather like a bell in shape, and as when covered with leaves and flowers it weighs about 12 stone, it naturally calls for an extremely powerful man to carry it. Robin Hood's bower may have been the same kind of thing.

'The bower is made of flat lathes of wood, as for the hoops of a barrel. At the top was a circular piece of wood with a hole in it about an inch in diameter. Into this the topknot of Queen...was inserted, made of the choicest flowers... mounted on a wooden knob... Two men standing on barrels then lift it on to the head of the chosen King, as he is now called, though formally he was know as the Man. He is accompanied by a woman wearing a crown and called the Queen, though formally she was known as the Woman....'

The King then mounts on a horse, which he cannot guide, so that he is lead about by a figure called the Ringer. Morris dancers follow and the Queen brings up the rear, and they proceed through the village, pausing for the dancers to dance before every inn.

'At last the procession reaches the church. The queen...is removed, and the King enters the churchyard alone upon his horse, and stands under the south wall of the tower. On the tower are the ringers who, using a projecting piece of masonry as a pulley, lower a rope and to the King, who fastens it into the hole left by the removal of the topknot. The garland is then drawn up to the top of the tower, where it is fastened to a pinnacle, and there remains until next year, or until it is blown away by the winter gales....'

This leaves me in little doubt that it contains a last surviving echo of a time when the King would have been sacrificed and hung up, decapitated, and his head hung on a tree. It is also not without significance perhaps that many of the Green Men carved on roof bosses in medieval churches have their tongues sticking out - a not unusual feature of someone who has been hung or strangled.

The question still remains whether Robin may be seen as a type of sacrificed king. Lewis Spence certainly thought so:

'In my view (he wrote) the games of Robin Hood represented the last shadow of an enacted rite which narrated the life and adventures of a god or wood-spirit, and ended with the sacrifice of his human representative, who was dispatched by a flight of arrows... [which] represented the rain-shower, for in all parts of the world the flint arrow-head is the emblem of rain....'

Whether or not there is any truth in this remains to be seen. That the Games did indeed retain the last vestiges of a more ancient ritual celebration I have no doubt, any more than I would question that Robin is the inheritor of the story of a woodland spirit. Spence is right, also, about the symbolism of flint arrow-heads (the elf-shot of faery tradition), and about the association of the games with archery, while Robin himself seems to have been regarded as almost the patron Saint of archers.

As we saw earlier, Robin met his death at the hands of the Prioress of Kirklees Abbey, who bled him to death while supposedly treating him for illness. This method of treatment was common during the Middle Ages, but it is also significant for our argument in that it represents ritual mode of death. In the ballads the Prioress is represented as an evil woman in league with an old enemy of Robin's, but it is much more likely that she represents a memory of the priestess whose task it was to let out the blood of the sacrificial King to fructify the earth.

All of this leads me to the conclusion that 'Robin Hood' or 'Robin-o-the-Wood' were the May King's original, secret names, which became known with the passage of time and as the old mysteries ceased to be as important or so closely guarded. Robin was the King of the May and Marian his Lady - and his consort. Together they ruled over the mysterious games, which welcomed in the season of plenty and signalled an end to the harshness of winter. They began with the bringing in of garlands and branches which signified the bringing of the greenwood into everyday reality, and ended with the nuptials of the Lord and Lady of the Wood, celebrated, in similar fashion, by their followers and supporters. Once, the sacrifice of Robin (the King of the Wood) may have been part of this: but by the time of Robin Hood (the Outlaw) in the 13th or 14th centuries, such things were no more than a memory, all but forgotten save in certain neglected corners of the land such as Castleton and parts of Wales. Robin Hood still reigned supreme, as he had through the ages, but in a new form. Ever renewing like the Greenwood he represented, he could not die, only change and take on a new disguise as 'the merry outlaw of Sherwood'.

If Robin is the King of May then most assuredly Marian is his Queen. This fact overrides any evidence to the effect that Marian is a latecomer to the Greenwood. The Green Man requires a Flower Bride, and it is as such that we shall come to recognise Marian. A central aspect in any proper understanding of Marian's part in the May Day celebrations is the theme known as the rape of the Flower Bride. It appears most clearly defined in an episode from 'The Story of Culhwch and Olwen" in the Welsh Mabinogion.

> 'Creiddylad the daughter of Lludd Llaw Ereint, and Gwythyr the son of Greidawl were betrothed. And before she had become his bride, Gwyn ap Nudd came and carried her away by force; and Gwythyr the son of Greidawl gathered his host together, and went to fight with Gwynn ap Nudd. But Gwynn overcame him...When Arthur heard of this, he went to the North, and summoned Gwynn ap Nudd before him.... and made peace between ...[him]...and Gwythyr the son of Greidawl. and this was the peace that was made: that the maiden should remain in her father's house, without advantage to either of them, and that Gwyn ap Nudd and Gwythyr son of Greidawl should fight for her every first of May, from thenceforth until the day of doom, and that which ever of them should then be conqueror should have the maiden.' (Trans Lady Charlotte Guest)

Clearly, there can be no final overall winner 'until doomsday', because the two adversaries are really the representatives of winter and summer. Later this reappears in accounts from as late as the 19th century in which mock battles take place between rival groups of villagers.

Here the elements of the ancient story and its part in the May Day revels leaps into focus. The struggle of the Lords of summer and winter, whether for Crydellyad or Marian, is the same - an enactment of the spiritual dimension underlying the natural turning of the seasons.

The need to ensure the safe continuance of the seasonal round was always in the mind of our ancestors. It was from such fears and shadows that myths of the sacrificed god arose, and with it the embodiment of the principles of nature such as the Green Man and the struggle for the Flower Bride.

There is not enough time to look at the individual members of Robin's Merry Men - but I can say that both Little John and Friar Tuck are guardians of river crossings - an ancient and important role which is much in keeping with ancient traditions. Much, as a Miller, is one of the guardians of the Quern of the Heavens, Scarlet may have been a nobleman or even more anciently a ritual assassin. It is also interesting to note that the outlaws seem almost to reconstitute the principle aspects of the outside world within the forest. Robin and Marian represent the court; Tuck the Church; Much the husbandry of the land; John the warrior; Allan- a-Dale the ballad maker, and so on.

Robert Graves made an interesting additional speculation about Robin's followers, which I'd like to share with you. The Merry Men, he thinks, were really 'Mary's Men' the followers of Mary, a curious turn of affairs brought about by some possibly deliberate confusion between the words 'Mary', 'Marian' and 'Morris' (as in Morris dancers). This last word, according to Graves, was first written 'Maris' thus equating with 'Stella Maris' Star of the Sea, one of the many symbolic names for Mary - the earliest spelling of whose name in England was - Marian! Furthermore, the name is a good deal closer to 'Merry' than we might suppose. With a poet's subtle understanding of the true meaning of words Graves proposes that the Merry Men were once Mary's Men, and that the Morris Dancers were once similarly called - both deriving their importance from the fact that they were the followers of the cult of Mary - not necessarily the Virgin, but either the Magdalen or Mary of Egypt, both of whom had a considerable - if unorthodox - following in the Middle Ages.

If we are right to believe that Marian was always the name of the May Queen - and therefore of the Green God's consort - then to suggest that her followers (as well as Robin's) were actually 'Mary's Men' seems less out of the way. Robin's own particular devotion was said to be to 'Mary', which would have been interpreted as the Virgin by medieval authors but which probably refers to an earlier figure - Marian or May, the consort of the Green Man.

To sum up, there is really no adequate historical evidence to associate Robin Hood with any historical personage or period before the emergence of the ballad as a literary genre in the 13th and 14th centuries. We may suppose that oral tales of the Lord of Sherwood were circulating before that time (just as, I believe, earlier than that there were traditions relating to the Green Man which became fused with those of the Outlaw of Sherwood).

A whole mixture of events thus came together to create the character of Robin Hood as outlaw and as champion of the people. The time was right for the social injustice of landowners toward their tenants to become the setting for the ballads - even if we discount for the moment the natural animosity that existed between Saxon and Norman. If ancient pre-Christian traditions were still flourishing in parts of the country, as seems likely, it was natural that the figure of the Green Man should reappear in a new guise which could be openly discussed and whose stories became popular on the lips of a hundred ballad makers. The many folk traditions (including those surrounding the May Day Games) preserved elements that passed through the channel of the Robin Hood myths and emerged with new characteristics acquired from the ballad characters.

I remain convinced that Robin originated in the character and tradition of the Green Man, and that he only gradually developed into the Outlaw of Sherwood, shedding certain characteristics and gaining others, until he is, on the face of it, a far cry from his origins. Yet, even here, traces remain which hark back hundreds, even thousands of years to another time and another culture, in which the Green Man was honoured as the most powerful force in the cosmos, the spirit of Nature itself.

It is this spirit that informs the ballads and plays, the songs and dances of Robin Hood. It enlivened the dark days of winter for our medieval ancestors, and it helped them welcome back the spring. It is still with us, still present in our hearts and minds even as we perhaps wander far from the fields and rivers, woods and valleys of the old land. Robin and Marian represent a freedom we have lost, the freedom to escape to the woods and live at peace there. They remind us of the times when, in our childhood, we made bows and arrows out of pieces of stick and played at Robin Hood and the Sheriff of Nottingham.

The mystery which lies at the heart of the Greenwood is a green mystery - when the greenness is brought inside - as in the Green Man carvings in churches - it is pent, it dies. Robin sets it free, and with it all who seek to experience the joyous celebrations of May Day, when Robin and Marian come together and are crowned with the blossom that signifies the birth of the new season. If we are lucky, if we look deeply enough within ourselves, we can still join in that celebration.

Chapter 23:

MERRY ROBIN: THE NATIVE BRITISH TRICKSTER

This essay grew out of my researches into the figure of Robin Hood, the famous outlaw of Sherwood Forest whose archetype stretches back to the even more ancient Green Man. While I was working on the book which became Robin Hood: Green Lord of the Wildwood (Gothic Image,1997) I found myself fascinated by the figure of a character who seemed to represent native British trickster figure. The resulting essay found its way in part into the above named book, and reappeared more recently, in the revised form include here, in the on-line journal of the wonderful Mythic Journey Institute.

Robin Goodfellow is the archetypal prankster and trickster of Britain. Almost everything we know about him comes from a curious 17th century pamphlet which rejoices in the title *Robin Goodfellow, alias Puck, alias Hob: his mad pranks, and merry jests, full of honest mirth, and is a fit medicine for melancholy*. It was printed in 1628 but almost certainly drew on a whole range of earlier faery lore as well as lore concerning Robin Hood and the Green Man. The story contained in the pamphlet may be summarised as follows:

Robin's nascence is described in a manner very reminiscent of the birth of Merlin. Oberon, the Faery King, visits a maiden at night, but in the day vanishes 'wither she knew not, he went so suddenly.' As with Merlin's mother, the outcome of these nightly visits is a child, who shows no unusual traits until, aged six, he began to be so troublesome and to play such knavish tricks upon the neighbours that his mother was in despair. Finally she promised him a whipping, and since this did not please him he ran away. A day from his home he settled to sleep in a field, and there dreamed of bright-eyed folk who danced around him all night to music he deemed as fair as Orpheus might have made. In the morning he woke to find a scroll beside him on which was written, in words of gold:

"Robin, my only son and heir,
How to live take thou no care:
By nature thou hast cunning shifts,
Which I'll increase with other gifts.
Wish what thou wilt, thou shall it have;
And for to fetch both fool and knave,
Thou hast the power to change thy shape,
To horse, to hog, to dog, to ape.
Transformed thus, by any means,
See none thou harm'st but knaves and queans:
But love thou those that honest be,
And help them in necessity.

Do thus and all the world shall know
The pranks of Robin Goodfellow,
For by that name thou called shall be
To age's last posterity;
And if thou keep my just command,
One day thou shall see Fairy Land."

Robin at once tested the promise of wish granting by asking for food; a dish of fine veal was set before him. He wished for plum pudding: it appeared. Then, being weary, he wished himself to be a horse. At once he became a fine spirited beast, and thereafter changed himself into a black dog, a green tree and so one, until he was sure he could change himself into anything he wished. Then he wished to try out his newfound skills by playing more of the tricks for which he had been recently chastised, and forthwith he set forth into the world, where he began to play so many merry jests that soon his name was known throughout the land. He played tricks on clowns, on burgers, on old and young; he turned himself into a chimney sweep (for which reason he was a patron of sweeps until the Victorian era and appeared in procession with them in the May Day Games). Finally, so great was the noise about the world complaining of Robin Goodfellow's trickery, that his father Oberon summoned him to Faery with these words:

 "Robin, my son, come quickly rise:
First stretch, then yawn, and rub your eyes:
For thou must go with me to-night,
And taste of Fairy-Land's delight".

Robin rose from his bed at once and went where he was called. Here he met with Oberon and many other fairies, all clad in green. Throughout the night they danced to faery music, and as they danced Oberon said:

"Whene'er thou hear the piper blow,
Round and round the fairies go!
And nightly you must with us dance,
In meadows where the moonbeams glance,
And make the circle, hand in hand -
That is the law of Fairy-Land!
There thou shalt see what no man knows;
While sleep the eyes of men doth close!

After this Robin is said to have remained in Fairyland for 'many a long year'.

The great folklorist Kathleen Briggs catalogues this Robin, together with Puck, as a type of Brownie, a hobgoblin or sprite whose characteristics were chiefly to cause trouble for mortals and to clean up houses where they were made welcome. This is generally in line with the instructions he is given in the scroll by his father, that he harms none who do not deserve it. Generally, the victims of his pranks are indeed unworthy people, and despite the anger he causes by his at times outrageous deeds, there is little or no real spite or cruelty in them. Indeed, like Robin Hood he more often helps the poor at the expense of the rich.

Like other heroes of myth, such as the Welsh Taliesin or the Irish Fionn, he is able to change shape at will - not only into animal, bird and fish, but also into such things as trees, bushes, rocks and clouds. In this, and by the nature of his birth, he proclaims himself more than a simple fairy. Like Robin Hood he is a hero of the common people, with powers far greater than his pranks would suggest. Indeed, it seems that he really never grows up, but remains forever the little six-year old boy, even after he has attained his rightful place beside his father in Faery. Like the young Merlin and the youthful Taliesin he loves playing tricks that more often resolve mysteries or which display his abilities to make things happen. His characteristic 'ho,ho,ho' is reminiscent of Merlin's laughter, while his shape-shifting abilities are like those of the famous Welsh bard. Alfred Nutt, in his essay on *The Fairy Mythology of Shakespeare* even compared him to the Irish God Manannan mac Lir, who was also the son of a mortal and a human mother, and who eventually attained the Celtic otherworld after being watched over by his father.

There are many other descriptions of Robin Goodfellow that show that he was seen in a remarkably unified way - as witness the following extract from Thomas Rowlands' More Knaves Yet:

'Amongst the rest, was a good fellow devil,
So-called in kindness, cause he did no evil,
Known by the name of Robin (as we hear)
And that his eyes as bigge as sawcers were,
Who came a nights, and would make kitchens cleane
And in the bed bepinch a lazie queane....'

Lewis Spence, in his study of the seasonal games, argues that 'many of the Mad Pranks and Merry Gests recounted of Robin Goodfellow in the old pamphlet of that name make it clear that the goblin in question had more than a nominal connection with Robin Hood in his 'tricky' stories.' He goes on to discuss the belief in the 'great dead' or tribal ancestors, who were believed to preside over the growth of vegetation - hence, perhaps, the attribution of the colour green to the world of the dead - and with whom the faeries have a close association.

'Of such a type, I believe, was Robin Hood, or Rob, or Hob of the Wood or Forest, who presided over that particular demesne, whence both timber and venison were forthcoming... The facts that his traditional tomb was situated among a grove of trees, and that it consisted of a standing stone which was capable of self-propulsion and miraculous motion...bring him into line with those other spirits who haunt such standing stones, and who were formally worshipped at them. In a word his gravestone behaves like the traditional fairy monolith... Robin Hood I believe, then, is a reminiscence of an early departmental deity or godling associated with afforested places, and as such his festival would be celebrated at the seasons of vernal growth. That Robin Goodfellow, the Mad Hob, or wild goblin, is a later and more elfin phase of him appears more than probable.'

Whether we see Robin Goodfellow as an elf, a fairy, a hob-goblin, or an ancestral guardian of the land, we can be sure that he was at one time recognised as a far more powerful being than we can ever imagine today. Folklorist Sydney Hartland reached the same conclusion when he wrote in his book *The Science of Fairy Tales*:

'Do you imagine that Robin Goodfellow - a mere name to you - conveys anything like the meaning to your mind

that it did to those whom the name represented a still living belief, and who had the stories about him at their fingers' ends? Or let me ask you: Why did the fairies dance on moonlight nights? Or: Have you ever thought why it is that in English literature, and in English literature alone, the fairy realm finds a place in the highest works of the imagination?'

This makes it clear that we should see Robin Goodfellow as a native British trickster figure akin to the Native American Coyote, or the West Indian Anansi.

(2006)

Chapter 24:

GUARDIANS OF THE LAND

This is the second of the two talks I gave at different Robin of Sherwood conventions. This one begins with an extended joke. I had been given a bizarre report from the National Enquirer that claimed to have found Robin Hood's body in a grave in Britain. Later a further report claimed even odder and more unlikely things. The laughter echoed around the room in the hotel near Heathrow airport where the convention was held and I remember I had difficulty continuing. The substance of the talk is one that has fascinated me for many years – that the spirits of great heroes become indispensable guardians of the land where they once walked during their lives.

Some of you may remember that when I spoke at a Robin of Sherwood convention in 1995 I had just been given a wonderful report by the *National Enquirer* that announced the discovery of Robin Hood's grave in Sherwood Forest! No one was really surprised to find that the remarkably well-preserved body was dressed in Lincoln green (including tights) and had a gold medallion round his neck that read 'With grateful thanks from Richard I'. Unfortunately this priceless piece of literature has gone missing among my papers, so I can't quote it to you in full for the benefit of those who weren't there on that earlier occasion. However, I though you might like to hear the update, from the same eminent journal and the same 'historical expert' a Mr Guy Ratcliffe of Arkansas, Kansas, who has been occupied in following up his persona line of enquiry in and around the area of Sherwood. Following on his initial startling discoveries he apparently obtained permission to do some more digging, and found - to his astonishment, that in a place very nearby the grave site, was an ancient wooden casket which had somehow been preserved through the centuries and which, when opened, revealed a cache of letters and other documents (Mr Ratcliffe is shy of identifying them all). In fact he has so far failed to publish anything further than a list of the contents, in a report dated the 3rd August 1997, in which he mentions a number of letters ' of a personal nature' from someone signing himself Robert Hode to one Maryon of Leaford. In addition to these there was a small bag of gold coins dating from the era of Richard Lionheart, and last, but by no means least, a charter giving 'the land and entitlement of the manor of Huntingdon in the Paryish of Nottinghame' to the same Robert Hode' and ratified once again by King Richard. I know you will all await the full revelation of these documents and their eventual publication as eagerly as I, since they are bound to add to our knowledge and understanding of the Outlaw of Sherwood and especially to his relationship with Maryon of Leaford....

In the meantime, I thought it might be of interest to you all to look at the figure of Robin as a mystical Guardian of the Land, since my own interest, as it so often appears in Robin of Sherwood, is in mythology. So to begin with we should look back at the history of this unique role.

The idea of the Guardian really goes back to an extremely ancient time, when the Celts began to

213

settle in the British Isles from around 2000 BC. They almost certainly brought with them the concept of sacred kingship, which involved the idea that the king must marry the land over which he was to rule, and that he must be physically perfect without a blemish anywhere on his body. Thus when the Irish king Lugh lost a hand in battle he had a false one constructed by the magical smith of the Gods, Goibnu, but this was not enough to ensure him the kingship, and he was forced to hand over (pun intended) the kingdom to a substitute. Indeed the idea of a substitute or surrogate who literally stands in for the king dates back to the time when the king was sacrificed every year. At some point a stand-in was appointed to be sacrificed in the ruler's place, and this idea continues in the idea of the guardian who holds the land in trust for the king.

The land itself is often personified as an actual figure, the goddess Sovereignty, who holds the power of the land and grants it to the King only if he enters into a contract that is indeed a marriage. The test that goes with this is repeated in a number of stories and usually involves the young contender for the crown having to kiss or sleep with a hideous hag who guards the access to a spring. Symbolically she represents the land and soon reveals herself in more beautiful guise to the future king.

But one of the earliest recorded stories of a guardian who becomes almost an embodiment of the spirit of the land is Bran the Blessed, who comes to us from Celtic mythology. His legend is briefly told as it appears in *The Mabinogion* story of 'Branwen, Daughter of Llyr', further corroborated by *The Welsh Triads*. It describes the troubled times of the legendary Bran, King of Britain; the unfortunate marriage of his sister, Branwen, to the King of Ireland; and the subsequent war between the two lands. At the end of this story Bran, mortally wounded, charges the seven men who are the remnant of his army:

> "And take you my head,' said he, 'and bear it even unto the White Mount, in London, and bury it there, with the face towards France. And a long time will you be upon the road. In Harlech you will be feasting seven years, the birds of Rhiannon singing unto you the while. And all that time the head will be to you as pleasant company as it ever was when on my body. And at Gwales in Penfro you will be fourscore years, and you may remain there, and the head with you uncorrupted, until you open the door that looks towards Aber Henvelen, and towards Cornwall. And after you have opened that door, there you may no longer tarry, set forth then to London to bury the head, and go straight forward." (Trans. Lady Charlotte Guest)

Needless to say, the forbidden door is opened, the head begins to decay and the seven men recall the sorrow of the tragic events in Ireland. This Otherworldly sojourn in which the natural processes are suspended is called 'The Entertainment of the Noble Head' and was one of the prime stories told by bardic storytellers. What is significant for our purposes is the fact that Bran is voluntarily beheaded in order to become a sacred palladium for Britain. According to the traditions surrounding this idea, the body or head of the king fulfils this role of inner guardian. As long as the king's head is buried at a certain point, the land cannot be conquered.

The Welsh Triads present us with weighty evidence for this tradition. Triads are terse mnemonic sentences, arranged in groups of three; they are the remnant of an extensive oral tradition in which bardic poets, storytellers and druids preserved ancestral lore. Triad 37 records a tripartite British tradition about its sacred palladia. Only the first of the three need concern us here.

> "Three Fortunate Concealments of the Island of Britain.
> The Head of Bran the Blessed, son of Llyr, which was buried in the White Hill in London.
> And as long as it was there in that position, no Oppression would ever come to this island.

This is juxtaposed by:

"Three Unfortunate Disclosures of the Island of Britain... Arthur disclosed the Head of Bran the Blessed from the White Hill, because it did not seem right to him that this Island should be defended by the strength of anyone, but by his own."

Arthur's hubris in electing to become the *sole* guardian of the land may well account for his own early demise. But the story did not end there. Bran's name means 'Raven', and to this day, the Tower of London keeps a few ravens, whose wings are clipped to prevent them from flying away. Even in this time the old legend of the guardian of the land is honoured, even though most people have forgotten its origin.

It is perhaps appropriate that the next Guardian of the Land is Arthur himself, who is described as sleeping beneath the hills of Britain awaiting the day he is recalled by the need of his countrymen. All over the land there are stories of unsuspecting people who have entered caverns in search of treasure only to find the King and his men sleeping in as great circle. In one story, set in Cheshire at Alderley Edge, a man named Potter Thompson finds his way into a cave and finds a sword and a horn lying on a great stone table. Uncertain what to do he picks up the horn and puts it to his lips. At once Arthur stirs and raises his head. 'Is it time?' he asks. 'No', cries the terrified Potter Thompson, and the king returns to his ancient sleep. As the bewildered fellow speeds out of the cave he hears a voce telling him that had he drawn the sword rather than attempting to blow the horn he would have earned himself a great treasure.

Robin Hood is really the next great Guardian of the land after Arthur. In the story of his death this is made clear. You all know the traditional version of the story I'm sure, with Robin Hood going to his 'kinswoman' the Abbess of Kirklees, to seek healing, and being bled by her until he is too weak from loss of blood to survive, and of shooting the arrow into the woods to be buried where it falls. After this of course, thanks to the important work of Mr Ratcliffe, we know what happened, but until the discovery of Robin's grave (there was an earlier one in the Middle Ages) it remained a mystery which was wholly in keeping with the idea of Robin as a guardian of the Land - since it is generally the case hat the grave site must remain a mystery. Of his death we can see that it places him within the category of sacred kingship, the ruler who gives up his life voluntarily for the good of the land. The fact that he bleeds to death, and that we can recognise aspects of the Washer at the Ford in his slayer confirms this.

After the time of Robin we begin to move away from the idea of the Guardians of the Land. But even though the people of Britain no longer outwards acknowledge such superstition things the idea lingered on - much later than one might expert. When the great sailor Sir Frances Drake died people refused to believe that the hero of the Armada was gone. They believed that he had entered into a place where there was no time, from whence he would return at time of need. The drum that had been carried with him on many an adventure was taken to his old home at Buckland Abbey near Plymouth and was heard tapping the call to arms as recently as World War II. You may still see it there today.

Towards the end of the first great world war, Lord Kitchener, the chief of the allied armies, was killed when a torpedo hit the ship on which he was sailing. But the British people refused to believe this and were herd to say that Kitchener was not dead but only sleeping until he should be recalled.

Finally the same story was told about Winston Churchill. When his funeral procession wound its way through London in 1965, an old man was heard to remark that the coffin was empty and that 'Our Winnie' would come back when he was needed.

215

In the USA the same story is told of President Kennedy. Not only was there a giant conspiracy to disguise the nature of his death, we are told, but in fact it is said that he did not die all but was spirited away into hiding until such time as he was needed. In Russia no one believed that Tsar Nicholas II and his family were really killed and the debate continues to this day, despite efforts on to prove this the contrary.

All of these stories perhaps have a element of wish-fulfilment in them - reluctance to believe that a brace and powerful hero has died. But behind it all is the notion that there is some kind of magical quality invested in these great leaders, and that they cannot die until they are no longer required. Perhaps we shall yet see the likes of Bran, Arthur, Robin and the rest ride back into our lives, bringing with them wondrous tales of the Otherworld, and the gift of healing for the ravaged land.

Chapter 25:

TO CATCH THE SUN

In 2002 I was invited to give speak at the annual NAPRA breakfast. (NAPRA is the Network of Alternatives for Publishers Retailers and Artists). I gave the following speech to a hall full of some of the best writers on new age spirituality in the world. I chose the theme of Midsummer because it happened to be Midsummer's Day, and I had just recently completed a book on the Midsummer Solstice. I'm glad to say it seemed well received, despite the fact that I was suffering from jet lag.

Well, it's wonderful to be here, even though this is probably the earliest address I've ever given. In fact for the first time ever I'm actually glad of jet lag, because it means that while it's 8.30 here, by my clock it's already past noon!

But thereby hangs a tail. Because the fact that we suffer from jet-lag at all has a lot to do with the light of the sun - which is what I have come here to talk to you about this morning. I'm aware that drought and forest fires burning not so far from here may well make the idea of honouring or calling upon the sun not particularly popular, but there are as many positive as there are negative aspects to the sun's light, and we have been celebrating them for centuries.

It's also true that we've had an increasingly ambiguous attitude towards the sun in recent times. We know that its rays, unfiltered thanks to the holes in the ozone layer, cause skin cancer and forms of glaucoma, and the increasing number of forest fires in various parts of the world are not unconnected to its rays. But at the same time, we all know, as we have always known, that without its light and warmth we would not be here at all.

It was this aspect which our ancestors focused upon, and which motivated them to see the sun as god and to worship it with all the ritual and panoply available to them. This is why we have Stonehenge, Avebury, New Grange, Tihuanaco, Heliopolis, Ankor Wat and dozens of other ancient temples and sacred sites around the world. All were, to a greater or lesser extent, built not only to celebrate but also to call down and capture the sun's rays, to anchor them in the earth, so that the harvests would grow and greenery flourish.

When I was just starting out in my career as a writer, wanting to be a famous novelist - still haven't managed that yet - I used to dream of the day when I would write my own autobiography - something else I haven't done yet, though I have made a start on it! Anyway, I decided its title would be: To Catch the Sun, because that was what I somehow always knew I wanted to do in my writing - capture the sunlight, fill my words with it. I'm not sure if I've managed to do that, or anyway to what degree, but I've always tried - because light - both real and metaphorical - is so immensely important to us all. Whatever the light means to you - in the Middle Ages it meant God, pure and simple; to those of the Jewish faith it manifested in the mystical imagery of the Qabala, the Book of Lights; while a

217

contemporary Hindu sage described the sunbeam as the straightest road to God.

All these things are products of light, and without sunlight we'd not last very long, nor would anything else on our planet. But light brings us something more than photosynthesis, or warmth, or illumination - it also brings wonder - something else we really can't do without for long. That's something else I've been trying to capture in my writing - that sense of wonder that's both childlike and that touches us all, children and adults alike, when we experience something that changes us or enlightens us. The very word enlightenment, so much used in the literature of the New Age, encapsulates the need for the presence of light within us. That's where we find wonder - the astonishment and delight that comes from appreciating a wonderful morning, or a great painting, or a mighty piece of music, or simply each other ... because that wonder is all about light too, and it's an important aspect of the whole mythology and religion of the sun.

To so many people of the world - both past and present - Midsummer's day itself, and the night that precedes it, are acknowledged as times of magic and wonder. On this night many believe that the curtain which separates us from the Otherworld grows thin, and sometimes even parts, allowing beings both strange and wondrous to visit us. On this night too the gates of the faery realm open and the magical beings such as those immortalised in Shakespeare's A Midsummer Night's Dream, come forth to dance beneath the moon. Human beings also may pass into that otherworldly realm, some never to be seen again; while those who do return are forever altered by the experience.

But it is the celebrations that have attended the period around Midsummer, along the with the stories that are still told, and the setting up of monuments like Stonehenge, that tell us most clearly how important the sun was to our ancestors - not only at Midsummer but throughout the year - and how much of that primal understanding has been passed on to us today. As a Druid I would have spent last night at Stonehenge, waiting in silence with maybe a hundred others for the moment when the first rays of the sun struck the hele stone (from Helios) at which time the Chief Druid would blow a long blast on an ancient bronze horn called a Dord, a note to welcome the sun.

When the world was still young, our ancestors constantly watched the sky, looking for signs and asking questions about the nature of the stars and the sun's journey. Where did it go when it disappeared below the horizon? Would it continue to return? The importance of such matters was enormous in a world that conducted much of its life by attending to a series of heavenly events - especially those which focused upon the seasons and the harvest.

Two dates in particular - the solstices of Summer and Winter - divided the year into times of plenty and scarceness. To ensure the seasonal round ritual observances were devised to propitiate the elements, or the gods who stood behind them.

As Midwinter saw the death and rebirth of the New Sun, so Midsummer saw the rising of that Sun to its zenith, followed by a gradual waning of its power as the year turned once again towards winter. The period between early May and the end of September came under the influence of the sun in all its aspects, with rituals designed to encourage and draw upon its luminous power, to keep pace with its journey across the heavens.

In our own time these ancient traditions continue to influence in way we are scarcely aware of. At Midsummer we see the sun reach its highest point in the heavens, and know, with more than just our conscious minds, that its power is essential to our well being. Despite the spectre of global warming and the widening hole in the ozone layer, which have taught us to fear the rays of the sun if we are exposed to them without protection, we still acknowledge the mystery of Midsummer, just as we find it more natural to walk deosil or sunwise, following the path of the sun, rather than widdershins or against the sun, which is widely believed to be unlucky.

Just as Midwinter fires were kindled to encourage the return of the sun, so at Midsummer they marked the sun reaching its period of greatest strength. To light a fire at this time was a hugely significant act, since it was felt that even a tiny light conjured forth by ourselves would help draw back the greater light of the sun, and we can understand just how important the secret of fire became, and how much power was given to those who knew how to call forth flame.

Despite the disparate cultures and places where the solstices were honoured, a great deal of continuity exists between the ceremonies and festivities that took place around this time. Most often these concentrated on the lighting of fires, which served both to purify and to drive away negative forces, and to honour the sun.

In recent times huge, communal fires were still being lit in villages across rural Ireland and was is considered lucky for local farmers if the smoke from these drifted across their land. Individuals also lit their own fires, and chains of these may still be seen in Ireland from May Eve to Midsummer Night. Throughout the Northern world in general, the lighting of the Midsummer fires was seen as essential to the health and well-being of everyone. In Sweden a Midsummer Tree is set up and decorated for people to dance around, while throughout Norway, Germany, France and Spain Midsummer fires are still ignited with a sense of devotion that spans the ages.

The solstice time, when the sun appears to stand still above the horizon every night, is caused by the rotation of the earth's axis, which is tilted slightly in relation to the sun, causing us to experience the seasons. To our ancestors this was a miraculous pattern that, if it were to vary, could cause all kinds of disasters to follow, hence the importance placed on the procession of the seasons and the return of the sun on a daily as well as yearly basis.

In this way the sun came to represent cosmic order. There's a wonderful story from the Jewish Talmud (dating from around 500 AD) that illustrates this perfectly.

One day Rabba bar-Hana, a famous traveller of antiquity, was guided by an Arab to the edge of the world, which was really the horizon. Here everything seemed to come to an end and the world fell away to nothingness, but there was a window through which one could see the movement of the planets. Arriving at the hour of prayer, Rabba put down his basket of food on the celestial windowsill. When prayers were over he looked for the basket only to find it had gone. "Who has stolen my food?" he demanded. The guide replied: The Wheel of the Heavens turned while you prayed, the world had moved on. Wait until this time tomorrow and it will return. You can eat then." What the sky ploughs under in the west will rise again in the east. Rabba's dinner becomes his breakfast through the movement of the heavens.

Observing the comings and goings of the sun was a constant reminder of the cyclically of life itself. For ourselves today as much as for our ancestors, things apparently lost can return to us, and experiences that happened yesterday can sow seeds that sometimes do not bear fruit until long after.

Thus light and wonder are connected, nowhere more closely than at the time of the Midsummer Solstice, when the sun appears to stand still for a moment in its climb across the horizon, and when it is visible to us for the longest period of time in any single day. For as long as we have any knowledge of ourselves as a species we have been celebrating this moment, worshipping the newly risen sun as a god, making prayers and pilgrimages to ensure that, wherever it went in the long winter nights, it would come back. Everyone knew, even then, that without the sun we would all wind up dead - so our ancestors went to great lengths to make sure it returned each day. This became a cornerstone of religion practice in most parts of the world.

Myths and stories were compiled to explain where the sun went at night. For the ancient Egyptians it went in a boat that sailed through the underworld all night until it returned, bringing the day with it. In Mesopotamia there were two gates through which the sun passed at night and returned in the morning - both guarded by fearsome monsters. In other cultures the sun is always getting stolen, kept for the pleasure of one individual. Which in turn meant that someone else - any likely hero would do - had to go and steal it back. In Classical mythology its Prometheus who steals the power of fire so that humanity can live; in the myths of the Inuit people the sun gets stolen by an evil sorcerer, and it's up to Raven, the ancient trickster god, to go and steal it back.

The sun has remained a central image for what is essential to life. Today it can still teach us to stand still, to consider, to be receptive of its light and warmth, to warm and grow golden in its rays. Nor is the acknowledgement of the sun - especially at Midsummer, which is being celebrated in many parts of the world as I speak - restricted to the distant past. Apart from the many neo-pagan groups who follow the path of the sun and celebrate rituals to honour it, there are other signs of sun-worship which are more surprising. Did you know, for example, that Fifth Avenue in New York is aligned in such a way that the rays of the rising sun on the 21st of June strike exactly down the length of the avenue? Or that the Obelisk at the Washington Memorial is also aligned to the rising of the Midsummer sun? And of course you have only to look at a $ bill to see the empowering rays of the sun shining out from behind the enigmatic pyramid bearing the all seeing eye of God.

Calling out to the sun then, inviting its light to dwell within us, to fill us up, is as old as time itself. As a species we have always done it, whether through the lighting of fires (in Scotland these are known as 'need' fires, no accidental emphasis there!) through prayer and visionary awakening. Another way is to sing - but I'm not going to do that today - for which you should all offer thanks - nor am I going to ask you to sing either. But I will invite you to join with me in invoking the sunlight by sounding your own note of joy and wonder.

I'll need you to stand up for this.... now I want you to face the East, the direction of the Sunrise... now close your eyes... and think of all that sunlight means to you... Now reach down deeply within yourself, to the very centre and heart of your being.... and sound a note that represents you and your relationship to the sun... Don't worry if everyone else's note sounds different, because when we all do this it starts out like a cacophony but sends up sounding like a choir. So, when you're ready, one long sustained note. Keep it going as long as possible... until it stops naturally... Then, still with your eyes closed, imagine that you are looking at a great lake of fresh water with the sun striking off it, dancing in its ripples ... imagine that water spreading out across the dry land around us.... so much water that even as it is absorbed, there is still enough... dousing the fires that rage nearby, cooling and soothing the enflamed heart of the earth.... Keep that image in your mind for a moment... then sound that note again.... see if it comes out differently this time.... hold the note and the image of that spreading lake of water.... and with every breath, breathe in the coolness of the water and the brightness of the sun's light... feel it filling you up... and if there are any dark places in your heart or soul, or any places that have gone dry, feel them being lit from within, moisturised ... feel yourself touching into the wonder of the moment....

Midsummer, 2002.

Chapter 26:

BREAKING THE CIRCLE

This was originally written as part of an anthology edited by my wife Caitlin Matthews and Prudence Jones (Voices from the Circle: The Heritage of Western Paganism, Aquarian Press 1990). I had been asked to say something about my experiences with a group of people who were following as very ancient path with whom I had trained for a period of time in my teens. Some would call these people witches, though they themselves laughed when I suggested this. In the brief time I spent with them I learned a very great deal. My still very untrained psychism was honed and sharpened until I was able to make a full and proper use of it. Looking back now almost forty-five years on I see that I was lucky enough to stumble (though noting is ever accidental) into the last dieing flicker of a tradition as old as anything I have encountered since. Now, I would call it shamanistic – though even this word does not entirely cover it. Even seventeen years ago I found it hard to write about this – not from any sense of a desire to protect the secrecy of the group, but more because I had moved on so far from those times that I scarcely knew what to say about them. In the end I decided to write of my experiences in the form of a story. What is described is not fiction, but the memory of a moment that changed my life forever. It is the most personal thing I have ever written, and reading it now is like looking in on the life of someone else. Somewhere under the envelope of this almost 60 year old lies the person who once climbed a hill in Sussex and changed his life forever.

The Ways of Tradition

There were, until recent times in Britain, a number of groups following an ancient path that has no name. Most would describe them as Pagan, simply because they do not follow any of the prescribed religions of the Book. Others would use the term 'Traditionals', thereby seeking to categorise what ultimately cannot be categorised. Actual definitions are simple enough: they meet in a rural setting which they have probably used for generations, and which is their own native space; their members are drawn from local, rural communities (with occasional exceptions); they are concerned with the seasons, with the right relationship of mankind to the earth. They are not interested in power, either personal or general; nor do they work needlessly or from habit. What they practise is neither exactly a religion, nor is it exactly magic; yet both labels, if applied in their broadest sense, describe something of the way such groups function.

Their observance of the seasons is as precise as their ancestors', whom they remember, fondly, as links in a chain stretching back into the distant past. They are thus, in as much as they are like anyone, closest to the hereditary families of wise folk who, like them, seem to have no roots but to gravitate to a particular place and lock onto its energy centre. They themselves scorn labels, seeing what they do, and are, as so much a part of life that it needs no categorizing. Many are Christians, who attend local church services and honour a god who is younger than theirs but who nevertheless stands for many of the same principles. They see nothing strange in this being, above all, supremely adaptive and knowing that all gods are one god. Nor are they to be confused with the medieval idea of 'Witches', who were burned in their thousands by zealous Christians. Most of these were harmless old women with nothing to fuel them but the horrific images conjured up every day in the local church. The Traditionals were always there, following a path that is at least as old as the bones of the earth Herself.

It is no longer possible to say with any certainty how much their practices have changed with the centuries. Sometimes, one might say, hardly at all. Yet they have ever been adaptive, taking what they needed from each successive influx of peoples into these islands, so that one may hear more than one archaic language in their chants.

This lack of definition is perhaps summed up best by say that the Traditionals follow the laws and customs of the land, dressing, speaking and behaving like everyone else in their locality. They blend into the landscape and, though their fellow villagers probably know that they follow older ways, they are neither offended nor scandalized by this; it is considered as much like a public duty as jury service or sitting on the district council.

All in all, there is nothing special about being a Traditional. Enthusiastic followers of the current revival in Wicca may demand to know about glamorous rituals and strange, antique practices; the only problem being that there are none. It is not even a matter of being unwilling to share the old wisdom; the sheer impossibility of communicating a sense of belonging to the land and its subtle, ordinary rhythms creates its own barrier. Finally, there is really no need for dialogue between the revivalists and the traditionalists. Despite having almost no common words with which to do so, they are both still speaking the same language. The distance between the one and the other is indeed vast, but the unifying principles, in whatever form these may be worshipped, are still the same. It is to a better understanding of this that the work that follows is dedicated.

More than this it is difficult to say. What follows is an attempt to record the incommunicable in a manner that can be understood by all. It is also a deeply personal response to a set of images, dreams and memories stretching back some 25 years. Sometimes, indeed, the edges are blurred - but the essential feeling of deep joy and primal energy experienced remains as clear now as then. Traditionals remain active because there has always been a need for them, a function for them to fulfil. If ever that need ceases to be, they will quickly follow suit. When, if ever, that happens, the earth will be made poorer by their absence.

Breaking the Circle

They used always to meet on hilltops - to be between the earth and the sky - and because of the *numen* of the place, whose influence was to be felt in all that they did. There was no sense of worship, simply of respect. Higher devotions were kept for the principles of earth and sky, usually referred to as 'she' and 'he', or more often 'Her' and 'Him', said not with disrespect, but with a jerk of the head or a lifted hand in acknowledgment of the shaping powers.

Meetings were regular, moving with the seasons. The chang-ing moods of the land dictated the mood of the celebrations - to call them rites would be wrong. There was, though, an under-lying savagery about them, something itself born of the imper-vious earth, which knew nothing of the sufferings of humanity, but which yet knew everything, was mother to them all. Thus they always wore some scrap of green about them 'in token that the Mother keep her fair face'; and this memory brought others, that 'wearing the green' meant something else, but also the same thing.

The green door was for the Otherworld, the red door for Para-dise; and it was through the green door that he went, over and over again, to meet in a place that was part of a far greater land-scape, where there was a 'version' of the hill itself.

There, they did many things to 'help the flow', to 'set the sea-sons in their places', to 'spin the wheel and turn the weaving until the pattern is complete'. That was how he remembered it, afterwards - the healing and the putting of things in their natural place. For within their own universe they were supreme, kept to the laws that ruled there, tried never to offend those who shared it with them, who were, by definition, Other.

The red door was less often used, a more private entry point into another kind of Otherworld. Here, Paradise was the home of the dwellers' own soul, where he or she fought personal bat-tles, won or lost, honoured or dishonoured, in the place of the Gods. There were no hierarchies within the group, no' higher' or 'lower' powers. Paradise, through the red door, was in no way superior; it simply was. There, he saw and understood the mean-ing of his own visions, heard the song of the ineffable spheres, and joined with them in a song of his own devising.

He came upon them by chance as it seemed, cycling through deepening dusk to come at length to the foot of the hill. Look-ing up through clustering branches, leaning outwards into the air like crones at a wellhead, he almost turned away. But some-thing, curiosity perhaps, or a stubborn streak that refused to relent after the long ride, pushed him on. Somewhere, at the top, was an ancient temple of Roman Gods - his purpose for coming. There would be little enough to see, even by day, but still ... He pushed the bike into the shelter of some bushes and began to climb.

There, near the summit, was the circle; a random grouping of trees and bushes that made a place set apart. There he saw figures move, silhouetted in firelight. He heard them chant-ing, the rise and fall of sound, the calls and the answers, male voices pitched against female, then joining together in a rich harmony.

Hesitating, he almost turned away, until one came through: the circle towards him, arms outstretched, welcoming. 'You are awaited. Enter.' Four words only to change a life. Yet from that moment his was never again the same.

Two years of training followed, often at a distance because he 'lived away'. Books were distrusted, some that he showed then laughed at. Sometimes, a dream would come, and he would walk again through the green door, and learn what he could and strive to retain it afterwards, in the cold light of day. He learned to fly, in these dreams - not on some twiggy besom, but on his own wings of thought, fleeing across the green land, seeing it - the same, yet different - with new eyes. And he learned the chants. Some of them wordless, ancient, springing from the deepest roots of the earth herself; others, a strange mixture, some Greek words that he knew, some Latin, others unknown: 'We take what we find and make it ours.'

These chants could do many things; conjure rivers from dry rock, split boulders or raise a storm - all of this in the green world where its effects were like the merest shadows on the surfaces of the world outside, but where the people met and talked and discussed the way of things, as they had always done, in awesome timelessness.

Regularly, in those two years, a summons would come, an envelope containing a single sheet of paper on which was writ-ten in fine copper plate handwriting, his name, the new name they had given him: 'A passing name, until you be ready for another.' Then he would go, and be permitted to watch, as he had done that first time, apart and yet part of, sometimes asked, suddenly, for a comment, a pronouncement. 'Shall we call upon the Swift Steed or on the Slow?' - 'Is it time yet to show the Dream to those who know it not?'

He learned the words he was taught. There were few since spells and stuff of that sort are for the latecomers' by which they seemed to mean anything from the Romans to more recent walkers of the Old Way. Only once did he ask for knowledge of their history, to be told: 'Not taught. Not remembered. We were drovers' wives once, that came together to do what men forgot. But the way is older - no names, no times. We are what we are and nothing more.'

But they were something more: dreamers who never dreamed, teachers who never taught, thinkers who never thought. And yes, there was a kind of unconscious cruelty about them - they were impersonal and did what they did, not only because they had always done it, but because it was always meant so to be done. Thus the 'initiation', a foreign concept they found hard to accept until he told them more, at which it was said: 'Ah, the key in the lock; the opening of the door'. The initiation he underwent, which he afterwards thought of as re-learning the things he had been born knowing but had forgotten, had its own share of savagery…

He paused in his memorizing of these things and fingered the green man head that hung on a thong at his neck. They had no images of their god, nor of their goddess. These were two impersonal polarities that held the whole of life in balance. The initiation then - the only time for nakedness, because 'it is only right that you enter as you were made', entering this time between the sturdy legs of one of them - a rebirth of sorts - into the bright and burning circle.

Then the words, murmured in his ears though none stood close: 'Be that you be, see that you see; shine, and in the shining, show what you be.' Ancient words? Perhaps an echo? But by whoever or whenever first spoken, potent now as then. He felt enclosed, safe, yet at the same time set free, poised on the breath of a great beginning.

Other words, forgotten now, that spoke of the year's turning, of the part each must play in its continued restoration, its endless making. Then, the touch of hands on his back and arms and thighs, a summoning, and more words, whispered now, that he could not catch. Then the thonged punisher 'To remind you always, what you are.' The seven strokes and the three, and then the five, and with the last, released from the hand that had held it in check, a thong on which was tied an arrowhead of long-past time. Brief, burning pain. Some blood, soon cleansed, salve applied that brought swift relief and healing. Gentleness now in the hands that touched brow and shoulder and foot. Last words, half remembered: 'Shallow is the shadow world… deep the world of earth and stone, where the Seasons turn…' Like a waking dream he hears them again, remembers the thoughts they conjured, that between the two worlds lay very little space, and often overlapped. That was only a part. Other truths followed: that to be part of life was to feel the flow of the earth's own blood, through the feet, mounting to the body, until the head was filled with its fire; that to be one with Creation was the greatest gift, though little known and rarely understood,

They had always known, had always sung or chanted, its rhythm, celebrating the round of the year in all its patterns, below ground and above. Thus there could be no set initiations in the understood sense; the coming in was merely the open hand, the word 'welcome', which had its own magical volition. Beyond this, he was considered ready, ready to have the key turned in the lock, so that his understanding flowered within him and he was attuned to the inner harmony of the group, where no one, man nor woman, spoke of having greater authority, the seal of man-strength or woman-power. He saw again, more clearly now, the balance within the group, the polarized strengths that worked for one direction and that all theirs, the 'will' of Creation.

Thus, they each 'acted out' that will, singly and in chorus, as the laws governing chant allowed for one voice or two, three or many, according to the song of the hour. Earth sang, the Mother sang in answer, and the stars fell into alignment, those above reflected by those below.

He reflected, briefly, that there was greater similarity between the concepts of 'High Magic' and the work of the family, than most would acknowledge; the working in harmony with the inner realms was at the heart of all their work.

The last night, remembered still with difficulty and some pain. A big night, a season-changer, a night of song and story. Then, a summoning, all of them, and he, drawn close and tight in the circle, chanting the end note and the dawn note in changing harmonies, drunk with the sounds, drawing ragged breaths full of the night. And he, focused, no longer aware of anything but the circle of light before him and the power he sought to fill it with ...

But, what came there, what filled the circle, overflowed across the hill, drove back the rest, overwhelming them, was something other. A man-shape cut out of the night, a vast-seeming darkness that shut out the moon and the stars, a great voice roaring his head: COME!

Just as violent was his response, his silent-shouted NO! Then the reverberation, the tearing aside of the curtain, and the circle of faces, some shocked, some bewildered, two angry. He remembered the anger for a long while after, the muted words: 'Be darkness and be fear and be not of us' . . . After, long after, when he could think again of these things, and seek interpretation and meaning, he wondered what really occurred. Was it his own psychism that had acted as a catalyst to some waiting energy, releasing it like a volcano from within the hill? Or were they to blame, as someone had suggested after; had they sought him as a gift to the numen of the hill? But would they not, at the least, have asked him? To go unwillingly was not to go at all - or so he believed.

Was it simply the unexpectedness of the thing, for none had foreseen it, least of all he? For many years he was to wonder, pursuing another course that yet brought him back to that broken circle, to that hilltop night. Often, he was asked the question 'come, give up yourself, be part of the circle again meaning other circles, never the first which was forever closed). Always he refused, until she came, who knew all the ways of intuition, who smiled and was gentle and taught him again the meaning of the Way, until he was able, in part, to teach her.

But all was fragmentary, forcibly suppressed through the years of being dark, of being fearful and 'not of us'. Only now, writing this, he remembers the deepest joy of all, the quickening earth beneath him, the answering heartbeat when his hands, their hands, struck it in rhythm; or when their voices, rising and falling, seemed to snare the moon.

And he remembered the trees, that seemed more than trees, and that beyond the green door were more than trees. Best of all remembered the meetings on the inner hill, beneath a moon that was always full and yellow, where he saw and understood the blurring of many tracks into one, and saw that he and his were truly appointed guardians of the earth, to see that it always held true to them and they to it. Right relationship with the living earth was their true calling - his also now.

Then he remembered, too, something else. That theirs was a religion of love and of light, just as much as the Christian God's; that they celebrated the natural world, its greenness an its brightness, because these were sacred things. That knowledge brought its own release, and he recalled some words from a book, supposedly meant for children, but that yet said all that he would wish said of these things:

Long ago, when the world started, there was magic everywhere; every race and country, every tribe and tributary had its magic--handlers, its wise witch people. Magic is another word for Creation, for the creation of the world was the biggest magic of all.
(The Witches and the Grinnygog by Dorothy Edwards
London, Methuen, 1983)

Section Five:

Neglected Masters

Chapter 27:

MIRRORS INTO MAZES
MICHAEL AYRTON & THE MYTHIC LANDSCAPE

I met Michael Ayrton at a London gallery showing an exhibition of paintings and drawings by Picasso. We literally bumped into each other and dropped the books we were carrying. They turned out to be the same book, a study of Picasso, and after we had stopped laughing we began to discuss the exhibition. I was only 15 at the time, and very shy, but Michel drew me out and we ended up having tea in the gallery's café and discussing not only art, but much else beside. I discovered that Ayrton was an artist himself: a painter, sculptor and writer, with a particular fascination for Greek myth. Being somewhat interested in this myself we had a fascinating conversation and at the end of the day swapped addresses. After this, until only a month or so before his untimely death, Michael and I kept in touch. Often I would not see him for several moths, but then he would call me and we would meet up and continue our ongoing 'conversation' as if it had never ceased. Over the next 12 years I learned a great deal from this brilliant and extraordinary person, who has rightly been called a 'Renaissance man' because of his multi-talented mind and deep fascination with the past. I gave the talk printed here as part of an art class at a London art school in 1979, to a group of students who barely knew of Ayrton's existence. I am happy to publish it here for the first time – unfortunately without the many slides that originally accompanied it. I encourage anyone who loves are, literature and myth to seek out the works of this neglected 20th century genius. It is followed by a poem I wrote in 1975 at the time of Michael's death.

Minotaur Risen by Michael Ayrton

228

When he was in his 50s the artist Michael Ayrton (1921-1975), made a self-portrait in which he depicted himself facing his own reflection in a mirror. This was typical of a man who once suggested that he was himself, in all probability, a fabrication, 'done with mirrors' - a remark which illustrates his life-long fascination with reflections, mirror-images and mazes, as well as with his refusal to accept things as they were presented. He did several drawings to illustrate what he meant, and published a "posthumous autobiography" of one " Lameich Trojan", in which it is maintained that the person known as Michael Ayrton, whose name is, after all, an anagram of Trojan, merely deciphered the life (written in mirror script - that is, backwards) in order to fabricate his own. Eventually, Trojan "meets" Ayrton in a mirror, the "Life" proves to be a palimpsest, and in the interplay of images he is not surprised to see "an infinite number of inimitable, multiple, blind, but smiling simulacra of the face of Jorge Luis Borges." So Ayrton/Trojan is perhaps only a fabrication of the Argentinean writer, an arch-fabulator, whose stories, particularly those collected in the book *Labyrinths* (1964), Ayrton greatly admired.

This is not to suggest that Ayrton's concern was with unreality. On the contrary he wanted to discover what was real, beyond the accepted criteria. He sought an objective truth, believing that it lay at the centre of the symbol known as the maze or labyrinth, the image of which preoccupied him more than any other over a greater length of time, and produced an extraordinary proliferation of work in almost every medium open to a multi-talented man with an endlessly enquiring mind.

In his lifetime Michael Ayrton produced hundreds of drawings, paintings, etchings and sculptures; he made several films, wrote books of art criticism and history, short stories, novels and poetry, executed designs for the theatre and ballet, wrote TV programmes and designed a life-size maze. Yet he remains neglected and largely ignored in major historical surveys of twentieth century art.

Reasons for this are twofold. In the first instance Ayrton did not seek critical acclaim, and cared nothing for selling himself or his work - which, being largely in the figurative tradition, set him against the increasing preoccupation with the abstract and formless in the movements which dominated his life-time. In the second instance he was gifted with a remarkable facility with words, and his critics found it disconcerting to find an artist capable and willing to answer back. His ability to write so clearly, not only about his own work (he is still his own best critic) but that of others, earned him the stigma of being "too clever by half", and critics who ought to have known better dismissed his best work as over-intellectual or precious - thus failing to recognise the high degree of self-mocking honesty, coupled with a ready wit and truly majestic feeling for the subjects which, literally, possessed him as he sought, in words and paint, bronze and collage, to interpret his particular vision.

This ability to work in so many disciplines only caused him to be tagged, unfairly, as a latter-day 'Renaissance Man', and many critics who did try to grasp what he was doing, found themselves brought up short by the bewildering proliferation of expertise in so many fields. Also, from 1956 onward, the central themes of his work were drawn from the world of Greek mythology, making knowledge of the classics a necessity for the full understanding of his achievement. The sensual quality alone of the sculptures is not enough to make them accessible, and many were not willing to make the necessary effort to bridge the gap.

A word must be said here about Ayrton's background, which was unusual in that it fitted him well for the career he chose to pursue. His father was Gerald Gould, poet, essayist and critic, but his death when Michael was fifteen meant that the strongest influence in his early life was that of his mother. This redoubtable lady was Barbara Ayrton, socialist politician, sometime chairman of the Labour party and M.P. for Hendon. Michael's schooling was broken by long periods of illness and he attended a number of schools until he was fourteen, after which he was allowed to travel widely and to attend various art schools. It was during this time that he first met Henry Moore, who was to have such a marked influence on his later career. At one point, the story goes, when he was barely fifteen, he ran off to take part in the Spanish Civil War, and lying about his age was present at the bombardment of Barcelona by Franco's troops, before Barbara Ayrton discovered his whereabouts and he was sent home. As a result of this incident he was sent to Vienna to stay with his cousin Millie. This remarkable lady was Amelia Levetus, who had once been a governess to the Arch Duke Rudolph of Austria, and the artistic circles in which she then moved enabled her young nephew to gain much valuable experience and establish an unusual degree of independence. Years after, when cousin Millie unwisely remained in Vienna after the Anschluss, she was shot in the Ringstrasse, aged 91, after hitting a Waffen SS officer with her umbrella!

To begin with, writing and public speaking came more easily to Michael Ayrton than drawing, and it required some discipline to bring his hectic mind, so full of ideas, to bear on the translation of images to paper. But in 1938 he took a studio in Paris with John Minton, and worked for a time in the studio of Georgio de Chirico. One of his earliest surviving paintings 'The Bull-Ring' shows the influence of de Chirico - and it is interesting also that the subject, which depicts a bull fight, reflects another theme which was to be at the centre of his major work from 1956 onwards.

A slightly later picture 'The Mask-Maker' of a mysterious masked individual, shows the first signs of Ayrton's individuality, and while the precise theme of the piece remains uncertain, if one looks closely at the arm of the figure, one can see a figure apparently reaching up towards the sun - an image which we shall be seeing again later on. In the character of the Mask-Maker it is also possible to foresee the archetypal craftsman, the creator who holds the key to meaning, who was to be embodied for Ayrton by the figure of Daedelus.

Soon after moving to Paris Ayrton met Diaghilev's conductor Pierre Monteaux and worked on a series of designs for a hypothetical production of Purcell's *Dido and Aeneas*. This in turn led to an exhibition in London, which caught the attention of Sir Hugh Walpole, and through him of John Gielgud, who commissioned Ayrton to design the sets and costumes for a new production of *Macbeth*. This was in 1941, and as Ayrton was called up in that year, the designs were finally executed in collaboration with John Minton, during several 48-hour leaves, and the production staged in 1942. In the same year Ayrton was invalided out of the RAF, and shortly after obtained a post teaching life drawing at Camberwell School of Art - a job that he held until 1944.

During this time he completed his first major work, a painting entitled 'The Temptation of St Anthony'. This is an amazingly mature work for an artist still only in his twenties and shows the way in which his style was already beginning to develop towards sculptural forms. The weight and density of the figures and their precise anatomical structure again strongly foreshadows later work. The method he used to obtain the correct delineation for the figure of St Anthony is particularly important. Painting his own arms and legs to shadow the muscles and give emphasis to the veins, Ayrton then used a mirror, making himself the model and demonstrating that he was already thinking in terms of three-dimensions as well as the degree of identification with the character of St Anthony. The crisis he was undergoing and which caused him to see himself in the light of the tortured saint is less important than the way in which he identifies with the subject of the painting. Throughout all his work, Ayrton's possessed the ability to become one with the character or theme he was expressing. This is developed to a marked degree in the paintings, sculpture and collage he executed concerning the myth of the Minotaur, Daedelus and Icarus, where this sense of oneness with the artefact is such that it becomes almost impossible to separate the man from his work - a position far removed from the work of most his contemporaries who strove to keep themselves distanced. The use of mirrors also figured largely in his later work.

During the next few years Ayrton continued to produce a steady output of paintings, mostly studies of tree-roots and landscapes. He also spent a period in Sussex and Wales, moving for a time in a circle of English artists who include John Piper, Paul Nash, John Craxton, and Victor Passmore. This 'group' - though it was hardly that - has been termed the 'English Neo-Romantics,' and is the only time Michael Ayrton could be said to belong to any school. Most of his life he remained a maverick, an artistic outsider who created his own world and was content to inhabit it alone.

In 1944 at the age of 23 he became one of the youngest art-critics to write for the *Spectator*, and at the same time began to illustrate books. He also formed a lasting friendship with the composer Constant Lambert, and I must digress for a moment to relate a story typical of Ayrton's playfulness as well as his obsession. Travelling to Stoke-on-Trent by train, where they were to see a performance of the Sadler's Wells Ballet, the two men began a discussion as to the relative merits of cats and fish and their representation in Oriental Art.

"As the train began to move, Constant produced paper and pencil and executed in outline a small but lively carp. Between us, alternating, we drew cats and fish for some time until the available paper was exhausted. As dusk fell, Constant inscribed in pencil above the carriage door a small goldfish seen head on. Gradually fish of many varieties and cats posed in numerous ways, came to decorate the available wall space. Night came and we worked like the Cro-Magnon man in total darkness. Occasionally, by the light of matches, we inspected our work. Small cats appeared riding large fish. Small fish were revealed inside large cats. Fish bit cats. Cats sat on fish.

In due time, only the ceiling remained virgin and it was not without difficulty, for we were both heavily built, that we climbed each into a separate luggage racks to continue, like twin Michelangelos, to design upon the vault. At some time during this creative frenzy, the train drew up at a station, and an elderly lady entered our carriage. Seeing no seat occupied, she relaxed comfortably and took out her knitting. Poor lady, she had assumed that the carriage was empty. She was wrong. The luggage racks were filled with reclining draughtsmen, but it was not until Constant observed to me that the ceiling was becoming over-crowded that she became aware of this. She left hurriedly and one can only be thankful that the train was still standing in the station."

It was at this time that Ayrton became widely known through his appearances on the BBC radio programmes *Brains Trust*, and *Round Britain Quiz*. Paradoxically, as his popularity grew, his standing with the critics fell, and James Laver's book on his paintings, published in 1948, remains the only full-length study of Ayrton's work published in his lifetime.

The next important development in Ayrton's life was his first visit to Italy in 1947. Here he was at last brought face to face with the Renaissance masterpieces he had studied at art school and after. It is from this period that the influence of painters such as Massachio and Piero della Francesca began to be apparent in his work, and the general impact of the Italian light in his painting became immediately apparent.

On his return to London he began work on two paintings, 'Afternoon in Ischia' and 'Approaching Thunder'. The most notable thing about these two fine paintings is their innate sense of form, and the sculptural quality of the figures. In a statement in the catalogue of his first retrospective exhibition in 1949 Ayrton shows how his interest is beginning to turn away from painting.

'I am not really gifted with painterliness,' he says ' I am concerned with rendering images as simply and austerely as I am able and not introducing delectable or succulent pictorial dishes. The work of sculptors was the most potent single influence on painting during the formative years of the Renaissance ... sculptural form realised pictorially by drawing ... is the significant factor in the 19th century art of Ingres, Degas and Surat and the 20th century art of Juan Gris and Wyndham Lewis ... herein my main interest lies ... I aim, rashly enough at the creation of monumental images as timeless as impersonal, and yet as human as those of Piero della Francesca and Giovanni Pisano.'

This marked the beginning of great changes in both Ayrton's life and work. Though he was to execute many more paintings, among them 'Vines before Easter' he did not advance, technically, much further than 'Afternoon in Ischia' or its companion piece 'Approaching Thunder', which carries such a marvellous sense of brooding silence, with only the merest patch of cloud to suggest the sudden Mediterranean storm which is about to break.

During a stay in Paris in 1950 Ayrton first declared a wish to sculpt, and consequently spent much of his time in the studio of the Swiss surrealist painter and sculptor Alberto Giacometti (1901-1966), a significant choice in that both men were much concerned with form - a concern which was to evince itself later in Ayrton's preoccupation with the stress and strain of the human body under conditions of enormous pressure. In 1951 he moved to Essex and set up a studio in one of the outhouses of Bradfield's Farm, which remained his home almost to the end of his life.

He did not begin sculpting immediately however, but executed a number of fine paintings which reflect the sense of expansion and freedom he derived from escaping from the atmosphere of London for the open air of the Essex countryside.

Further visits to Spain, Italy, and America followed, and in 1955 a large retrospective collection at the Whitechapel Gallery was received with mixed feelings. In 1952 he visited an exhibition of bronzes by Manza, and there he saw a blind girl reading the sculptures with her fingertips. He recorded this in a painting 'Blind Girl With Sculpture' but he had still not made the transition from paint to bronze, though he wrote, at this time: *There are times when one's drawings, coming out from the paper, insist on becoming sculpture, at the next stage, rather than painting. Over this one has no control unless one deliberately ignores the dictates of one's vision.'*

By 1954 he was no longer prepared to ignore these dictates. He made a sculpture called 'Snowbird' from bone and wood, which was used as a prop in the painting he was working on at the time. Two years later he cast it in bronze. The head of the bird is formed by a rat's skull and the body by the skull of a rabbit, and it can be seen that Ayrton already displays a remarkable sureness of touch and handling of materials. This was due largely to the help and advice given to Ayrton by Henry Moore, who gave a great deal of time and technical know-how to the younger man. He also taught Ayrton how to work directly in plaster on iron armatures, and demonstrated the use of wax for modelling small maquettes that could be cast directly into bronze. The result of this was 'Scavenger I', depicting a spavined dog poised as if to leap. This was Ayrton's first attempt at a sculpture wholly independent of painting. Moore gave encouragement, and it was followed in 1954 by 'Figure on a Wall', which showed a man balancing on a knife edged line. Of this Moore remarked: *'That's a bloody good idea, I'll use that.'* Indeed the two men continued to meet and exchange ideas for a number of years and eventually collaborated on a book on the Italian artist Giovanni Pisano (1250-1314). The story is told that when Moore came to visit Ayrton in his studio some years later and observing a large sculpture, said: 'that's good, but its a bit sharp there' - pointing to a raw edge in the bronze. For answer Ayrton picked up a file and handed

232

it to Moore. 'All right, file it down' - which Moore proceeded to do!

The relationship between the work of the two men, artists and great friends, is subtle. Both understood, perhaps uniquely in this age, the sensuous nature of bronze; and despite their widely differing approach to the subjects they chose, there are certain parallels. But where Moore's work increasingly relied on weight and depths to express his feeling for nature and the human form, Ayrton tended to move more and more towards lightness and the spatial concerns pertaining to a solid body moving in air or vacuum. While Moore's sculptures seem always firmly rooted to the earth, Ayrton's strive to escape into the sky-maze of which he was shortly to begin so exhaustive an exploration.

Amongst the most interesting of the early bronzes is 'Orpheus Seeking 1', foreshadowing remarkably the later work. The base was cast in bronze from an animal bone, and the way in which it is used as if to weigh down the poised and straining figure of Orpheus, who stands upon it, leaning downwards with his lyre held before him, is both a profound metaphor of the myth and displays the feeling Ayrton possessed for his materials. He was learning fast, studying Donatello, Degas, and Rodin, and during the next years produced a remarkably varied series of bronzes. 'Falconwatcher', like the figure in 'Orpheus Seeking', has all the poised anguish and desolation of the seeker after the unattainable. He stands in a moment of pause, turning his head skyward in search of the bird and perhaps longing to follow it into the air.

And in the series of bronzes that followed, this is exactly what happens. Ayrton's figures literally took to the air - or almost. A long series entitled 'Figures in Balance' were studies of acrobats in flight. One of the finest is 'Handstand', which depicts a dancer balancing on her hands, her body poised in the air. This fascination with violent movement, with the activities of the bodies' musculature and the compensations of balance were given a shaper edge by Ayrton's growing immobility due to arthritis. He freed himself in the flowing momentum of his bronzes.

But the great watershed of Michael Ayrton's artistic life was approaching. In May 1956 he travelled to Italy again and spent three days at Cumae near the bay of Naples. The effect of the place upon him was fundamental. Its associations were many and varied, especially in terms of mythic landscape. As Ayrton said later: *Its sense of genius loci came out at me.'*

Cumae was the site of the cult of the ancient sibyl, whose oracle once spoke from the honeycombed tunnels beneath the virtually impregnable city on the rock. (Virgil called them 'her thousand mouthways') Here Aeneas first landed after his escape from Troy, and the music of Berlioz' opera cycle *The Trojans* echoed in Ayrton's ears as he walked there. But it was also, traditionally, the landing place of Daedelus, who in the myth made wings for himself and his son Icarus, to escape from Crete and the anger of its king, Minos, for whom he had built the greatest labyrinth in the classical world. According to the myth, during their flight Icarus flew too close to the sun so that the wax holding his wings together melted and he fell into the sea and was drowned. Daedelus flew on and on landing at Cumae built a temple to the god Apollo and made an offering of his wings. He also cast the story of his flight and of his son's fall on a pair of great bronze doors that became one of the Seven Wonders of the World.

It was this story that began to haunt Ayrton. The doors of Daedelus recalled those made by Ghiberti, an artist Ayrton greatly admired, for the Florence Baptistery in 1401. Where one had recalled the fall of Icarus, the other recalled the fall of man. He thought of the words of Michelangelo in one of his sonnets:

'This is the way Daedelus rose.
This is the way the sun rejects the shadow.'

These words were to have great meaning for Ayrton and he eventually used them to preface his book about the myth. Meanwhile, he made a series of superb landscape drawings including 'The Acropolis at Cumae', and began to trace the story backwards through Crete to the mainland of Greece. The following year he returned as adviser to the filmmaker Basil Wright who was filming *The Immortal Land*. This led to the prize-winning documentary *Greek Sculpture,* which Ayrton co-directed, and it was the making of this film that clinched his feeling for the classical world. 'It was" Wright said later, 'in making this film... that Ayrton learned to know the subject!'

On his return to England the immediate result of his Greek experience was 'Figure in Landscape' in which the seekers of the earlier 'Orpheus' and 'Falconwatcher' are combined and set amid a searing image of the dry, baked landscape of Greece.

For the next few years Michael Ayrton worked on a series of wax and bone reliefs which moved between painting and sculpture, and in 1959 produced the first in a long series of works based on the Icarus theme. In 'Icarus Falls 2' we see for the first time one of the connected themes that were to dominate his work for most of his life, and upon which his stature as an artist must ultimately rest. The subtle combining of wax and bone is used to convey the stark figure who, having flown too close to the sun, falls, stripped of his feathers, blackened by the fiery embrace of the sun, which is half hidden in the smoky trail left by his plummeting body. Like Milton's Lucifer, Icarus has flown too high and been cast down. The story might have ended there, but to Ayrton's inquiring mind it was only just beginning to open out.

Icarus. Daedelus. The Minotaur. The labyrinth. Step by step Ayrton proceeded to extract fresh meaning from the myth. He began to identify with Daedalus, an artist more than half legendary, whose works had perished but whose name lived on in the myth of man-powered flight. Where artists before had been content to picture the story simply, Ayrton strove to find a meaning in it all. Typically, he did not stop with images of paint and bronze. He proceeded to write a series of poems which grew into a short novel *The Testament of Daedalus* (1962) a fragment told in the first person by Daedalus himself, relating the truth of his life and that of his son. From this beginning eventually came *The Mazemaker* (1967), a long novel which used the material gathered for the earlier book and expanded it into a full length account of Daedalus' life.

As the greatest craftsman and artist of his time Daedalus is called to Crete by its king, Minos, who has a strange request. His wife Pasiphae has become enamoured of a great white bull which came out of the sea and is believed to be Poseidon, God of the Waves, in bull-form. Daedelus must somehow make a contrivance whereby the bull may mount the woman. He does so, building a false cow in which the queen can lie and be impregnated by the bull. The description of this from *The Mazemaker* must rank as one of the most extraordinary pieces of writing in our time. Suffice it to say that the congress is successful, and that the result is the birth of Asterion, the Minotaur, half-bull, half-man. Horrified by the birth, yet fearing to kill what may be the son of a god, Minos orders Daedelus to build an enclosure for it. This is the famous labyrinth - so-called from the labrys or double-axe that was the symbol of the Cretan royal house. It became the subject of countless depictions throughout history.

Once the labyrinth was built, Minos decided he could not let Daedelus or his son leave Crete, and imprisoned them. Daedelus then hit upon the idea of making wings so that they might escape. What happened during the flight you already know - but Michael Ayrton was unable to accept the primitive account of the melting of the wax that held the wings together. In his interpretation Icarus is a 'hero' - a type for which he personally had little time. Icarus saw himself as making an attack, deliberate and explicitly sexual, on Apollo the sun god. He wanted to become one, through copulation, with the sun and in his attempt was destroyed. Ayrton described the event in word and image. 'Icarus l' shows a jaunty figure mounting into the heavens, to climb and soar effortlessly towards the sun. What happened to him is described in *The Testament of Daedalus* (and in the image called 'Icarus at the Climax') in a way that leaves one in no doubt as to the fate of those who challenge the might of the god.

> *'At his tip of time, at his apex, he moved upon the sun and joined the god. At his summit, his moving mass changed its form. His trunk splayed outwards, expanding, and the jointed projections of his limbs, disordered in the fission of his body, became the vectors of an energy beyond mortal strength. His proportions altered and his structure was transformed.*
>
> *The cage of ribs passed through the ribs of wing. Each performing an identical function, affirming the ascent implicit in the descent. The wings of his pelvis spread from the spine and in their bowl the duration of his flight was contained like a liquid. At maximum velocity, the sequence of modifications to which Icarus was subject, appeared simultaneous. A compact projectile and yet spread across the sky, he evolved in that instant a sequence of related anatomies, each designed to succeed and doomed to fail. In these anatomies, the embryo co-existed with the fish, the lizard with the bird and disintegration of ultimate fatigue moved with the impulse towards birth.'*

Icarus falls. Daedelus, scarcely able to comprehend what has happened, flies on and lands at Cumae. Ayrton made a bronze recalling his desolation. Daedalus sits, staring at nothing, the hands of the maker open before him, empty. He begins to see that all his life has been a maze, one that he has constructed about himself. Even Icarus was part of it, his flight a passage through the heart of the Sun-Maze, from which he has passed, emerging into the maze of death.

Still working backwards into the heart of the story-maze, Ayrton began to concentrate on the image of Daedelus as craftsman and maze-maker. In a large bronze actually called 'Maze-Maker' he depicts Daedelus in the act of constructing a maze that is really a projection of himself. He is connected by an umbilical cord to the point of the maze that emanates from the brain - a confluence of images combining two kinds of creation, physical and intellectual. In the later myths, which include the story of Theseus and Ariadne, the famous red thread with which the hero found his way to the centre of the maze is an ambiguous image. To Ayrton it represented the birth-cord and Ariadne, who was half-sister to the Minotaur, holds this key to the heart of the maze/ womb/ entrails of the labyrinth.

Before I go on to discuss the nature of Ayrton's maze and of the brooding figure that lurked at its heart, I should perhaps say a little about the history of mazes and labyrinths generally.

They are, of course, immensely ancient symbols, Mazes were amongst the first images carved or painted upon rocks by our earliest ancestors, and as symbols they have continued to haunt us with the suggestion of a preconceived pattern buried in the confused and often incomprehensible labyrinth of existence. There are basically two sorts of maze: the unicursal, which is more truly a 'meander,' beginning at the beginning and taking one by a winding route to the centre. (An example would be that which is laid out on the floor of Chartres Cathedral, traversed by the faithful on their knees, thus earning it another name, the 'penitential' or 'Jerusalem' maze, and used by those unable to go on crusade, for whom it became a symbolic journey to the holy city.) This is by far the most common type to be found throughout the world, pictured or carved, or laid out in turf or stone - a pointer to an age where the journey of life was more simple, a beginning and an end joined by the winding patterns laid down by the gods (or the Fates) which must be walked by everyone. Later, another kind of maze, the 'multicursal,' became more widespread, and there is some evidence that its appearance coincides with the emergence of philosophical reasoning, the understanding that life was less certain of direction, less rigorously laid down for those who journeyed it. The multicursal maze takes a markedly different form to that of the unicursal; it offers choices at every turning, many of which lead nowhere, or to dead ends from which may only turn back - the reflection of a state of mind which sees life as other than a simple journey from A to B.

So we have the maze as penitential path, a way of symbolically traveling that avoids the rigors of the real journey; and as an expression of the dark, labyrinthine voyage of life, which is both uncertain and subject to arbitrary change. To this may be added other images called forth by the idea of the maze: the womb, with its attendant suggestion of rebirth, (in ancient times the maze was danced through to symbolize the journey of the soul from chaos to life, and from life to the realm of the spirit); the brain, through which the thoughts are processed towards articulation, and which may bear as many variables and changes of direction as it is possible to imagine; and the intestines, which add another dimension of process and reduction which may suggest that the end of the journey, (in this case defecation,) may be projection into another dimension. This shows the maze as a gateway, implicit in the notion of the soul's journey. The idea of escape, the natural colleratives of imprisonment, is demonstrated by Daedelus and Icarus, who in order to escape the maze must take to the air, only to discover that the sky is itself a maze, an extension of the labyrinth of life. Icarus falls into yet another dimension, the sea, which is the origin of life, another womb, or maze, itself. (This is not to say that the maze is inescapable; only that there are no short cuts.)

But at the centre of Michael Ayrton's maze is the Minotaur, that sometimes terrifying, sometimes pathetic being which is at once an embodiment of the beast-in-man and of the evolutionary urge of beasthood towards a higher self. The bronze called 'Evolution of the Minotaur'(1964), is one of the earliest Ayrton executed. It seems to express both the agony of the beast struggling to understand its own nature, and the rage it feels towards those who have imprisoned it. At this stage Ayrton was still experimenting with the form of the Minotaur. The head is still without horns, more that of a gorilla than a bull; and it possesses hoofs rather than human hands and feet. But this line of approach reached a dead end soon after and from there on the evolution of the Minotaur was towards the human.

In 1968 an American millionaire, Armand G. Erpf, approached Michael Ayrton with a commission. The exchange (according to Michael) went something like this:

Erpf: You make mazes?
Michael: Yes.
E: I want one.
M: All right. What size?
E: Life-size.
M:(Slightly surprised) Why?
E: To prove to my colleagues in business that the easiest way
from A to B isn't necessarily a straight line!

So Michael Ayrton accepted the commission and began work on the maze which is probably the largest ever built since classical times - perhaps since the one Daedelus himself made. It stands at Arkville in the middle of the Catskill Mountains outside New York, and consists of 1,680 feet of stone pathways with brick walls 8 feet high and 18" thick. Overall it measures 200 feet in diameter and took 2 years to build. There are two centres, each containing one of Ayrton's finest sculptures. In one chamber, lined with red stucco (suggesting the womb) is the monumental 'Arkville Minotaur', the culmination of a long series of smaller bronzes. Standing over 7 feet on its stone plinth, it looms above the spectator and seems to contain all the suppressed power and anger of the trapped beast; trying to raise its too-heavy head and terrible horns on its too-feeble man legs.

In the second chamber is the Daedelus/Icarus Matrix 2. Here we see Icarus on the point of mounting into the air, but still attached both to his father and, through him, to the maze by the now familiar umbilical cord. The walls of the chamber are lined with polished bronze mirrors, which create another kind of maze, compounded both of the sculpture and anyone who enters the chamber. Here, Ayrton seems to be saying that the centre of the maze is only the entrance to an infinite number of further labyrinths, other dimensions into which one may project oneself. (Here, one cannot help thinking of the movies built around the central them of the 'Matrix', which seem to reflect Ayrton's themes at several levels) As he wrote: 'To escape from it [the Labyrinth] is to return, wishing to return.'

The imagery seems complete. But Ayrton could not escape his own maze that easily. In 1971 he executed a suite of 10 etchings in which he chronicled the story more fully than ever before. They are inscribed thus: *'Asterion was thus born, consecrated, mazed and isolated. Rising, he found himself part man, pent-up. Revealed, he saw himself alone, part bull. Fallen, in darkness, he yet endures.'* The etchings begin with the Minotaur as 'Embryo' in which Asterion crouches inside the first, primal maze, from which he must emerge into the world and be consecrated. At this stage he is still uncomprehending, his state that of any newborn infant, human or animal. But as 'Calf' he is taken to the entrance of the maze, and led by his own birth-chord passes beneath the labrys, (which is, you will remember, the symbol of Crete, and like Asterion himself, ambiguous) into the maze where he is to remain for the rest of his life. As 'Yearling' he crouches in his dark, empty world, struggling to understand, accepting what comes without knowing why, or how, it comes. Only one woman, his nurse and sister Ariadne, will stay with him as he grows stronger and his horns become weapons. In 'Rising' we see him at last beginning to take his first clumsy steps, bellowing defiance against the darkness of his personal maze. In number 6 of the suite, 'Risen' (ILLUS 1) Asterion stands at last fully upright. He regards his own hand, with its opposable thumb, with which he has done nothing but tear at food and scrabble in the earth of his prison. Inevitably, as a full-grown male, Asterion's next discovery is sexual - Ariadne becomes more than his nurse. But even here the ambiguity continues. One can see the anguished/tender look in his eyes, yet he is bewildered, and there is the danger also that his great strength may harm or even kill the object of his desire. Also of course, Ariadne is his sister, a further dark strand in the skein of his fate. Certainly, in the next etching, called simply, 'Pent' we can see that Ariadne either will not or dare not get close to Asterion any longer. Nor must we overlook that she holds in her hand another symbol of the maze, the spindle from which she weaves the red thread of life. But there is yet one further act that must be accomplished. Asterion must be shown his own image. In the ninth etching, 'Revealed' Ariadne confronts him with a mirror; and here at last there is understanding and acceptance, as well as horror, in his look. Lastly we see him 'Alone', crouching at the heart of the maze, holding his 'terribly strange head,' finally aware of the fate that must be his; always to be alone, to be racked with the vague, unclear images of his brain, prey to the actions and reactions of a beast grounded in his animal nature. In darkness he yet endures.

In a poem he wrote some years later, Ayrton put these words into the mouth of the Minotaur:

'What is man that I am not a man
Sitting cramped pupate in this chrysalis?
My tongue is gagged with cud and lolls round words
To speak impeded of my legend death.
My horns lack weapon purpose cannot kill
And cannot stab the curtain of the dark.'

Though he continued to execute further bronzes and many drawings of the Minotaur until the end of his life, Michael Ayrton never went further than in this magnificent group of images. His Minotaurs are always most human in their anguish and their plight becomes more terrible in so being. Ayrton's own grandchildren, when still young, used to put out food for the minotaurs which stood in his garden, and when a little older used the horns of the largest bronze to swing from.

But Ayrton was still not free from the labyrinth. Plans were made to extend the Arkville maze. A unicursal turf maze was laid out near the entrance/exit and Ayrton began work on a new series called 'End Maze', a larger version of which was to have stood at the centre. But Armand Erpf died and the project remained uncompleted. None the less the smaller version of 'End Maze 2' was completed, and is interesting for the way it brings together several themes on which Ayrton was working on at the time. He had often used the nautilus shell to represent the maze, and here he shows a figure emerging from such a shell, straining forward towards some new goal. And with this Ayrton himself seemed to have emerged from his obsession.

He found, however, that it would let him go so easily. From 'End Maze' he was led to explore, in a series generally called 'Emerging Figures', the idea of an evolving figure that never quite succeeds in freeing himself from the neutral background of bronze or space in which he tries to become completely manifest.

Approaching this from still a different direction Ayrton executed a bronze called 'Troy Maze', in which the figure is shown as entering (or trying to enter) through a crack in the wall. The work takes its name from the inscription TRUIA (AIURT in mirror writing on the reverse side) which is both a punning reference to the first four letters of the artist's name, and identifies the situation of the entrance as being a doorway to the maze, which was often referred to as a 'troy'. But, in both showing that there were still aspects of the maze which remained to be explored, and in setting up the ambiguous contrast of the entering/ emerging figures, Ayrton was preparing the way for a final sortie into the matrix of the image.

In 1966 he had completed a bronze entitled 'Mirror Maze' in which a crouched figure, locked in a bronze box, is extended, spatially, almost indefinitely though a series of carefully angled reflections. Ayrton was to use this idea again in the reflecting walls of the Daedelus/Icarus chamber in the Arkville Maze, and as he meditated on this he began to see larger possibilities for extending the theme. He stated this as follows:

'The labyrinth is at once ambiguous in its form and its nature. To Daedelus its walls were dense and impenetrable, translucent and illusionary. It may also be as implacable as stone or 'as impalpable as smoke.... In 1969 a small piece of neutral perspex, a substance at once dense and translucent, yet with the power reflect, extended my means to give physical expression to metaphorical form as to the idea of what lies within or behind the mirror... In ancient legend, it was some times believed that a man's image, reflected in clear water, was possessed of a separate spirit from his own. While all of us see ourselves in the looking glass not as we are but in reverse, a maze concept

because, although the mirror reflects the image and may even suggest the journey, it gives no clue to its destination. The mystery of the mirror was defined in 10th century China when it was pronounced that at 100 yards the mirror can see the man, but the man cannot see the mirror and also that the mirror can exist without the image but is incomplete because it is alone, whereas the image can exist without the mirror, but is not itself empty.'

This riddle Michael Ayrton set out to solve, using neutral perspex that, under normal lighting conditions, transmits an image through the smoky sheet, of the same intensity as that reflected from the surface. Thus, in the simplest instance, a figure placed in direct relation to a sheet of perspex creates a double image, which is not a reflection, and this can be exploited to create even more complex effects, as in the work called 'Impact', which by placing a Minotaur on one side of the perspex and the figure of a man with raised arms on the other, creates an illusion of interaction between bull-man and man. In another of the reflector series, 'Mirror-Twins', two figures face each other, but the perspex is so placed that a third, ghost figure, appears. When the sculpture is turned through 90 degrees a complex interplay exists between the figures, and a degree of merging and emerging takes place which is a continuation of the earlier emerging/entering figures already referred to.

If we look at this study for 'Discovery of Nautilus 2' we can see the degree of sophistication to which these reflectors can be developed. Three half-heads are presented, divided by two sections of perspex, and are completed by their own reflections and also appear to regard each other, while the figure which stands before (or is he inside?) one of them, faces a nautilus shell, again referring to the maze. As he points to its centre we can see, in the finished sculpture, that his reflection causes him to point to another image of himself which in turn points to him.

With these reflectors Ayrton challenges the accepted view of reality. Images are half presented, to be made whole by the enigma of the ghost in the glass. Nothing is what it seems. The mirror exists alone and is completed by the reflection that is completed by the mirror. The riddle solved indeed!

The culmination of all this was the huge work 'Reflector-Head' commissioned for the outside of the S.S.Kresge Company in the aptly named Troy, Michigan. Over 22 feet high, it is the largest single sculptural form created by Michael Ayrton, and it is a summary of his life work. Two huge bronze half-heads are divided by a polished bronze-glass screen and set in a high faceted plinth. As one walks around it, the heads are completed; the smile on the face of one is met by its smiling self. Through openings in the cheeks and the back of each head, smaller masks can be seen, facing each other in endless colloquy. Ayrton said of this that it was his intention to convey the principle that ' it is in the conjunction of heads that human beings relate and combine to formulate concepts.' Certainly the maze of interchanging faces recalled his earlier work, but the concept had become simpler, though no less complex in its depths of statement.

In setting the head where he did Ayrton was also aware that the highly polished surface of the Kresg building would itself act as a reflector, so that as with Daedelus/Icarus matrix in Arkville, the heads are themselves duplicated.

With the reflectors there seemed to be an end at last to the maze /Minotaur/Icarus themes, though Ayrton continued to work occasionally in this area, and as late as 1975 (the year of his death) produced two small images, one in bronze, 'Minotaur Erect', and the other a drawing, 'Minotaur Surprised', which show his continued fascination with the subject. These were the last Minotaurs he completed.

Early in 1975 he was at work on a series of TV programmes on the subject of mirrors, and at the same time became interested in an ancient Greek poet named Archilochus. Though he knew little classical Greek, with the help of two scholars he produced a series of translations from the fragments that are all that remains of Archilochus' work; and a set of etchings to accompany them.

These were his last completed work, and in their starkness and simplicity they are amongst the finest contemporary etchings. There is, to my eyes anyway, something more than a little reminiscent of Asterion about the figures who are included here - as though the Minotaur had finally become fully human.

The introduction to the book, containing the translations and etchings, and which came out posthumously in 1977, begins like this:

'I seem to see in my mind a hard and heavy man, raising
himself after a heavy sleep and lifting his head from
his crossed arms as if his elbows were tired. Yet
from where I sat opposite to him, across the table,
he could reach my right hand and this he did, locking
it in his own and casually bending my wrist and elbow
back against their joints. Such a table-contest is not
new among drinkers who are neither friendly nor at
particular odds.'

We should not be surprised by this degree of personal identification with the subject. After all, did not Ayrton write the autobiography of Daedelus, and of that other character, Lameich Trojan?

The Maze Maker is still the most important document we have for an understanding of Michael Ayrton. The comments and asides are more often than not as applicable to him as to his alter ego. Indeed the degree of identification with his 'characters' is one of the most important themes in Ayrton's work. He made only two straightforward self-portraits, but he put himself into many of his drawings and sculptures. One of the last of these was the cover to the catalogue to a retrospective show he was preparing at the time of his death, and it is unusually revealing. There is Ayrton, holding before him the skull of a bull- the mask of the Minotaur indeed. And in a bronze from 1970 called 'Point of Departure', he created an image rich in personal symbolism. On the reverse of the wall is a crouching Minotaur, with Icarus in flight above him. The double-axe to one side identifies the place as the Cretan labyrinth, while on the other (within or without) the sculptor prepares to move forward into (or out of - who can say?) the maze. It is a fitting memorial to a remarkable man and one of the greatest sculptors of the 20th century, whose work in the mythic landscape has, in my belief, yet to be equalled.

Note: For more about Ayrton see *Michael Ayrton: A Biography* by Justine Hopkins, (Andre Deutsch 1994); *Michael Ayrton: An illustrated Commentary* by Peter Cannon-Brooks (Birmingham Museums and Art Gallery, 1978); and *Myth and the Creative Process: Michael Ayrton and the Myth of Daedalus* by Jacob E. Nyenhuis (Wayne State University Press, 2003). For a fully rounded view of this multi-faceted man see also the special edition of the magazine *Labrys 3, 1978* (Ed John Matthews and Grahaeme Barrasford Young)

(1979)

Oracle
(For Michael Ayrton)

Heavy with unborn words,
(fruit of her unploughed womb)
head thrust forward and down,
chin jutting, elbows at her sides,
she crouches on the bronze tripod,
fingers knotted in a cats-cradle maze
through which she follows
the mad, dream-strung destinies
of all who seek the burden of her words.

Gravid, she rests in the quick of earth;
the walls of her cell engulf her:
harsh grey granite swallows
the dream she spins round her in the dark.

Shadows grow round her eyes,
which are blind, vestigial:
her breasts like stone,
her flesh heavy with ponderous weight;
and across her arms and thighs,
among the winding of her fingers,
hot red lines are scored, as though wires
bound her invisibly to the stool.

There is the look of the statue about her,
half formed, heavy with unborn child –
her womb a gape of darkness
round which she slowly evolves.

(1975)

Chapter 28:

DAVID JONES AND THE MATTER OF BRITAIN

Since 1985 until the present I have been involved with the Temenos Academy, founded by a group of people who constellated around my great friend the poet Kathleen Raine, and which has continued since her death in 2005. It numbers among its patrons HRH Prince Charles. Dedicated to keeping the light of wisdom and pure knowledge alive an a world of increasing philistinism Temenos Academy produces a journal containing some of the best thinking and poetry of out time. It was my privilege to teach several seminars there over the years and to give several lectures. One of these follows here. It concerns the work of one of the truly great poets and painters of the 20th century, David Jones (1895-1974) whom I first met in the 1960s and continued to visit until his death. His work profoundly captures the essence of Arthurian and Celtic lore, as well as the highest regions of spirituality and the very human experience of the life of a soldier in the First World War – which David Jones experienced at first hand. Jones' work is often said to be difficult, though T.S. Eliot and W.H. Auden admired it. It is well worth seeking out and brings great rewards to the reader willing to make the effort to follow the work. It was given in a slightly revised version at the David Jones International Conference, in Cambridge, 1998. It is dedicated here to the memory of Kathleen Raine.

For David Jones the myths of Britain, specifically Wales, represented a spiritual history of this land. As Blake said, in a phrase David often liked to quote: 'The Acts of Arthur are the Acts of Albion', referring to the deeper, inner Britain, sacred Albion, whose presence is felt, though deeply buried, even now. Thus David Jones' Sleeping Lord, and Blake's Giant Albion are closely related, brothers perhaps, even farther and son, and when he recalls the carnage of the Western Front, it is to the madness of Merlin that he refers, who ran into the wilderness after witnessing the death of family and comrades:

Merlin in his madness, for the pity of it; for
the young men reaped like barley.' (IP. p.24)

Later he was to write to Harmon Grisewood:

'I tried very hard to make a lucid, impersonal statement with regard to those things which have made us all - of this
island.' (Dai Great Coat)

From the beginning *In Parenthesis* is signposted by its links with the Matter of Britain. The quotation that prefaces the whole book is from the great native Welsh myth-book known as the *Mabinogion*. It refers to the moment when one of the followers of Bendigeid Vran (Bran the Blessed) having been entertained by the mysterious singing head of their Lord, is tempted to open a door which they had all been specifically forbidden to do:

> 'Evil betide me if I do not open the door to know if that is true which is said concerning it. So he opened the door...and when they had looked, they were conscious of all the evil they had ever sustained, and of all the friends and companions they had lost and of all the misery that had befallen them, as if all had happened in that very spot ... and because of their perturbation they could not rest.' (Pedyr Keinc Mabinogi)

The reference is clear enough - this is a kind of Fall - and the writer sets out to open the door upon his own memories. These, often terrible, are chiefly of the Waste Land, the place where, in the words of Thomas Malory':

> 'there increased neither corn, nor grass, nor well-night no fruit, nor in the water was here found any fish. Therefore men called it...the Waste Lande.'(Morte D'Arthur XVII,3.)

In David Jones' work this becomes a metaphor for the war-scarred area of no-mans-land, whose blasted trees and broken buildings are so powerfully described in his own paintings. This landscape has a voice of its own also, one which David Jones laboured to express in his writing. Thus in the preface to *In Parenthesis* he says:

> 'I think the day by day in the Waste Land, the sudden violences and long stillnesses, the sharp contours and unformed voids of that mysterious existence, profoundly affected the imagination of those who suffered it. It was a place of enchantment. It is perhaps best described in Malory, book iv, chapter 15 - that landscape spoke 'with a grimly voice'. (pp x-xi)

This is echoed later in section 3 of the work, 'Starlight Order' where the platoon of soldiers, make a long night-march to the trenches. As they proceed, with mounting terror and discomfort, through the deadly waste, Jones refers directly to Malory's description of Lancelot at the Chapel Perilous, a dreaded testing place for any knight who came near it, where skeletal figures with glowing eyes rush out of the night with levelled swords:

> 'Past the little gate
> into the field of upturned defences,
> into the burial yard -
> the grinning and the gnashing and the sore dreading - nor saw he any light in that
> place.'
> (IP p31)

This episode, together with a later one in the sequence of the Grail Quest, was especially important to David Jones. During the time he was in Flanders, he came upon a ruined farm building and looked though a hole in the battered wall. Inside a Catholic priest was celebrating the Mass. In a letter to Rene Hague, he wrote:

> 'I can't recall at what part of the Mass it was I looked through that squint-hole and I didn't think I ought to stay

243

long as it seemed rather like an uninitiated bloke prying on the Mysteries of a Cult.' (Dai Great Coat, p249)

This image, which he later caught in the painting entitled 'A Latere Dextro'(1943-49) clearly recalled the episode of Lancelot who, standing before the chapel of the Grail, sees the priest struggling to hold up the body of a crucified man, and desiring nothing more than to help, rushes forward. He is struck down by a tongue of fire and temporarily blinded. It was not appropriate for a sinful man to enter this place of Holy mysteries. That David Jones felt this passage deeply is reflected in this passage from the later poem 'The Grail Mass':

> *Lake-wave Lawnslot*
> > *beats against that*
> *varnished pine*
> > *his quillon'd cleddyf-hilt*
> *fractures the notices for the week*
> *hew would see*
> > *right through that chamber door*
> *he would be*
> > *where the Cyrenean deacon*
> *leans inward*
> > *to relive the weight*
> *he too would aid the venerable man*
> > *surcharged with that great weight....'*

(The Roman Quarry p110)

Returning to *In Parenthesis*, later in the same sequence comes a whole thicket of Arthurian and myth-laden reference. A soldier is observed, keeping watch over his sleeping fellows. This evokes a whole series of images: of

> *'Spell-sleepers, thrown about anyhow under the night.*
> *And this one's bright brow turned against your boot leather,*
> *tranquil as a fer sidhe sleeper, under fairy tumuli, fair as Mac Og sleeping.'*
> *(IP p51.)*

Here Jones remarks in his own notes to the work, he was thinking of 'the persistent Celtic theme of armed sleepers under the mounds' of the sidhe or faery folk of Ireland, of the Mac ind Oic, the love god of Ireland, of the Greek god of time and space, Cronus, who according to Plutarch, sleeps on a golden stone beneath an island which is identified with Britain. And of course there is Arthur himself. In the first of many references to the Sleeping Lord - culminating in the fragment of that name not published until 1967 - Jones makes reference to the idea of the mighty leader who sleeps beneath the land awaiting his country's call to arms.

This is an important theme both in Arthurian myth and in the writings of David Jones. It is tied to the belief that the person of the king is sacred, and that its sacredness must remain inviolate. Thus, in Celtic tradition, when the king is wounded or maimed the land over which he rules suffers also.

This is the meaning of the theme in the Matter of Britain that refers to the Wounded King. In Malory we read how this comes about through the actions of the pagan knight Balin le Sauvage, who while on a quest set him by Arthur, encounters Garlon, a knight who rides 'invisibly' and uses his gift to attack and kill his enemies. When Balin discovers him in the castle of King Pellam, he attacks without warning and dispatches the cowardly knight. However, unbeknownst to Balin, Garlon is the King's brother, and Pellam now pursues him through the rooms of the castle. In one of these Balin discovers: *'a table of clean gold with four pillars of silver that bare up the table, and upon the table stood a marvellous spear strangely wrought.'* (Malory Bk II, ch. xv.)

Having lost his sword, Balin takes up the spear and uses it to defend himself. He strikes down king Pellam, wounding him through the thighs - a term generally accepted to mean in the generative organs - which renders him impotent and, at the same time causes the Waste Land. This stroke, we learn, leaves the king with a wound that will only heal when the Grail is achieved, specifically when a ritual question is asked which will 'free the waters', healing land and king.

This is the Dolorous Stroke referred to several times in *In Parenthesis*, particularly in the section titled 'King Pellam's Launde', where at the very beginning we find a reference to Pellam's Castle, who falls down as a result of the Dolorous Stroke. The quotation referring to this, which opens this section, is again from Malory:

'So thus he sorrowed till it was day and heard the foules sing, then somewhat he was comforted.' (IP p59)

But it is in the famous passage towards the end of this section, which is generally known as 'Dai's Boast' that the references begin to coalesce, and to draw upon the imagery of the Grail Quest.

The character of Dai is important to the structure of the work as a whole, because in this long section, David Jones gathers together many of the strands with which he has been working, and signposts a whole cluster of mythological references.

The boast itself is meant to recall the supposedly boastful nature of the Welsh bards, as well as a most famous boast - that of the 6th century Welsh poet Taliesin, a number of whose poems are extant. In particular Jones refers to the *Hanes Taliesin*, a 14th century poem attributed to the ancient bard, in which is a listed a lengthy catalogue of places, things and events which the poet has variously been, seen or experienced. A passage will serve to illustrate both style and content:

Primary chief poet
Am I to Elffin.
My native country
Is the place of the Summer Stars.

John the Divine
Called me Merlin,
But all future kings
Shall call me Taliesin...

I was the instructor
To the whole universe.
I shall be until judgement

On the face of the earth.

(Hanes Taliesin. My trans)

Set alongside 'Dai's Boast' the similarities are clear.

> *I was the spear in Balin's hand*
> *that made waste King Pellam's land....*
> *I the adder in the little bush*
> *whose hibernation-end*
> *undid,*
> *unmade victorious toil:*
> *In ostium fluminis.*
> *At the four actions in regione Linnuis*
> *by the black waters.*
> *At Bassas in the shallows.*
> *At Cat Coit Celidon.*
> *At Guinnion redoubt, where he carried the Image.*
> *In urbe Ligionis.*
> *By the vallum Antonini, at the place of boundaries, at the toiling estuary and*
> *strong flow called Tribruit.*
> *By Agned mountain.*
> *On Badon Hill, where he bore the Tree.....*

After the reference to the Dolorous Stroke comes this long list of battles. All are attributed to Arthur in the few historical documents concerning him that have survived. At Guinnion, he is said to have carried a shield on which was painted an icon of the Virgin (the 'Image' of the poem); at Badon, the great battle in which the historical Arthur finally routed the invading Saxons, his shield bore the image of the crucified Christ, In this battle Arthur carried all before him. The other reference, which significantly comes before the list of Arthur's victories - to the 'adder in he little bush', refers to the last battle fought by Arthur, in which he received his death-wound. It began when an adder woke and bit the heel of a knight, who drew his sword and thus precipitated the conflict. Arthur's end is thus seen to have been laid down even before his victories, and in the poem we learn of the reason - Arthur's overweening pride.

The passage reads as follows:

> *I saw the blessed head set under*
> *that kept the narrow sea inviolate.*
> *To keep the Land,*
> *to give the yield:*
> *under the White Tower*
> *I trowelled the inhuming mortar.*
> *They learned me well the proportions due -*
> *by water*

by sand
by slacked lime.
  I drest the cist -
the beneficent artisans knew how well to keep
  the king's head to keep
  the land inviolate.
    The Bear of the Island: he broke it in his huge pride, and overreach of his
imperium.
  The Island Dragon.
  The Bull of Battle
    (this is the third woeful uncovering).
  Let maimed kings lie - let be
  O let the guardian head
  keep back - bind savage sails, lock the shield-wall, nourish the sowing.
  The War Duke
  The Director of Toil -
    he burst the balm-cloth, unbricked the barrow
  (cruel feet march because of this
      ungainly men sprawl over us).
  O Land! - O Bran lie under. (IP pp81-2)

This refers again to the story, found in *The Mabinogion*, of the great Celtic hero-god Bran, who has the epithet 'bendegied' (blessed). He earns this because, when he is wounded with a poisoned dart - much like the Maimed King of the Grail myths, whom he predates - he orders his head cut off by his own followers and after various adventures, instructs them to bury it beneath the White Mount, now the site of the Tower of London. It was to be set in place with the face towards France - because of which no enemy will ever overcome this land.

This is done, but when Arthur is king he orders the head exhumed, because no one but he should guard the kingdom. In the collection of gnomic wisdom collected under the title of *The Welsh Triads* this is reference to as 'one of the three woeful uncoverings' - because, of course, the Island is overrun by the Saxons for a time, and after Arthur completely so.

There is a sense here, that David Jones is making a parallel between the pride of Arthur - Bull of Battle, Director of Toil. Island Dragon: all are titles from the Celtic stories - and the subsequent overrunning of the Island of the Mighty by the Saxons, with the wastefulness of the war-effort, which sacrificed so many for the cause of National pride, and which so nearly ended with a new invasion of 'Saxon' enemies.

Several other Arthurian references follow, including one concerning the failure of Lancelot in the Quest for the Grail, from which he is turned back because of his sinful relationship with Arthur's Queen. This, as we have seen, was a matter of some moment to David Jones, who saw it as a parallel to human failure in general. In addition there are references to the great hunt of the boar Twrch Trwyth, which was later to become the subject of another of the fragments collected under the title *The Sleeping Lord*.

But by far the most extended and powerful Arthurian references appear in the final section of In Parenthesis, 'The Five Unmistakable Marks'. Again, as elsewhere throughout he work, the opening quotation is from the old Welsh heroic poem *Y Gododdin*, which tells of a hopeless assault by a handful of Celtic tribesmen against a vastly superior force. This in fact gives a backbone of reference to the whole work, which parallels it in many ways.

Arthurian and Celtic references inform the whole of the battle described in this section. Aneurin Lewis, the gunner whose death is recorded here, 'sleeps in Arthur's Lap', while the battle itself is compared both to Catraeth (the battle described in *Y Gododdin*) and to Camlan, the last battle fought by Arthur against his son Mordred. Lancelot's fearful encounter at the Chapel Perilous is invoked next, then the Dolorous Stroke - though the latter is dismissed as irrelevant - 'who gives a bugger for the Dolorous Stroke' - in the face of the naked extremity of War. A list of chiefly Arthurian heroes follows, including:

> 'Tristan,
> Lamorack de Galis'
> Alisander le Orphelin
> Beaumains who was the youngest....
> or the sweet brothers Balin and Balan
> embraced beneath their single monument.'

The latter, a reference to the mutual deaths of these two brothers, who slew each other, not knowing, until too late, their truer identities, adds to the catalogue of worthless death, while the enemy, 'lurkers who pounce', are 'like Garlon's truncheon that struck invisible.' Almost the last image in the book, which refers to

> 'Oeth and Annoeth's hosts...
> who in the night grew
> younger men
> younger striplings' (IP p187)

is a complex reference to the graves of the heroes listed in *The Englyns of the Graves*, a 12th century Welsh text which lists the resting places of many Arthurian heroes, and perhaps also to the Cauldron of Annwn, which gave back life to dead warriors, restored in all but speech.

Throughout *In Parenthesis* the Matter of Britain provides a deeply-laid structure which gives a degree of meaning to the senseless carnage of the war. It is as though, by remembering Malory and the heroes of ancient Celtic Britain, David Jones found a way to unprocess the horror and devastation he has witnessed.

However, *In Parenthesis* is not about the glory of war, still less about its victory. It is about he futility of war in the face of the Eternal. As Thomas Dilworth has written in *The Liturgical Parenthesis of David Jones* (   ): 'Liturgy endows life with meaning by uniting in a dramatised hypothesis the ordinary experiences of life with the fullness of belief and desire.'

David Jones meant to write about the way in which the 'creaturely' is subsumed in the world of order, brought into harmony like a ground string resonating in sympathy with subtle counterpoints being played outside the range of human hearing or understanding. Meaningless acts - such as the deaths of thousands on the field of battle - become meaningful within the framework of the Mass. Even the apportioning of rations becomes an instance of the Eucharist:

'Come off it, Moses - dole out the issue.
Dispense salvation,
strictly apportion it,
let us taste and see,
let us be renewed'

No action is too mean not to have its liturgical counterpart. In some places the liturgy is not always Christian, but shadows an older experience. The men are fodder for a darker sacrifice:

'for the northern Cybele.
The hanged, the offerant:
himself to himself
on the tree.'

while in the references to Arthur there are more echoes of the sacrificed Lord.

Attis, Odin, Christ or Arthur, the sacrifice is indistinguishable, and here the quality of David Jones' faith is most interesting: profound sympathy between man and his fellow being, the relationship of man with beast or inanimate object is mirrored forth in his understanding of the immanence of redemption.

In his next published work, *The Anathemata*, the presence of the Matter of Britain is still there, still felt, but has gone deeper. The whole poem is concerned with the act of remembering made by the priest during the saying of the Roman Mass, who is himself prefigured by 'the cult-man' who performs a ritual of his own which is also a prophetic recollection of the history of the Island of Britain. The epigraph, which appears on the title pages, makes this clear - it is a quotation from Shakespeare's *King Lear*:

'This prophecy Merlin shall make for I live before his time'.

The first section, 'Rite and Fore-Time', evokes this older figure who

'... stands alone in Pellam's land: more precariously than he knows he guards the signa: the pontifex among his house- treasures, (the twin-urbes his house is) he can fetch things new and old: the tokens the matrices, the institutes, the ancilla, the fertile ashes - the paladdic foreshadowings: the things come down from heaven together with the kept memorials, the things lifted up and the venerated trinkets' (AN p50)

Pellam is the Lord of the Grail, its guardian. And, in guarding the signa, the signs or sacred things, the Hallows of the Land, he guards more than he knows. For these things, of which the Grail is one, are nothing less than the memorials of time and place which lie in the landscape itself, the hills upon which, in ancient times, rituals took place which honoured the land as Mother.

These are the same 'colles Arthuri (that is, the Hills of Arthur) beneath which Cronos, Bran, and Arthur himself are said to sleep. They are also the 'Buarth Meibion Arthur! 'The Enclosure of the Children of Arthur' where lie 'dragons and old Pendragons', the ancestors of Arthur himself. 'Searching where the kitchen midden tells of the decline which with the receding cold marked the recession of the

Magdalenian splendours' uncovers not only the disjectia of ancient times, but the living bones of myth:

...the dish

> *that holds no coward's food*

...the hound-bitches

> *of the stone kennels of Arthur*

that quested the hog and the brood of the hog

> *from Pebidiog to Aber Gwy?*

These references are to the beginnings of the Matter of Britain, specifically to the ancient 9th Century poem 'The Spoils of Annwn', in which Arthur, accompanied by seven fabled heroes, stage a raid on the Underworld itself, to bring back the Cauldron of Annwn, a vessel which 'will not boil the food of a coward' and which, when dead men are put into it, gives them, back living - but dumb, unable to speak of what they have seen; and to the great hunt of the boar Twrch Trwyth, the subject of David Jones later work *The Hunt*.

All of these references build into a vast pattern of association with Arthur, the Grail, and the spirit of place itself. For, it is impossible to remember one without the other, to perceive any single sign without becoming aware of the power of all signs to place those who honour them into a special state of being - what we might choose to call a stare of grace.

The fifth section of *The Anathemata*, 'The Lady of the Pool' is really a long reminiscence of the history of London. But the lady herself is clearly one of the Ladies of the Lake who appear at so many crucial points in the history of Arthur, advising, beguiling, betraying and supporting according to their lights. Thus we hear of ' Taffy Merlin's mistress', who is Nimue, the maiden upon whom the great magician is said to have doted, and who, by dint of offering him her favours, acquired his secrets and then shut him beneath a stone- where he becomes yet another 'voice of the land' calling plaintively 'the *cri du Merlin*', from his place of imprisonment.

Such figures are themselves guardians, re-memberers, who, like Arthur and Bran, lie under the earth but eternally guards the walls of the city and the land, and who, as the Lady tells us:

> *'... have ward of us that be his townies -*
> *and certain THIS BOROUGH WERE NEVER FORCED,*
> *cap-tin!!....*
>
> > *and these slumberers*
> *was great captains, cap'n:*
> *tyrannoi come in keels from Old Troy*
> > *requiescant.*
> *For, these fabliaux say, of one other such quondam king*
> *rexque futurus.*

Here Arthur is the 'quondam King', upon whose tomb the words were written, '*Hic Jacet Arthurus Rex quondam Rexque Futurus*'- here lies Arthur, the once and future king'. So that he is another who exists both in 'the fore-time' and in the future time, the time that is, as the poet tells us 'the sagging end and chapters close' of Western history.

In 'Mabinog's Liturgy' comes a remarkable and unforgettable description of Gwenhwyfar (Guinevere), Arthur's Queen, who is compared to Selene, the Blessed Virgin, and Helen of Troy. Her elaborate costume is described in such sensuous detail that one can almost feel it.

Physically, she is described in terms of barley, marble, and pale Welsh gold.

> 'If her gilt, unbound
> (for she was consort of a regulus) and falling below her
> sacral bone, was pale as standing North-Humber barley-corn,
> here, held back in the lunula of Doleucothi gold, it was
> paler than under-stalks of barley, held in the sickle's lunula.
> So that the pale gilt where it was by nature palest, together
> with the pale river-gold where it most received the pallid candle-sheen, rimmed the crescent whiteness where it was
> whitest.' (AT 196ff)

This is taken up directly by the description of the linen that drapes the alter-stone on which are the Chalice and the holy things of the Mass. The connection with the Arthurian Grail mysteries and the parallels between Arthur and Christ, and between Christ and Apollo, and the Grail Winner, who fees the waters of the wasteland, are then evoked:

> 'What says his mabinogi?
>   Son of Mair, wife of jobbing carpenter
>   in via nascitur
>   lapped in hay, parvule.
> But what does his Boast say?
>   Alpha es et O
>   that which
> the whole world cannot hold.
> Atheling to the heaven-king.
> Shepherd of Greekland
> Harrower of Annwn.
> Freer of the waters.
> Chief Physician and
> dux et pontuifex.' (AN. p.207)

Finally, we come to 'Sherthursday and Venus Day', which at once evokes the Arthurian connection with the Grail story, which is linked closely to the Mass throughout. 'Sherthursday', the old name for Maunday Thursday, is a direct reference to Malory, where Christ, appearing to the Grail winners says of the vessel that: 'this is the holy dish wherein I ate the lamb on Sherthursday' (XVII,20).

In the passage beginning:

> 'Grown in stature
>   he frees the waters...'

Peredur, the Welsh form of Perceval, is conflated with Christ, and his childhood in the forest, where he is brought up in ignorance of human ways, becomes a pattern of innocence. But the youth encounters two of Arthur's knights, whom he thinks are angels, and from that moment will not settle until he has himself become a miles, a knight. He thus puts on the armour of a man, and takes his place in the world. This act will result in the death of his mother, from sorrow, but also, ultimately, brings about the healing mystery of the Grail. For Peredur, or Perceval, is he who asks the all-important question: who is it that the Grail serves, which reverse the effects of the Dolorous Stroke and 'frees the waters which in turn cause the refructification of the Waste Land.

All of this is summed up in the passage that reads:

> Her Peredur
> vagrant-born, earth-fostered
> acquainted with the uninhabited sites.
> His woodland play is done, he has seen the
> questing milites, he would be a miles too.
> Suitor, margaron-gainer.
> Tryst-keeper
> his twelve-month-and-a-day
> falls tomorrow.
> He would put on his man's lorica.
> He has put it on
> his caligae on
> and is gone
> to the mark-land....
> Unless he ask the question
> how shall the rivers run
> or the suitors persuade their lovers
> or the erosion of the land cease?' (AN 225-6)

Finally, the poem reaches an almost elegiac close. The sacring of the Mass, the oblation, the offering of gifts, is depicted, as Christ himself says mass with the Holy Cup:

> Here, in this place
> as in Sarras city
> (where the maim was ended
> at the voyage end)
>
> . . .
>
> Here, in this high place
> into both hands
> he takes the stemmed dish
> as in many places
> by this poured and that held up
> whatever their directing glosses read:
> Here he takes the victim.
> At the threshold-stone
> lifts the aged head?
> can the toothless beast from stable come

252

discern the Child
in the Bread?' (AN p242)

In *The Hunt* and *The Sleeping Lord* both parts of a longer work provisionally entitled The Roman Quarry and left unfinished at the time of his death, David Jones returned again to the Matter of Britain in an even more direct fashion. Taking up themes that had been mentioned both in *In Parenthesis* and *The Anathemata*, Jones extends the parallels between Arthur and Christ and Arthur as guardian of the sacred Land. *The Hunt*, his most clearly Arthurian work, returns to the theme of the hunting of the great boar Twrch Trwyth, described in the medieval story of 'Culhwch and Olwen'. In the notes to a recording made in 1967 he prefaced the work as follows:

'The great boar is the personification of destructive potency, so that the tale is largely one of the immemorial struggle between what is salvific and what is inimical - 'cosmos' against 'chaos'....I tried to evoke something of the feel of the stress, urgency and effort of the war-bands of the island lead by an Arthur-figure in pursuit of their formidable quarry across the whole of South Wales. What distinguishes this native prose-tale from the subsequent great medieval Arthurian Romance-Cycles is its vivid sense of the particular, of locality and site...Though the theme itself is a common mythological theme stretching back to remote prehistory, here in this Welsh tale, its setting is a knowable, factual, precisely defined tract of country.
In short, for all its marvels and numinous powers, its many strata of mystery. its narration 'proceeds from the known to the unknown'....'

Here the wonderfully rich strata of Celtic and Arthurian myth are evoked and overlaid with a background of emergent Christianity. The war-bands learn from the Cumaean Sybyl 'the Change Date and the Turn of Time' when the message of Christ comes to Britain; and the whole of the long description of Arthur's riding across the land forms a striking picture of both the Wounded King, the 'stricken numen of the woods', and the crucified saviour.

Arthur rides

'with the trophies of the woods
upon him
who rode
for the healing of the woods
and because of the hog.' (SL p69)

This beast has become, like Garlon or the Dolorous Stroke, the active principle of evil, the cause of the Waste Land, which must be healed. Arthur, as its guardian must suffer also, and thus his riding causes him to be wounded, like Christ, for the sake of the land and its people. He is

' the speckled lord of Prydain
in his twice-embroidered coat
the bleeding man in the green
and if through the trellis of green
and between the rents of the needlework
the whiteness of his body shone

253

so did the dark wounds glisten.' (SL p68)

In *The Sleeping Lord* this parallel has become even stronger. The themes of the Waste Land and the Wounded King are explored through the notion that the king must be perfect in every limb before he can rule, and that if he is wounded then the land is also. The whole of the poem is really a huge single image. The Lord, be he Arthur or Christ or Bran, sleeps beneath the land - is the land. He is invoked by these named and others: Cunedda Wledig, proto-ancestor of the Celts, Ambrosius Aurelianus, the last of the Roman lords of Britain and Arthur's uncle, Cronos the sleeper who is imprisoned beneath the Island of Britain, Mabon the *puer eternis* of the Celts, who shared his imprisonment with Arthur.... These and all the

'many, many more whose names are, for whatever reason, on the diptycha of the Island; and vastly many more still, whether men or womankind, of neither fame nor recorded nomen, whether bond or freed or innately free, of far back or of but recent decease, whose burial mounds are known or unknown or for whom no mound was ever raised or any mark set up of even the meanest sort of show the site of their interment...' (SLp85)

Thus the Sleeping Lord becomes a container of memory, a living anamnesis who recalls, within himself, the history and myth and story of the land. It is David Jones' purest statement of his art, and it is rooted most deeply on the Land that gave birth to Arthur. In the final passage from the poem, this is set forth in a series of questions, which are one with the Grail question, and with the great Question of life itself.

With this David Jones brings into focus all the themes he has been exploring from *In Parenthesis* onward: the question of the ordinary and the particular, the named and the un-named, the nature of salvific signs, the re-membering, the wasted land and the search for the Great Theme which is the human quest for meaning, which was for him found in the life and teachings of Christ.

In these works, and in paintings such as 'The Lord of Venedotia', 'Lancelot and the Three Queens', 'Trystan ac Essylt', and 'Lancelot in the Queen's Chamber', David Jones distilled the whole of the Matter of Britain. In so doing he also showed how it fit within the pattern of a greater whole, the heritage of Western Spirituality and history, and the literary heritage of the Middle Ages.

I can think of no better way to end than with the words that form a prayer that sums up, for me, all of David Jones' work. It comes from the fragmentary poem 'Cailleach' published posthumously in *The Roman Quarry*, and the reference is once again to that moment where Lancelot, standing before the entrance to the Grail Chapel, sees the 'venerable priest' lifting the body of the crucified man at the oblation of the Mass. It might well stand as a fitting epitaph not only to David Jones himself but to all artists and writers living at the 'sagging end and chapters close' of the twentieth century:

'Holy and Eternal Lord, Gwledig Nef, I ask but that one microscopic fraction of this world's time of you, who within the vast Wheel of Eternity created time as not illusory but of realitas. No more I ask but that, not any amelioration of what is adjudged me, on the in favilla day, As David and the Sibyl have it. Nil intultum remanbit - but I too would aid the venerable man surcharged with that great weight, and it is but for that brief moment I ask it.' (Roman Quarry p105)

Brief Biography of David Jones

Born: Brockley, Kent in 1895, the son of a Welsh printer's block maker and the daughter of a Thames-side mast and block maker. Attended Camberwell School of Art from 1909 to 1914 and Westminster School of Art in 1919. From December 1915 to March 1918 served as private in the Royal Welsh Fusiliers on the Western Front. Invalided out with lung problems and general ill health, which dogged him thereafter. Received into the Roman Catholic Church in 1922 and joined Eric Gill as part of the Ditchling Community in Sussex in 1922. Moved with the community to Capel-y-Ffin in the Black Mountains of Wales during the mid 1920s. He published *In Parenthesis* in 1937 having begun it in 1927, and *The Anathemata* in 1952. His essays were collected in *Epoch and Artist* (1959) and this was followed by '*The Sleeping Lord*' in 1974. After his death in 1974 *The Kensington Mass* and *The Roman Quarry*, fragments of a longer work-in-progress, were published, followed by a further selection of essays *The Dying Gaul* in 1978. Paintings, etchings and lettering are to be seen in the Tate Gallery, London, and Kettles Yard, Cambridge.

(1993)

Chapter 29:

SAGGING END AND CHAPTER'S CLOSE:
David Jones in the Zone

This was another talk given to the David Jones Society, this time in Oxford 2000. As with the preceding essay, I wanted to take the opportunity open up the knowledge of David Jones' incomparable work to a wider audience.

David Jones, on his own admission, was neither comfortable nor 'at home' in the modern world. To him, the period of history through which he lived, particularly the two world wars and the period between them, was a time of darkness and destruction, characterized by loss of religious faith, a failure to recognize the importance of symbol and sign, and an increasing neglect of the sacramental in Modern Art. It was indeed a Wasteland, like that whose outlines he delineated in so much of his writings. It was this that he described, in the opening passage of the *Anathemata*, as 'the sagging end and chapter's close' - the end of history, particularly as it is defined in the writings of Oswald Spengler, whose work was familiar and important to David throughout this period in his life.

Jonathan Miles, in his book *Backgrounds to David Jones,* (1990) draws attention to the wide knowledge of Spengler which is evidenced throughout a great deal of Jones' work. Indeed, he quotes from a letter to Harman Grisewood written in 1942, in which David said that reading Spengler was: 'as if one were reading one's own exact thought for the past twenty years put down by someone who could think clearly and who had the power of expression and elucidation'.

David Jones' own copy of Spengler's seminal work *The Decline and Fall of the West,* is dated Aug. 19th, 1941, a date which might seem to carry its own weight of significance, at a time when Europe was reeling under the repeated hammer blows of Hitler's assault. Jones' marginal comments, written throughout, have been ably studied by Dr Miles, but I would like to mention two key passages, along with David Jones' comments, by way of an introduction to the main aspect of this paper - his characterization of the modern world as 'The Zone' as it appears in *Balaam's Ass.*

Among the many key passages which are marked and underlined in David Jones' copy of *Decline and Fall*, many revolve around the split between 'civilization' and 'culture', as in the following:

"The present is a civilized, emphatically not a cultured time, and ipso facto a great number of life-capacities fall out as impossible... Of great pointing and great music there can no longer be, for Western people, any question. Their architectural possibilities have been exhausted these three hundred years." (Decline and Fall)

or again

"Culture-man lives inwards, Civilization-man outwards in space and among bodies and 'facts'."

Under which David has written

"If this is true and I think it is, it seems to follow that 'man' will be nostalgic and wretched in any 'civilization' - yet S[pengler] urges in the introduction and elsewhere that one is a third-rate person if one has such nostalgia for a 'culture'. He can't have it both ways."

Spengler even offered a statement concerning the isolation of artists in the modern age which David Jones must have found telling:

'artists, poets, philologist and philosophers ... feel themselves to be out of their element in the ... present.' Choosing rather "in this or that past epoch a standpoint... from which to condemn 'today'. "

This is certainly what David Jones did, placing himself firmly in the past of Arthurian Britain, the Roman Empire, and, in the *Anathemata,* even further back in the geological past of the planet. To what extent he was 'condemning' today' is a moot point. Certainly there is little opprobrium in Jones' writings about the present in the arts - and by extension (nowhere perhaps as strongly as in **Balaam**) there is a deep distrust of what Spengler termed the 'Faustian' culture of the 20th century.

I do not think it is stretching things too far to say that David saw himself as a solitary, embattled figure holding out against the tide of materialism and nihilism which he saw as one of the key aspects of the 20th century, and that, through his writings and paintings he was, in a certain sense, striving to re-make the world. Not for nothing is his greatest work called the *Anathemata*, a word that means re-membering, literally putting back together the lost and forgotten fragments of creation. It is for this reason that Jones' work could only ever be fragmentary - a factor which he emphasized again and again in his commentaries, in the subtitle of the **Anathemata** - 'Fragments of an attempted writing' and in the very nature of his work itself - so many incomplete attempts at the recreation of time and space, at the rekindling and restitution/restoration of a world which had gone mad.

There are so many variations of this theme that one discovers them wherever one looks in David Jones work. In his essays for example, I found the following statements:

In 'Past and Present', a letter written in answer to a critique of his work in the Cambridge magazine *Granta*, he wrote:

*"My contention, stated in the preface to **The Anathemata** and also hinted at in the Preface to **In Parenthesis** (1937) is that for a number of quite objective reasons over which ewe have no control, our present civilizational pattern in its essential and determining characteristics has occasioned a dichotomy which effects to some extent the 'doing' of man (Aristotle's praxis) and to a much larger extent all his 'making' (Aristotle's poesis) an which effects to a unique extent and in a special manner, those makings which involve certain specific arts, e.g. painting and poetry.*

What I have suggested is that man-the-artist, finds himself, willy-nilly, un-integrated with the present civilizational phase. I regard this as a regrettable matter of fact. I also say that there have been phases when this was less marked and that there have been true culture-phases when this was not marked at all, when man-the-artist was as integral to the pattern as is man-the-mechanic or managerial man to our pattern today." (Epoch & Artist: pp139-140)

This is almost dystopian. And nowhere is it so forcefully depicted than in the work we have been looking at today. David Jones himself described *The Book of Balaam's Ass*, in the brief introduction note to the extract published in *The Sleeping Lord and Other Fragments'* as 'seeming to afford a link of sorts between the two widely separated books: *In Parenthesis* and *The Anathemata*.' The former was written under the pressure of his war-time experiences, and was itself an attempt to explain to himself the reasons for the madness and carnage he had witnessed in the trenches. The latter, begun in 1938 and not published (I do not say completed, because in a sense it was never completed) until 1959, is a work of deeper maturity, though still worked on almost from the moment the earlier book was finished. It contained David Jones' answer to the question he had asked in *In Parenthesis* and elsewhere - an answer that takes place within the framework of the Roman Catholic Mass, in which all of time is remembered and recalled.

Between these two points, sits *The Book of Balaam's Ass'*, a curious and often rambling account of Jones own reactions to the world in which he found himself between the wars. A word with which he was distinctly out of joint, and in which he sought (perhaps without success) to discover a point from which he could operate.

When he chose to give this title to his work in progress he may well have been thinking that artists, like prophets, are most often unwelcome in their own land. But unlike Joyce he choose not to leave his homeland - indeed he would almost certainly not have survived anywhere else - but to remain, almost in hiding, producing a body of work that reflects his love of tradition, and the guiding principle of its continued importance.

Balaam's Ass immediately refers us back to the Biblical story of the prophet whose beast of burden was able to see the Angel of God when he could not, and was beaten for it. Unsurprisingly, this image has stood for the plight of artists everywhere, who have consistently been the visionaries of our culture and just as consistently ignored or belittled.

The Book of Balaam's Ass constantly refers us back to animals, sand to the way they could teach us a thing or too, or as David Jones puts it:

She'd teach you manners; for she has part in the patrimony...
She'd show you a classless society. She'd thrust you on your origins.
She'd break down and nozzle to your foundations and toss high for the windy advent day a thousand middle-walls of partition.
She'd rend your temple veils...
She'd make your exploiting governance wither away all right...' (BA p189)

Here are references to the denial of our common origins, (human and animal and by extension the many segregation's of the human species) which are brought together under God's covenant. The 'exploiting governance' probably refers to the Fascist leaders of the day, but can stand for any dictatorship to which you care to apply it.

But it is the final passages of the work where he finally cuts loose and delivers a powerful salvo at the modern world of what Spengler called 'technocratic man'. The passages in question, for those with copies of the book, are from p 207 to p 211, and I would like to read from these at some length, because as with all David Jones work understanding comes with hearing the work - and also because I want to comment on some of the passages as we go.

Until this point we have heard much about the beauty and grace of animals. Then, suddenly, we get the following passage, in which the real sub-text of the poem is finally laid out before us:

"Well, Mrs. Balaam, how do you do? ... you'ld laud a dunghill for the children to gain their tributes from its fetid slopes. You've fair danced a jig for all your informed disillusion.

You would to me a tale unfold of this unhoused and unchrism'd flesh whose end is bare of sweet reason.

In each slow turning of each fold in the miserable garment of our sorrow you would show a mockery and grim futility, where lice for woven beauties crawl. You would show apeheads for fair princes when they lift their beavers up, and Geraldine's terrible paps for a sweet queen's embroidered bodice, and leprous wood to crumble in our trusting fists -as illusory as, that fungus-barter which Gwydion's magic made (when he effected the rising of the south to obtain for his brother the bed he was after).

You would cry wolf, and portray his loping flanks, his hunched malicious twist, his grinning maw, as though he were conceived outside love's covenant. But look! where he stands to mock your anthropomorphic prejudice, see where he regards you, his grey beauty flaming, his strong pelt praising the Lord of all glistening hair on lion, on fox, on tunneling badger. See him lurching his glory, see his loose limbs stretched familiar on the predella of the throne, with the nine choirs to stroke him. And hear his grim voice that his erect throat trumpets out among the flock of the elect; see him, the ravager of folds, redeemed and foldkeeper. (p202)

Mrs. Balaam is a false Prophetess, who, as Rene Hague points out in his notes on the text,

'.... is the disillusioned person, the person who 'cannot see the angel', as Balaam could not until his eyes were opened, who does not recognize the 'sweet influence', who sees things in a purely factual and utilitarian way, who ... would be at home in the Zone.' p277

But the above quoted passage is immediately followed by a powerful evocation of Wisdom: Sofia, the Divine 'Bride of God', here remembered in the form Minerva and her owl. She is also the *poesis* of Aristotle, which you may remember David Jones introduced into Spengler's equation. Wisdom balances the presence of Mrs. Balaam, and leads us into a wonderful catalogue of numinous offerings-up of things that out-weigh the negative aspects of human development. Thus what might on one hand be seen as the loss of a Catholic spirituality to the Protestant faith is seem to have given us Milton and

'For all God's children, a consummate prose style.' (P205)

But almost at once we are into the Zone. This place is both, to borrow David's term, the world of the utile, the godless, the mechanistic - and also the army camp near Winchester where he was stationed before embarking for France in 1915, and which here serves as a microcosmic vision of the 'real' world. It forms a bleak, sometimes funny, often frightening view of the Wasteland of the West, that world of which Spengler had written and to which David Jones found himself exiled.

Let me read you some extracts:

259

" .... you can't say much about the Zone. We all know the Zone we all weep in the Zone. It's a great crust runs there about, they beat his messengers in the Zone. It never distils a balmy shower on the heath. He's naked in the Zone. You would perhaps have a good case in the Zone. If you went to the Zone to curse you might manage it .... It's always 3 p.m. on the heath, you are always in civvies walking the tired tracks between the cigarette cards, there are discarded contraceptives to drape the fern roots on the heath, the viper's dry belly draws out between the torn late-pass and the Odeon counterfoil, two one and threepennies Block D - that's for bread and circuses and that's for a lot of fun. These trophies of innocent recreation are surely pleasant discoveries to any humane person on the blasted heath ... It makes your bosom swell with proper pride to think of the tempered discipline practiced by those who will some day be called up to defend our beautiful country. The Zone is a prepared womb from which they spring, fully conditioned for such a task.

All the doors are shut in the Zone.
All roads intersect in the Zone.
They've swept and garnished the Zone....
They never complain in the Zone.

When their teeth break on the dark stone they say to themselves: We're the boys of the bulldog breed. This is the price of our freedom. We can take it, you can't have jam on everything, there is a price to our enlightenment. After all it's the twentieth century.
0 they don't know it's the Zone.
They're as mercifully conditioned as a limbo child.
Yes, some of them no doubt do - yes but there's a lot they can praise and anyway they know it's necessary to the defence of the realm - it's obvious you can't have National Parks everywhere - you must have the works somewhere. We can't all indulge our fine feelings -and think of other nations - they have Zones - there are a lot of Zones up and down Europe you must have Zones you know. I don't say they are - but I only know this Zone and that's the bugger I'm going to talk about.

Oswald Spengler, whatever one thinks of his reduction of the 20th century, having seen the pyre on which the culture of millennia had been almost consumed, nevertheless began to seek for hope among the ashes. In a similar fashion David Jones saw, among the detritus of the Zone, the glimmerings of revival and restoration. His work is almost nowhere more bleak than in **Balaam's Ass**, but as he saw an answer in the glimpse of the Mass through a chink in the wall on the Western front, so he continued to offer glimpses, through the brief gold of older times, through his luminous paints and inscriptions, a hope for the future. In his last years he was less sanguine about the way the 20th century was headed, but he never lost touch with the riches of the past, and all they had to offer. Even in the Zone he found signs of hope. The end of the passage I read to you just now will be familiar from the extract printed at the beginning of **The Sleeping Lord** as 'A, a, a, Domine Deus'. In the fuller version to be found at the end of **The Book of Balaam's Ass**, it shows David Jones coming to terms with the 20th century and seeing something there that could not be killed off - even by the deadly vacuity of the Zone:

"I said: - Ah, what shall I write. I enquired up and down. (He's tricked me before with his manifold lurking places.) I looked for his symbol at the door, I have looked for a long while at the textures and contours. I have run a finger over the trivial intersections and felt with the hand under and between. I have journeyed among the dead forms causation projects from pillar to pylon. I have tired the eyes of the mind regarding the colors and lights.

I have felt for his wounds in nozzles and containers. I have wondered for the automatic diversions that rattle for a dropped coin when she calls for another, when he suggests a soft water. I have tested the inane patterns, without prejudice, for it is easy to be blinded by pre-conceived opinions. It is easy to miss him at the turn of a civilization. I have been on my guard not to condemn the unfamiliar. I have refused the tests of theorists who come with manuals. I have opened my heart to sterility when she said: Ain't I nice with me functional flanks - the sockets of my joints go free of your handiworked frills: you can, given the equation, duplicate me any number of times. I'm very clean very good. All the merchants adore me. I'm bought and sold in the whole earth.... (p210)

The final lines are troubled, but I believe not without the hope that gave David Jones himself the strength to survive the Zone, and to transform it from within.

(2000)

Chapter 30:

DEFENDING OSSIAN

This is the text of a talk I gave at one of the Merlin Conferences, organised with R.J.Stewart in London from 1986 to 1988. I had long felt that the subject of this – James Macphearson, was unjustly neglected. Though seeing old fashioned to our modern ears, he had succeeded in distilling the essence of Celtic myth and poetry in an age when these had been almost forgotten. It is followed here by a mediation I wrote for the conference that took the listeners on a journey in to the lands of the ancient Celtic faery race, the Sidhe. Looking back on this, I am amazed at how close it comes to the more recent work I have done with these powerful enlightened beings.

"Star of the descending night! Fair is thy light in the west! Thou liftest thy unshorn head from thy cloud: thy steps are stately on thy hill. What dost thou behold in the plain? The stormy winds are laid. The murmur of the torrent comes from afar. Roaring waves climb the distant rock. The flies of evening are on their feeble wings, and the hum of their course is on the field. What dost thou behold, fair light? But thou dost smile and depart. The waves come with joy around thee, and bathe thy lovely hair. Farewell, thou silent beam! - Let the light of Ossian's soul arise.

And it does arise in its strength! I behold my departed friends. Their gathering is on Lora, as in the days that are past.' Fingal comes like a watery column of mist; his heroes are around. And see the bards of the song, grey haired Ullin; stately Ryno; Alpin with the tuneful voice, and the soft complaint of Minona! How are ye changed, my friends, since the days of Selma's feast! when we contended, like the gales of the spring, that, flying over the hill, by turns bend the feebly-whistling grass.

Minona then came forth in her beauty; with downcast look and tearful eye; her hair flew slowly on the blast that rushed unfrequent from the hill. The souls of the heroes were sad when she raised the tuneful voice for often had they seen the grave of Salgar, and the dark dwelling of white bosomed Colma. Colma left alone on the hill, with all her voice of music! Salgar promised to come: but the night descended round. Hear the voice of Colma, when she sat alone on the hill!" (The Songs of Selma)

These words were written by James Macphearson, (1736-1796) who, when he published his Poems of Ossian between the years 1760-63, created a storm of controversy that, if it is often forgotten in or own time, has still not completely died away. The books sold in a way that is difficult for us to believe today, when poetry has been relegated to the realm of polite hobby. McPhearson's book was a best seller - more than 80,000 copies being sold in the first year of publication. The works themselves were romantic, colourful, and visionary. They had titles like: *Cath-Loda, Fingall, The Death of Cuthullin, The Battle of Lora,* and they dealt with episodes from the lives of the great heroes of the Celtic world. In their time they were the favourite reading of no lesser person than Napoleon Bonaparte himself, who declared that they were one of the reasons why he wanted to conquer England! But, as various authorities on the literature of the Celts soon began to ask - were they genuine?

Undoubtedly, most present day authorities would state unequivocally that they are not. The truth of the matter is, that like his equally famous and equally notorious Welsh counterpart, Iolo Morganwg, Macphearson began as a translator and collector of genuine Gaelic poems, and ended as a forger. Where there were "gaps" her filled them in from his own imagination and from a liberal knowledge of Celtic myth and legend.

So, if we regard the works as, in a certain sense, "fictions" we are correct. But - and this is a very big but -we should also be aware of the contribution they made to Celtic art and literature. Not only did they - as did Iolo's work - help to focus the attention of the world upon Celtic literature - writers as famous and distant as Goethe defended them - with the result that we have far more Celtic literature today than we might have had - he also added a dimension to the old stories which they had always possessed, but which had been hitherto neglected - that of the visionary, the magical, and the wondrous.

Like his younger contemporaries, Fiona Macleod and 'AE', Macphearson saw that beyond the Celtic myths and legends lay spiritual and magical qualities that had something to say to all people. His works - which are admittedly often difficult or ill written, carry a charge of Celtic magical energy which is still of value.

James Macphearson was born at Ruthven, in the parish of Kingussie, Invernesshire, on October 27th 1736. His father was a poor farmer, and his mother a more well to do woman, and when James showed an aptitude for learning she saw to it that he was educated up to a standard which would enable him to study for a law-degree. He entered King's College Aberdeen in 1753, but soon after went on, probably as a student of divinity, to Edinburgh University. But, although he prepared for the Clergy, he almost certainly never took holy orders. He seems to have drifted through life after this, acting at various times as a private tutor - work he apparently hated - as a hack writer for Edinburgh booksellers, and as a teacher at village schools. But it was at this time that he composed over 4000 poems, some of his own devising, others "translations" of old Gaelic songs and ballads.

In 1759 he met John Home, a successful Scots author, who read some of McPhearson's works and saw fit to encourage him - even showing them to Carlisle who urged him to publish them. With some reluctance James agreed, and eventually published a volume in 1760 under the title Fragments of Ancient Poetry Collected in the Highlands. An eminent literary figure Dr Hugh Blair, wrote the forward, and referred to a longer, epic poem on the subject of the great hero Fionn or Fingall. This created so much interest that a subscription was taken up to allow Macphearson to make two long journeys around the Highlands to "collect" further information and sufficient versions of the story to compose his "epic".

He certainly visited a number of eminent authorities on ancient Gaelic literature, and from them, obtained a large amount of late Gaelic poetry, as well as some undoubtedly genuine bardic material. He returned to London and set about translating these into a form that would be acceptable to lovers of literature.

The result, published in 1761 in Edinburgh, with the financial support of Lord Bute, to whom the poems are dedicated, was Fingall, an epic poem in six books describing the invasion of Ireland by the Danish King, Swaran of Lochlin. In his own foreword he compared it with the epics of Homer and while this is certainly an exaggeration as to quality, it makes a point that the work is much closer to the Greek epics than to let us say the *Gododdin* which we know to be a genuine Celtic poem.

Fingall received mixed reviews, but sold well. Various critics cast doubt on its authenticity, but others were equally strong in their praise. It was followed, in 1763, by a further volume, *Temora,* in eight books. This told the story of *the* usurping prince Cairbar and involved a mixture of Druids, warriors and lovely women. It was received with an even stronger degree of disbelief. Even the eminent Dr Johnson was required to comment and gave as his opinion that Macphearson had borrowed names, phrases and stories from genuine sources, but had done no more than write these up in barely adequate verse. To his amanuenses James Boswell, who asked him if any "modern man" could have written the poems, he responded: "Yes, sir, many men, many women, and many children!"

Macphearson responded with a challenge that appears to have been of a physical nature, and Dr Johnson bought a stout stick and declared that he would answer violence with violence if the need arose. But Macphearson seem not to have been serious, and blood never actually flowed!

The controversy raged on, while Maphearson's sales mounted and more and more critics took sides on way or the other either in his defence or attack. Macphearson at first declined to produce the originals, which he claimed to have obtained on his journey to the highlands. Then, as the attacks on him mounted, he claimed that he had already offered to publish them if anyone would care to sustain the expense, and that he had deposited certain MS with his publisher, Beckett and De Hondt of the Strand. Apparently no one had offered to do so, and the papers were returned to their owner. After this, and Johnson's attack, Macphearson declined to publish any more of the works and withdraw from the affray, leaving everyone, if anything, more puzzled than before.

Macphearson kept his word, and no further ancient poems appeared in his lifetime. He went on to follow a not undistinguished career as a government official, being at one time the personal secretary to the Governor of Florida, and holding several posts in England. His other works include *A History of Great Britain from the Restoration to the Accession of the House of Hanover* and the more racely titled *Original Papers, Containing the Secret History of Great Britain, from the Restoration to the Accession of the House of Hanover*! He died, wealthy and respected, on his Highland estate in his native Invernesshire, in 1793, and was buried in Westminster Abbey - not far, indeed, from Poet's Corner.

After his death the controversy was opened again and his papers, on examination, declared to offer proof that his poems were based on liberally edited and amplified versions of some genuine ballads and folk-tales. The great epics were forgeries indeed; the stuff on which they were founded, proved to be genuine.

So much for Macphearson. What of the work itself? It is, by nature, uneven. There are whole passages that are unlikely to raise more than a yawn today. But these are offset by passages of considerable power, such as the following, from *The Death of Cuthullin* (not to be confused with the other, more well-known, Irish hero!)

"Is the wind on Fingal's shield? Or is the voice of past times in my hall? Sing on, sweet voice, for thou art pleasant, and carriest away my night with joy. Sing on, O Bragela, daughter of car-borne Sorglan! Is the white wave of the rock, and not Cuchullin's sails? Often do the mists deceive me for the ship of my love! When they rise round some ghost, spread their grey skirts on the wind. Why dost thou delay thy coming, son of the generous Semo? Four times has autumn returned with its winds, and raised the seas of Togorma, since thou hast been in the roar of battles, and Bragela distant far. Hills of the isle of mist! When will ye answer to his hounds? But ye are dark in your clouds, and sad Bragela calls in vain. Night comes rolling down: the face of ocean fails. The heath-cock's head is beneath his wing; the hind sleeps with the hart of the desert. They shall rise with the morning's

light, and feed on the mossy stream. But my tears return with the sun, my sighs come on with the night. When wilt thou come in thine arms, O chief of mossy Tura?"

This is Macphearson at his most splendid and declamatory. In *Temora* he goes to even greater heights, describing a strange ghost-ridden mist that arises from the lake of Lego:

"From the wood-skirted waters of Lego, ascend, at times, grey-bosomed mists, when the gates of the west are closed on the sun's eagle-eye. Wide, over Lara's stream, is poured the vapor dark and deep: the moon, like a dim shield, is swimming thro' its folds. With this, clothe the spirits of old their sudden gestures on the wind, when they stride, from blast to blast, along the dusky face of the night. Often, blended with the gale, to some warrior's grave, they roll the mist, a grey dwelling to his ghost, until the songs arise."

But what about the people he describes. Who were they really? Well, "Fingall" is really Fionn mac Cumhail, one of the most redoubtable heroes of Ireland and Scotland. He may well have existed in around the 3rd century AD, and his band of roving adventurers, the Fianna, have been compared with the war-band of the Dark Age Arthur - they were famous riders, famous fighters, and possessed huge appetites - both for food and for love. In Ireland, as well as Scotland - the Scotti having migrated there from Ireland - the names of Fionn and the Fianna are well known. Unlike most heroes of folklore, the traditional story- tellers are still adding to the legion of tall tales concerning "Finn Macool", as he is popularly known. We can read how the giant Fionn built the Giant's Causeway off the coast of county Antrim because he got tired of getting wet feet every time he crossed the water to steal cattle. We can hear how her married a faery woman, who turned into a deer later on and went back into the Hollow Hills, and we can read of his accidental eating of the flesh of the Salmon of Wisdom, which gave him the same kind of universal knowledge and understanding as the other great poet, Taliesin, had in Britain.

Oisín, of whom Macphearson wrote so much, was actually Fionn's son, and a genuine poet whose songs were so magical that he was believed - like Orpheus - to be able to charm birds and animals. Indeed, Fionn himself was no mean poet, as the following indicates:

The Song of May

May: fair-aspected
perfect season:
blackbirds sing
where the sun glows.

The hardy cuckoo calls
a welcome to noble Summer:
ends the bitter storms
that strip the trees of the wood.

Summer cuts the streams;
swift horses seek water;
the heather grows tall;
fair foliage flourishes.

The hawthorn sprouts;
smooth flows the ocean -
Summer causing it to sleep;
blossom covers the world...

The true man sings
gladly in the bright day,
sings loudly of May -
fair-aspected season. (My trans.)

This shows both the similarities and the differences between McPhearson's works and his genuine sources. The former are more stilted and artificial, the latter have a lyrical quality we can still appreciate hundreds of years later. Both have a magical quality about them that comes from acknowledging the power of nature and the Otherworld.

One of the most fascinating things about the Fionn stories is the way they were preserved. The story is told that when St. Patrick came to Ireland, he met one of the old heroes of the Fianna, who had come riding out of a strange mist one day, and, in helping a farmer move a huge stone that was blocking his plough, fell from his horse and touched the earth - at once turning into an old, grey haired man. Intrigued by this story, Patrick is said to have interviewed the old warrior, who turned out to be Caoilte mac Ronan, one of Fionn's closest companions, and from him learned all the stories of the Fianna, which the saint ordered to be copied out and bound into a great book, thus preserving the stories into historical times. He is said to have done this because he saw, in the bravery and free-spiritedness of the old heroes genuinely Christian values. Whether the truth was not that he actually liked to hear a good old story we cannot say, whatever the reason wee must be grateful - for the total surviving literature of the Fionn stories would easily fill three large volumes - before one got onto the folk-lore of the old heroes!

I hope you might be persuaded to seek out a copy of the *Poems of Ossian* for yourself - they can still be found in second-hand bookshops, or from libraries, and are well worth a read. The passage I want to leave you with comes from the end of *Temora*. Fingal has won his battles and sings of his gladness and the high regard he holds for his son Ossian.

"Sudden bursts the song from our bards, on Lena: the host struck their shields midst the sound. Gladness rose brightening on the king, like the beam of a cloudy day when it rises, on the green hill, before the winds. He struck the bossy shield of kings; at once they cease around people lean forward, from their spears, towards the voice of their land.

'Sons of Morven, spread the feast; send the night away on song. Ye have shone around me, and the dark storm is past. My people are the windy rocks, from which I spread my eagle-wings, when I rush forth to renown, and seize it on its field. Ossian, thou hast the spear of Fingal: it is now the staff of a boy with which he strews the thistle round, young wanderer of the field. No: it is the lance of the mighty, with which they stretched forth their hands to death. Look to thy fathers, my son; they are awful beams. With morning lead Ferad-artho forth to the echoing halls of Temora. Remind him of the kings of Erin; the stately forms of old. Let not the fallen be forgot, they were mighty in the field. Let Carril pour his song, that the kings may rejoice in their mist. To-morrow I spread my sails to Selma's shaded walls; where streamy Duthula winds through the seats of roes."

Chapter 31: A Meditation

THE HOSTING OF THE SIDHE

Close your eyes. We are going on a journey together. May you see all that you wish and experience all that you may.

You see before you the entrance to a cave. Though it is dark within you enter without fear and walk directly into its deepest recess. The ground beneath your feet is smoothed by the passage of countless other travellers, and as your eyes adjust to the dimness you become aware that the walls give off a faint luminescence...

Suddenly, the path you are following bends to the right, and as you turn a corner you come face to face with tall, golden gates, fine as spider's webs but stronger than the strongest steel. Beyond them swirls a golden mist, through which you glimpse curious drifting lights. You walk forward and, placing your hand upon the gates, utter a single word... What that word is only you will know, but you must remember it if you can, for it is your password to the lands beyond...

The gates swing open and you pass through, at once absorbed into the golden mist, which clings to your skin like dew and has a faint scent not unlike that of honey. You walk forward, unafraid, for there is a feeling of great peace and gentleness to this place between the worlds...

Then before you, appears a light, which gradually manifests itself as a great, ornately carved lantern, hanging from the roof of a vast cavern, which opens out around you as the mist begins to draw back. You catch a glimpse of a soaring roof, vaulted like that of a cathedral, but made by no human hands...Walls of glimmering silver and golden stone lead off on either hand...

Coming towards you, is a tall figure... His hair too is golden, a shimmers like a river. It tumbles about his shoulders as he walks... He is garbed in a mail shirt of the most delicate making, which fits him like a second skin. Beneath it you catch a flash of the distinctive saffron-coloured shirt of a warrior of the Fianna of Eriu...

The warrior greets you. He is Oscar, grandson of Fionn himself, and son of the great bard Oisín. He bids you welcome to the halls of the Sidhe, the people of the Hollow Hills, and invites you to come with him... Deeper you pass now into the realm of the Otherworld. From somewhere beyond sight comes the sound of singing, a high and majestic sound that fills you with unspoken longing... for what you can scarcely think...

The cavern seems to stretch forever, but gradually you become aware of a change. The roof, far above, changes gradually from stone to sky, blue and cloudless as the clearest summer's day ... and in the distance you become aware of a great tree ... but a tree such as you have never before imagined. Its trunk is so vast that it would take several minutes to walk around it; its branches reach upward into the sky itself, and are lost to view; its roots grasp the earth like the fingers of a huge hand ... The leaves of the tree are of green and gold, and seem ever to move as though in a gentle wind...

Gathered about the foot of the tree is a strange and wondrous company. Tall, handsome, and splendid, they are garbed in rainbow colours, beneath shining shirts of mail. They carry swords that seem like living things, leaf-shaped weapons of fiercest beauty. Indeed, you are aware that these are a folk truly terrible in their beauty, which is from the dawn of the world, before darkness ever showed upon the face of the earth ... For these are the people of the Sidhe, the Aes Dana, the Lordly Ones. There, among the rest, stands one who is taller than all the rest, whose golden hair streams out from beneath a cap of bronze with a crest of gold. At his side is a slender figure that seems no more than a youth.... until you see in his violet eyes the changing patterns of a thousand summers... In his hands he carries a harp, strung with gold, from which he plucks the notes of a song that you hear as the centre and source of the unseen singing, which seems to continue forever in that place ...

These are Fionn himself, and Oisín his son, and around them stand many others of the Fianna: Gol Mac Morna, Fiachna son of Conga, Caoilte mac Ronan and Conan Maol, Dairmuid o'Duibne, Culaig and Cuchulainge... There, too are the women of the Sidhe, fairer than the fairest flowers that grow beside the river in the land of Tir nan Og. Sabha, Fionn's wife, and Grainne, for love of whom men might easily die; Aine and Milucra, Muirne and Ele...

And Oscar son of Oisín leads you into their midst, and at that moment a horn-call rings out which sets all your blood dancing, and sends shivers through every part of your body. It is the call to the Hosting, when all the people of the Sidhe, the Fianna and their women, ride forth in joy upon the land, blessing and saining it with their passing... And, on this day, you are to ride with them...

Glorious, high-stepping steeds, caparisoned in shimmering cloths of gold and silver, are brought forth, and amid cries and jests the gorgeous company mounts. You, who have come upon this journey, mat each choose a man or woman of the Sidhe with whom you will ride... strong, golden hands reach down and lift you into the saddle behind a glimmering rider... then, with a cry, the whole great company sets forth, the music of their harness spilling forth in a river of bright sound, which mingles with the eternal singing of the Lordly Ones, and the gentle, plangent strings of Oisin's harp...

Bright as a hundred shooting stars the company rides forth across the green land of the Otherworld. On either hand you glimpse palaces of impossible beauty, orchards and meads and sparking streams where the salmon of wisdom leap and play amid the glittering spray...

Faster and faster rides the company, your breath is snatched back from your lips by the wind of their passage. You want to shout and sing for the very joy of the journey, feeling the power of the faery steed beneath you, smelling the perfume of the otherworld upon very side...

Slowly, the landscape changes. The colours that seemed almost too rich to your starved eyes, grow dimmer, the sound of singing grows faint upon the breeze. You realise that you have left the land of the Sidhe and are back in your own world. But because you ride with the host of the Sidhe, you see it with different eyes, are aware of the exhaustion and darkness that covers more and more of the land. Wherever the host rides there is a brief ray of light, like sun in a darkened room, but on every side are the marks of human endeavour: exhausted soil, diseased trees, animals and birds forced into smaller and smaller areas of land. The wild places grow less with every moment that passes, and the dirty sprawl of house and factory covers the earth like a scab...

As you ride you see that more and more of the people of the Sidhe are falling behind. Some turn back to their own place, their bright faces dimmed by what they see. Others linger for a time, seeding light once more upon the tired earth, nurturing and giving back strength to trees and rocks, rivers and streams, which have grown sick and polluted with the refuse of human living...

Great sorrow and perhaps some shame fill you and you long to do something... As if in answer the rider who carries you points to some detail in the flowing land, some place in need of re-awakening, of cleansing and purifying. This will be your place to care for, in dream or actuality, for as long as you will. For this act you received the thanks and the blessing of the Lordly Ones, and the rewards of the land itself, which will be renewed and grow strong again through your love and care.... And, too, another service will be accomplished, for you are made to understand that if the sick earth is not soon restored the People of the Sidhe will no longer wish to ride in the world, and, in time, they will come no more, and begin to fade... If you would prevent this from happening, you must do all in your power to make the sacred places holy again, to restore the life that he been selfishly sucked from the earth...

Now it is time to take your leave of the Faery Host, who scatter across the landscape like stars, scattering fire and light upon every side, then fading, fading, back into the Hollow Hills. Your own rider hands you down to the ground, and as your feet touch earthly soil, the scene grows dim and begins to fade... You hear the farewell of the rider echoing back down to you, and catch a final glimpse of him or her leaping back towards the sky like a fiery star... remember the place that has been given to your keeping ... Remember the word that will enable you to open the gates of the Hollow Hills again, and to enter there...

Our journey is ended. Return to the place from which we began, and become aware of your surroundings.

Section Six:

Stories Along the Way

Chapter 32:

THE TENTH MUSE

I started out wanting to write fiction and though most of my career as a published author has lead to in other directions, I have managed to complete several stories, some of which have been published and others not. The one that follows was written for an unusual collection called Tarot Tales, edited by my wife Caitlin and the renowned Tarot expert Rachel Pollack. (New York, Ace Books, 1989). The idea of this collection was to ask a number of writers – mostly of Science Fiction and Fantasy, to write a story by selecting a number of Tarot cards and then basing the story on these. It was a fascinating way to go about composing a story and the result is certainly one of the stranger tales I have written.

"It is said that there are nine circles or spheres which surround the world, which is naturally at the centre of all Creation. Each has a name and a meaning, each is ruled by a goddess or a god, and each follows its own implicit laws. It is also said that people of singular race live upon the surface of each sphere, walking and talking in the firmament above us. Some hold them to be inferior, others, superior, and there is much debate in the halls of wisdom regarding these and other matters. Yet none knows for certain, and if there be such folk, then they are most assuredly strange and given to pursuits such as we of Earth would find wholly repugnant, and quite foreign to our way of thinking. Suffice it, therefore, to say, that whilst we may speculate upon the existence of these supernal realms, they are as petty and lacking in meaning as are those idle folk who profess to tell the future in the stars, or prophesy events to come with cards."

Hygestus Prognosticator: **The Book of Blech.**

Middleman used to hear voices. Or rather, a voice. It wasn't something he talked about of course - on Draconia such things were frowned upon, if they were believed at all, which more often than not they weren't. Apart from which he could never really remember what the voice said to him - only that sometimes it was there, inside his head, speaking quietly about one thing or the other, perhaps answering a question.

That was something else Middleman did that he kept quiet about - he thought deep, questioning thoughts. In his line of work - he was a letter-carver working mostly on tombstones or monuments to the mighty dead - there was plenty of time to think, even though it was discouraged on Draconia.

On this occasion Middleman was thinking about the girl he loved. Her name was Bettina and Middleman loved her with all his heart and soul. Which was unfortunate, because there was no way that he could ever have got to do more than think about her, were it not for an extraordinary chain of events.

Bettina (who was, by the way, a talented musician, dancer and singer) came of a good Draconian family. Her parents, Trebuschino and Olinka were both extremely rich, as well as extremely miserly. They held onto their money as though they expected to wake up one morning and find that everything they possessed had vanished in the night through some mysterious agency - perhaps from one of the lower spheres, and they would no more have considered Middleman as a prospective son-in-law than they would have considered giving away all they possessed.

Their miserliness was out-matched by only two other people on the whole of Draconia - Duke Tollicos and his wife Udoxia, who were not only extremely wealthy, but also greedy, lustful, avaricious, gluttonous and sybaritic - in short all the worst aspects of Draconian nature.

The trouble began for Trebushino and Olinka (or more particularly for Middleman and Bettina) when Tollicos happened to catch sight of the girl in the street. Of course he immediately wanted her, and having sent spies to discover all they could about her and her family, he went to see Trebuschino and demanded to know how much he would take for his daughter's "services".

This put Trebuschino in a quandary. On the one hand he wanted Tollicos' money very much; on the other he was, in his own way, genuinely fond of his child. The idea of her lovely pink and white flesh being pawed over by Tollicos filled him with disgust. But he was also afraid of the Duke who could, without difficulty, ruin him. So he asked for time to consider what sum he might require and went to talk to Olinka. She, in turn, was horrified; though there was a gleam in her eye as she mentally calculated how much they might screw out of the Duke. They were still deliberating when they received a visit from the Duchess Udoxia. She was a large, well-built woman in her forties, who had a habit of stroking her belly as she talked in a manner that was somehow both suggestive and repulsive. She wasted no time in coming to the point, which was that she knew what Tollicos - "That rancid pig!" - was about, and demanded to know how much he had offered for "that twig of a child".

Trebuschino managed to stammer out that no price had as yet been agreed on. Whereat the Duchess laughed heartily and made the couple promise to ask for more than even Tollicos would pay.

"Why does she care?" demanded Trebuschino when the Duchess had swept out again, "Everyone knows they both carry on like this."

"Never mind why" said Olinka, "The question is what are we going to do?"

"We must get her away - far way - so that the Duke can never find her."

"But if we do that he will crush us. We might - lose everything."

"If we don't, then she will crush us. And what she leaves undone he will finish. We can't win."

A large tear welled in the eye of Olinka. It followed an unaccustomed course down one furrowed cheek. "Then - what are we going to do?"

"Middleman."

"What, that horrid letter-carver who's always hanging about trying to see our dear Bettina?"

"Just so. He thinks he wants to marry her. Well, let him have her. He may be a low-born jackanapes, but its better for him to have her than Tollicos. If we pay him a little..."

"A very little..."

"...Enough to get him away. At least he'll care for her."

So it was that an astonished Middleman received an urgent summons to the house of Trebuschino and Olinka, where he received an amazing offer - that he should run away with Bettina, marry her if he wished, and get paid - if not handsomely at least well - for doing so.

Middleman thought quickly, then asked, quite plainly, what the reason was for this sudden change in his fortunes. Trebuschino answered just as shortly:

"You've no need to know the reason - just see that you get far enough away so that no-one from around here is likely to catch up with you."

Middleman wondered briefly who "no-one" might be, but refrained from asking. He looked at Trebuschino and Olinka and said: "All right. I'll do it. Providing Bettina agrees."

Since there was small likelihood of their daughter not agreeing, Trebushino and Olinka allowed smiles to relax the tension in their faces and the bargain was struck. Middleman did not volunteer where he intended taking Bettina - indeed he could not since as yet he had no idea - nor did her parents demand that he tell them.

In the end, it was the girl herself who decided their route and so precipitated their great adventure.

Bettina, of whom we have heard much but know little, was more than merely a pretty face. She was, as remarked, a talented musician, besides which she also had a head on her shoulders. It so happened that she had, quite by chance, overheard the discussion of her fate between Tollicos and her father. She had never really doubted that Trebuschino would decline, but it came as a delicious surprise when they put their plan regarding Middleman to her. It was, of course, an ideal solution to her, and she lost no time in agreeing. She was married to Middleman, in a terribly quiet ceremony, by an ancient priest who could scarcely mumble the words past his toothless gums, and only a day later the couple left the city and headed out into the country.

They took with them enough money - painfully counted out by Trebuschino - to pay their way all round Draconia if need be, and to set up house wherever they chose. That "wherever" was finally decided by Bettina herself.

Less than a day on the road she told Middleman the reason for her parents sudden change of heart, and added her own thoughts on the matter, together with their solution.

"No matter how far we go, Tollicos is bound to catch up with us sooner or later. I don't care what father and mother think - he's going to see through the whole thing. And if by chance he doesn't they will certainly say you ran off with me. What else can they say? So, we must get right away. Not just anywhere in Draconia, but - onto another sphere."

"Another sphere!" Middleman trembled at the mere thought. People might not even have letter-cutters on the lower worlds. As for the higher - one just did not go there unless invited. Then he thought some more and realized they really did not have any choice. If they were going to escape Tollicos, or worse, Udoxia, they had to go somewhere no one would follow. Getting off one sphere onto another was not so difficult, probably because no one in their right mind ever wanted to do it. All one had to do - which Bettina and Middleman did - was go to any one of a dozen places where the worlds were more or less permanently aligned, and let oneself down from one to the other.

In this case they found a large iron bucket on a kind of pulley attachment, which had presumably been left there by another mad Draconian, and having checked that it was securely fastened to a great rock which arched out into space, Bettina and Middleman climbed into the bucket and began to lower themselves down.

Once over the edge they were in shadow. Above them they could see the massive, endless-seeming underside of the Draconian sphere; below was nothing but fat clouds, greyness and a darkly spinning vortex of light and shadow that seemed to indicate the next level.

Unfortunately, before they were more than half way, and still suspended between the worlds. The rope to which their conveyance was attached gave way and they began to plummet down at great speed.

Air rushed past them with a shriek; lights danced and swung on ever side. Middleman clutched

Bettina and had no time to think anything except: "This is it. The end." But in this he was mistaken.

The bucket landed softly, with a great plop, in what was evidently a huge pile of dung - from what animal they could not tell, but there was no mistaking it. They clambered out and staggered away as fast as they could.

They place in which they found themselves was not at all what they had been lead to expect. No one on Draconia did much in the way of speculation about the lower or higher spheres - they had no call to do so. Current theories did not exist therefore, but dated back to much earlier times. The most popular claimed that all the lower worlds were denser than the upper levels, and that consequently any life forms dwelling there must consequently be squat and ugly: trees or bushes stunted, flowers short of stem, animals thick legged, humans (if you could so call them) squat and probably hairy. The air, too, must be considered as polluted, and it was probably very hot since the sun, moon and stars fixed to the bottom of each sphere must be much closer to the surface than on Draconia, which only had the higher (therefore loftier) spheres above it.

Whatever expectations Middleman and Bettina may have had were shattered at once by the world in which they had landed. It was certainly greener than Draconia, and there were perhaps some different kinds of trees, but in almost every other respect things were the same. The same roads meandered between green hills; the same small houses dotted the landscape; the same birds (more or less) sang in the heavens, and what looked like an identical sun (beginning to set) shone down out of a familiar blue sky.

Indeed, so alike was the place to which they had come that for a moment Middleman wondered if he had not fallen asleep and dreamed the whole descent. Then, as they made their way over a field of long grass, Bettina pulled at his arm and pointed to where a figure could be seen advancing towards them.

It seemed woman-shaped, though dressed in a strange close- fitting costume that enclosed both limbs and trunk. On its head was a wide-brimmed hat that shaded its eyes and made it impossible to see the face beneath at all clearly. However she (for it most assuredly was a she) seemed in no way threatening, and the hand she extended was clearly in greeting.

"Hello, you must be the new comers. Glad to meet you. Name's Sportinoza. Welcome to Bidewell."

"Er...thank you. I'm Middleman and this is my - wife, Bettina."

"Hello to you both. Didn't know you were bringing your wife. Still you are both welcome of course. Good. Well, I expect you'd like to settle in. The Contest does begin tomorrow after all. First come, first light, eh?" Chattering on, she lead the way across the field to a gate beyond which was a large house with gabled roof and several chimneys from which smoke rose lazily into the evening air.

Middleman had no idea what anything the woman had said to them meant, but he was anxious not to betray the fact that they were from another sphere, since one could not tell if the natives were friendly or not, despite appearances. So he said nothing beyond an occasional "yes" and "no".

They were shown into a bright, airy room, in which, once alone, they discussed the situation in lowered voices.

It was evident that Sportinoza had mistaken them for another couple, and that she expected Middleman to take part in some kind of contest. Though whether of strength or skill they could not say. Whatever it was, Middleman decided he would just have to try and bluff his way through. "Somehow or other I have the strangest feeling this was meant to happen. Though I don't know how, or why."

They were woken next morning by a smiling Sportinoza, who offered to escort them to the Contest. With no idea what to expect the two Draconians followed her, chattering all the way about the weather and the excellent turnout of people. Long before they arrived at the site they could hear what sounded like a large crowd. They arrived at last at a natural bowl-shaped amphitheatre, around which were set a number of massive upright stones. Each was gaily painted a different colour and decorated with spirals and zigzags. Only one was plain, a huge black basalt pillar more than twice the height of a man, which looked oddly forbidding, perhaps because it was the only one with no-one standing before it. The rest had a collection of assorted people gathered about each of them. All were gaily dressed and none of them squat or hairy. They were talking, or rather shouting, at the tops of their voices. Straining to hear something that would offer him a clue to what was going on Middleman could pick out only a few phrases from the babble. He heard: "...far outclasses yours." "Such imagination!" "There's no doubt Mossdene can do better than anything Skilla can come up with." and a number of "Wills" and "Wonts", "Cans" and "Can'ts"" bandied about between the supporters.

As they hesitated at the edge of the crowd Middleman and Bettina saw that there were ten of the huge stones, and that in front of each one was a chair set up facing it. In each of these the contestants sat, silent and concentrated. The rest of the noisy crowd thronged on all sides, or went in and out of some brightly coloured tents set up close by. Judging by the merry sounds within, some kind of alcohol was being served there.

The only stone which did not have anyone sitting in its chair was the undecorated black pillar, and after a moment's hesitation Middleman lead Bettina over to it and looked up at its massive face.

It was, he now saw, carved all over with a faint tracery of intricate spirals and interconnected lines. Something about it made him shudder, and he was about to turn away to join one of the other groups, when he realised a hush had fallen and that everyone was staring at him.

Then Sportinoza thrust her way through the crowd. Her normally smiling countenance was downcast. You are quite certain this is what you want?" she asked. "I mean, it's not too late to withdraw."

Something in Middleman wanted very much to say that he had made a mistake and to ask what was going on; but the feeling that "all this was meant to happen" was still with him, so instead he smiled at Sportinoza and said simply: "No, this is where we will stay." He wasn't really sure why he said this; in fact, the moment the words were out he wished them unsaid, but by then it was already too late. Sportinoza turned to face the crowd with hands on hips and said loudly: "There's no need to stare. This gentleman has chosen to represent the tenth Muse as is his right"

Middleman felt Bettina's hand on is arm. "But there is no tenth muse" she whispered. "Not unless these - these people have invented one." She added, not without reason, "Middleman, I'm afraid."

"So am I," he admitted. "But I don't see what we can do."

"We have to try something," said Bettina. "Wait here!"

Before Middleman could say or do anything to prevent her, Bettina hurried after the retreating figure of Sportinoza. When she caught her up, Bettina called: "Wait! Can I speak to you a moment please?"

Sportinoza turned her friendly countenance to the younger woman." Of course, dear. Can't spare long, though. Contest begins in a few minutes."

"About that," Bettina said. "I know it sounds silly, but there's been a mistake."

"Mistake, dear? What's that?"

"It's just that, well - Middleman and I aren't from around here. We just happened to arrive at this moment, but we don't really know what's happening."

Sportinoza looked taken aback. "You mean you didn't come for the contest at all? ... But we were expecting you..! " Then, as light dawned, she became anxious. "Then your man didn't mean to choose the Black Stone at all? Dear me!"

"What's going to happen?" demanded Bettina. "Please tell me."

"Well… you really don't know? About the contest, I mean? Oh dear…! Well, every year people come from all over Astronica, to meet and hold this contest in the name of the Muses."

"Calliope, Urania, Terpsichore, Erato, Polyhymnia, Thalia, Melpomene, Euterpe, Clio," listed Bettina.

"Yes. And Her we don't name. The one your Middleman has chosen."

"What does he have to do in the contest?"

"Fancy not knowing that! You must come from a very distant part of Astronica. But it's very simple. Each of the contestants has to think a Perfect Thought. It goes into the pillar and is recorded there. Then the Muses judge and the winner gets a prize."

"The Muses themselves are judges?" exclaimed Bettina. You mean they actually appear?"

"Well, of course! How else could they do the judging? - Oh, sometimes they send a messenger. Once Apollo himself came instead of Erato, but that's never happened since." She gave Bettina a curious stare. "You really don't know anything about it, do you?"

"Thank you" Bettina said hurriedly, "You've really been a great help." Before Sportinoza could say anything more she hurried back to Middleman and told him what she had found out.

He brightened visibly. "That's wonderful. Now I know what to do it won't be half as difficult. Thinking is something I do rather well," he added, with a certain shy pride. "The only problem is, we don't know who this tenth muse is, or why no-one else seems to want to represent her."

"Look", Bettina interrupted, "It looks as though someone is going to make an announcement. Maybe you'll be able to work it out from what he says."

A large, expansive figure had emerged from one of the bright tents and there were calls for silence. The newcomer, a man with a red face and a very loud voice, began to announce "The Great contest for the favour of the Muses. Give your support now for Terabinth, representing Clio, muse of History; Mossdene, representing Polyhymnia muse of Heroic Songs; Johnstondi, representing Thalia, Muse of Comedy..."

The voice boomed on, but Middleman was scarcely listening. He was thinking furiously, "However did I get myself into this," and wondering how he was going to carry off what seemed to be required of him, and what would happen if he failed. Then he heard his own name.

"...and finally Middleman, representing the Nameless One - the Muse of Death."

The word sank into Middleman's brain like a hot knife into soft wood. "Death". And he had chosen her. Well, it was too late to do anything now. Too late to withdraw. Too late to wish himself back on Draconia, where thinking got you a bad reputation. He stared at the stone in front of him and wondered rather foolishly what to do. As silence fell he stole a surreptitious glance at the other contestants. All of them had their eyes tight shut. Hopefully Middleman closed his. Nothing happened. Then a cool voice sounded in his head, which sounded strangely familiar.

"You are the first mortal on any of the ten spheres to choose me in a thousand years. You have pleased me greatly, Middleman. Listen, and I will tell you what to do. But I cannot help you make the Perfect Thought. That you must do for yourself."

Middleman's eyes snapped open, but there was no sign of the speaker. Yet there was no doubt - the voice was one he had heard often on Draconia while he worked on memorials for the departed. He closed his eyes again and tried to form a thought. "What must I do?"

"Let your mind be blank. Focus on the stone. Then, when you are ready, offer your Perfect Thought to the stone. It will be recorded there for all to see and judgement will be made by my sisters. But hurry, you have only a short time left."

Middleman struggled to obey, without success; then suddenly his mind cleared, the ordering of his thoughts began to flow again as they had always done at home on Draconia. He set himself to think, not of Death as it was portrayed in all the worlds, as a terrible spectre; but rather as a friend. He thought of the voice he had heard so often, and with that there came a picture, a woman's face of great and disturbing beauty, strong and noble and fearful at once, but with a deep sorrow underlying it that touched Middleman at the greatest depth of his being.

Slowly he opened his eyes, and there, mirrored on the black stone, which seemed now to be touched with silver, was the face he had envisioned. He heard a gasp from beside him and turned to where Bettina stood, staring with sudden tears in her eyes at the stone. "She is so beautiful. How could we have not seen this before?"

"Easy enough in a world without a tenth muse," he murmured, feeling suddenly weak. He looked towards the other contenders and saw that on each of their stones stood out a brilliant, coruscating image, representing the Goddess of their choice. Each one was extraordinary, a masterpiece, he saw at a glance. By their side, his own image looked poor and drab. A sudden shimmering in the air betokened the arrival of the Goddesses - among them one who wore a grey cloak with the hood pulled up to hide her face. They stood together in the centre of the bowl, a brightly glimmering group whom Middleman found it difficult to see or to look directly. Presently, she of the cloak approached him directly; with her came a Goddess of surpassing beauty and delicacy whom Middleman somehow knew to be Melpomene, the muse of Tragedy.

Middleman bowed his head at their approach and when he lifted his head he found himself looking into a pair of level grey eyes that he knew saw everything. The rest of the face remained in shadow. The voice he remembered in his mind said, "You have made an image of me that will change the thoughts of all people towards death. Yes he is fearful, yet from my presence come many things that my sisters cannot give. Desire to overcome, to cajole or supplicate death has inspired many great works of men - much poetry, many dreams and works of art that give men hope. No one may see me directly, until their time comes. But you have made my true face theirs for all time. For that I and my sisters, thank you and declare you the winner of this contest."

On all sides there were cries of "Middleman! Middleman!" Bettina was hugging him. Sportinoza was beaming. Then the Goddesses were gone and only Middleman heard the voice in his mind that said: "I can offer you no reward for what you have done, nothing beyond the approbation of your fellow mortals. Yet I promise you that your life will be blessed and that you will always have time to think."

And thus it was that Middleman became famous. He and Bettina settled upon the second sphere of creation known as Astronica, where they lived a long and happy life and had a large family. Middleman taught letter-cutting and Bettina the arts of music and dance. And sometimes Middleman talked of his perfect thought and what it meant to him and others. And when it came time for him to die, it is told that the Goddess herself came, and that she pushed back the hood of her cloak and allowed him to see her at last, unveiled.

(1988)

Chapter 33:

TRAVELLING NEAR & FAR

Like my good friend David Spangler I often feel the need to write a Christmas story – though in fact time usually makes it impracticable to do so. So, I generally end up writing a poem instead – some of which you will find in this collection. But in 1996, on Midwinter's Day, this particular story leapt out and caught me. I had to write it down there and then and it came out pretty much exactly as printed here. When stories are that strong they have to get written, and I'm especially glad of the opportunity to share this one here for the first time. It may seem strange, but after all, why not… ?

It was Christmas again.

They could not remember how far they'd been travelling. Nor why. Only that when they saw the Star, as they always did at this time of year, they knew it was Christmas.

There were two of them, a male and a female, though such distinctions no longer had any meaning for them. They had seen life dawn, seen it grow old and almost die; only to be revived gain. Now the world seemed empty, and it remained a mystery. There seemed no pattern, no sense in it any longer.

They had been travelling so long they no longer remembered why, only that it had something to do with Christmas, and with the Star, which was the only regular event in their journey.

But this Christmas was different. There was an air of expectancy about it that was always there, but this time seemed somehow especially charged. They could not account for it but they recognised it just the same.

- What should we do? the male thought (they had long since given up communicating with words).

The female thought nothing for a long time. Then she thought back

- Perhaps we should go and look. There could be something there.

Her thought was like a question, hanging in the still air. After a time the male thought back to her his agreement.

The cave was full of light and air and a sound not unlike singing. There was a stirring also, as though something had got up and was moving about inside.

They looked at each other and the male wondered if they should go inside.

The female went to the entrance and looked in. After a moment she beckoned to her companion.

Together they went into the cave and stood looking down at the creature that lay quiet and helpless on the floor amid some wisps of fern and straw.

They were surprised. It was not a child. Not even a young animal; but something else. Something they had not seen before.

- Do you remember this? thought the female.

- No. It's not...

- The same.

- No.

The creature opened its eyes and looked up at them. In its grey skin its eyes were the colour of exploding suns and light streamed out of them.

It opened its mouth and uttered a cry.

All time stood still.

The heavens trembled.

The male and the female fell back before the sound and were filled with wonder.

'Now I remember,' said the woman.

'Yes', said the man.

'It all began like this that other time, before we began the journey.'

'Yes, but then it was another child.'

'As this is, but different.'

'Different, yet the same.'

They both looked down at the infant, and received the light of its lambent eyes.

'Shall we?' asked the man.

O, yes', said the woman.

She bent to lift the young one, and wrapped a corner of her garment about it.

They left the cave together.

The Star shone overhead.

The land looked new, as perhaps it was.

They still had far to go.

(1996)

Chapter 34:

TITUREL'S DREAM

This story was written in 1997 for a collection of stories featuring the Templars. I really enjoyed writing it and suggesting that the origin of the Templars might have been from somewhere much further away than medieval France. However, as is often the case with such things, the editor of the collection did not like it and it was never included. It is published here for the first time, and I would like to acknowledge the idea of the Collectors, which I borrowed from an unpublished story by David Spangler. Readers might also like to know that Titurel features in several Arthurian Grail texts, and that the story of his building of the Temple is recorded in Der Jungere Titurel by Albrecht von Scharfenburg, written in the 13th century.

[From the files of Ed'k'O, First Chronicler of the Tem'plar
In the 900th year after the Birth of Gol-Saad.]

The dreams began when Titurel had passed his fiftieth year.

Until that time he had spent much of his life in the service of Count Walter of Vogleweide, latterly as the seneschal of the great castle of Mewlesburg, his master's principle holding. His life had been neither more, nor less, eventful than that of any other knight in the period of the second half of the 11th century since the Passion of Christ; occasional wars, skirmishes with rival neighbours, raids by disaffected outlaws. Beyond this Titurel had lived his life in comparative obscurity; a quiet man who spoke softly when he spoke at all, which was as seldom as he needed to. Faded blue eyes watched the world about him with a faint look of wonder. He never married, having never found the courage, or the right woman.

Then, about the middle of his fifty-second year, the dreams began. At first, they were no more than flashes, brief glimpses of events that he could not wholly remember in the light of day. Then came a dream he could not forget. A disembodied head floated before him, its mouth opening and closing as if in speech, though Titurel could hear nothing of what it said. He woke amid tangled, sweat-soaked sheets, and that day felt only half aware the events that went on around him.

When he had dreamed the same dream for five nights he went to the priest, Father Bernard, and confessed his fear that he was being troubled by an evil demon.

Once he had established that there was no element of self-abuse involved, and that the head had not commanded the knight to perform any evil acts, the phlegmatic priest prescribed a herb to aid sleep and urged Titurel to prey fervently every night.

For a single night the dream ceased.

Next night it returned, and this time Titurel could hear and understand what the head was saying.

280

'We are coming. It is time to wake and prepare for us.'

This repeated over and over until Titurel woke with a cry and found himself still in his bed.

He arose and paced about his small chamber for a time, praying aloud. Then he got back into the bed and drew the covers over him. As soon as he slept the disembodied head returned. It spoke the same message, over and over: 'We are coming. It is time to awake and prepare for us.'

This time, somehow, Titurel forced himself to look at the head directly. To his surprise he found that it was less terrible than he had thought. A broad high brow rose above a finely shaped face, in which were set eyes of cobalt blue. The mouth was thin but not unpleasant, and the voice, now that he listened to it rather than to what it was saying, was low and resonant. The head even, now that he looked at it, was not disembodied at all. He could perceive shoulders below the neck, which had merely been clad in some dark material. Finally, in his dream, Titurel plucked up the courage to speak.

'Who are you?' he demanded.

At once, to his fresh terror, the head responded.

'I am Kor-in-Tar, Second Preceptor of the Tem'plar. We are coming. It is time to awaken and prepare for us.'

At that Titurel woke in earnest. Starting up in his bed for a moment he could still believe the figure from his dreams stood before him. Then the illusion faded and he was looking at the banner draped on the wall of his chamber.

Sleep had left him entirely now and he rose and dressed with unaccustomed haste. Before cockcrow he had saddled and bridled his horse and rode out alone from the grey castle that had been his home for so many years.

The morning was fresh and clear, and without thinking Titurel turned his mount towards the open lands that lay to the south. He rode for an hour, letting the feel of the animal beneath him and passage of air against his face rid him of the worst of the dream's aftermath. At length he reigned in and dismounted, allowing his mount to graze while he stretched himself out on the greensward and gazed up into the blue circle of the heavens.

After a time, tired from lack of sleep, he drifted off, only to see before him again the head of the being who had called himself Kor-in-Tar. This time, the vision did not speak at once, but merely stared at Titurel with what seemed a measuring look. Then it said:

'Are you worthy of the prize?'

'What do you mean? What prize?' answered Titurel, too astonished to keep silent.

'The greatest prize of all. The salvation of your world.'

'I do not know what you mean,' said Titurel again, and tried to wake himself.

To his terror, he could not.

'What are you? What do you want with me? ' he cried, making the sign against evil.

For the first time the stranger seemed to hesitate.

'You must not be afraid', it said at last. 'Soon you will understand.' Then it repeated once again: 'We are coming. Soon we shall be here and you will know all that you need to know.'

Then, of its own accord it broke the dream. Titurel found himself lying on soft ground with his horse still cropping the grass nearby. He was stiff and chilled and saw from the height of the sun that several hours must have passed. Wondering and still fearful, he mounted his horse and turned back towards the castle. As he rode he found his gaze drawn to the bulk of the mountains which rose off to the East. One peak in particular, an oddly shaped mass known locally as Galensburg, seemed to stand out from the rest, seemed almost to beckon to him. Titurel shuddered and crossed himself repeatedly.

For the next few days the dreams ceased. Thankfully Titurel tried to put all thoughts of them behind him. He busied himself in the daily minutiae of running his master's castle, attending to the needs of the other knights who held fiefs from the Duke, and with matters as hum-drum as ordering a new cooking spit to replace the old cracked one in the great hall, and to dealing with complaints from the local blacksmith that he had been badly treated by one of the Duke's men.

Thus the days passed until a few weeks before the harvest was due. That night Titurel dreamed again, but this time the dream was different. He found himself in a place that seemed made of light. He could not tell whether he stood within a building or in the open air. The walls, if there were walls, must have been made of some strange reflective material that gave back the light so brilliantly that he could do no more than blink and shade his eyes. He stood upon a firm floor, but it too was bright and smoother than any surface he had ever walked upon.

Fear made him want to crouch down, to cover his head against that terrible light. Then in a moment, his fear left him, so suddenly that he was shaken by it.

Two figures emerged from the light and stood before him. Both were tall and dressed alike in robes which were as white as their surroundings, but which yet seemed somehow to absorb some of the brightness. One, Titurel recognised at once as the figure he had seen so often before in his dreaming. The other seemed older, though neither of them possessed the characteristics associated with age in his mind.

It was this figure that spoke now.

'You are Titurel.'

It was not really a question, but he felt compelled to answer, 'I am'.

'Do you know who we are?'

'You are things of my dreaming. Or else demons', answered Titurel.

'We are neither. You have forgotten us. It is essential that you remember.'

'I do not understand' said Titurel. 'What do you want with me?'

'Only what was always intended' said the one who had named himself Kor-in-Tar. 'This is Jar-in-Tel. In two more days we shall be with you. Tonight you will remember.'

With that Titurel awoke. Now more afraid than ever he tried to think of what he should do. He knew that he should go to the old priest and tell him everything, but something prevented him. Would not anyone that he told of his dreams believe him either mad or possessed? Thoughts of what this might bring upon him filled his mind and brought with them a determination that he would tell no one, that he would somehow survive the trial alone. With this came something like calm. Having made up his mind how to behave Titurel was free to consider all that had happened.

The beings with whom he had spoken in his dreams seemed to offer no immediate threat. The place in which he had found himself in the last vision had seemed - now he thought of it - oddly peaceful. The Devil, he knew, was cunning, but surely there would have been some smell of brimstone?

Titurel reviewed the last dream and wondered at its content. If he was to believe the words of Kor-in-Tar something momentous was about to take place. What, and how, he could not say, though it seemed to involve the coming of these brings into the earthly realm. If so, where could they be coming from? Were they somehow part of that place that he had heard mentioned by old women in the village, a place where beings made of light dwelled beneath the rounded hillsides of the land? The mere thought of this should have made Titurel shudder; yet somehow he no longer felt any fear from the dreams. Whatever was about to happen would happen anyway, and nothing he could do would prevent it.

That night he spent a long while in prayer before retiring to bed. For a while he lay awake, staring at the ceiling, thinking that he was too old for this kind of thing and wishing he had a good woman lying next to him to whom he could turn for words of comfort.

At last he slept, and the dream began almost at once.

This time, it was different. He found himself standing in a rock-strewn valley. It was a place he could never remember being in before. The sides of the place were sculpted into fantastic shapes resembling nothing so much as frozen water. Sparse soil covered the ground on which he stood. Reddish in tinge, and sprouting strange fern-like plants that were no more familiar to him than anything else in the dream. And yet, in some way, there were not unfamiliar at all. Something in him recognised this place, though he could give it neither a name nor a setting.

Then, turning from the strange rock walls, Titurel saw the building.

It was so white that it seemed to start out of the reddish cliffs in which it was set. Nor did it resemble any other building he had ever seen, in dream or in life. Low lying, pillared along the front like the cloisters in the abbey church of Worms he had visited long since, it seemed not so built of stone as to be almost organic. It glowed with such purity of light that he at once knew that this was akin to the place in which he had found himself two nights since.

Turning at once in that direction Titurel walked towards the building, which grew larger as he drew closer. At length he stood beneath the portico and looking ahead saw where two great doors opened into its interior. Again, light spilled forth as though from a thousand lamps or torches - but this light was steadier than any he had ever seen.

Knowing he must enter whatever occurred, Titurel walked forward and found himself standing in a vast hall, the proportions of which were such that he could scarcely encompass them. Briefly he thought that whoever had built this place must have had to tunnel far back into the hillsides, and that this must have required a vast army of people. But just as quickly he knew that the dimensions of the structure within were very different from its outer shell. How he knew this he could not have said, save that with every moment that passed the place seemed more familiar. Yet he also knew that he had never been to this place before. The sense of familiarity came from elsewhere.

With this realisation came another. Looking down at himself Titurel found that he was dressed in the same white robes as the beings with whom he had spoken previously. Nor was he surprised, upon looking up, to find both Kor-in-Tar and Jar-in-Tel standing again before him.

'Where is this place?' he asked.

'It does not exist upon your world at all' came the reply.

Somehow, this did not suppress Titurel.

'Then is this heaven?'

Jar-in-Tel smiled for the first time. 'Not as you would understand it, Tit-ur-el' he said, pronouncing Titurel's name oddly.

'Then you are not angels?'

'No. Neither are we demons. We have come to fulfil a promise, made long ago, before the birth of your world. We bring the great prize that has always been the rightful heritage of your species. You were sent before, seeded with others, to prepare for our coming. It seems,' he added with what might have been a trace of sadness, 'that you have not remembered us at all.'

Titurel bowed his head in shame, for suddenly he felt that to fail in anything these beings asked of him could only be a most terrible failure.

As though aware of this thought Kor-in-Tar said: 'Be at peace. There is still time to set right what

283

has only begun to fail.'

Titurel found these words so comforting that tears sprang to his eyes. 'What must I do?' he asked.

'Tomorrow you must go to the mountain which you know as 'Galensburg', said Jar-in-Tel. ' We shall come to you there and make a new beginning.'

With that the dream faded, and Titurel awoke in his bed, but calm this time, and with a new sense of purpose that he had never felt before.

He slept, dreamlessly, and as the first rays of the sun were warming the grey walls of the castle he rose, dressed and prepared himself for the journey to the mountain.

The way was long and gruelling, much of it uphill through the dark and impenetrable forest that clothed the lower slopes of the mountain range. But Titurel's heart was lighter than he could ever remember, and he made good speed, passing though the barrier of trees and emerging onto the upper slopes of the mountain.

It was, as such places are judged, of no great height, and though steep in places proved less of an obstacle than Titurel would have believed a day earlier. Despite his age he found himself moving easily up steep trackways, until at length he was forced to leave his mount behind and continue on foot. The evening light was only just beginning to fade when he arrived at the foot of the main outcrop, a sheer-sided bluff that rose another three hundred feet above him. The sight of this gave Titurel no cause for alarm. He knew that he was not meant to climb this yet, and instead he made camp in the shelter of some tall stones. Without fear of either man or animal he slept deeply and dreamlessly until woken by the sunlight falling slantwise across his face.

Throughout the day he remained in that place, watching the sun mount into the heavens and begin its descent. Often, he looked up at the sky as though in some way he expected his visitors to arrive from there. Why he did this he could not say, yet as time elapsed he was aware of a subtle change in himself, of a desire to understand things that had never even entered his mind before. He wondered about the beginnings of things, about the way the ages were shaped. He even turned his thoughts towards the stars and considered how they made their course through the heavens. And though only days since he would have deemed such thoughts blasphemy, now he felt only a stronger and stronger urge to look beyond the circle of his life into a vaster appreciation of the wondrous creation in which he found himself. And he thought of the beings of his dreams, who claimed to be neither angels nor demons, and who were somehow not of his world at all.

It was evening when they came, not with any sudden flash of light, strange noise or disturbing smell. One moment Titurel was alone, crouched close to the small fire he had made, and the next Kor-in-Tar and Jar-in-Tel were beside him. In the natural setting of the mountain they seemed somehow less human, their white robes seemed to gleam with supernatural light, and their long serious faces had an alien cast. Yet Titurel felt no fear as they approached, not even they each took one of his hands and he found himself lifted away from the mountainside.

How this might be he could not have told, but after a moment of dizziness which forced him to close his eyes, he opened them again and found himself in the midst of the bright place that he had visited twice now. Bu this time he was not dreaming - he pinched himself surreptitiously to be certain of it - and to his eyes there was a new dimension to the place. No longer did it seem foreign, or strange; rather it was somewhere that Titurel had always longed to be, and now that he was there it felt wholly right to him.

'Now you must see', said Jar-in-Tel, and as his companions released his hands Titurel turned and saw, without surprise, that several more of the white-robed beings had appeared. Together they looked towards one wall of the great hall, and there, as Titurel stared open-mouthed a picture began to form there.

Such a picture as he had never imagined, or such as had never entered even the deepest recesses of his mind. A wonderful image that he knew was indeed as real as himself - no picture at all, but a window onto another aspect of creation.

At first he could scarcely make sense of what he saw. A vast blackness peppered with flashes of white fire, and below, filling the lower part of the window, a great half circle, a blue and green ball covered with swirls of white that moved and shifted constantly. Then he felt as though something in his mind had been opened, and he knew, with absolute certainty, that he was looking down at his own world, and that the blackness surrounded it on every side, and that it was filled with other worlds, and that the white flashes in the midst of the dark, were stars.

Titurel had no words as yet for what he saw. He drank down the wonder of the revelation like a man who has been in the desert and arrives at a water hole. And, as he did so, he became aware that other white robed figures had appeared and joined them in contemplation of the infinite vista. Titurel felt profoundly connected to all of them, as though they were somehow related. To witness the glory of the revealed world with them was to share in something more than miraculous.

At length he turned to Kor-in-Tar.

'That is my world,' he said, half way between certainty and question.

Kor-in-Tar nodded. 'One of many - more than you or I could count.'

'Tell me', said Titurel, 'how it is possible for us to be so high that we can see so much?'

It was Jor-in-Tel who answered. 'We are even now in a great ship that sails between the stars. It moves faster than thought itself, yet so vast is the universe that it has taken us many years to travel here from our home.'

'Then, you are not of my world?'

'No, indeed. We are but one of many races who inhabit the deep regions of the universe.'

'Then why have you come here? And why have you chosen to reveal yourself to me?'

'That, good Tit-ur-el, is a long tale and will take much telling,' replied Jor-in-Tel gravely.

'I am ready to learn,' said Titurel.

'And there is much indeed that you must learn' answered Kor-in-Tar. 'But first, we must show you the Hall of Great Truth. Come'

It was with difficulty that Titurel turned away from the window through which he could see the world and the stars. He followed Kor-in-Tar out of the first great hall and into another space which seemed to him even greater, but which was lit with less brilliant light. Where the Hall of the Window (as Titurel thought of it) had been rectangular, the Hall of Great Truth was longer and narrower. At regular intervals along its great length were alcoves, some covered by curtains, others open to view. With Kor-in-Tar at his side he moved slowly along one side of the hall, pausing before some of the alcoves and looking within. At first he was hesitant, but gradually his desire to see more overcame his reluctance.

Each alcove contained an object, many of great and unearthly beauty, housed on simple stands or in carefully contrived boxes or racks. Titurel marvelled at them all with equal wonder, and yet, try as he might, he could not understand their purpose. Some resembled vessels, others weapons, while still others seemed designed for uses he could not begin to conceive of. Many were made of substances that he could not recognise, and some seemed almost alive, as though they hovered between animate and inanimate form.

Finally he came to a halt about half way along the vast room, before an object of such strangeness that he could not comprehend it. Looking along the rest of the alcoves, and across to those which lined the further side, he turned to Kor-in-Tar.

'What are these...things?' he asked.

'They are gathered from a thousand worlds. Brought here and preserved against time of great need. There are still many to find, many others to bring to the worlds where they belong.'

'But, what is their purpose?'

'They are many things.' replied Kor-in-Tar. 'They are luck, they are spirit, they are life itself. Every world posses such a one, something upon which to focus in time of need. Imagine that you were threatened by a terrible darkness, to what sign would you turn in search of comfort and strength?'

'Why to the Cross of Our Saviour.' answered Titurel.

'Then think of all these objects as 'crosses'. On each world from which they came they were revered as holy and sacred, something to be turned to at need.'

Titurel was silent for a moment. 'But surely' he said at last ' they should remain on the worlds where they belong. Is it not blasphemy to remove them.'

'It would be so only if we intended to keep them, or if we took them in time of need. But that is not the case. Indeed, we have often been the bringers of such objects, which we have seeded through the universe as we have seeded children such as you, Tit-ur-el.'

'I', Titurel stammered. 'What do you mean? Are you saying that I am of your race?'

'No' replied Kor-in-Tar. 'We have simply selected those among your race who are best suited to receive the message we bring. While you were still a child we implanted certain information within you. So deep that you were never aware of it until you began to dream of me. I was the one deputed to waken you and to prepare you for this moment. In spite of which' he added, 'many have begun to forget completely.'

'What is this message you speak of?' demanded Titurel.

'That a time of danger and change is coming to your world, and that yu must prepare for it.'

'That may well be so' answered Titurel slowly. 'But what is my role in this?'

'Why to become the guardian of your own world's greatest treasure.'

Bereft of speech, Titurel stared at his companion. Kor-in-Tar allowed one of his rare smiles. 'Come. All shall be explained. It is time for you to meet the Grand Master.'

Titurel followed Kor-in-Tar from the great hall and through a maze of softly illumined corridors to a smaller chamber. As they entered a figure turned to greet them. Tall, powerfully muscled, with wild reddish hair, the being who faced them was built like a warrior. Yet his expression was mild, and his voice, when he spoke, was soft.

'Welcome Tit-ur-el' he said, again pronouncing Titurel's name oddly. 'You have visited the Hall of Great Truth?'

'I have,' answered Titurel, 'And there is much that I would know concerning it.'

The Grand Master indicated that Titurel should be seated and took his own place opposite him. Then stretching forth his hands took Titurel's own in them. At once something like a pulse of warm light passed through the knight. He started back, but the Grand Master released his hands with a smile.

'Do not be afraid, my friend. No harm will come to you here. You are as much one of our children as if we had begotten you. '

'Then tell me what you want of me, and what brings you to my world.'

The Grand Master nodded. 'We are an ancient race', he began, 'who found our way to the stars long ago. We have been dedicated to the way of the spirit for even longer than that, and when we first set forth on your voyages between worlds, it was natural to us to wish to study the beliefs of other species. Over the centuries we discovered that every world where sentient life had evolved, possessed a sacred object, a talisman in which much of the soul of the race resided. For many ages we studies these objects for afar and in time came to understand their function. Then, some nine thousand years ago as you measure time, one of our number, Gol-Saad, whose name we revere, discovered that in every case these sacred objects were in danger from a being we know only as 'The Gatherer'. This being, seeking absolute power, was seeking out the sacred things and carrying them off. We believe it is the Gatherer's desire to possess all such objects, and that if this ever occurs it will spell the doom of many worlds, perhaps of the universe itself.

Thus Gol-Saad founded the First Order of the Tem'plar, whose task was to discover the sacred things and to take them to safety until they were needed. His studies had taught him that once such a special object had come into being it was often dormant for many hundreds of years, only coming to light in time of great need or of spiritual crisis. It was at such periods of dormancy that they were at greatest risk, for while active they were preserved against the Gatherer. Thus the Order began to seek out the sacred objects of every world we had ever visited, and many more besides. In our archives was preserved knowledge of every such artefact we had ever encountered. So we journeyed, at first under the leadership of Gol-Saad and with his passing many others, ever seeking to reach new worlds ahead of the Gatherer and to snatch away its sacred thing before it could be carried off by our adversary. Many thousands of your years have gone by, and many hundreds of sacred artefacts have we preserved; many more remain, awaiting our search. And, each time we have visited a new world; we have sought to discover when the object might be required again. Once we have placed it in the Hall of Great Truth we continue to monitor the world where it belongs, until such time as it is needed again. To do this we have 'seeded' a number of beings on each world with memories that can be activated when the time is near. You, Tit-ur-el, are one such being.

Wide-eyed as a child Titurel stared at the Grand Master. 'Then, the time is near for my world.' he said.

'Our researches show that a time of great spiritual upheaval is soon to dawn. For your world this is a time of great moment and great danger. Many factions will vie against each other for control of the souls of your fellow beings. The sacred artefact that belongs to your world will soon be needed. It is time for it to be returned. And, for this time, it will require a guardian. That guardian is you.'

Titurel drew in his breath. 'Surely one greater than I should carry out this task' he said.

'There is no other,' answered the Grand Master. 'This is the work for which you have been prepared. You and you alone may carry it out.'

For a long while Titurel said nothing, his mind a whirl of thoughts and emotions. But at length he bowed his head. 'What must I do?'

The Grand Master rose from his seat and crossed to the further side of the chamber, to a curtained recess. Drawing back the curtain, he took something from within and turning back to Titurel held up an object covered with a white veil. Light issued from it and seemed to pulse as if with the beating of a great heart.

'This is the sacred artefact of your world' the Grand Master said quietly. 'It came into being more than two thousand of your years since and it remained on your world for another five hundred years.

During that time it underwent many changes, including that of form. It has been many things to many people, and it carries within it the power to bring about great land lasting good within your world. Its last change occurred a little while before we took it into our keeping. It seems that one of your gods used it as a symbol of his return from death. It is a most remarkable object.'

Titurel stared at the gleaming thing beneath its veil. He could scarcely bring himself to speak aloud the thought that had entered his mind.

'It is the Grail', he said at last, trembling. 'The Cup used by Our Lord to celebrate the Last Supper. It has been lost for generations.'

'Not lost, only in safe keeping' said the Grand Master. 'Now it has come home, and you must prepare a place suitable for its housing, for soon its influence will be required, and it must be again within reach.'

'What must I do?' demanded Titurel.

'You must build an edifice to contain it. At the top of the mountain, where you first met Kor-in-Tar. We will help you as much as we can. Others will come.'

Titurel rose to his feet and bowed his head before the Grand Master and that which he held.

'I am ready,' he said.'

In the weeks that followed miracles occurred in the mountains to the North of Mewlesburg. A great light was seen in the sky above the mountain called Galensburg. Its oddly shaped peak was sheared off as if by a giant sword, and building work began which was swiftly brought to a conclusion, though there seemed no sign of human masons.

It was widely believed that angels carried out the work; for how else could a building of such beauty and majesty as that which soon rose there have been accomplished. Soon word began to spread aboard of a wondrous castle, built to house a relic of such holiness that none dared speak its name aloud. And, too, there came word of a new Order who dwelt there, a band of knights dedicated to preserving the sacred thing, lead by a man of great sanctity named Titurel. Angels had visited him in vision and had called him to this great task, had then helped him to build the great foundation on the mountain.

That mountain soon acquired a new name, its old one fast forgotten. Muntsalvache, the Mountain of Salvation, and throughout the world word of it reached out, bringing men and women who felt the call of the sacred vessel housed there. The Order of the Knight's Templar, so called because they were the guardians of the 'Temple' of the holy thing, became a focus for goodness and truth, warrior monks dedicated to the service of God. For many many years, during which the world saw much of the spiritual upheaval that had been prophesied, Titurel was their leader, taking the title of 'Grand Master'. After him came others, all of them remembered in the archives of his world as men of courage and goodness.

And so the Grail once more played its part in the history of that world, and many wonders were told of it. Many sought it, though few found their way to the doors of the chapel on the mountain where it stood. In time the Order established by Titurel foundered in jealously and hatred, and with their passing the Grail once again vanished from sight. But for many ages after the name of Titurel was remembered, and his dream remained long after the walls of the first Templar castle fell into ruin.

(1997)

Chapter 35:

FOLK STORY

I have always loved folk tales and more than once have tried my hand at writing some new ones. The folk tale is a slippery form and does not always lend itself to literary intent, but sometimes the results can be interesting. I wrote this one in 1989 after a particularly vivid dream and it seems to me to be saying something that more people might appreciate. I revised it slightly in 2006 and it is this version that appears here.

There was once a young farmer who lived alone and tilled his fields and watched over his few sheep and nurtured the land as best he might. But one day there came a blight upon his crops, and a murrain upon his sheep, and within a week of this he lost everything.

He sat in the doorway of his poor house and looked at the desolate scene, and he wept for the waste of the green corn and the young beasts. Then he heard a voice that said to him:

"Farmer, do not weep, for though there seems no life here, yet there is still life beneath the surface, and in time your land will be fertile again".

He looked up and saw standing before him a young maiden with brown hair and eyes that laughed, and she said: "Come. Smile again. I will stay with you".

And thus it was. The farmer and the brown girl lived together in his house, and she swept the floor and made bread and sang as she did so. And soon the farmer was so deeply in love with her that he could not even speak of it to anyone - least of all to the brown girl herself.

In time the land was reawakened and the farmer sold corn and bought new sheep with the money; and, to add to his joy, the brown girl gave him a child, a son with bright laughing eyes and gentle ways.

Then one day, in the dead of winter, the farmer woke one morning to find that his love had vanished. All through the day he sought her, calling and calling, but she came no more.

So the Farmer took his young son and set out to look for her through the world. For long years he searched without finding what he sought; the boy grew to manhood and went away to make his fortune in the world. And, because he was a merry man, he made a good life and was much loved and respected by everyone. And sometimes he would send word to his father, and join him for a while as he carried on his unceasing quest.

Wit time the farmer grew thin and wasted, and the ice which had formed around his heart the day the brown girl left, grew thicker and began to squeeze until he could scarcely breathe.

Then one day he came to the door of a cottage and begged some food from those within, and the master of the house took pity on him and let him sleep in the barn. And as morning broke, the farmer found himself lying in the doorway, looking out at the sunrise. And a shadow fell across him and a well-known, dear voice said:

"Do not be so sad farmer. There is still life in the land, even though it seems dead".

Filled with joy the farmer sprang up and took the hand that was held out to him - a strong brown hand that led him away across the hills to a far distant land where he found peace at last and understood all that had happened to him.

Written 1989
Revised 2006

Chapter 36

MERLIN REMEMBERED

At the turn of the millennium my good friend David Spangler and I dreamed up the idea of writing a book about Merlin, a figure who had fascinated us both for many years. It was to be called **Merlin Remembered** and would consist of a number of tales written from the view point of those who had known the great man at various times throughout his long and varied life. In the end, other tasks lead us way from this idea. I went on to write a full-length study in **Merlin: Shaman, Prophet, Wizard** (Mitchell Beazley, 2004). But I had already written three of the stories, 'The Princess of Dyfed', which imagines the reflections of Merlin's mother in her old age; 'Vortigern's Architect' which presented the famous tale of the building of Vortigern's tower from the viewpoint of its chief builder; and a brief squib called 'The Esotericist' which poked gentle fun at those claiming to incarnate and channel Merlin's message for our own time. I am glad to include these three little tales here, and hope that one day David and I may still get to write the whole book.

Part 1: The Princess of Dyfed

Sometimes, when I am alone, I still hear his voice speaking to me from the darkest part of the room.

Not that it is he, of course. Not yet, at least. But it reminds me of that other time, when I was still young. It murmurs, kind and gentle things, words of comfort that give me hope - not just for myself but for my son also.

My son. Merlin. How strange the word sounds, even now. Though it is more than thirty years since I gave birth to him, fed him milk from my breast, and though I have rarely seen him in all that time, it seems that he has seldom been far away.

So many things I have heard about him. Things that seem fearful to me, as well as wondrous. Things that make his raising of the two dragons, his prophecy of the death of that evil tyrant Vortigern, seem as nothing. Golden wonders that remind me of his father.

I have never told the full story of those enchanted nights, when the one whose name I still may not utter came to me. I was every inch the princess then: strictly raised, shy, ignorant of the secret ways of men and women. It was my romantic heart he touched first, and only later my body.

But I remember the beauty of him, how his skin seemed to radiate light, how he spoke to me of wonders beyond my understanding; of another world, rich in unearthly beauty. Many times he sang to me, in a voice more lovely than anything I have ever heard. The songs he sang were of older, simpler times, when the world was other than it is now, when strange creatures roamed the earth and beauty clung to the trees like stardust. It is strange that now, when I am older, many of those old tales and

291

songs come back to me, and seem somehow more familiar than when I first heard them, as though some part of me remembered them from another time.

But O how clearly I remember that first night, when I sat by the window in my father's house, looking out over the moonlit meadows that fell away from the tower and met the shadows of the wood. (That ancient wood that has so many names, and where so many of my son's deeds have been brought to birth).

I remember how, as I watched, I became aware of a light that shone out from amid the high old trees. A golden light, as if a star had fallen there and veiled its glory (I cannot help but see starlight as warm and golden rather than while and cold as many would have it).

As I looked the light grew briefly brighter, then vanished completely, though I strained me eyes to see it. Then I heard a voice behind me, a voice like no other, which spoke my name. And when I turned about he stood there, shining and unearthly, smiling at me, his voice a spell that took away my fear and left in its place peace and fulfilment.

It is hard now to remember what we spoke of. The impression I have is of one long dialogue that continued through the hours of darkness, and again the next night, and the next, until it seemed that it had gone on forever and would never cease. (Perhaps it never did). Nor can I recall at what moment, within that time, we became one flesh. Yet I know that our loving was like no other, and that to say this is all I can say.

Every day I longed for the night to come, grew thin and distracted. But when my father spoke his concern I made no answer, retreating into silence that only added to his worry.

Then one night my golden one came no more. Nor the next night. Nor the next. The pain of it was such that I thought I must die. Then, on the fifth night, he came again, solacing me with his voice and gentle touch. Until, just before dawn, he told me that he must return to the place from whence he had come, and that I would see him no more. "But", he told me, "we shall meet again, be assured of that", and through the spell of his voice, and the strength of his presence, I was able to accept the fact. Not easily, but with none of the pain I might have expected to feel. Then he was gone, and the night seemed emptier than ever before.

As the weeks passed, my life began to return to normal, and there were times when everything that had happened seemed like a dream. Then things began to take place within my body, which though at first I did not understand soon became open evidence of my condition.

Then it was that I learned for the first time of the cruelty of men. First my father, then his advisors, then the women and even the children of the court, vilified me. Physically I was not harmed, and though some would have had me soundly beaten, my father spared me this at least. But the humiliation I suffered was far worse than this. Small things, perhaps, but I have never forgotten them, nor will I, though with time the pain has become but a distant memory.

No longer the pampered child of the royal line I was hidden away in the darkest corner of the tower and left to dwell upon what was called my 'shame' - though I could see nothing shameful in the love I had known with my golden stranger.

So in time I gave birth, and from the moment I looked into my son's eyes I knew that he was different. For there I saw reflected all the wonder I had learned from the songs of my lover - and something more. For an ancient wisdom shone out of my son's eyes that was not of this world at all, but of that other place I knew only in my most secret heart.

And, as I looked at him, I knew that he could have no other name but Merlin, and that this was his name, as perhaps it had always been, and surely always will be.

But now, when I think of my son, it is not of Merlin the Wise I think, but the child I nursed at my breast, who lived with me for the first twelve years of his life.

He was always a strange one, speaking little, but always looking, watching, listening. Sometimes I thought he listened to things no one else could hear, but only once did I find the courage to ask him what he saw. And when he turned his strange grey eyes upon me and said: "Only the spirits of nature, mother", I grew afraid and asked no more.

There were other things, too. The way that he seemed always to know what I was thinking or feeling, so that he could would respond in such a way that I was comforted or soothed, or informed however I needed to be. So that our years together were kindly, even though I was no longer the Princess, but a woman whose child had no father.

Once, when he was no more than ten years old, we went together to the market at Carmarthen - one of the few times we went out into the world, for I remained fearful of recognition and of the old whispers beginning again - and here he showed me of what he was capable.

He spoke up in defence of a girl accused of adultery (a raw enough subject for me) proving the magistrate's own wife guilty, and offering evidence in the shape of a leaf caught in her hair when she had lain with another man, and how the girl had been falsely accused because she had witness their tryst.

Another time, not long before Vortigern's man came for us, he laughed to see where a ragged beggar sat at the roadside - and when I reproved him sharply for his unkindness, told me that the man sat where a hoard of riches were buried.

From these and many other signs I knew that Merlin had inherited his father's knowledge, which was truly otherworldly, and that my son was, indeed, only half human. But only once did he reveal to me something of his true nature and purpose. And that was but two days before the soldiers came to take us both to Vortigern.

I remember how he stood before me, looking at me with those extraordinary eyes, and how he said: " Mother, there are men coming to take us away from here. But do not be afraid, for I promise you than none shall harm us."   In that moment he looked so much older than his twelve years that I almost drew away from him. Then he spoke some words that I have never forgotten:

"The time of my ministry is almost come. I am to be the guardian of this land for a time, and a guide to its greatest king. You will hear many things told of me that may fill you with fear. But never forget that I love you, and that all I do is for the good of the world and the people in it. "

Now that I am old, hiding away from prying eyes in this house among the hills of Dyfed, I think of those words often. I have heard much of my son's achievements. Of his guardianship of Arthur, the once and future king; of the miracle of the Sword in the Stone; of the coming of the glory that man call the Grail.

This and much else I have heard. And as I think on these things, I believe the time is near when I shall understand them better. Perhaps I shall meet again with my golden lover. For I have heard it said - and I believe it to be true - that those who have been touched by a lord of Faery return to them in the Hollow Hills, and there find youth again. I pray this may be so, and that there I shall learn more of my son's work, in this world or any other.

(2000)

Part 2: VORTIGERN'S ARCHITECT

Another tale from the uncompleted collection **Remembering Merlin**, written in 2000. I have lost count of the number of times I have retold this story, either at story telling events or as parts of longer books. But it continues to be a favorite and it is one of the best ways of introducing the character of Merlin. The original version dates from the 9th century, in a book called the Historia Brittonum, attributed to a chronicler named Nennius. Here I gave it a twist by telling it from the viewpoint of the man given the job of building the tower that will not stand.

My credentials are the best you will find in the whole of Britain. I have constructed buildings for Princes and Warlords right across the land. Nothing like what I am about to describe ever happened to me before, I can assure you!

I suppose I should have known things would go wrong right from the start. Vortigern was a tyrant and I don't care who hears me say so. "Build me an impregnable tower," he said - as though such a thing was easy. "Make it somewhere high and make sure it has a view over at least thirty leagues". Let me tell you, there are few builders who would undertake such a commission - but I had my reputation to think of, so I said yes. (Not that one says no to Vortigern anyway, not if he values his life.)

Of course, we all knew what it was he was afraid of - or rather who - Ambrosius and Uther, the two sons of King Constantine who some said Vortigern had ordered to be killed just before he declared himself High King. He musty have been careless to let the two princes slip away to Amorica, because now everyone was talking about how they were raising an army across the channel and that pretty soon they'd be back - and looking for Vortigern. Hence the tower.

Anyway, I set to work. The site was easy enough. Vortigern wanted it to be remote, high up and inaccessible (no thought for how we were supposed to get timber and stones all the way up there!) We settled on a high spur of rock in the shadow of Y Wydffa. At that time it had no name; now people have started to call it Dinas Emrys - after *him!*

I started to draw up plans. When I showed them to Vortigern he was well pleased. "Waste no time," he said, "I want it finished by the end of the summer." Of course I knew that was virtually impossible (it was already well into Spring), just as I knew that the chances of being paid were slight, but I said yes anyway (what else could I do?) and set to work organizing things. First I had to get enough men to do the work - and that turned out to be another problem, because Vortigern insisted on drafting a hundred men from his war-band to do the job.

Let me tell you now, soldiers do not make good workers. First they think they are too noble and high up to do such menial tasks; then they spend half the time fighting amongst themselves. Even after Vortigern had hung a couple of troublemakers and threatened the rest with a beating, they were still surly and dangerous. I had to insist they leave their weapons behind - I didn't want to end up with a sword in my guts some dark night!

So, we started digging. The foundations needed to be deep enough to support the very thick walls that Vortigern had demanded. While this was going on I had another let of men felling and trimming tress and a third lot away to the nearest quarry - which was fortunately close buy - to start bringing back the huge blocks of dressed stones I was intending to use for the tower.

The nearest wood was several leagues away, so the trees had to be dragged all the way to the foot of the hill, then carried up it. The ground was soft to the foot and we lost a couple of men when they

294

slipped and allowed a tree to roll over them. But at last we get the scaffolding up and then began the exhausting work of dragging the stones up there as well.

It took two weeks to get enough of them up there to lay the foundations and set the first two courses of the walls. That brought the tower only waist high to a tall man and we still had a long way to go.

It was mid way through April by then and preparations were already afoot for the Beltain celebrations. The men were grumbling all the time - more than usual that is - because they wanted time off to visit their families ands prepare for the feasting. But I knew we had little chance of getting the work done in time and I pushed them as hard as I could - invoking Vortigern's name every time they were inclined to give up. Some slipped away anyway, and I had to make do with a reduced work force. But still the tower proceeded. We got it up to three courses before disaster struck.

One night it rained heavily, which would not normally have been a problem. But sometime in the middle of the night there came noise which sounded like ea giant turning over in his sleep and then all hell broke out, with men and horses screaming and yelling, and several more huge crashes and the sound of trees being broken apart.

At first I though we were being attacked, but the noises were the wrong sort for that, and I realized with a sick feeling that something had gone wrong with the tower. By the time some sort of order had been restored and we had enough torches to see what had happened it was already getting light. In a mixture of smoke and pre-dawn blur I surveyed the mess.

And what a mess it was. The whole wall had simply fallen down as though it had been pushed over. Great cracks spread though the earth and down the hillside and most of the blocks of stone were back at the bottom of the hill. At least two men had been crushed, and several others suffered minor injuries. The scaffolding was wrecked and new trees would need cutting.

None of it made sense. As soon as it was properly light I went to walk the ground and examine the whole sorry mess. On the face of it, nothing added up to what had happened. I know my job well enough to have made sure the foundations were well sunk and that the hilltop was stable enough to take the weight. The stones had been well cut and dressed and I had overseen the construction myself - every inch of the way. I knew about Vortigern's famous bad temper and hadn't wanted to experience it for myself. Now I was going to have to.

To my surprise he was less angry that I had expected. Maybe his mind was on the latest news of the Princes - that they were about to set sail for Britain. Instead of ordering me to be punished he simply stared at me with those dead, flat eyes of his and told me to get on with it. He also drafted another fifty men to help.

Even with them it took another ten days to restore the damage done by whatever freak of nature had cause the walls to tumble. This time I made sure that everything was doubly reinforced with wooden props. Nothing short of an earthquake would shift the walls this time - I would have staked my reputation on it.

It was just as well I didn't, because two nights after that the whole thing started again. The same groaning of the earth, the same crashes and cries, and in the morning the same result - the walls were down, the blocks of stone carving huge scars down the face of the hill.

I have to admit that I was beside myself with a mixture of fear and anger. Fear for what Vortigern would do to me, anger that the impossible had happened despite everything I could do.

Vortigern must have really wanted that tower to be built. Because, where most men would have given up and looked for another site, he came back with a command that I should continue with the work. Along with the man who brought this message came someone else - and I knew it was going to mean more trouble as soon as I saw him.

Vortigern's chief druid.

His name was Maugant and he had an evil reputation as a cruel and contentious man. Of course he insisted on inspecting the ruins of my work, pacing round the broken stones, muttering and shaking his staff over the cracks in the earth. Eventually he called me to him. " There are evil spirits in this place" he said. "A sacrifice will be required. You are commanded by my lord Vortigern to do no more work until he gives you permission." An unpleasant smile slid over his face. " He also bids me tell you that he will be here by sunrise tomorrow to inspect the site personally."

That was all I needed to know. To have the druid poking and prying into my business was bad enough; the presence of Vortigern himself seemed like a potential death-warrant. Then there was this matter of the 'sacrifice'. Such things always make me uncomfortable, though I realized the gods require it from time to time. Then again, when I considered the events of the last week I began to think that Maugant might be right. There was no good reason for the stones of the tower to fall, and no good reason meant there had to be a bad one.

So work stopped. We waited for Vortigern to arrive - which he did, next day; then we waited again while he and Maugant consulted, walked about and prodded the earth on the hilltop, then waited some more while Maugant went through a series of divinations to discover what was wrong. Finally, word filtered down that Maugant had declared that only the blood of a fatherless boy would seal the stones. My instructions were to prepare the foundations again, and then to wait until such a child could be found. Vortigern sent out a number of search parties through the surrounding county - Maugant having assured him that the required sacrifice would be found nearby.

The next few days I was busy enough, marshalling my teams of reluctant workers to prepare for the task of restoring their broken down walls and then, when all was ready, to continuing with the rest of the job.

Then I heard that one of Vortigern's search parties had found a boy who had no father. He and his mother - who was apparently a princess of the area, were being brought there.

Everything was set, and Maugant began his preparations for the sacrifice.

I saw the party arrive, the woman and her son muffled in cloaks and taken straight to Vortigern's tent.

Soon after I received a summons to attend upon the High King myself. I made my way to the richly decorated tent and was ushered in. There were a number of people there. Several important-looking men whom I guessed to be Vortigern's advisors and generals, Maugant, with three others of his kind, as well as various lesser hanger-on. The air was stuffy and hot, and I could tell at once that I had entered in the middle of an argument.

In the middle of the tent stood two others - a woman of middle years whose face, though not beautiful, had a certain quality about it which made her seem fair; and a youth of maybe twelve years, slightly built with long dark hair cut raggedly around his face.

As I came in the youth turned his head to look at me, and I saw that his eyes were a curious pale grey colour. But, more than that, it was the way he looked at me - as though he could see right inside of me - that made me want to look anywhere than into those eyes.

Almost at once he looked back at Vortigern, who sat frowning in a heavily carved chair. The king turned his most baleful stare on me. "This.... child ... tells me he knows why my tower will not stand. I want you to hear what he has to say."

To my secret relief the boy did not look at me again, but kept those strange eyes fixed on Vortigern. His voice had a clear light tone that seemed at variance with the measured way he spoke. " The tower will not stand because there is a pool of water deep within the hill. At the bottom of this pool is a stone casket ands within the casket are two dragons. Every night they struggle against each other and their movements cause the hill to shake."

"Well, master mason, what do you say to this?" demanded Vortigern.

I thought quickly. I had of course taken soundings of the hilltop, but had I gone deeply enough? Of course, most of what the boy said was pure nonsense - probably invented in the hope of saving himself from certain death - but the pool could be a possibility.

Finally I said: "I would have to dig more deeply to see if this is true or not."

"Then do it," ordered Vortigern. "But be quick."

As I left the tent I caught sight of Maugant's face. He looked angry and - yes - something else ... was it fear? I had no time to think of it because I was already shouting for men to come and bring tools to dig.

Several hours later I stood on the edge of deep pit looking down and seeing water seeping up between rocks and earth. The boy had been right - though how he had known I could not fathom.

I sent a messenger to Vortigern who decided to come and look for himself. In the end most of the court were standing around the edge of the pit. The boy and his mother had been brought there as well.

"I see no stone chest." Vortigern said.

"Nor any dragon's", added Maugant with a sneer.

"Nonetheless, they are there", said the boy.

Vortigern turned to me. "Dig," he said.

And dig we did, for several more hours, at then of which time, the lid of an ornately carved stone sarcophagus measuring nearly ten feet in either direction was revealed. The hair on the back of my neck prickled as I looked at it. I thought Vortigern looked uneasy for the first time. But he quickly hid it.

"Open it" he said.

So pry-bars were fetched and the lid slowly raised. It took fifteen of my strongest men to shift it, but finally it slip sideways with a crunch and we were looking into the stone coffin.

I will never forget what we saw there.

Dragons indeed. Or at least what are commonly known as dragons - though a good deal smaller than the storytellers would have us believe. I would say they measured no more than the height of two men from nose to tail. But they had wings, thin membranes stretching back from just below their shoulders. Serpentine necks, long barbed trails, heavy clawed feet - they were dragons all right. And, just as the boy had said, one was red the other white.

No one said anything. But as we watched in utter silence the dragons began to move and stretch, then they flew up into the air with a cracking and creaking of wings that echoed from the surrounding mountain slopes. Ignoring us completely, they began to fight.

I suppose we stood there for an hour while the two dragons fought, held like spell-struck people, watching with a mixture of horror and fascination. At the end the red dragon won. It bit through the neck of its adversary, which fell down out of the sky and struck the earth with the sound of something much larger than it appeared. Then the victorious red dragon flew down and breathed fire from its mouth, utterly consuming the body of its adversary. Then, apparently satisfied, it flew off to the South.

Silence fell, and seemed to go on for a long time. We stood there amid the smoke and stink of charred flesh. Then the child stepped forward - suddenly no one wanted to restrain him or indeed come to near him at all. I saw Maugant with open fear on his face and even Vortigern looked shaken.

" You have seen that everything is as I foretold", the boy said. "Now hearken to this. The red dragon betokens the Pendragon line, and the sons of King Constantine. The white dragon betokens you, lord Vortigern. Like it you shall perish in flames. The red dragons will become the lords of Britain, and prepare the way for another who shall be the greatest king this land had ever seen."

As we stood there around the broken hilltop, the boy held out his hand to his mother and together they walked away. No one tried to stop them.

As soon as I could I packed up my equipment and left the place. Afterwards I heard how Vortigern retreated deeper into the mountains and how he tried to hide from the young princes. He even managed to build a fortress of sorts - though it was of wood not stone. There, eventually, Ambrosius and Uther caught up with the tyrant and set fire to the place. Vortigern perished in the flames just as the boy had said he would. After that Ambrosius became king, and the rest is history.

But I have never forgotten the events on the hill. I heard that soon after they began to call it Dinas Emrys, the fort of Emrys. I never knew the name of the boy until then, but by then he was already being called by another name - Merlin. Yes, he was Merlin Emrys, and I was witness to his first great prophecy. I hear he made many more thereafter and that they came true as well. People say he is the greatest wizard ever to walk the earth, and for myself I think they may well be right.

(2000)

Section Seven:

Myths, Poems and Translations

Chapter 37:

FOOLSONGS

I've written poetry for most of my life but published very little of it. Such writings seem somehow too personal to share or are simply not good enough. But there are some I do feel are worth putting into print. One is a long, and still ongoing, sequence of poems about the Celtic Bard Taliesin, some of which appeared interspersed between tales in two volumes of stories: Song of Taliesin and Song of Arthur.

The other is a set of poems inspired by the visionary paintings and drawings of the British artist Cecil Collins (1908-1989), whose work is not only powerful and moving but also strangely comic. His many paintings of the Fool – a medieval figure employed to keep a smile on the faces of royalty – represented, for Collins, all humanity. It is a vision that somehow deeply appeals to me. The poems that follow were inspired by a visit to a retrospective exhibition of Collin's work that I visited in London in 1981, with three more added some time after. I met Collins only once, through my friend the poet Kathleen Raine in the basement of whose Chelsea house he lived for many years. He seemed to me not only wise but also tranquil in a way that I could not explain. His work shows him to have been a true visionary, on a par perhaps with William Blake. This sequence of poems is dedicated to his memory.

Fool woke in the morning
met a bird on the way
bade the bird good day
Fool
with a kick
made air his own

Fool
woke in the evening
sang a song
slept
his song kept going
'till morning was again

*   *   *

Foolishly
Fool
nodded at a reed
reed nodded back

Fool sang
piped on his fingers -
thought
I am piper of dawn
in evening clay
nodded
slept

*   *   *

Fool stept
out of a window
into green woods wild

*   *   *

Fool got up
couldn't remember
who he was
listened for a moment
hummed a tune

Dreamed he was sleeping
found himself awake
"always oldways"
he said
and fell asleep

*   *   *

Fool oped
his heart to everything
lifted
his soul to treetops
and saw
mirrored there
his god

*   *   *

Fool looked in the mirror
saw his soul imprisoned
broke it with his finger

blood flowed
he sobbed
O fool…

*   *   *

Fool carried
his heart in one hand
with the other he sketched
a figure in the air
from it he took
a silver net
laid the heart within it
tossed it away

*   *   *

Fool saw
a goddess in the steam
waited for her to speak
she said:
Look away Fool
Fool looked away
He waited
looked back
saw her
gone

*   *   *

Fool went marching
saw no change in the light
felt like singing
just the same

*   *   *

Fool met an angel
JOY!

*   *   *

Fool met a boy and girl
thought them foolish

winked
slept
dreamed he met a girl and boy
who sang how once they
met a Fool upon the way

*   *   *

Fool and the Lady
danced for all to see
Fool and the Lady
in a high tree

Fool and Lady
in a boat
Fool and Lady
afloat

Fool and the Lady
in a high tree
Fool said the Lady
come kiss me

Fool and Lady
fell to earth
Fool and Lady
began a birth

*   *   *

Fool wore a mask
he laughed
the mask laughed too

(poor Fool)
alarming him

*   *   *

Fool sat in the darkness
polishing a star
plucked
he said
from a spire

Fool set it high
in the branches of a tree
walked backwards through the woods
admiring his work

*   *   *

In the rain
dancing
three fools

"Let us look
for the Great City!"

Dancing
three fools
in the rain

"There!" On the hill!
The spires! The domes!"

three fools
dancing
in the rain

"Golden! Golden!
golden golden
golden-golden!"

rain
fools
dancing

*   *   *

Aiming his smile
at the sky like an arrow
Fool slipped on the green
lay beneath his shadow

Fool met Death
he didn't know her
tried a joke

302

Fool set it high
in the branches of a tree
walked backwards through the woods
admiring his work

*   *   *

In the rain
dancing
three fools

"Let us look
for the Great City!"

Dancing
three fools
in the rain

"There!" On the hill!
The spires! The domes!"

three fools
dancing
in the rain

"Golden! Golden!
golden golden
golden-golden!"

rain
fools
dancing

*   *   *

Aiming his smile
at the sky like an arrow
Fool slipped on the green
lay beneath his shadow

Fool met Death
he didn't know her
tried a joke
Death laughed

live another day Fool
she said

*   *   *

Fool went into
a tower of glass
shivered it
curved it
broke it in two

inside looking out
Fool grinned
his shadow danced fantastically
imprisoning the sun

*   *   *

Fool in quest of…
in quest of the City

found a door
a door in the wall
found a friend there

Fool on quest
for a journey
to a place

Fool walking
Fool dancing
Fool travelling

found a dream
found a journey
found the City

Fool set off…
Fool's still travelling

THE END OF THE BEGINNING
OF THE SONGS OF FOOL

Chapter 38:

BETWEEN DARKNESS AND LIGHT

Every year I write poetry at Christmas – trying to capture the elusive quality of that magical time. Sometimes the efforts are reasonably successful, as in the case of the first of these two poems, which I wrote in 1995 and 1999 respectively. More recently, in 2002, 'Between Darkness and Light' was set to music, by David Seitz for the Camerata Singers of the First United Methodist Church of Mishawaka, Indiana. It seems to have become something of a perennial favourite there and was recorded live in 2006. All the poems that follow were written around Christmastide and Midwinter and are in some sense responses to the time and the feelings it evokes.

Between Darkness and Light (for Emrys)

It is within the darkness and the silence
That the magic of Christmas starts;
Somewhere between the glimmer of lights
And the first breathless moment
When children come
Stumbling like new-born angels
Into morning light.

Within the darkness and the silence
We sit, watching wonder
Evolve into form; where we
Enter the ringing silence
In which the first bells of Christmas
Sound the music of the soul;
Where the morning joy begins
With a single carol
To a half-forgotten tune.

It is here, between the darkness
And the light,
That we wait, uncertain,
Seeking the moment
That challenges us to believe
In a freshly minted miracle
Born every Christmas Day.

(Christmas, 1995

WINDSONGS

1

Sometimes, when the wind
Storms down the chimney,
Its voice a raw song of rejoicing
Sometimes - then -
I too rejoice:
To know the freedom
Of the wind's soul,
And yet to feel
Secure in the net of night
With walls and roof
And a red fire
dancing in the grate.

2

This Christmas
The lights gleam out
Brighter somehow --
Shining out
Across the snow
Shadowing
The New Year.

The Child -
The Young One --
The Winter Lord --
Is with us again
Dancing on the Wind's back,
Beckoning us
From the bright dream of Christmas
To the dawn of a new day.

(Christmas 1999)

TO SEE THE QUEEN

Three men came
out of the crystal night
to kneel
at the feet of the queen.

All were kings –
coming to see
her beauty revealed -
her motherhood
bright as candles,
her face a long dream.

Not for the babe they came -
but for her; to worship her glory
in the cold still heart
of winter's night.

Three kings came
to see the Queen;
to utter their song
of what has been.

WINTER WORLD

"Snowbound Britain!" the headline read.
I rushed outside.

Bright walls were gathering
burdens of snow.
Sighing, they lifted their stones
to receive the benison.

In this bleak midwinter
I came home to the world.

(2005)

THE GREEN KING

The Green King's a-hunting
Again in the Wildwood
Drawing swift tracks
Like traces through his hands.

The Green Lord's a-hunting
Again in the Waste
Watching the patterns
Of birds across the sky.

The Green Man's a-rutting
In the ancient mast,
Rooting out the old dreams
From the Wood's heart.

(2005)

THE SONG OF THE GREEN MAN

The Green Man flares in my head
like a song of seasons
and Robin is come to the Green again
singing:
O, I am in
the Greenwood
alone, so alone.

The May King dances in my head
like a bough in blossom
and a trumpet blows in the woodland
singing:
O, I am in
the Wildwood
deep, so deep.

The Faery-King dances on the green
like a Summer blessing
and I am transformed in green and gold
singing:
O, I dance
in faery land
forever.

(1993)

Chapter 39:

GRAIL

A Work for Two Choirs and Soloists
(With Caitlín Matthews)

The extraordinary power of the Grail story to move us profoundly is in that continued to haunt me as it has generations of others before and doubtless to come. In 2003 my wife Caitlín and I were approached by an exceptional composer to write the words for a Grail Mass. We were very excited by this since we felt that the subject transcended any simple religious impulse, and worked hard to complete the text that follows. Unfortunately this project came to nothing at the time, but the words have remained and we still hope one day to hear them set to music. The incomparable phrases of the Latin Mass are set here against words drawn from several medieval Grail texts mixed poetry of our own. I feel this stands up to a reading even without music. I am grateful for Caitlín's permission to include the work in this collection.

Celebrant: Bass
Quester: Alto (Male)
Lady of the Waste Land / World: Mezzo-Sop.

1: Kyrie

CELEBRANT:
In the evening
In the twilight of the day
A voice sings
Out of the starlit places:

CHOR.II:
Here is the book of thy descent.
Here begin the terrors.
Here begin the miracles...

CHOR.I:
How shall we be deserving?
How shall we be at peace?

The end is not a beginning
The path lies at our feet ...

CHOR.II:
The beginning is the struggle
The endless place of pain
Daily are the terrors
Tears of acid rain.

QUESTER:
Where are my beginnings and what is my quest?
Why do the shadows turn their coats to my back?
Which road is the best one to set out upon?
Who am I? Who was I? Why was I born?

CHOR.I:
The heart has five changes
Five questions to seek
For the answering peace
And the turning cheek.

CHOR. II:
The land is a waste with nowhere to hide
We ask no forgiveness wherever we ride;
The skills of the strong and the ploys of the weak
Our captains, our sergeants, our keepers of peace.

QUESTER:
Give me time to answer,
Make space for my thought
Find me the freedom
That cannot be bought.

LADY:
I am pain
I am torment
I am empty hearted.
I birthed you
I taught you,
We are one, you and I.
Yet guide you I will
And keep you I must
Till you find your beginning
And ransom your trust.

QUESTER:
The thirst to find consumes my mind.
I fear the gathering, the garnering,
Will not be mine.
What has been sown must be reaped -
Beyond my keeping, beyond my catching,
The path is trod by others.

LADY:
I will show you a story.

CHOR I.
Kyrie ....

LADY.
I will set you free.

CHOR.II
.... Eleison

LADY
 I am your beginning and your birth.

CHORS I & I
Kyrie eleison, kyrie eleison, kyrie eleison,
Christe, eleison, Christe eleison, Christe eleison,
Kyrie eleison, kyrie eleison, kyrie eleison.

The CELEBRANT enters, lies upon the earth. During the singing of the Kyrie he kneels and knocks
three times on his breast to signify the Mea Culpa implicit in the Kyrie. The QUESTER begins the
Quest, shadowed by THE LADY OF THE WASTELAND, cloaked so that she is not obvious to the
audience.

CHOR. I.
We bring the shadows

CHOR.II:
But the light is abroad

CHOR. I
We ask no forgiveness

CHOR.II
Yet the offering is made.

QUESTER (to LADY)
Why do you keep in darkness?
Why do you weep?

LADY:
Exiled from wholeness
My tears are for you.

THE CELEBRANT at the altar stands as Christ Pantocrator, hands outstreched.

2: Gloria

CELEBRANT:
In the midst of the morning
In the half-light of the day
The Graal appeared
At the sacring of the Mass
In five shapes
It is not meet to speak of,
The last of which
Was the shape of the world.

CHORS I & II.
Gloria in excelcis Deo
et in terra pax hominibus bonae voluntatis.
Laudamus te,
benedicimus te
adoramus te
glorificamus te,
gratiam agimus tibi propter magnam gloriciam tuam,
Domine Deus, Rex caelestis,
Deus Pater omnipotens,
Domine Fili unigenite, Iesu Christi
Domine Deus, Agnes Dei, Filius Patris
Qui tollis peccata mundi, miserere nobis;
Qui tollis peccata mundi, suscipe deprecationem nostrum,
Qui sedes ad dexteram Patris, miserere nobis.
Quoniam tu solus Sanctus, tu solus Dominus, tu solus
Altissimus.
Iesu Christe, Cum sancto Spititu; in gloria Dei Patris.

CHOR. II:
There is no glory.

CHOR.I:
Gloria in excelcis Deo (reprise)

CHOR.II:
There is no peace.

CHOR.I:
In terra Pax hominibus bonae voluntatis ... (Reprise)

LADY:
There was a glory once
You do not remember it
But it shone,
All life was aflame with it.
Only you can make it come again'.

QUESTER:
Since there was wilderness,
I have known no better.
I have drunk the cup and torn the meat.
I am alive.

LADY:
The path before you winds away.
We will meet once more.
Tread softly on my heart.
(Exit LADY)

QUESTER:
Was there ever a world
Where we could live?
A world where living was for now?
A world not far removed
Beyond the starry realms ?
There are two many answers.
And still the quest goes on.

3. Sanctus

CELEBRANT:
In the midst of noon,
In the shadow of the day,
When they went to the chapel
They saw the Lady

Take her Son upon her knees
And say to him:
You are my Father & my Son   (solo)
And my Lord,
Guardian of me
And of all the world.

ALTAR now becomes a table and the CELEBRANT welcomes all and invites them to share the divine feast. Members of the choir come around him.

CHOR. II
There are no welcomings.
Home is beyond.

CHOR.I.
Where the Table is spread
Be welcome.

The Graal procession winds through to the accompaniment of a wandering SANCTUS, with THE LADY taking the part of the Graal Maiden and bringing the Cup. Candles are born in to light the darkened stage. THE QUESTER watches.

QUES:
I thirst.

CHOIRS I & II
SANCTUS ....

QUESTER.
I hunger

CHOIRs I & II
.... SANCTUS

QUES:
I thirst.

CHORS I & II:
.... SANCTUS

QUEST.ER:
I hunger.

CHORS I & II:
.... SANCTUS.

QUESTER.:
I want.

CHORS I & II:
SANCTUS, Dominus Deus Sabaoth.
Pleni sunt caeli et terra gloria tua.
Hosanna in exchelsis.

CHOR I: (Jubilant)
Benedictus que venit in nomine Domini.
Hosanna in Excelsis.

The lights dim and the stage is revealed empty and forlorn. The QUESTER falls to his knees in weakness and loneliness.

QUEST.ER:
The cup passed from me.
The dancing gone.

CHOR.II:
There is no holiness.
The will to live is all.

CHOR.I.(faint)
Beyond holiness
Live to do the will.

QUESTER:
Questions, answers.
Exile and defeat
An end that is no beginning
Stretching out its hands to emptiness.
Where, am I? Why do I seek?
No purpose, no meeting, and now no retreat.
You promised me freedom
You promised ...you promised... (failing)
There is no changing things.
I am the same!

THE LADY (voice off)
Where do you stand?

315

How do you call?
What is your question?
Why do you fall?

(Lights out)

CHOR. I & II.
The heart has five changes
Five questions to seek.
For the answering peace
Is the healing ....

4: Consecration

CELEBRANT:
In the noontide
At the height of the day.

Lights up to reveal QUESTER lain upon on altar. CELEBRANT lifts him up tenderly and sings:

They looked within
The place of the Graal
And saw come forth
A man out of the Vessel,
That said to them:
My knights and my sergeants
My loyal sons.
You who in this mortal life
became my spiritual creatures
Who sought me out so diligently:
I will no longer hide myself from you,
But you shall see
A part of my mysteries
And of my hidden things;
And you shall hold and receive
The meat you have desired.

As CELEBRANT sings members of the CHOIR appear in a pool of light around him The QUESTER is fed from the Graal by THE LADY and CELEBRANT. He revives.

LADY   (to Quest.)
You are whole for a moment and a moment
For the healing of the world is your birth and ending.

QUEST.ER:
I am mortal, of the world -
Yet I know the citadel of stars.

LADY.:
For the healing of the world -
This moment and this moment.

QUESTER.
Of the deepest things I have knowledge.
I have touched the heart and all its changes.
LADY.
There is one change more.

She reveals herself as THE WORLD, an expression of all human pain, sorrow, weakness, and self-inflicted woe.

CHOR.II:
There is no healing.
The Vision fades.

CHOR. I.
Earth is mother.
Earth is home.

5: Agnus Dei

QUESTER seizes the Graal and gives it to the LADY to drink.

CHOR I & II.
Agnus Dei, qui tollis peccata mundi: miserere nobis
Agnus Dei, qui tollis peccata mundi: miserere nobis

QUESTER.
Miserere nobis ...

CHORS I & II
 Agnus Dei, qui tollis peccata mundi: miserere nobis…

QUESTER. (and LADY as she revives):
Dona nobis pacem.

QUEST ER & LADY:
The heavens spin their purposes.

To tear the meat, to drink the cup
Is not to eat.
Although we win, we lose.
Tread gently, tenderly.

CELEBRANT.
And in the morning
At the rising of the day
He heard a bell
Sounding from the sea...

CHOR. I:
The heart's five changes
For the healing of the world.
Your cup, to win or lose -
But always yours to give.

CELEBRANT:
And in a while
The ship drew far away,
And he was within it,
And a voice commended
All men to God.

CHOR.& SOLI.:
Benedicat vos, omnipotens Deus.
Pater, et Filius, et Spiritus Sanctus....

Sanctus
Sanctus
Sanctus
Sanctus   (fading).

(2003)

Chapter 40:

THE FAERY WORLD

This short piece was written as the introduction to a collection of writings about Faery that my wife and I edited in 1992. Published as A Faery Tale Reader (Thorsons) it remains one of our favorite anthologies. That book is now out of print, but as we still felt the introduction said things that were worth saying, it is reproduced here with the permission of Caitlin Matthews.

It is more than fifty years since J.R.R.Tolkien gave his justly famed lecture 'On Fairy-Stories' at St Andrews University, in Scotland - a land well known for its continuing belief in fairies. Professor Tolkien's remarks are as appropriate now as then, and serve as a fitting place from which to begin this brief account of the faery traditions.

"The realm of fairy-story is wide and deep and high and filled with many things: all manner of beasts and birds and are found there; shoreless seas and stars uncounted; beauty that is enchantment, and an ever-present peril; both joy and sorrow as sharp as swords. In that realm a man may, perhaps, count himself fortunate to have wandered, but its very richness and strangeness tie the tongue of a traveller who would report them." (Tree & Leaf)

There are many different reports of visits to Faery, some of which are more or less tongue-tied than others. Professor Tolkien would probably not have approved of all of these. Some, like the classic stories, "Sleeping Beauty" and "Beauty and the Beast", would have seemed too literary, too contrived even, in style, betraying a sorry lack of faith in the skill of the oral storytellers who transmitted the tales from ancient traditions. However, each of the writers whose work is represented here shares a deep awareness of the reality of Faery. They wandered there themselves, and their perceptions were forever changed.

As Tolkien himself noted, the best stories of Faery concern the wanderings of human beings within the realm of the otherworld. The division between the two distinct realms of ordinary and Faery reality blurs in faery tale, so that Faeries experience our world and we experience theirs.

The way in which we view both the Perilous Land of Faery and those who dwell there, has varied so much over the centuries that it is at times difficult to get a clear look at what is really involved. Tolkien drew attention - as indeed have several other writers - to the fashion for diminutive Faeries. This is even reflected in the Oxford English Dictionary definition of a fairy as: 'One of a class of supernatural beings of diminutive size, popularly supposed to have magical powers, and to meddle for good or evil in the affairs of man'. This is a very narrow and misleading definition that we hope that this book will amplify and correct. It could be said, indeed, looking at the best known examples of faery-tales, that though the denizens of faery are accused of meddling in the affairs of humanity, it is humankind

319

who does the meddling - since it is more often than not the human creatures who enter Faery - usually at their own behest and desire, to steal gold, wisdom or some other empowerment from Faery. Faeryfolk and human beings live in neighbouring realms which have their own interconnections, so it is hardly surprising to find plenty of meddling on both sides of the fence: we are each interested in the other's lives.

We have chosen to use the spelling 'Faery' throughout, to apply both to the realm and to those who dwell there, except where the meaning would be unclear or where a quotation gives 'Fairy'. This is in line with the first recorded usage, in John Gower's Confessio Amantis (c1450) in which the hero is described as being 'as if her were of Faerie.' (v7065ff). 'Fairy' is a later spelling and has unfortunate modern connotations. It could be argued that the majority of misconceptions about the appearance and behaviour of the Faery race are due to the diminishing of all the Faery races to minute beings by popular Victorian writers: as witness the number of winged and vapid sprits peering coyly from the pages of Victorian children's books. However it must be said also, that while their presentation of faeries is a great deal more powerful than their Victorian counterparts, such writers as Shakespeare, Dryden and Johnson, played their own part in establishing the faery race as small, mischievous and comical, as in the 'Tale of Robin Goodfellow' which is certainly a key text in the literary history of Faery, and may well have a good deal to do with the way they have been perceived since the 16th century.

That they once possessed a more powerful set of attributes is easily shown by reference to a handful of the existing portraits of faery people and acts. We would hardly see the Queen of Elfland in the Ballad of 'Thomas of Ercildoun' as a diminutive sprite when we read of her:

"Her shirt was o the grass-green silk,
Her mantle o the velvet
At every tip of her horse's mane
Hung fifty silver bells and nine."

Nor indeed do we find Argante, in Layamon's thirteenth century *Brut* as either laughable or whimsical, for she is 'A very radiant elf, the fairest of all maidens' to whom Arthur repairs to be healed of his grievous wounds.

Argante, of course, is the Lady of the Lake familiar from Arthurian romances. Another figure from the same source: Morgan le Fay, who originates in the fearsome battle goddess of ancient Ireland, is scarcely either gentle or picturesque. Her title "Fay" derives from the French 'Fée' and she is only one among many such wondrous and terrifying women who inspire at very least a healthy respect in all who encounter them.

Andrew Lang, one of the foremost collectors of Faery Tales, clearly shared Tolkien's view when he wrote, in the introduction to The Lilac Fairy Book to the contemporary authors who always began their books with 'a little boy or girl who goes out and meets the fairies of polyanthuses and gardenias and apple blossom.' And, he added, 'These fairies try to be funny and fail; or they try to preach and succeed.'

This was very much a phenomenon of the time, but the truth of the matter is still that the Faery race has been systematically and deliberately diminished by generations of largely Christian authors, who saw in them a last vestige of Pagan belief, enshrined in innocent-seeming fairy tales. That they were at least half right is certainly true, as is the belief that faeries were once regarded in a very different light.

The Faery once evoked tremendous respect and it would have been a brave soul who would have mocked or offended them without fear of reprisal. The Faery were the original, ancient race that remembered the old way of communion with the natural world. They did not seek to control or manipulate it by the use of iron, which is traditionally a metal that is inimical to them. If people see fewer of the Faery today, it is the prevalence of concrete and electricity that keep them cushioned against their appearance. The Age of Reason and the Age of Industry have both contributed to the diminishment of Faery, which has almost faded from the consciousness of our race. But though we have scorned the enrichments of Faery, we still have to pay the tithe of our imagination. Without the communion and otherworldly exchange between Faery and our own world, we grow sick in soul.

Though we tend to think of Fairy Tales as intended primarily for children, this association is of comparatively recent origin. Certainly up to the 19th century fairy tales were considered as part of the traditional heritage of lore and wisdom among native people the world over. There was nothing inherently 'childish' about those stories, which in fact display elements of cruelty and violence and quite frequently deal with adult subjects. (One has only to look at Robert Bly's bestseller *Iron John* or Bruno Bettleheim's *The Uses of Enchantment* to see how much relevance for adults these stories can have). The idea that Fairy-tales are childish and therefore somehow unworthy of adult attention seems to have grown up at about the same time as the image if Victorian tinsel-winged flower-fairies of the type decried by both Land and Tolkien. The present collection is made with a view towards an adult readership (though not excluding children) and for this reason contains a number of commentaries or personal accounts from those who have indeed wandered in Faery.

Tolkien himself did much to restore the faery folk to their rightful place. His wonderful and terrible elves are far closer to the true nature of the fair folk than the diminutive sprites that are still invoked by Walt Disney and in far too many illustrations of traditional folk and fairy tales even to this day. The elves seen by the hero of Tolkien's story 'Smith of Wooton Major' restore our race's ancient vision:

> *'He saw a great ship cast high upon the land, and the waters fell back in foam without a sound. The elven mariners were tall and terrible; their swords shone and their spears glinted and a piercing light was in their eyes. Suddenly they lifted up their voices in a song of triumph and his heart was shaken with fear, and he fell upon his face, and they passed over him and went away into the echoing hills.'*

People have been saying goodbye to the faery race for centuries: Chaucer, in 'The Wife of Bath's Tale' said they had vanished in King Arthur's time; Bishop Corbet in the 17th century claimed they had gone; Hugh Miller, a nineteenth century folklorist, recorded their final departure from Scotland, while in Oxfordshire A.J. Evans told that an old man of his acquaintance had seen them departing down a hole near the Rollright Stones. Yet despite this sightings continue to be reported and the belief in the fair folk, among all kinds of people is as strong as ever.

The reason for this is not hard to find. The universal appeal of the stories has little or nothing to do with the Faery race. The majority of faery-tales do not concern faeries at all, but more often the actions of kings, queens, princes and princesses, step-mothers, witches, animal helpers and, above all, ordinary people. The truth of the matter is that the term 'faery tale' is a catch-all for a vast treasury of lore, belief and mystery teaching. It is for this reason that the faery tradition has recently become the stamping ground of psychologists, mystics and anthropologists, who have found, within the world of faery, a reverence for, and a deep understanding of life, in all its myriad forms. Faery-tales can teach us a great deal about the world in which we live and the wonders that are hidden just beneath the surface of 'reality'. J.C. Cooper sums up the essential themes of faery in her 1983 book *Fairy Tales: Allegories of the Inner Life*:

> *'The most constantly recurring themes are those dealing with the descent of the soul into the world, its experience in life, initiation and the quest for unity and the trials and tribulations that beset its journey through the world. Possibly the best known and most frequent of motifs is that of Paradise Lost and Regained. of which the story of Cinderella is the classic example, though the theme runs through most fairy tales in the form of initial misfortune leading eventually to a happy ending'*

The happy ending is perhaps the single most important in all of the Faery Tale tradition. Tolkien coined the word 'eucatastrophe' or 'happy outcome' to describe it, referring to the sense of overwhelming relief and joy which accompanies the reading of many of the classic faery tales. These stories offer hope, a chance for the littlest brother or sister, the poorest farmer or fisherman, the obscure child or the ugliest woman, to succeed, to change their lives, to aspire to greater things and to succeed.

It was to this that the great psychologist Bruno Bettleheim referred when he wrote that, with rare exceptions, 'nothing can be as enriching and satisfying to child and adult alike as the folk or fairy tale'; and it is this, more than anything, which has kept the classic faery tales alive for hundreds of years, just as it is part of the fascination with unknown possibilities which still sends people off in search of the reality of Faery itself.

The fleeting nature of Faery gifts, such as faery gold, which is supposed to turn back to mushrooms or leaves, is a reminder to our materialist world that there are other forms of wealth without which we are poor indeed. The enrichment of Faery is a gift we should not look in the mouth, but rather treasure with all our hearts and share with others that the enchantment shall never fade.

The writers assembled in this collection are people whose lives were dedicated to this sharing: the Grimm brothers, Jakob and Willhelm, Charles Perrault, Andrew Lang, J.F. Campbell, Ruth Sawyer, from each of whose collections we have included a story. As well, we have provided extensive passages from some of the many august authors who have written about Faery itself: Thomas Keightly, whose 18th century account of the mythology of Faery has still to be surpassed. Lewis Spence, the Scots writer who single-handedly did more to revive an interest in the Faery traditions of Britain, provides two long chapters filled with fascinating information. Joseph Campbell, perhaps the finest writer on mythology in recent times, contributes a brilliant chapter on the world of the Grimm bothers; Alfred Nutt, better known for his studies of Celtic and Grail myths, offers us insights into the fairy mythology behind Shakespeare's work.

All of these writers have one thing in common - they take the world of Faery seriously and they take it as they find it - not attempting to put in meanings that are not there or extract significance where there is none. They do not seek to preach or to make fun of the Faery race. In this they align themselves with a great tradition that has been stronger in this country than almost anywhere else in the world. They have helped us assemble this Faery treasury and we hope that they will help retune your senses to hear once more the music of Faery and to perceive the People of Peace in the words of Fiona MacLeod's song from the text of the opera he wrote with music by Rutland Boughton:

> *How beautiful they are,*
> *the lordly ones.*

Who dwell in the hills,
In the Hollow hills.
They have faces like flowers,
And their breath is wind
That stirs amid the grasses
Filled with white clover.

Their limbs are more white
Than shafts of moonshine:
They are more fleet
Than the march wind.

They laugh and are glad
And are terrible;
When their lances shake
Every green reed quivers.

How beautiful they are,
How beautiful,
The lordly ones
In the hollow hills.
(The Immortal Hour)

(1992)

Chapter 41:

THE GODS ARE OUR FAMILY

At the turn of the new millennium I started work on a book called **The Oldest Wisdom in the World,** which explored the fact that the Sumerian people, who lived along the Indus Valley more than 2000 years ago, had put forward some of the most profound truths to enter human consciousness, as well as producing the first great epic – **Gilgamesh.** I have always loved mythology for the wisdom it enshrines, for the humanity it displays, and for the deep truths expressed by its heroes and heroines. Myth represents the first attempts of our species to explain the universe to ourselves. Homer drew me in my teens; then I discovered the Celtic and Arthurian traditions that illustrate my native landscape - inner as well as outer. But in all the years I have spent studying and writing about these subjects, I have never forgotten a moment when, in London on a research trip more than twenty years ago, I wandered into the Mesopotamian gallery in the British Museum. I stood in front of a case filled with delicate seals and enigmatic clay tablets with their birds-feet markings and felt something stir within me - a tiny flicker of excitement which rapidly became a flame. Still uncertain what it was I was seeing, I wandered from case to case, reading the printed transcriptions of some of the ancient tablets.

I quickly knew that I had stumbled on a source of wisdom, twice or three times as old as Celtic, but which shared some of the hallmarks of the tradition I knew so well - a deeply practical wisdom that showed how men and gods interacted with each other; how humans were truly the offspring of the ancient deities in a wholly surprising way; how the world of nature and the worlds of the divine overlapped. I remember that I felt a shiver of recognition then, a feeling of closeness to the people who had made these objects, who had written the words I was reading more than 2000 years ago. Across that seemingly vast gulf of time these ancient people spoke to me, saying: 'Tell our story; let us share our wisdom with you.' I knew then that I had to write something about the Sumerians, to share the extraordinary body of wisdom I had discover with others.

In the end the book never happened (though I hope it will one day) but I did produce a chapter on the theme of immortality – an important one for the Sumerians as it remains for us today. I include it here – along with my retelling of the Myth of Adapa and a new translation of an ancient poem that seems to say everything about this ancient world.

The Search for Immortality

'To him had been given wisdom -
immortality had not been given to him'.
- The Myth of Adapa

From the beginning of human history the idea of immortality - its getting or its loss - has been a central theme in the myths and stories of every culture. In the Tablets of Lore it occurs many times, especially in the story of Gilgamesh, where the hero at first seeks the immortality of fame, flying in the face of the gods to achieve it, and then, when he at last meets death face to face when his friend Enkidu dies, by seeking actual immortality of the body. In this story, as in the one that follows here, the mortal hero is offered the gift, in the shape of the plant of eternal life that grows beneath the sea. But, just as in the story of Adapa, the gift is lost.

It is very clear that to the people of Sumer the gift of life was acknowledged as supremely important, as something to be both honoured and cherished. Living, as they did, in a land where the most precious gift of water had to be persuaded to flow into fields and wells, they were well aware of the fragility of their existence. And, while there is no doubt that they possessed a belief in an afterlife, they approached this in the same pragmatic way they brought to everything. It is this that brings special poignancy to the story of Adapa, as to the epic of Gilgamesh - for in both the gift of immortality is offered, only to be snatched away again before it can be gained.

ADAPA AND THE BREAD OF LIFE

The man was named Adapa, and he alone was permitted to serve at the Gods' table. Ea had given him great wisdom, enough to understand the shape of creation itself. Every day he baked bread, fetched water, and fished in the sea. With his skills he stocked the temples and brought good things to those who lived in the city of Eridu. So he was considered the wisest among men, a pattern of the Gods' creation, subtle and astute.

But, though Adapa was wise and skilful, he was also mortal. Death would find him in the allotted time, and he would vanish into the realm of the Underworld.

Now it happened that one day the stocks of fish in the temple of Ea fell short, and Adapa saw this and was mindful to catch some more. He went to the quayside and boarded the moon-boat that lay at anchor there. A fresh wind blew and Adapa let the craft run before it. Soon he was far out in the ocean, and there he cast his nets.

Then the South wind began to blow. So strong was it that Adapa's boat capsized and he was thrown into the world of the fish. As he struggled in the grip of the waves Adapa called out in anger: 'South Wind, may your wings break!'

As he spoke the wings of the wind broke indeed, and the ocean became still. Adapa righted the Moon Boat and sailed safely back to the city.

For seven days thereafter the wind was silent, until at length it came to the attention of the King of Heaven.

'Why has the South wind stopped blowing?' demanded Anu of his servant Ilabrat.

'Lord, the man Adapa, Ea's son, has broken the South Wind's wings with his anger.'

When he heard this Anu rose from his throne and went to speak with Ea. 'This man, Adapa, has done an evil thing and must be punished', said Anu. 'Fetch him hither.'

So Ea summoned the man and spoke with him. 'Anu is angry', he said. 'He will destroy you if you do not do as I say.' And he advised Adapa to go in rags, with his face scratched and his hair uncombed as if in mourning. 'Follow the path to the gate of heaven. When you arrive there you will see two gods waiting for you. They are Tammuz and Gizzida. Do not be afraid. They will ask you why you look like this. Tell them you are in mourning for them, who have left the earth. They will smile upon you because of this and will speak well of you to Anu. Do you understand this?'

Adapa trembled but nodded.

'Then', said Ea, 'When you stand before Anu, he will offer you the bread of death. Do not eat it. Next he will offer you the water of death. Do not drink it. Next he will offer you a garment of light. Accept this, and anoint yourself with the oil that shall be given to you also. Do not forget this!'

The messenger came to bring Adapa before the King of heaven. He led him up the roadway until they stood before the Eastern gate. There they met the two gods, Tammuz and Gizzida, just as Ea had foretold.

When they saw Adapa in his torn garments, with his hair uncombed and his cheeks scratched they said: 'Why do you appear before us looking like this?'

'I am in mourning for two mighty gods who have left our land' said Adapa.

'Which gods are these?' they demanded

'Why, Tammuz and Gizzida', answered Adapa.

Then the two gods looked at each other and smiled. 'Come.' they said, 'Let us go before great Anu.'

When they stood before the throne of heaven Anu looked down at Adapa and frowned. 'Why did you break the wings of the South Wind?' he asked.

'Lord', replied Adapa, 'I was fishing to bring more stocks to the house of my master, Ea, when the South Wind rose and capsized the boat of the Moon. In my anger I cursed the wind.'

Anu frowned on the man, but Tammuz and Gizzida spoke kindly of him, and soothed the anger of the king.

Anu sighed. 'What was Ea thinking about to make this creature like us, and to gift him with wisdom equal to ours?' He looked at Adapa, and said: 'Well, now that you are hear there is only one thing to do. Bring the bread of life.'

So they brought the bread of life, but Adapa, mindful of what Ea had told him, refused it.

Anu said: 'Bring the water of life.'

So they brought the water, but Adapa again refused.

Then they brought him the garment of light and oil to anoint himself and these Adapa took.

Then Anu laughed. 'What a strange creature you are to be sure! Why do you refuse my gifts? Now you will never have eternal life.'

'Lord, it was Ea who instructed me', answered Adapa.

Anu laughed again. 'The loss is yours Adapa, as it will be of all who come after you. ' Then he showed the man the whole breadth and height and depths of heaven and gave him command over his own life and of those who came after. Then he sent Adapa back to the world of men.

And so, because of this man, who broke the wings of the South Wind and went into heaven to stand before the throne of Anu, humankind are mortal, and after the span of years decreed to them, they die. And sickness is theirs, that can be cured only by Ninkarrak, the Lady of Healing. And Ea was sad, for he had a liking for the creature he had formed, but even he dare not go against the decree of Anu.

The anguish of death and dissolution is something most of us encounter at least once in our lives. Some dwell on the thought of their own death, or that of a loved one, increasingly as they grow older. The inevitability of the moment cannot be denied, and is the same whatever ones belief in an afterlife. We face the thought in different ways - by pushing it to the back of our minds and avoiding all mention of it, or by addressing the idea of our own, or others', deaths head on.

Right at the beginning of the Adapa story the crux of the matter is stated. Ea had granted Adapa almost god-like status, gifted him with skill and cleverness. But, he has also made him finite. Death will come for him in time. We are not told how Adapa feels about this, or if he has even thought of it. Perhaps, like Gilgamesh, when he is reminded of his own end, he will face it with a mixture of courage or fear. Perhaps he sees it as an inevitable aspect of the life he has been given - for he is, in a sense, the first man, the nearest equivalent to Adam that we find in Mesopotamian culture.

At any rate, when he is offered the bread and water of life he refuses, apparently because he misunderstood the meaning of Ea's advice. Perhaps, as can so easily happen in our own lives, he failed to pay enough attention to the words of the god, hearing only what he thought was an injunction not to eat or drink anything. The outcome is that he is denied immortality, as are all his descendents. There is no second chance. The original text ends on a note of sorrow: ' As for him, the man child of man, who broke the wing of the South Wind in his arrogant brought upon us the sufferings of mankind.' (Trans. N. K. Sanders).

So it is Adapa's arrogance, his pride and anger, which bring the curse of mortality down upon all of mankind. This is a theme that occurs throughout ancient myth. Again and again humanity is tested by the gods and found wanting, the gift of immortality held out to them, only to be withdrawn as the result of some act of hubris. Yet it might also be said, that while Adapa does indeed act out of the heat of the moment - he has just been upended into the sea! - he is not entirely to blame for this. Everything turns on a fact of which we have a less certain knowledge. Does Adapa know when he calls out in anger against the wind that his words will be so powerful as to actually cause the wind's wings to break? If so, if his intent was to bring harm, then the fault is truly his. He ought, we might say, to have had the patience and understanding - part of the astuteness given him by Ea - not to strike out against a force of nature.

But again we see how the man is loved by his creator - enough for Ea to devise a means by which Adapa will avoid the anger of the lord of heaven. He does this by appealing to the natural arrogance of the gods rather than by speaking up for his own creation - a fact which says something about the relationship of the gods themselves, as does the scene which follows, where Tammuz and Gizzida are flattered by Adapa's appearance as a mourner bewailing their withdrawal from the world (we are not told of the reason for this.) Perhaps it is this failure on the part of Ea to stand up for his creation (and which emphasises his own humanity) that causes Adapa to forget the more important instruction not to eat or drink the bread and water of death. We are, after all, told that the man was made as a pattern of the God's creation, which implies that he inherited flaws that they too possessed. (Or are we meant to think that Adapa himself bent the divine pattern to his own ends? At this point he seems not to have free will, though this is granted by Anu in the closing lines of the text).

In this story, there is no sense of the man trying to trick the gods into giving him mortality - as in so many traditions around the world. Adapa seems to accept this mortal state as a matter of course (perhaps he knows no better?) and indeed scarcely seems to understand what he is being offered: another point at which his famed wisdom apparently fails him.

What, though, are we to make of the garment of light and the oil for anointing which he is offered and which he does accept? Traditionally such a garment represents a transformation from an ordinary state of being to something more - often the calling of the human spirit to put off its fleshly form and dwell forever at the side of the gods. Oil, too, in many cultures, is both a bonding with deity and a sign that a deeper relationship - that of worshiper and worshipped as in the chrism of Christian baptism - has been reached. Again and again we read of worshippers being anointed as a means of being received into the service of a particular god or goddess. So from this we may assume that Adapa accepts the bond that exists between himself and the company of heaven. And we should note that after Anu has told him that he and his descendants will never have immortality, he shows him the whole of heaven, from the heights to the depths - surely a promise that he will return there rather than a demonstration of what he has lost!

In the end the story is touched with the sorrow of all humankind - the feeling of being somehow outlawed from the state of immortality and the wonders of heaven. It is probably that here we have a first sight of the theme which was to dominate much of Biblical writing: the exile from Eden and the loss of a deeper relationship to deity which permeates Genesis - much of which was to be composed while the memory of Sumerian and Akkadian traditions were still fresh.

But the offer of immortality means more than the gift of eternal life. It also means becoming open to an awareness of our own infinite potential. We can be immortal even within the finite world in which we live, not just by making a name for ourselves or being remembered by our surviving family, but by living beyond the moment, outside the confines of ordinary time, in what we might term 'soul time'. In most instances we are prevented from doing this by the attitude we take to time itself. For most of us time is something that stretches out before us, waiting to be filled, and with the dark immensity of death at the end. Perhaps because we want to put off that inevitable moment for as long as possible we constantly try to stretch time so that we can fit more in, achieve more, experience an increasing number of different states of being. This has the effect of driving us ever more deeply into matter - into the experience of the world - and of reducing the amount of time we spend in communication with our own souls.

At a soul level there is no time. We can experience an entire lifetime in a single second of 'soul time'. And yet we consistently run away from this deeper level of experience, preferring the frivolous pleasures of outer time. As the philosopher Jacob Needleman has so eloquently said in his book *Time and the Soul*: 'Our relationship to time is what it is because we lie to ourselves about what we are and what we can do and we hide from ourselves what we are meant to be and what we are meant to serve.' The lies we tell ourselves are those that limit us, which bind us forever to the ordinary and the everyday. Because we tell ourselves that we are time-bound and that we begin to die from the moment we are born, we have limited ourselves and our consciousness into a form or mortality that is at least partially an illusion.

Adapa is like a blank sheet of paper when we first encounter him. Given skills and wisdom by the god he acts without real thought or consideration, breaking the wings of the wind in a moment of anger (he seems never to be in real danger) and without a moment's compunction about the possible effect his action may have. In the story we scarcely feel any real sorrow for him; we may even think that the got what he deserved. It is an unfortunate consequence that the rest of humanity is denied immortality as a result. We may well recognise aspects of ourselves in this unthinking action, in the carelessness with which we behave towards our fellow men and women as well as what Needleman calls the lies we tell ourselves. If we were only able to spend more moments in the timeless place of the soul we would become more fully aware and take more thought before we acted.

The rewards of this are immeasurable. If every moment we lived was virtually infinite, is this not itself a form of immortality? Certainly it would make the moment of our own passing less fearful, closer to Peter Pan's 'awfully big adventure.' Once we are no longer bound by the limits of time we become freed to experience the extraordinary wonder that is life more fully and unreservedly. Without the lies that tell us we are subject to the inevitability of death, the actual fact of our demise ceases to rule over us. 'And death shall have no dominion' has more than one interpretation. If we no longer give mortality power over us we are truly free - free to return, like Adapa, to the city with another gift - one just as important as that of endless life - the freedom of ordering our own lives, to choose who and what we are, to lift the burden of time from our shoulders.

HYMN TO THE GODS OF THE NIGHT

(Translated from the ancient Mesopotamian)

The Great Ones have lain down,
Shot the bolts and dropped the bars of heaven;
The people sleep and the gates are locked tight.
The gods and goddesses
Shamash and Sin, Adad and Ishtar,
Sun and moon, restlessness and love
Sleep now in high heaven.
Even the judgement-seat is empty,
For no god is working now;
Night's curtain is drawn down,
Temple and sanctuary, dark and still.

In this hour,
The traveller calls to his gods,
Defender and plaintiff, cause laid to rest;
While Shamash - judge and father,
Is chambered in sleep:
'O great ones, lords of night,
Gibil of the furnace,
Irra of the Underworld;
Bow of the Gods,
Orion, Pleiades, Dragon,
Bull, Goat and Bear -
Stars of the Gods -
Stand by me now,
Accept this lamb I offer -
Show me the truth!'

(2000)

Contact Details
for John Matthews

The Foundation for Inspirational and Oracular Studies (FíOS) founded by Caitlín & John Matthews and Felicity Wombwell, is dedicated to shamanism and the oral and sacred arts. Each year the most inspiring exponents of living sacred traditions give practical courses. As do Caitlin and John themselves. FíOS also offers a progressive program of shamanic training worldwide. For more details of events and courses, write to Caitlín Matthews *at BCM Hallowquest, London WC1N. 3XX, U.K.* Membership of FíOS is currently (in 2007) £35/£45 a year, giving members four issues of the *Hallowquest Newsletter* and discounts on special events. We accept PayPal payments to Tigerna9@aol.com .Alternately send a Sterling cheque or a Stirling International Bank Draft for £35 (within Europe) or £45 (world rate) payable to Caitlín Matthews to the above address.

Hallowquest Newsletter: For details of forthcoming books and courses with John & Caitlín, send for their quarterly newsletter. Current subscription: £8 or 15 Euros (UK) or £16/$25 (World). Send sterling cheque payable to Caitlín Matthews or U.S. dollar bills (no foreign cheques please) to Caitlín Matthews, BCM Hallowquest, London WC1N 3XX, U.K. Alternatively, see their website at www.Hallowquest.org.uk

Lorian Press

Lorian Press is a private, for profit business which publishes works approved by the Lorian Association's board of directors. Current titles can be found on the Lorian website www.lorian.org.

The Lorian Association is a not-for-profit educational organization. Its work is to help people bring the joy, healing, and blessing of their personal spirituality into their everyday lives. This spirituality unfolds out of their unique lives and relationships to Spirit, by whatever name or in whatever form that Spirit is recognized.

The Association offers several avenues for spiritual learning, development and participation. It has available a full range of face-to-face and online workshops and classes. It also has long-term training programs for those interested in deepening into their unique, sovereign Self and Spirit.

For more information, go to www.lorian.org, email info@lorian.org, or write to:

The Lorian Association
P.O. Box 1368
Issaquah, WA 98027